THE
PUPPET

The New Tool of the Global Forces

The Hizmet Movement

REŞAT PETEK

kopernik

REŞAT PETEK: He was born in 1955 in Burdur, Turkey. After completing his seven years in Burdur Religious Vocational High School (Imam-Hatip Lisesi) as a pupil, he studied an additional year in Burdur High School. This is because at that time period those students that went to Religious Vocational High Schools did not have equal opportunities when entering Universities, so he had to study an additional year in Burdur High School in order to get admission to the university. After graduating from Faculty of Law at Ankara University he held office in 9 different provinces and districts as a candidate judge, deputy public prosecutor, public prosecutor and chief public prosecutor.

While he was a chief public prosecutor in Yozgat, he became known in the public eye by launching an investigation on the President of the University of Erciyes and the Dean of Faculty of Arts and Sciences at Yozgat University on the charges of *"preventing the freedom of education by giving unlawful orders"*. This was the first time in history that such a charge was filed as a civil law suit. As a result of this case, he received several negative reactions from those that were involved in such illicit activities, but at the same time he was acknowledged with several positive reactions from entirely diverse groups in society that esteemed civil rights and human freedom. Due to the indictment prepared by him in accordance with the laws and the constitution, all investigations opened against him during the 28th of February period remained inconclusive. However, due to the pressures that were a result of unlawful practices of the 28th of February post-modern coup, he retired from duty in 1999.

He went onto conduct scientific research on Constitutional Law, Penal Law, Civil Right, and Fundamental Rights and Liberties. He wrote for numerous magazines and daily newspapers. As well as being a columnist on a website called *Haber7.com*, he was also assigned as a commentator in several television channels and radio programs.

Moreover, he participated in non-governmental organizations such as *Hukukçular Derneği, Uluslararası Hukukçular Birliği, Hukukun Üstünlüğü Platformu, İGİAD (Türkiye İktisadi Girişim ve İş Ahlâkı Derneği), Sivil Dayanışma Platformu,* and *TGTV (Türkiye Gönüllü Teşekküller Vakfı)*. He also registered a legal grievance so that the 28th of February coupists could be put on trial wherein he had the status of a plaintiff, the intervening party and the intervening party delegate.

In the elections of the 7th of June 2015 and the 1st of November 2015, while he was a practising lawyer, he was elected as the Burdur MP for AK Party. He was the Deputy Chairman of the Constitution Commission of the Grand National Assembly of Turkey, the Chairman of the AK Party Group Disciplinary Committee and the Chairman of the Parliamentary Inquiry Committee when the 15th of July Coup Attempt of the *Fetullahist Terrorist Organization (FETÖ)* took place. Reşat Petek has also written a book entitled *"İhanet ve Direniş"* on the same topic and he is currently serving as an MP for the 26th Parliament. He is married and a father of three children.

First published by Kopernik Inc.
®Reşat Petek 2019

Editor-in-Chief: Abdülkadir Özkan
Advisor: Prof. Halil Berktay
Series Editor: Dr. Yaşar Çolak
Director: Dr. Cengiz Şişman
Translated by: Rahim Acar
Design: Ali Kaya
Application: Sinopsis

Kopernik Publishing House
Kopernik Inc.
108 Olde Towne Avenue Unit: 308 Gaithersburg Maryland 20877 - USA
www.kopernikpublishing.com

Certification no: 35175
ISBN: 978-605-80697-3-2
First Edition: August 2019

Printed in ISTANBUL
Bilnet Matbaacılık - 42716

ISTANBUL - LONDON - NEW YORK – WASHINGTON DC

THE PUPPET

The New Tool of the Global Forces

The Hizmet Movement

REŞAT PETEK

kopernik

CONTENTS

PREFACE

For centuries the Turkish Nation, who encountered Islam in the steppes of Central Asia, carried the banner of this blessed religion. In the Battle of Talas, the Turkish Nation won a great victory with the Muslim Arabs fighting the Chinese. Later, Sultan Mahmud of Ghazni carried the religion of Islam to the Indian subcontinent, and was instrumental in bringing forth the prayers of nearly six hundred million Muslims today. Moreover, the Karahanids transformed the cities of Samarkand and Bukhara into one of the greatest science and culture centers, not just in the Islamic world, but in the world.

While the Seljuks established the world's first university and carried the flag of science, they brought the Middle East into an era of peace and tranquility. The dreams of the Crusaders, who rushed to the lands of Islam from the remote corners of Europe, were crushed under the Seljuk commanders. During this period of Karahans, Ghaznavids and Seljuks, numerous scholars such as Birunî, Khoja Ahmad Yasawi, Al-Farabi, Ibn Sina and, many others brought forth numerous scholarly works for the benefit of humanity.

The peak of Turkish history is undoubtedly the Ottoman period. Through the ingenuity of Ertuğrul Gazi, the sincerity of Sheikh Edebali and the prudence of Osman Gazi, one of the largest states in history was created, and the homeland of Anatolia was opened to the Turks, and made the everlasting Turkish home. Since that time, Anatolia has seen many days. It was elevated by the conquest of Istanbul, gushed into Europe as a flood through Mohach and Preveza, and in turn crushed the Crusaders in the Mediterranean. Great scholars, poets and philosophers were educated in Anatolia. Mevlâna, Yunus Emre, Hacı Bektaş and Veli, all embraced the blessed the message of Islam into their hearts.

Still, Anatolia also saw its days of gloom; incursions, plunder, massacres, riots, disorders...

However, every time, the Anatolian people managed to survive and stand on their own feet. Even if everything was taken away from them, they still confronted the enemy and all kinds of difficulties, with faith in God.

However, Anatolia never saw such a betrayal. It would never have imagined that such a mischief would occur from within, and it did not...

A movement of malady which tries to drain the last religion of Allah, by shaking the foundation of Islam...

A movement seeped in treachery attempting to remove the name of the Prophet from the words of testimony...

A movement of disloyalty that is able to state, "*it is not precarious for the Crusaders to invade your country*"...

An unethical, an unlawful and unprincipled movement that believes that the ends justify the means...

A movement of exploitation which regards the bold youth of Anatolia as unthinking slaves...

A satanic movement that sold its soul to the devil...

But this time, as always, the Anatolian people managed to survive and stand up on their own feet. Under the leadership of "*Reis*", the Anatolian people wrote an epic that that will set an example to the world.

They did not let the so-called masters of '*hizmet*' (service) oppress the sacred relics of Mahmud of Ghaznavi, Alp Aslan, Osman Gazi, Fatih Sultan Mehmed, Yavuz Sultan Selim, Kanuni Sultan Süleyman, Abdül Hamid II and innumerable servants of Islam.

They did not let the so-called the merchants of "tolerance" to oppress the sacred relics of Khoja Ahmad Yasawi, Sheikh Edebali, Mevlana along with innumerable figures works of knowledge, wisdom and the truths of faith that have been formed through the ages and beyond their time, which is embraced in peoples' emotions and thoughts.

Revealing the truth behind the most insidious act of betrayal and the cruel coup attempt in Turkey's history is a service to this country, and it is a debt that must be paid as soon as possible.

Of course, many studies were carried out, books were written, reports were prepared and scientific works were published on the issue. Every effort was put forward and it has made a great contribution to a better understanding and analysis of this insidious and treacherous coup attempt, and to the endeavor of raising awareness and sensitivity that is required in society.

We have also made a modest effort to reveal the hidden sides of this movement of treachery that went as far as zealously bomb its own people, and to reveal the truth of the inhumane coup attempt on the 15th of July 2016.

We have tried to create this work by taking up a pen and write as much as Almighty God has granted us.

Our greatest request from God is for this work to contribute in showing all aspects of the disreputable Fetullahist Terrorist Organization.

I would like to offer my deepest gratitude to everyone who has contributed to the preparation of this work, and to Turkuvaz Media Group's valuable members for publishing this work.

REŞAT PETEK

AK Party Burdur Deputy

ABBREVIATIONS

op. cit.	In the same work
EU	European Union
USA	United States of America
AKOM	Afet Koordinasyon Merkezi (Disaster Coordination Center)
AK Parti	Adâlet ve Kalkınma Partisi, AKP (Justice and Development Party)
ANAP	Anavatan Partisi (Motherland Party)
ANASOL-D	Commonly used abbreviated name that indicates the coalition government made up by the Motherland Party, Democratic Left Party, and Democrat Turkey Party.
ANASOL-M	Commonly used abbreviated name that indicates the coalition government made up by the Motherland Party, Democratic Left Party, and Nationalist Movement Party.
APA	Asian Parliamentary Assembly
ARFF	Aircraft Rescue & Firefighting
pbuh	Peace be upon him
JSC	Joint-Stock Company
BBC	British Broadcasting Company
BBP	Büyük Birlik Partisi (Great Union Party)
BDDK	Bankacılık Düzenleme ve Denetleme Kurumu (BRSA - Banking Regulation and Supervision Agency)
BDP	Barış ve Demokrasi Partisi (Peace and Democracy Party)

BIS	Bank of International Settlements
Bist-100	Borsa İstanbul 100 Endeksi (Istanbul Stock Exchange)
UN	United Nations
BOTAŞ	Boru Hatları ile Petrol Taşıma Anonim Şirketi (Petroleum Pipeline Corporation)
ByLock	The secret communication system that has three different cryptographic components; it was developed and used by the FETÖ/PDY.
CIA	Central Intelligence Agency, USA
CD	Compact Disk
CDS	Credit Default Swap
CHP	Cumhuriyet Halk Partisi (Republican People's Party)
CMK	5271 sayılı Ceza Muhakemesi Kanunu (Criminal Procedure Code, number 5271)
Major Bill of Indictment	Bill of Indictment concerning the 15th of July coup attempt carried out by the Fetullahist Terrorist Organization. The indictment was prepared by the office of Ankara chief public prosecutor (Ankara Cumhuriyet Başsavcılığı) (Date: 06.06.2016, E. No: 2016/24769) and approved by the Ankara 17th high criminal court (Ankara 17. Ağır Ceza Mahkemesi)
DAP	Doğu Anadolu Projesi (Eastern Anatolian Project)
DASİDEF	Doğu Anadolu Sanayici ve İş Adamları Dernekleri Federasyonu (Eastern Anatolia Federation of Industrialists and Businessmen Associations)
ISIS	Islamic State of Iraq and Syria (designated as a terrorist organization)
DEİK	Dış Ekonomik İlişkiler Konseyi (Council of Foreign Economic Relations)
DHKP – C	Devrimci Halk Kurtuluş Partisi Cephesi (The Front of Revolutionist Popular Party of Independence – designated as a terrorist organization)
DHMİ	Devlet Hava Meydanları İşletmesi (Administration of National Aviation Bases)
DİBS	Devlet İç Borçlanma Senetleri (Government Domestic Debt Securities (GDS)

Assoc. Prof.	Associate Professor (Doçent)
Dr.	Doctor
DTK	Demokratik Toplum Kongresi (Congress of Democratic Society, an institution connected to a terrorist organization)
DVD	Digital Versatile disc
ed.	Editor
EDOK	Kara Kuvvetleri Eğitim ve Doktrin Komutanlığı (Army Training and Doctrine Command)
EGM	Emniyet Genel Müdürlüğü (General Directorate of Security Affairs)
EPDK	Enerji Piyasası Düzenleme Kurumu (Energy Market Regulatory Authority)
EÜAŞ	Elektrik Üretim Anonim Şirketi (Electricity Generation Corporation)
FBI	Federal Bureau of Investigation (USA)
FEM	Fırat Eğitim Merkezi (Fırat Education Center)
FETO	A popular derogatory label to refer to Fetullah Gülen
FETÖ	Fetullahçı Terör Örgütü (Fetullahist Terrorist Organization)
GAP	Güneydoğu Anadolu Projesi (The South-eastern Anatolia Project)
GATA	Gülhane Askeri Tıp Akademisi (Gulhane Military Medical Academy)
GSM	Global System for Mobile Communications (The global system that allows for communication via mobile communication devices, such as cellular phones)
HAVELSAN	Hava Elektronik Sanayii (Air Electronics Industries)
HDP	Halkların Demokratik Partisi (The People's Democratic Party)
HKP	Halkın Kurtuluş Partisi (The People's Party of Independence)
HSYK	Hakimler ve Savcılar Yüksek Kurulu (Council of Judges and Public Prosecutors)
HTS	Harmonized Tariff Schedule (the report that includes detailed information about one's phone calls)
IHH	İnsan Hak ve Hürriyetleri İnsani Yardım Vakfı (The Foundation for Human Rights, Freedoms and Humanitarian Relief)

ISBN	International Standard Book Number
JFAC	Joint Force Air Component
KCK	Kürdistan Topluluklar Birliği (Unity of Kurdish Groups - designated as a terrorist organization)
KHK	Kanun Hükmünde Kararname (Legislative Decree)
KKTC	Kuzey Kıbrıs Türk Cumhuriyeti (Turkish Republic of Northern Cyprus)
The Commission	It is the Parliamentary Investigation Committee that was established to investigate the July 15 2016 Military Coup Attempt carried out by the Fetullahist Terrorist Organization and to investigate all the activities of this terrorist organization in order to identify relevant preemptive measures against its activities.
Report of the Commission	It denotes the report prepared by the Parliamentary Investigation Committee that was established to investigate the July 15 2016 Military Coup Attempt carried out by the Fetullahist Terrorist Organization and to investigate all the activities of this terrorist organization in order to identify relevant preemptive measures against its activities.
MAK	Muharebe Arama Kurtarma (Combat Search and Rescue)
MASAK	Mali Suçları Araştırma Kurulu (Financial Crimes Investigation Board)
md.	Madde (A legal article/clause)
MEB	Milli Eğitim Bakanlığı (Ministry of National Education)
MGK	Milli Güvenlik Kurulu (The National Security Council)
MHP	Milliyetçi Hareket Partisi (Nationalist Movement Party)
MİLAD Partisi	Millet ve Adâlet Partisi (Nation and Justice Party)
MİT	Milli İstihbarat Teşkilatı (National Intelligence Organization)
MOBESE	Mobile Electronic System Integration (Mobil Elektronik Sistem Entegrasyonu)
MTA	Maden Tetkik ve Arama Genel Müdürlüğü (General Directorate of Mineral Research and Exploration)
MÜSİAD	Müstakil Sanayici ve İşadamları Derneği (Independent Industrialists and Businessmen's Association)
OHAL	Olağanüstü Hâl (State of Emergency)

NATO	The North Atlantic Treaty Organization
ÖSYM	Ölçme, Seçme ve Yerleştirme Merkezi Başkanlığı (Presidency of Assessment, Selection, and Placement Center)
PDY	Paralel Devlet Yapılanması (Parallel Government Structuring)
PKK	Partiya Karkerên Kurdistan (Kurdistan Workers' Party, designated as a terrorist organization)
Prof. Dr.	Profesör doctor (Professor)
PYD	Partiya Yekîtiya Demokrat (Democratic Union Party (Syria) - designated as a terrorist organization)
RTÜK	Radyo ve Televizyon Üst Kurulu (Radio and Television Supreme Council)
Pbuh	Peace (and blessings) be upon him.
SAS	Su Altı Savunma (Turkish Underwater Defense and Security)
SAT	Su Altı Taarruz (Turkish Underwater Offence Command)
SBS	Seviye Belirleme Sınavı (Placement Test)
SGK	Sosyal Güvenlik Kurumu (Social Security Institution)
S&P	Standard and Poor's Financial Services
SPK	Sermaye Piyasası Kurulu (Capital Markets Board)
STK	Sivil Toplum Kuruluşu (Non-Profit Organization)
TBMM	Türkiye Büyük Millet Meclisi (Turkish Grand National Assembly)
TCK	5237 sayılı Türk Ceza Kanunu (Turkish Penal Code, number 5237)
TCDD	Türkiye Cumhuriyeti Devlet Demiryolları Genel Müdürlüğü (General Administration of Turkish Republic State Railways)
TEDAŞ	Türkiye Elektrik Dağıtım Anonim Şirketi (Turkish Electricity Distribution Company)
TEİAŞ	Türkiye Elektrik İletim Anonim Şirketi (Turkish Electricity Transmission Company)
TEOG	Temel Eğitimden Orta Öğretime Geçiş Sınavı (Placement Exam Test for High Schools)
TETAŞ	Türkiye Elektrik Ticaret ve Taahhüt Anonim Şirketi (Turkish Electricity Trade and Contracting Corporation)

TİKA	Türk İşbirliği ve Koordinasyon Ajansı Başkanlığı (Presidency of Turkish Cooperation and Coordination Agency)
TİM	Türkiye İhracatçılar Meclisi (Turkish Exporters Assembly)
TKY	Taktik Komuta Yeri (Tactical Command Center)
TL	Turkish Lira
TMB	Türkiye Müteahhitler Birliği (Contractors Association of Turkey)
TMK	3713 sayılı Terörle Mücadele Kanunu (Anti-Terror Law, number 3713)
TMSF	Tasarruf Mevduatı Sigorta Fonu (Savings Deposit Insurance Fund of Turkey)
TOKİ	Toplu Konut İdaresi Başkanlığı (Presidency of Housing Development Administration)
TRT	Türkiye Radyo Televizyon Kurumu Genel Müdürlüğü (General Directorate of Turkish Radio Television Institution)
TSE	Türk Standartları Enstitüsü Başkanlığı (Presidency of Turkish Standards Institute)
TSK	Türk Silahlı Kuvvetleri (Turkish Armed Forces)
TUSKON	Türkiye İşadamları ve Sanayiciler Konfederasyonu (Confederation of Businessmen and Industrialists of Turkey)
TÜBİTAK	Türkiye Bilimsel ve Teknolojik Araştırma Kurumu Başkanlığı (Presidency of Scientific and Technological Research Council of Turkey)
TÜİK	Türkiye İstatistik Kurumu (Turkish Statistical Institute)
TÜSİAD	Türk Sanayicileri ve İşadamları Derneği (Turkish Industrialists' and Businessmen's Association)
UYAP	Ulusal Yargı Ağı Bilişim Sistemi (National Judiciary Informatics System)
YAŞ	Yüksek Askeri Şura (Supreme Military Council)
YPG	Yekineyen Parastina Gel (People's Defense Units (Syria) - designated as a terrorist organization)
YSK	Yüksek Seçim Kurulu (Supreme Electoral Council)

LIST OF PHOTOS, FIGURES AND TABLES

INTRODUCTION

A nalyzing all aspects of the treacherous coup attempt that Turkey faced on July 15 2016 is of utmost importance for our country, our nation, our state, and the survival and security of the entire Muslim world. It is necessary to study in detail a person who claimed to have been a "religious preacher", but became so by carrying out disreputable actions, and in time presented himself with the appearance of being a "Hoca", a "Hocaefendi" and a "religious scholar". Moreover, in the last few years he went as far as to claim characteristics of a "Mahdi" and a "Messiah". In addition, the movement, which he is the leader of, should also be carefully examined since it is a responsibility upon us to prevent the emergence of such individuals and the growth and development of such movements in the future.

In order to reach a comprehensive understanding of the 15th of July tragedy, where the country was literally just turned back from the brink of annihilation, all the phases of the Fetullahist movement should be examined, starting with its founding during the 1950's, its nesting period during the 1960's and 1970's, its fledgling period during the 80's and 90's, and its offensive period during the 2000's.

Fetullah Gülen has a flawed personality, and this trait of his led him at an early age to be dismissed from the Alvarlı Madrasah. This expulsion was based upon his ill conduct contrary to the customs, traditions and morals of religious education. His warped associations triggered by his flawed personality lay the groundwork for a journey full of questionable and dubious deeds that extended to the intelligence units in a very short time. In spite of having limited religious knowledge that was deemed insufficient even for the middle of the twentieth century, the creation of the perception of the "religious scholar" that led hundreds of thousands of people, is a undertaking that exceeds the capacity of a person of this caliber, and is rather a natural result of a step-by-step implementation of a much larger project that spans decades.

The structure that was established by Fetullah Gülen under the auspices of domestic and foreign intelligence organizations grew in a very short period of time and reached a volume that made it prominent even in the 1970s. In this period and during the 1980s, the attempts of infiltrating its people as staff within the state continued to increase and reached a mass level during the 1990s. In the 2000s, the organization infiltration process was completed to a great extent in the main critical positions and in the units of public institutions, such as the Turkish Armed Forces, the Ministry of National Education, the Ministry of Interior, the Directorate General of Security, the Judiciary. Thus, the critical positions and units in these institutions were handed into the hands of the Fetullahist Terrorist Organization. The organization, unlike any other illegal structure ever seen in the history of the country, took over the management of the critical institutions of the state as well as formed a parallel hierarchy parallel to the official hierarchy; however, this one was deemed to be above the official hierarchy. Thus, a parallel state structure within the state was established and secretly operated. This situation was reflected in the first reports about the organization and it was named as "Parallel State Structure" (PDY).

Fetullahism, which started out as a so-called virtuous movement, became a congregation in a short time, but it was organized separately from the other religious communities in terms of its methods. It made use of terror and criminal activities in order to realize its secret agenda and ultimately became an armed terrorist organization. Thus, in a short time it was counted as a *"terrorist organization"* in various cases filed, in administrative decisions regarding the organization and it labeled officially as the Fetullahist Terrorist Organization (FETÖ). After the judicial coup attempt in December 17-25, 2013, it was called FETÖ/PDY and this classification was adopted by the society.

In the beginning our people looked up at the organization that was known as a religious community, where people were praying; that was known as righteous, tolerant and virtuous movement. People who had the financial opportunities supported the organization in the form of; alms, zakat, charity, cash donation, donation of land, building, technical equipment and donation of animal skin. People who did not have the financial opportunities in order to please God worked in schools, dormitories, other buildings, and collected donated charity and animal skin. Those who did not have the power to do any of these prayed to God.

While the grass root base of FETÖ/PDY considered the service towards the organization as a form of *"worship"*, the executives of the organization started to take full control of the system by taking over the standard functioning of the country in the bureaucracy, the private sector and non-governmental organization. Thus an endeavor was made to transform the FETÖ/PDY into a form a dictatorship, and it is for this reason that they initiated the *infiltration, cartelization and monopolization* of every field in Turkey. While the grass root base of the organization was engaged in *worship*, the executives of the organization begun to engage in treason.

The fact that the FETÖ/PDY infiltrated public Institutions in mass and took over those institutions, that they stole exam questions, that they dismissed other religious community members from public offices, and that they acted as a cartel becoming a monopoly in the free market, made getting closer to this organization a necessity for several people. This situation made it seem as if the organization was more powerful than it actually was, and formed the perception in both the public and the politicians that the organization had "*millions of members*". Some parties wishing to receive the support of the organization's root base provided room for FETÖ/PDY members in both their headquarters and provincial districts and municipal offices of their parties, and made memberships or presidencies in the administrations, audit and disciplinary committees, and elected them as mayor, municipality/provincial general assembly member, or even a deputy.

The organization's interest in politics gradually increased to the level of obsession and they began to demand a large number of deputies and mayors from many parties. Some of the parties' chairmen, deputy chairmen, group deputies, and deputies were plotted against and bumped out of the race. Moreover, some of the deputies that the organization had control over were ordered to establish a new political party, and others were forced to enter the election as independent candidates.

Blackmails based on false evidences, witnesses and scenarios, sabotages, slanders, traps, conspiracies, plots, torture, countless murders, and the stealing of exam questions, were all done in the name of the "*truths of faith*", and all the religious values and symbols were exploited and rendered inconsequential. All kinds of misdeeds were conducted by the organization in order to create social turmoil that would lead to an economic crises such as; establishing a parallel religion under the name of "*saving the faith of the youth and society*", trying to seize the most confidential knowledge of the state by targeting the MİT, sending state secrets obtained in various ways to foreign countries, and assassination attempts against Prime Minister Erdoğan in the past, the Gezi Park attempts, the disinformation reports, lynching campaigns and defamation activities, the December 17-25 judicial coup attempt, the curse sessions, stopping the MİT trucks, and the illegal intervention in politics. The FETÖ/PDY almost instituted evil and oppression, "*legitimized*" all kinds of aggravation in their own dark consciences such as attempting to scheme in politics, cooperating with terrorist organizations and foreign intelligence services and conducting the most dishonorable operations particularly with the PKK, DHKP-C, ISIS, PYD-YPG, and violating the law and moral principles.

It is interesting to note that the FETÖ/PDY is reminiscent us of the fate of Hassan-I Sabbah and the Hashshashins who are infamous and despised in the history of Islam. Nizam-ul-Mulk, the great statesman who lived in the same period, quoted "*A state may last while there is kufur (irreligion), but it will not endure when there is oppression*", which thoroughly explains the current situation. The accumulated practices of the terrorist organization have transformed any previous perception of them into a negative perception in the public mind. Their attempts to intervene in politics and not being successful except in one party, the AK party winning election after election except one, and the independent candidates of the organization receiving very low votes reveals that our people did not and do not actually support this structure. They reluctantly supported the organization to save themselves from the malevolence of the organization, to ensure that their relatives found jobs in the organizations' staffing procedures, and, simply in order to survive in the current free market. Before FETÖ/PDY's attempts to shape politics, it was claimed that the organization had 15% voting potential, and that their grass root base had a maximum of 5% voting potential. However, after each election it was discovered that even this percentage is too high, and that in reality the organization did not even cover more than 1% voting potential.

After the treacherous July coup attempt, the state became fully alerted and initiated a wide range of clean-up procedures, which was supported by the people. Thus, members of the organization were dismissed from several institutions. However, it should be noted that there still is a lot of work to be done, and the course of actions concerning this issue are not yet completed.

This book has been written with the modest hope of contributing to the success of the struggle against the FETÖ/PDY; a struggle that the whole society has a consensus on. The establishment of this armed terrorist organization, its development, its objectives and strategies, the methods and tactics it uses, its economic structure, the timeline of the coup attempt, and the measures taken against it and the measures planned to be taken against it are discussed in this comprehensive work.

The report entitled, "*The constituted Assembly Research Commission regarding the July 15 2016 coup attempt of the Fetullahist*

Terrorist Organization (FETÖ/PDY) and the determining of measures to be taken against it by inspecting all aspects of the terrorist organizations activities", and many other studies and information sources were used in the preparation of this work.

The book contains sixteen chapters in total, and in the first part of the book, information regarding the life of Fetullah Gülen is provided. In this context, his works in the Alvarlı Madrasah and Erzurum, his connection with Said Nursi, his religious preacher period in Trakya, his military service, his connection with the Association for the Struggle against Communism, his return to Trakya and his appointment in Izmir, his activities in the Aegean region, his trial at the military court, his departure to Germany, his psychiatric reports and his resignation for his post as a government employee, his relation with the intelligence organizations and other noteworthy issues are discussed in detail.

In the second part of the book, material regarding the overt and secret objectives of the FETÖ/PDY, the words (confessions) of Fetullah Gülen "behind closed doors amongst his friendly surroundings", his relations with dominant countries at the global level, his connections with politicians and political parties, and the methods applied in this context, the confessions of some of the top executives who are apprehensive of the situation of the organization and other issues have been addressed.

In the third chapter, the strategic approach of the FETÖ/PDY is provided. In this context, the basic strategies applied by the organization (defensive, equivalency and offensive) and tactical approaches are explained. Furthermore, specifics about the instructions given by Fetullah Gülen in this context as the leader of the organization, some of the behavioral codes ordered and some of the methods applied are discussed.

In addition, retired former Deputy Chief of the Turkish National Police, Cevdat Saral's, and the former Deputy Chief of Ankara Osman Ak's report on the organization is presented.

In the fourth chapter, the establishment and development of the FETÖ/PDY is discussed. The emergence and change of the name of the organization, the activities carried out between 1966-1983, known as the organization's "nesting period", the text of the oath written by Fetullah Gülen himself, his connection with Vehbi Koç and MİT, his connection with the CIA and foreign intelligence services, his religious radicalism, his concepts of the "*golden generation*" and "*ışık evleri* (light houses)", the publication of the Sızıntı magazine, his support of the military coup of September 12 and his purchase of the ranch in Pennsylvania are deliberated about in detail.

Moreover, in this section, activities that took place between the years 1984-2006, known as the organization's "fledgling period", are mentioned. In this context, the events and activities such as the opening of private schools and preparatory course centers, stealing of state exam questions and placing students strategically in military high schools, war schools, police colleges and the police academy, and the the staffing of the organizations members in critical institutions such as the Ministry of National Education, the Directorate General of Security, the TÜBİTAK and the ÖSYM are discussed. In addition, such issues as, Fetullah Gülen's letter to Pope John Paul II and his visit to the Pope, the initiation of the "*interreligious dialogue*" and "*Abrahamic religions*" projects with the Catholic Church in the Vatican, and the disintegration and manipulation of concepts in Islam such as *tawhid* and prophethood are evaluated. Other discussions in this section deal with the organization opening schools abroad, opening universities inside the country, their implementation of the board of trustees, their use of code names, their seizure of Zaman Newspaper, their establishment of radio and television channels, their publication of new magazines, their establishment of internet sites, their closer cooperation with political parties, and their Journalists and Writers Foundation and TUSKON's establishment, as well as hundreds of other foundations. Finally, this section discusses Fetullah Gülen's support of the February 28 coup, Fetullah Gülen's letter to the Deputy Chief of General Staff Gen. Çevik Bir, the organizations transformation into a corporation, the establishment of Bank Asya, the lawsuits declared against Fetullah Gülen, Gülen's escape abroad and self-exile, the Turkish Olympics and related topics.

This section also includes the activities carried out between the years 2007-2017, which is considered as the "offensive period". The FETÖ/PDY, who thought that it had control over several institutions and had reached a significant power in politics, began numerous illegal activities and committed many crimes during this period. These illegal activities discussed in this section include the assassination of journalist Hrant Dink and the journalist Haydar Meriç, the Ergenekon and the Balyoz cases, the Istanbul and İzmir military espionage cases, the cosmic room incident, the so-called *Tevhid-Selam* Jerusalem Terrorist Network, the theft of the Public Personnel Selection Exam questions, the Undersecretary of MİT called in for questioning, the Gezi Park incidents, the December 17-25 judicial coup attempt, the attempts to search the MİT trucks, the Istanbul Illicit Evacuation Initiative, and the attempts of manipulating the state of politics in the country.

The fifth section focuses on the management of the organization, the ringleader and founder Fetullah Gülen's non questionable dictatorial position, which is supposedly always full of miracle (*Fetullah Gülen's Throne*), the portrait of the organization's domestic vertical structuring units (Administrator of Turkey, Imam of Turkey, provincial Imams, district Imams, local neighborhood Imams, house Imams), and the Imams of critical public institutions (the Directorate General of Security, the National Intelligence Agency, the Turkish Armed Forces, and the Judiciary) who are referred to as '*hususiler*' (specialists). The horizontal structure of the organization is discussed which includes '*ışık evleri*', religious conversation groups, and '*mütevelli heyeti*' (the board of trustee's) etc. This section also deals with the staffing and infiltration of members within the strategic public institutions (The Turkish National Police, the Ministry of National Education, the Judicial organs, the Civilian Admiration, and the Turkish Armed Forces). This staffing and activities also took place abroad and both abroad and in the country they worked in clandestine, with precaution and engaging in deception. Through these structures, organizational practices, and methods they gained new members to the organization, applied illegal and unethical dismissal methods and cataloged even the organization's members' associations and marriages.

In the sixth chapter, examples of how religious values were exploited by the FETÖ/PDY are explained. In this context, it is demonstrated how such religious concepts such as the *mahdi*, the messiah, imam, scholar, religious preacher, *himmet*, community, *ashab*, and *belde-i tayyibe* (pleasant town: referring to Istanbul) were drained of any true meaning, how their meanings were altered, and how concepts such as dream, onomancy, *yakaza* (between waking state and sleep), and the bringing of knowledge from the unseen world were brought to the forefront. Furthermore, this chapter discusses how hadiths were distorted, how projects such as "*Interreligious dialogue*" and "*Abrahamic Religions*" were utilized to harm the religion of Islam, and in this context, how they attempted to separate the two phrases of the testimony of Islam.

In the seventh chapter, the transmission and communication methods used by FETÖ/PDY are deliberated on; the methods used in communication by the members of the organization (face to face communication, mobile phone and GSM number ruses, encrypted software, social media, internet programs, cryptic IP lines, despatchers, giving instructions through the media, organizational meetings), behavior codes applied during the communication process and points to consider, code names, lynching campaigns, subliminal messages in television-internet programs and commercials, blackmail and threats through the media, and propaganda operations conducted through films and television series are the subjects mentioned in this section.

In the eighth chapter, the financial structure of the FETÖ/PDY is emphasized. In this context, the main sources of income, economic and commercial activities, fraudulent and illegal operations in the companies that are connected to the organization and its affiliations; holdings, corporations, media organizations, schools, preparatory course centers, hospitals, dormitories, media organs, foundations, associations, universities, trade unions that provide income to the organization, the application of *himmet* which transformed more as a community tax and irregularities, mandatory subscriptions practices, structure of board of trustee's (*mutevelli heyeti*) and **treasurers** are discussed.

In the ninth chapter, the characteristics of the FETÖ/PDY as an "*armed terrorist organization*" and the cooperation with other terrorist networks are provided. The topics for this section include the judicial and administrative decisions that declares the FETÖ/PDY as an armed terrorist organization, crimes that have been committed by the organization, the existence of a sophisticated cooperation with PKK, ISIS, PYD-YPG and DHKP-C, and the brutality and treachery exhibited during the 15th of July coup attempt.

In the tenth chapter, the 15th of July coup attempt conducted by the FETÖ/PDY is discussed in detail. Important events that occurred prior to the coup attempt are discussed such as *the President's Erdoğan's rally known as the "one minute", the Mavi Marmara massacre, the pressurizing of MİT Undersecretary Hakan Fidan to testify, The Gezi Park incidents, the closure of the preparatory course centers, the December 17-25 2013 judicial coup attempt, the abolition of the assize courts assigned under Article 10 of the Anti-Terror Law, the general election of local administrations, the Presidential elections, the Kobani provocation, the election of the members of the Council of Judges and Prosecutors, the general elections of the Deputies, the appointment of the trustee to the Koza-İpek Group and the Zaman Newspaper, and Turkey's downing of the Russian warplane.* Moreover, the chapter describes the chronological time line of the coup attempt and the resistance against it, which began on Friday the 15th of July at 14.45 and continued till Saturday the 16th of July at 21.57. It includes events such as the assassination attempt on President Recep Tayyip Erdoğan, the leadership of President Recep Tayyip Erdoğan, Prime Minister Binali Yıldırım, and the Speaker of the Grand Nation Assembly of Turkey, İsmail Kahraman, regarding the suppression of the coup attempt, and the common attitude of the Assembly and the approaches of the political parties. It also goes onto describe the event entitled, *"The Democracy and Martyrs Rally"*, which was held in Yenikapı Istanbul after the coup attempt, and recounting some of the public institutions that were effective in suppressing the coup attempt.

In the eleventh chapter, the position of the media during the coup attempt is discussed in much detail.

In the twelfth chapter, the state of emergency and the emergency decree laws issued by the government are discussed. The legal background of the declaration of the state of emergency and the decisions taken, the emergency decree laws issued in the state of emergency (667-694), the regulations introduced by the emergency decree laws, and the rights provided to the relatives of the martyrs, the veterans and the relatives of the veterans are outlined.

In the thirteenth chapter, the impact of the coup attempt on economic and social life is discussed. In this context, the chapter illustrates the public support for the struggle against FETÖ/PDY, the public opinion on issues such as the coup attempt, statesmen and politicians, the coup attempts impact on capital and financial markets, and the unfair practices of the rating agencies towards Turkey.

The measures taken in Turkey and abroad in order to break the economic power of FETÖ/PDY are presented in the fourteenth chapter. The resilience of FETÖ/PDY (*strategies and tactics applied by the organization*) against the measures taken by the state following the coup attempt is then offered in the fifteenth chapter.

The sixteenth chapter concludes the book by offering measures that will be necessary to take in order to prevent any future rise of a structure like the FETÖ/PDY type organization. In this context, the chapter discusses in detail the restructuring of the intelligence system, the measures to be taken in the internal security system, the steps needed to be taken in the economic sphere, the restructuring of the public personnel system, the necessary measures to be taken in the education system and in the religious services, and, finally, the measures to be taken on an international scale.

WHO IS FETULLAH GÜLEN?

According to the official population records, Fetullah Gülen was born in Korucuk village, which is a located in the Pasinler district of Erzurum on the 27th of April 1941. He is the second of eight children of Ramiz Gülen, who was the imam of the village mosque and Refia Gülen, who was a housewife. Although official registration records indicate that Fetullah Gülen was born in 1942, he seems to have altered his birth year records from 1942 to 1941 in order to become a preacher. Many accounts have drawn attention to the deceptive nature of Gülen's birth records alteration.

It has been reported that he had to repeat the same grades over and over in primary school due to failing it every previous year, and only later by passing the exams was he able to complete his primary education and receive his diploma. In 1955 he attended Hodja (religious scholar) Alvarlı Muhammed Lütfi Efe's sermons in the Kurşunlu Madrasa. It is known that Gülen gave his first sermons in the village of Alvar. Interestingly, Gülen was forced to leave the madrasa after he accused Hodja Efe's grandson Sadi Mazlumoğlu of speaking against Atatürk. After Sadi Mazlumoğlu was taken into custody because of this accusation, Gülen was forced to leave the madrasa.[1] Afterwards Gülen took lessons from some of the religious scholars of that time in Erzurum, such as Master Sıtkı Efendi. In addition, when he was 17 years old, he met with some of the students of Said Nursi and started to attend the Risale-i-Nur classes, however, in contrast to popular belief he never met Said Nursi.

Fetullah Gülen, who travelled to Edirne in 1959, started to work as a preacher in Üç Şerefeli Mosque, and between the years 1961-1962, he served in the military at Ankara (Mamak) and Hatay (Iskenderun). Gülen is known to have completed his military service seven months early by acquiring a *"sick leave"* report[2] and returned to Erzurum to join the establishment of the Erzurum Anti-Communism Association,[3] and took up a managerial position in this association.[4]

Later on, Fetullah Gülen was appointed as a preacher to Kırklareli in 1965 and was employed to stay at Izmir in 1966. He preached in many provinces and districts of the Aegean Region as a mobile preacher. After the military memorandum of 12 March 1971, 54 defendants were arrested by the martial law court for acting against the principle of secularism in the Nurculuk Case, and Gülen remained in detention for seven months during this period. The verdict given by the Court was later reduced by the Military Court of Appeals and the penalty was decreased. Gülen was sentenced to three years of imprisonment, disqualified from public service for further three years and to be under supervision in Sinop for a year. However these sentences were also removed in May 25 1974 by the martial law court under the Southern Sea Area Command on the grounds that was is covered by the Amnesty Law (no. 1803)[5].

As his case in the Martial Law Court continued, Gülen

was appointed in 1972 as a preacher to Edremit, which is a district of Balıkesir. He was later appointed as a preacher in Bornova which is a district of Izmir. During this period, he gave sermons on religious life, creation, education and social issues in many of the cities of Anatolia, but mainly in the Aegean Region.

It is known that Fetullah Gülen was appointed to Germany temporarily for a duty in 1977. After returning to Turkey he continued his sermons and religious conversations in many Anatolian cities. On September 5, 1980, prior to the military coup of 12th of September 1980, he was granted sick leave due to a medical report. On 25 November 1980, he was appointed as the head preacher of central Çanakkale. Shortly afterwards the warrant for Gülen was issued and he went into hiding in various provinces, staying with his relatives and acquaintances. It is reported that he was diagnosed with "*reactive anxiety disorder*" and received a sick leave from the Psychiatry Clinic of Cerrahpaşa Medical Faculty in February 1981 and resigned from his duty as a preacher at the end of his sick leave.

Gülen's accusation" against Hodja Alvarlı Muhammed Lütfi Efe's grandson Sait Mazlumoğlu of "*insulting Atatürk*" might be the main cause for the reason why what has been labeled the "*deep state*" began to take an interest in Gülen. It is important to note that during that time period within the madrasa tradition and in an environment that so highly engaged in religious sciences, the complaint of Gülen with such an accusation was considered a very rare occurrence. The foundation of such a compliant in fact indicates that the person who made the compliant was far from being a self-disciplined and an ethical person. Moreover, it demonstrates that completely in contrast with the madrasa tradition, the accuser preferred to inform on the person in question without offering any prior advice or any kind of cautioning. In this case the accuser clearly exhibited unethical standards such as unscrupulousness, lack of clemency and duplicity.

It is clear that a person who displayed such attitudes and behaviors would have easily attracted attention of the intelligence agencies of the state, especially at a time when the Madrasa's were monitored closely by the state. A person who demonstrates this kind of moral weakness in the madrasa environment, which is engaged in religious sciences, will most likely not act morally and do anything necessary to attain position and authority.

It is evident that Gülen could not have altered his documentation of age in the official records all by himself considering that he had not received at all the sufficient education, and that he did not even complete his madrasa training. Therefore, by taking the context and time period into account it is obvious that this could only be completed with the assistance and knowledge of the intelligence agencies.

Moreover, it can be inferred from Gülen's involvement in the establishment of the CIA operation, the Anti-Communism Association, that Gülen was being closely monitored and that he was even assigned an active role in the association by the state intelligence agencies. It can also be argued that Gülen's enthusiasm in the association activities may have further attracted both the deep state's and the CIA's attention.

Gülen, unlike Said Nursi, in a short period of time began to establish a religious community around him, and in the 1960's his followers grew rapidly. However, this could not have been achieved solely by his ability and endeavors considering that this was a person who did not have adequate religious knowledge or a madrasa education, and who also displayed strong character weaknesses. There are reports that Gülen also had visitors frequently from foreign mission chiefs in Izmir during the 1970's, and this raises even more doubts over his connections and intentions overall.

A further assertion is that the Kestanepazarı mosque had been specially chosen for Gülen by Yasar Tunagur, who was the Vice-President of Presidency of Religious Affairs at the time.[6] It is well known that the Kestanepazarı Mosque has always been considered as one of the extraordinary mosques of Izmir and that across the mosque, there is the famous Havra Street, which the Kapani Jews have property in the Kestanepazarı region. In other words, Sabataists have always taken a special interest in this region.

The story that commenced with the complaint against a Hodja in the Alvarli Madrasah, continued with a deceptive increase of age in the official records, leading to a suspicious military service, the taking of a dubious sick leave, an irregular break from his civil service for a few years after his military service, and having taken an active role of in the establishment of the Anti-Communism Association established by the special order of the United States of America. He continued with his special role as a preacher in Kestanepazarı[7] which is a district of Izmir, where the Sabataists and especially the Kapani community[8] have a strong interest. Thus, a religious community established by an informant has opened schools, dormitories, and universities all over the world, and established companies, reached at a level of an effective media and lobbying power, and became an economical power that dominates tens of billions of dollars each year, and finally even reached such a state that he could coordinate a military coup in an attempt to take control of the government.

According to some, a religious community such as was formed in Kestanepazarı cannot have opened schools, sent teachers, manage this kind of monetary traffic and concealed itself without a cell-structure. Thus, the organization known as the Gülen community can be regarded essentially as the Muslim branch of larger Masonic Establishment, especially considering that several Mason lodges knew of the military coup on the 15th July beforehand.[9]

OBJECTIVES OF FETÖ/PDY

People who accept Fetullah Gülen as their guide and who are also bound to him as a disciple and obediently fulfill his orders were in the early years organized as a religious community. These people were called "*Fetullahist*" for many years. These people's ways of life have also been known as "*Fetullahçhk* (Fetullahism)". Fetullahism, which initially introduced itself as a moral and educational movement, evolved into a religious cult, then an organization and finally a malicious terrorist organization. As discussed later in this book, they are also known as "*Fetullahist Terrorist Organization*" and "*The Parallel State Structure*" (FETÖ/PDY) in legal texts (indictments, court decisions, and legal regulations) and administrative decisions (Decisions of the Council of Ministers, Decisions of the National Security Council, and Prime Ministry and the annexes of ministries, etc.), in many reports, books and printed works. This is not discussed separately in this chapter, as it is described in detail in the following sections.

When considering FETÖ/PDY's establishment and development phase, it can be noted that, it has two main objectives, which of one is clearly visible while the other is kept secret. The FETÖ/PDY, in open view, for all apparent purposes seems to be concerned with the development of a religious youth that mainly serves to fulfill the spreading of Islam in society, and establishing a hard-working, disciplined, and philanthropic community dependent on the country and state. Their volunteers have spread all over the world, working as a representative of their country abroad by making use of their foreign language skills and knowledge. They work in media outlets to bring peace and tranquility within the country and devote themselves to the country's development by opening schools and dormitories in the remotest corners of Turkey for the youth. They become role models everywhere by behaving accordingly and by succeeding in the workforce, being astute and knowledgeable, honest, moral, having good virtues, having a deep and profound view on the country's main issues, being balanced, discreet and being sensitive on variety issues, making sure their neighbors are not in need, competing to become more charitable, bringing understanding and knowledge to less developed countries, and they strive to teach the national anthem, language and culture of our country, creating a link with good impression between the host country and Turkey. The organizations' members have been convinced to believe that the examples given above are the main objectives of the organization.

Contrary to what is perceived in the society, this organization has two secret fundamental goals: Firstly, it is to become such a powerful force, and manage all the countries where it operates from the backstage. This has been done especially in Turkey. Their first plan is to seize power in the constitutional institutions and to install their own managers to strengthen their organization. After that, other Muslim countries that are also a target will be forced to surrender to this power in similar fashion. Achieving sufficient economic power to achieve this political power is their second plan.

These political and economic goals are actually means to serve the national interests of the USA, Israel and the UK, which in fact established and enabled the organization to thrive in the past. While the organization keeps its apparent goals on the forefront of the public, the secret objectives of the organization are only known by their top official mangers. Furthermore, the organization claims that its agenda consist of, "*spreading the truth of faith all over the world, saving the faith of mankind, spreading the religion of Islam, reciting the Turkish national anthem all over the world, and teaching Turkish and the Turkish culture all over the world*". These notions clearly appeal to the Anatolian people's hearts. On the other hand the organization uses concepts such as "*moderate*" and "*harmless*". These concepts have been given by the global powers, and the organization fulfills its mission by creating a version of Islam that is a version in line with the global powers.

In order to remove the doubts and hesitations in the public opinion, Fetullah Gülen claims that even though it seem they are in good terms with America and Israel, he is actually taking advantage of them. He makes this claim to prove that he is working for the realization of the supreme goals disclosed to the public. This is mainly because in today's world not much can be accomplished by standing against America.

Thus, FETÖ/PDY masks their political and economic goals by exploiting religious concepts. They also target other organizations by infiltrating them, and have made their followers believe that this is done under the names of religion, and it must absolutely be done. The mass takeover of the organization in public institutions and the state is aimed at realizing the goal of becoming a hegemonic economic and political power in society. This goal is only possible by infiltrating every institution and organization, and then converting it, making its main purpose to serve the organization.

In this framework, the organization has established nearly a dictatorship over the society. These people also have very bigoted views that are highly hazardous for Muslim societies. According to their main objective, the elected government will be under the command and control of Fetullah Gülen, which will be the leader of the organization. State policies will be determined by Fetullah Gülen, and the legitimate government elected by an election will implement these policies. In this structure, Fetullah Gülen will supposedly become the universal Imam, the so-called Mahdi and the Messiah for not only Turkey, but will also govern all the Islamic societies that the organization has taken over.

The structure that the organization desires consists of a universal Imam (Mahdi, Messiah), which has disciples and Imams (Abi) who are fully obedient to the universal Imam. The followers of the organization also have self-contained rituals and beliefs. They function in an authoritarian manner. Although they do not recognize the right of any other Muslim groups, they are submissive against other powerful countries.

FETÖ/PDY has prioritized education and has created a community perception that they provide education services according to national and spiritual values. The organization, which opened many schools both in Turkey and abroad, concealed its real purpose under the name of educational service. For a long time, the services of the schools abroad especially impressed and made our people proud, but in time it has been recognized that these schools have not contributed to anything at all.

When the organization reaches a sufficient level of economic resources and completes positioning of its own followers in public offices and excels its human resources to a certain level of competence, it will rise against the state. They will seize the state by a *"golden shot"* and a *"huruç operation"*. All plans were made in a way that would prevent any serious repercussions when the organization took over the state in the golden shot stage. All public institutions, non-governmental organizations and commercial companies would operate under the order of FETÖ/PDY.

FETÖ/PDY aim was to establish a unitary state order in order to keep the opposition under control. Fetullah Gülen did not establish a political party and therefore did not enter the elections. His main objective was to keep a strong bond with his followers that he has positioned in public offices. These followers were fully committed to Gülen, in such a way that they were ready to sacrifice everything in the name of religion. Fetullah Gülen made them feel as if they were *"God's chosen servants"*. In summary FETÖ/PDY intended to take over all political parties under its control and to manage all of them by the strategies mentioned above.

The organization has formed different alliances, led discourses, conducted projects and activities in different periods to make the best use of changing conditions.[10] This is mainly because of the strategy based on adapting to the changing environment both in the country and abroad in favor of the organization.[11] Because of this strategy, Fetullah Gülen created a followers based upon using his Risale-i Nur background in the 1960's. However, in the 1970's he claimed that he was not a Nurcu and that he did not have anything to do with Nurculuk (Followers of Said Nursi). He also supported the military coup of 1980 and praised the coup soldiers. Later on after returning to a normal civilian administration in 1983 he kept close relations with the Turgut Özal. After the 1991 elections he become closer to Demirel and supported the February 28 intervention. He called for the resignation of Prime Minister Necmettin Erbakan. He also supported the ANASOL-D[12] government, praised Bülent Ecevit who was the prime minister of the later founded DSP and the ANASOL-M[13] government. After the 2002 elections he started to support the AKP government. When he thought that he had sufficient economic and the bureaucratic power, FETÖ/PDY tried to capture the state.

Indeed, Fetullah Gülen following remarks reveals FETÖ/PDY's real intentions, *"We will infiltrate every area of this nation whether it be civil offices or not, and we will seize at least sixty percent of these institutions. We will also take part in all non-governmental organizations, political parties and ethnicities that exist in this country. One day we will come to such a level; that when I say 'the time has come', neither the state nor the nation will have the power to move!"*.

Gülen has chosen an opportunistic stance by acting in accordance with the time period and its current mood and has developed an appropriate discourse in order to achieve the objective of seizing the state. When we analyze his forty-year's discourse and his actions, it is evident to see that Fetullah Gülen masterfully disguised himself as a sunni, alawi, sufi, hurufi, radical, democrat, secular, liberal, humanist, dialogist, contemporaneous, modernist, nationalist and materialist. This disturbed personality has become capable of doing all kinds of wretched actions that are not compatible with Islamic morality. Even though it began with a religious community structure, in time it has become an organization that secretly planned and put into actions cloak-and-dagger projects. As a matter of fact, some of the senior executives who realized that FETÖ/PYD acted more as an *"organization"* than a religious community parted ways with this organization[14] and leaked the inside story of the so-called religious community.[15]

According to the statements of those who left the organization when they saw the true facade of the organization, FETÖ/PDY functions within a pyramid type hierarchy of individuals that are interconnected with networks of international interest. It is a deceitful organization that is formed in close contact with secret cell-structure and foreign intelligence agencies. Their main objective is not to serve Islam, rather it is to absorb various countries on behalf of this dark farce, especially in Turkey. These people have no regard for the country they were born and brought up in and the clearest evidences for this case is that they attempted a military coup without considering what kind of harm would befall on the innocent civilians. Furthermore, they are well known to have blackmailed different groups in the society, and there are documented unresolved murders committed in the past by the organization.

It is the religion, unfortunately, that has been used as tool and exploited by the organization to implement its secret plans. Fetullah Gülen has deceived the masses by making promises of fostering religious education. However at the end he ordered the mass murder of the civilians that acted against his plot to destroy the country. They tried to destroy the state institutions and to make our country ready for the occupation of foreigners. This was all done in a critical period, when the country was an in active struggle with global terror organizations.[16]

STRATEGIC APPROACH OF FETÖ/PDY

Fetullah Gülen divided his objective of seizing power into three strategic stages and developed a tactical approach for each stage. He also prohibited methods that did not comply with his approach. The strategies developed by Gülen are the defensive, the equivalency and the offensive stages.[17]

Defensive Strategy

The defensive strategy is the strategy implemented by FETÖ/PDY in the early period of the organization. It is based on infiltrating the state by attaining power without engaging in open politics. That is to say, the organization never created a political party in the electoral system. Its followers, who were trained in the houses, dormitories, classrooms and schools in the organization, started to be placed in the state positions by using both legitimate and illegitimate methods and thus in this way they attempted to take hold of the state positions. First of all, the organization actively infiltrated critical institutions such as the Directorate General of Security and the Ministry of Justice to prevent the prosecution and the suppression of the organization. In addition, it put pressure on groups who were thought to be hostile to the organization. Moreover, in this period, small and medium sized service producing companies and media companies were established to provide both financial resources and opportunities to manage its public relations. During the same period when the defensive strategy was implemented, the organization did not enter into a strategic relationship with any party and kept its relations at a tactical level. The policy of securing concessions from all parties, by staying close to all the parties that could become the ruling power was implemented.

The Equilibrium Strategy

When the infiltrations into the state had reached a certain level and it was decided that it had sufficient power within the judiciary and the security force, the organization began to focus on infiltrating the army, which is another major strategic institution. It also began to come closer to the ruling party in power during this period. The equilibirium strategy tried to keep a sense of balance between the defensive and the offensive strategy. Its attempt was to ensure integrating the masses within the security, the judiciary and the army branch and by keeping close relations with the ruling party. Thus the executive branch became completely besieged. While they prioritized infiltrating the military, critical positions were also occupied in the headquarters of the ruling party and its provincial branches. While the members of the organization tried to be positioned on the administrative and disciplinary committees, districts, provinces and headquarters branches, at the same time, by utilizing their membership of municipal and provincial council power, they tried to obtain the maximum number of mayors, and to insure this they also utilized the local administrations' power whom they had influence with.

Offensive Strategy

The last strategic move of FETÖ/PDY, which had almost completely seized the police force, the judiciary and the army, was the attempt to take over the state administration completely. First of all, in the 2011 general elections, a considerable number of (70-80) deputies in the parliamentary group of the ruling party were bidden to be under the organizations' control. The organization's executives planned to have the authority to force the ruling party to lose its majority in the parliament; this would take place at a determined time by making sure that these deputies under their control would resign at command. However, even after failing to this, they attempted to seize the National Intelligence Organization Undersecretary and attempted to assassinate Recep Tayyip Erdoğan, who was the Prime Minister at the time. Several plans were orchestrated by FETÖ/PDY such as; the Gezi Park incidents, the 17-25 December judicial coup, the detaining of the National Intelligence Organization's trucks, the alliances established with the opposition, the terrorist organizations in the local election of 30th of March 2014 and the general elections of 7th of June 2015 and 1st of November 2015. In this way they attempted to isolate Turkey by campaigning against it, and leading it into an economic and political crisis, thereby overthrowing the government. However, after all these plans failed, they resorted to attempt a final military coup on the 15th of July 2016. Thus, the power and management would be in the hands of the FETÖ/PDF members, and they would create "a *communal class*", where Fetullah Gülen would supposedly be the imam of the universe. A dictatorial structure would be established. Thus, a society would be shaped, where the purpose of the organization's existence of serving the interests of western powers would be achieved. The society would have members that are submissive, docile, supposedly reconciliatory, and harmless. Moreover, even though they would not have any Islamic virtues, they would be called a Muslim nonetheless. These Muslims would be completely spilt up from Islam's core values. Fetullah Gülen and his squad worked for decades as volunteer fighters of a destruction project that would have eliminated the Islamic world as a whole for the sake of worldly reign.

Tactical Strategy

The strategies implemented by the organization have been reinforced with a very strong tactical approach. At the beginning of this kind of approach, the organization did not openly engage with any political party, rather the strategy of infiltrating and manipulating all political parties, including the ruling party was implemented. This tactical understanding was intended to provide the organization with a very wide maneuver area and to ensure that all parties of the system entered into competition among themselves in order to make more concessions to the organization. Thus, FETÖ/PDY gained great advantage from this situation at almost every period. Not openly engaging with politics was implemented in order to make sure the organization accumulated enough capacity to seize the power later on. Since, entering into a political struggle without having sufficient power could have resulted in the loss of all the accomplishments of many years of hard labor.

In order to achieve its objectives and to implement its strategies successfully, the organization appraised children and the youth as *"human resource"* and the tradesman (*esnaf*) as *"money and logistics resource"* masterfully. Students that had completed their education in domestic and foreign schools, private tutoring institutions and dormitories that the organization operates, have been the basis of the human resources of the organization.

The organization is known to have targeted primarily the 13-18 age group since that is when idealism is at the strongest. In the following period, the organization started to operate kindergartens for 3-6 age group, in which their religious feelings start to develop and they put a lot of effort into raising young children in line with the organization's goals. The organization has a wide acceptance in society in general by conducting a comprehensive perception operation through educational institutions operating in Turkey and abroad. It was also able to camouflage its real intentions and to legitimize all kinds of illegal activities that it carried out. The organization finally created an illegal structure parallel to the state, and concealed itself behind values such as tolerance, peace, democracy, human rights and freedom.

In this way FETÖ/PDY managed to connect with people who had sympathy to them. However, they carried out this task by exploiting their religious-emotional bond, and manipulating them in in their regular religious conversations that were held across numerous households - where they conversed, and held meetings. The money collected under the name of "*himmet* (monetary donations)", real estate donations and aids provided the financial resources necessary for the organization to operate.

Some of the instructions given by Fetullah Gülen himself in the process of achieving the objectives of the organization are:

1. *Be flexible, swirl through their main veins without coming into existence.*

2. Proceed through the main veins of the system until you reach all the power centers without anyone noticing your presence.

3. Until the power and strength in Turkey becomes on your side, each step, each action you take is still too early.

4. The presence of our friends in the judiciary and the civil service sector, or any other vital institution should not be considered as individual entities, those friends in those units are our guarantees.

5. In a place where there is no balance of power, you shall not use any force.

6. When the balance is ignored, heroism is considered as a betrayal in cases where defeat and fiasco are inevitable.

7. Because a balance of power is not present, I personally prefer to disseminate my own thoughts and try to confiscate every side in order to achieve this.

8. It is not the right time. You must wait until the conditions are appropriate.

9. Until they develop and take office in high ranking positions, it is essential that they serve as they do.

10. Considering Turkey's state structure, until we confiscate all constitutional institutions and keep them really close to us, it will still be too early.

11. There is not a single person in this world, which is not willing to do anything for something. Everybody has a price. Only their prices are different. Some are costly some are cheap.

The tactics and methods applied by the organization can be summarized as follows:

1. To look moderate enough to reach enough power, to hide oneself, keeping oneself disguised by being cautious, and finally attacking when it reaches sufficient power.

2. To have the capacity to determine the agenda, to have the power to initiate and impact situations when necessary, and to have a general awareness of the events that occur.

3. Abusing social values to provide resource and legitimacy for the sake of the organization's interests.

4. Educating, especially, selected young people to create a human resource which is specifically obedient to the organization's decisions, which are always in line with the organizational ideology.

5. To infiltrate political and state institutions with a parallel organization that is in accordance with the current state model.

6. To find common ground with Christians and Jews by reforming Islam, through interreligious dialogue and Abrahamic religions project.

7. Leaving the companies and their affiliates unrivaled by revealing the weaknesses of competing companies, through the organization's security and financial intelligence networks.

8. To control the country's economy through its members corporations, federations and holdings.

9. To obtain the questions that will appear in public sector exams in order to assure that the majority of their followers enter public institutions and successful schools.

10. Opening judicial and administrative investigations by using false documents and evidence in order to remove those people that are not a part of the organization from public offices, thereby enabling the organization to place its own followers in these sectors.

11. To collect and archive information about the peo-

ple that the organization considers important, as well as the members of the organization.

12. Keeping close ties with the ruling government in each period to prevent actions taken against the organization.

It is also known that FETÖ/PDY entered into murky relations with terrorist organizations, mafia and other illegal organizations in order to achieve its organizational goals. The members of the organization that work in the military field have actively cooperated with PKK, PYD-YPG, DEAŞ, DH-KP-C and similar terrorist organizations. They have exposed MİT members that have infiltrated terrorist organizations which has led MİT members being executed. Furthermore. FETÖ/PDY has also carried out assassinations in collaboration with the terrorists and the mafia, and they have participated in illegal activities such as smuggling.

On the other hand, FETÖ/PDY has also allied itself with liberals, conservatives and democratic leftists, especially to get rid of the commanders in the military that are opposing FETÖ/PDY's position. Furthermore, the European Union's stance on this issue was neutral and did not act against it in this period since the organization kept highlighting the EU accession process of Turkey. The FETÖ/PDY has also reinforced the general perception that the main obstacle to implement democratic reforms is the army. It has also led several initiatives in the United States and the EU to create a political atmosphere both in Turkey and abroad to prosecute those that stand against the organizations goals. The FETÖ/PDY has mainly accomplished the removal of the groups in the army, which were also under pressure from the lobbying activities conducted by the national and international groups in this period. Thereby it has been able to place its members of the organization in many strategic positions.

The FETÖ/PDY has the strong belief that the ends justify the means. It believes that it is permissible to do anything to achieve its goals, and therefore its members were encouraged to engage in active deception, align oneself with different political views when necessary. Their members were allowed to do almost anything that is forbidden in religion and forbidden by law such as; lying, theft, arson, false testimony, murder, human trafficking, extortion, assaulting, keeping captives, organizing a lynch campaign, committing adultery, making false declarations, conspiring against someone, interfering with private life , gathering intelligence illegally, cooperating with foreign intelligence units, giving the secrets of the state to other states, producing counterfeit documents, forgery in official documents, assembling and producing fraudulent tapes/CDs, wiretapping, creating unjustified laws and implementing them, torture, abuse, giving or receiving a bribe, being unfair, stealing public exam questions, blackmail, engaging in collusive tendering, embezzlement and slandering someone.

Retired Deputy Chief of Directorate General of Security Cevdat Saral and former Chief of Ankara Police Department Osman Ak heretofore prepared a report on FETÖ/PDY. This report was sent to related units in the government on 16th of April 1999 and also to the State Security Court on the 21st of April 1999. In the report they predicted that, *"A critical uprising; such as the Babai revolt, Sheikh Bedreddin's Rebellion and Sheikh Said rebellion could occur if the measures are not taken in time"*. On the other hand, Zübeyir Kındıra who was removed from the Police Academy by the organization and who was one of the first people who wrote about this organization noted in his book that, *"This organization is actually a terrorist organization and it is very dangerous."*

FOUNDATION AND DEVELOPMENT OF FETÖ/PDY

The FETÖ/PDY, was established under the leadership of Fetullah Gülen, and has been called; *"Cemaat* (religious communal society)"*, "Gülen's Cemaat", "Fetullah Gülen's Cemaat"*, "Camia" (religio-social circle) and "the Serving Movement" until the end of 2013. It uses different names mainly because the organization management and its followers want to use the names depending on the time and the conditions in general. *"cemaat"* and *"hizmet* (Service)" have a religious aspect to them and therefore are generally used by the organizations lower base. However, the middle-top managers in the organization tend to use *"camia"* or "the Serving Movement". In both cases, the terms present special meanings and are used especially for the target group.[18]

Following the 17-25 December judicial coup attempts against the government in 2013, the organizations real intentions were revealed, and they started to be referred as a *"Parallel Structure"*, *"Parallel State Structure"* and *"Fetullahist's Terrorist Organization"*. The usage of these names became accepted and widespread after The National Security Council of Turkey passed decisions regarding the organization and lawsuits were launched against the organization.[19]

The development of FETÖ/PDY occurred in three main stages. The first stage, referred as the "*nesting*" stage was implemented in secrecy and continued until the end of 1983. The second stage, referred as the "*fledgling*" stage, involved the period where the organization heavily engaged in infiltrating the state institutions. The organization was actively using deception and trying to conceal their real intentions until the end of 2006. The third "*offensive*" stage, is the period where all of the State's institutions and corporations were intended to be seized.

The Nesting Period (1966-1983)

Although it is difficult to make a definitive determination about the establishment date of FETÖ/PDY, it can be said that the organization was founded in 1966 by Fetullah Gülen when he was appointed as a teacher in the Imam-Hatip Association and Theological Student Raising Association in Kestanepazarı district of Izmir. This association operated a dormitory where Fetullah Gülen was appointed as a director with a specific mission there. In the early years, he began recruiting people around him while operating within the "*Nurculuk*" movement. On the surface he seemed to be a normal "*Nur student who is a servant for faith and the Qur'an*". Whereas, the fact was that he had exploited the goodwill of Kestanepazari Mosque and the Quran course community, and started to form a group of sympathizers around himself during this period. His activities were mainly focused on students and young people in the age group of 13-18 and he went onto establish the community that is today known by his name. Blatantly, Fetullah Gülen who denied being a Nurcu, gave a plea in the 1971 Nurculuk Case, but repeated the denial whenever he had an opportunity in later years[20], still he did not hesitate to use the Risale-i Nur Collection as well. As a matter of fact, in his infamous cursing session, where Fetullah Gülen displayed his true colors and stopped hiding his real intentions, one can clearly see the famous books of the Risale-i Nur Collection such as, 'The Words', 'The Rays', 'The Flashes' and 'The Letters'.

Many of Gülen's first students who later became "senior older brothers" of the organization was in his core staff. In 1970, an oath was prepared by Fetullah Gülen himself. By taking the oath his core staff began acting on behalf of his organization.

The context and the background of the text of the oath written by Fetullah Gülen according to journalist Nurettin Veren is as following[21]

When 15 of us were staying in a student house in Izmir in 1970, this core 15-16 members took an oath prepared as a text by Gülen.

I am now writing the original oath in the following text.

Bismillahirrahmanirrahim (In the name of Allah, the compassionate, the merciful)

A: I will strive hard for my own excellence as well as for my community and my friends. I will honor them and I will devote myself entirely to the Qur'an.

B: I will express my gratitude when being criticized; however, I will stand against and defend my organization against all the assaults and critiques as if they were done to myself.

C: I will act accordingly to the decisions I have made, I will not question the duties assigned to me, and complete them without any hesitation.

D: I will keep faithful to the Qur'an and keep loyal to it under all circumstances. If I start to act for my own interest and defy the task assigned to me, I will leave this group and remain a normal student in the dormitory and act accordingly.

I TAKE THIS OATH, IT SHALL BE PERMANENT, AND GOD SHALL BE MY WITNESS.

In two places in the text of the oath, loyalty and the Qur'an are mentioned. In the original text of the oath; the "Qur'an" was not written in the oath, rather "Fetullah Gülen's name" was written. However, Fetullah Gülen realizing that having the text "being loyal to Fetullah Gülen" rather than having "being loyal to the Qur'an" would generate a strong reaction, he crossed his name out, and replaced it with Qur'an.

So at some point we took the oath as "being loyal to Gülen".

During the 80's revolution period Fetullah Gülen told these 14 friends to destroy the oath's text that was given to them and to burn them. If I am not mistaken, the only copy that survived belongs to me. I don't think that anyone else has an original copy. That is why I am writing this. ...

In 1971, a meeting was held in Vehbi Koç's house and it was claimed that Fetullah Gülen, Vehbi Koç, Fuat Doğu, who was the MİT Undersecretary of the time, Yasar Tunagür, who was the Vice-President of The Presidency of Religious of Affairs of the time, and other important members of the Turkish Armed Forces participated in this meeting.[22] Yaşar Tunagür was previously a manager of the Qur'an course in Kestanepazarı, a district of Izmir. He became friends with Gülen when Gülen was the preacher of Edirne Üç Şerefeli mosque. After Yaşar Tunagür left his position as a manager of the Qur'an course he appointed Fetullah Gülen himself as the manager. Moreover, several allegations have come to light with regards to Yaşar Tunagür's close relations with MİT during that time. In light of all of this data, it can be easily deduced that many critical topics must have been deliberated on during that meeting.

Gülen's attitude during his stay in the Alvarlı Madrasah, the altering of his birth date to appear older, acting as an informant when he was in the military, actively being engaged in the establishment of the Anti-Communism Association in Erzurum, being appointed as a manager after Yaşar Tunagür at the Qur'an course in Kestanepazarı, and participating in a meeting held in Vehbi Koç's house can all be considered parts of the US-MİT cooperation in which Gülen was set the duty (or perhaps Fetullah Gülen decided to this by himself) to form a religious community around him. Therefore, it cannot be claimed that Fetullah Gülen's purpose was to work on behalf of the Islamic World all along. In fact, this type of venture was commenced in Erzurum because the city's Islamic importance in Eastern Anatolia. Selecting a village Imam's son, who is ambitious in the sense that he wants to prove himself[23], who has a potential to establish good relations with upcoming politicians, and who was also brought up in a village may have been considered the most logical strategy for that time period.

According to retired Undersecretary Emre Taner, after Fetullah Gülen was appointed to central Izmir as a preacher, several members of the secret services of the foreign countries became interested in him all of a sudden, and started contacting him by using their "*diplomatic*" status. Their interest in him increased from the second half of the 1970's. The West has tried to pursue an experiment with their notion of a good-natured moderate Islam through Fetullah Gülen, and engagements and contacts with him were made within this context.[24]

In the 1970s, Fetullah Gülen presented himself as having a strict religious understanding. For example, he advised women to wear veils and chadors[25]. It is suspicious that Gülen once had the belief that "*wearing veils is essential for women*", and later on said, "*Wearing a headscarf is not a must, it's considered as more of a detail*"[26]. This is mainly because Gülen's positions on certain issues revolve around projected developments and the conditions of the time period. He basically takes an opportunistic approach, and pivots when necessary. During that time period it is clear that he was able to easily break even the most essential religious principles in order to carry out the tasks assigned by MİT and the USA. In the 1970's, his main focus was increasing his followers base, keeping a rhetoric that drew people who had strong religious sensitivity towards him in order to create a religious community. However, during the episode of the 28th of February, when conditions changed drastically, he began giving fatwas that said that wearing headscarves were not essential in Islam. Whereas, Gülen kept criticizing the United States at every opportunity that he had in order to mask his special task set by the United States. It is interesting to note that Gülen's preaching cassettes dating pre-1980's were destroyed by the organization in matching the change in his conjecture. This clearly displays his opportunistic and hypocritical approach. Keeping these cassettes in FETÖ/PYD's houses was even considered a treachery towards the organization.[27]

From the mid-1970s onwards, Gülen began to voice his "*golden generation*" idea and started using this terminology in his sermons. It was said that this *golden generation* was the expected generation that "*would have the Qur'an in one hand, and a computer in the other*", and that this generation would sprout and the *Age of Bliss* would take place once again. It was further contended that "*Hizmet*(Service)" will finally be complete under this generation, which is also referred to as the "*huruç* (dissident)" generation. Having such code names, like the "golden generation", the "*service privates*", the "*light cavalry*" and the "*dedicated spirits*", that have distinct connotations, clearly indicates that Gülen had formed a certain brand of organization, rather than a religious community.[28]

In the organization's Nesting Period, opening "*light houses*"[29] was prioritized. These houses are the places where the members of the organization were brought up under close supervision in order to be used as means to infiltrate the state and the civil institutions. Moreover, communal methods were used to provide economic resources to these *light houses*. These houses were launched rapidly, one after the other, and were maintained with the donations made by philanthropic affluent people.

In 1977, the number of light houses opened by Gülen in Izmir exceeded the number of sixty. The students living there were brought together with the notion of, "*ensuring equality of opportunity in education for peasant children*" and "*providing shelter and accommodation for Anatolian children who did not have the means necessary for education*". People who genuinely believed that Gülen's main purpose was to educate the youth, for the young generation to become successful, moral, committed to religious values, and being respectful to their families, basically becoming role models in the society; supported Gülen and thus the organization first dormitories started operating.[30]

It's pretty peculiar that since the 2000's only young people that come from good financial status were accepted to these dormitories created by the Anatolian people. These people's religious emotional states were exploited by Gülen in order to gather donations. The youth that did not come from such privileged financial standings were not accepted to such dormitories, especially, if they were not exceptional. This situation actually demonstrates that the statement, *"teaching the poor and the peasants"*, did not essentially reflect the reality on the ground, and that the organization had completely different intentions. This was actually a strategy implemented in order to set up the organization and its expansion. Later disclosures have revealed that this strategy basically was a type of debt. It left the person feeling obligated to pay back to the organization. This meant that the *golden generation*, which was expected to make the *golden strike*, was fully under the organization's control and were obliged to do anything that the organization commanded. Being in debt basically meant that, after a member of the organization was appointed in a governmental position, it was expected that these members would act in accordance with the interest of the organization rather that the State. During this period the public institutions began to be infiltrated by the organization's secret agenda. Since the intention of the organization was hostile and unscrupulous from the very beginning, the organization placed its members into public and state institutions very cautiously in a stealthy way in order to *"infiltrate"* these places.[31]

The first issue of the Fountain (*Sızıntı* -The root of the word "Sızıntı" is "Sız" which is actually a verb (sızmak) that means to infiltrate) magazine, which was published in February 1979, was one of the first and most powerful propaganda tools of the organization. In addition, considering the *"in-*

filtration" strategy of the organization, which mainly targeted important State institutions, it can be deduced that the name *Sızıntı* was particularly chosen for this magazine. In the June 1979 issue of Sızıntı, Fetullah Gülen concluded in his editorial, *"Soldier"* that *"His bayonet stopped us from wailing and comforted us a hundred times ... If the dark ambitions, which had prepared itself for many years, were not quickly prevented, we would have no choice but to curse and cry. Hail to the Tughra, hail to the flag, and hail to those who carry the flags"*. This indicates that Gülen was very aware of the military coup of 12ᵗʰ of September, 1980 beforehand. During a time period and in an environment where Fetullah Gülen's followers were not largely appointed in the army, and had almost no opportunity to receive intelligence from the army, it can be inferred that the deep state, both the domestic and the foreign intelligence agencies, informed him of the military coup. As a matter of fact, in his article titled *"The Last Post"*, written in the October 1980 issue of Sızıntı magazine after the 12ᵗʰ of September military coup, it is clear that Fetullah Gülen clearly supported the military coup and presented this very transparent message *"I am at your service"*: *"And now, here, we are very hopeful and delighted, we have waited a century for this, this last post's existence, this awakening is a miracle, we hail the military once again for a saving us when we had lost all hope"*. It is also well known that FETÖ/PDY voted "yes" for the 1982 constitutional referendum and as a result of this, it was also the least effected group from the martial law. Gülen confirmed this in an interview with a newspaper. He gave his support to the military coup, and claimed that, if Kenan Evren did not even have a single good deed, he would go straight to heaven.[32]

In his so-called religious conversations that he conveyed in the meetings of the organizations in Izmir in April and June of 1980, Gülen said the following words: *"The Huruç (Dissident) operation has begun, however this operation will be put into action in 35-40 years, this plan cannot be implemented considering our present state. Opening of dormitory buildings for middle and high school students in the whole country is essential for the success of the Huruç (Dissident) operation. The students that are trained in dormitories should start giving successful results, the publication of books and magazines in line with our own ideas should be completed, and especially a large force of teachers in Turkey is required to operate in our own favor in order for the Huruç (Dissident) operation to become successful."*[33]

Retired MİT Undersecretary Emre Taner, claimed that FETÖ/PDY rapidly expanded in the education sector during the 1980's. Their members that were working in schools put great effort in their work, and were paid very low wages as if they were legionaries. He also stated that they were accepted with tolerance by various circles inside and outside the country due to them having the image of being law abiding modern citizens.[34]

Due to the contributions of the public in 1981, the number of dormitories in the country rose to one hundred. The expansion of these schools ensued very rapidly. According to eyewitness sources, those students in the dormitories that graduated began to work in public offices. In the same years Fetullah Gülen started to gather illegal intelligence and began wiretapping; he even spied on his closest friends with wiretap during this period. A listening device was found in İlhan İşbilen's room in Altunizade, who was one of Gülen's core members and who had taken the loyalty oath. Later on several other listening and recording devices were found in residences in which İlhan İşbilen worked. There are several witnesses that claim that Gülen wiretapped numerous people other than Latif Erdoğan and İlhan İşbilen. Fetullah Gülen's 130-acre farm in Pennsylvania was established during this period. This also gives insight into the power and the attention that the organization gave to its cause even in those early times. Necdet Başaran, a close friend of Fetullah Gülen, established in the 1980s a charitable foundation under the name of *Golden Generation Foundation* and this charitable foundation purchased 130-acres land along with 8 villas on the land. This is a clear indication that the organization's plans were not short-term, and that it gained an international element soon after its establishment.[35]

The Fledgling Period (1984-2006)

National and spiritual values came to the forefront when the Motherland Party came to power after the general elections were held in November 1983. The country transitioned in to a free market economy at this time period. After some legislative regulations in 1986, private enterprises were encouraged to open schools. During this time the organization considered this as a great opportunity and rapidly invested in opening new schools. *Yamanlar College*, established in Bozyaka, which is a district of Izmir, became the first private school of the organization.[36]

The *Samanyolu High School* in Ankara, another school established in the same period, became one of the top-line educational institutions of the organization and it also carried a symbolic value. These two schools were put forward in various platforms in the following periods such as the Science Olympics and were used as the most important domestic and international publicity tool for the organization. These school played the leading role in the shaping the public opinion, as in, these schools created a perception of a "*charity movement that cultivates successful and moral students*". However, considering that the organization serves the dominant global powers, especially the USA, and that it engages in unscrupulous relations with these global powers, it is highly probable that the results obtained in the inter-high school Science Olympics are disputable These schools were brought to the fore in Turkey, and they were unrivaled. The demand for these schools rose abnormally. This may be because these schools were inflated to become models for undeveloped countries that possessed a very poor education system. This enabled the organization to easily enter the country under the name of investing in education. After all, no country would want to oppose investment in education. However, even though these schools seemed innocent, in reality these schools were filled with CIA agents, and these agents compiled and provided valuable intelligence to dominant global powers, especially for the United States.[37]

The achievements of these high schools in the national and international level may be questionable and fraudulent. It can be said that many groups in the national level and the secret services of the countries supporting the organization may have taken undertakings to make certain that the organization achieved successes that were undeserved. This was mainly accomplished in order to advertise the schools of the organization. For instance, the fact that we have learned recently is that the organization had infiltrated TÜBİTAK, which makes the majority of TÜBİTAK awards received by these schools suspicious and suspect. A system that is so successful in elementary, middle and high school education and is known for its investment in research should be expected to display the same success at the university level. However, FETÖ/PDY universities have almost no success to show at the national and the international level, which proves that there is a major inconsistency in the high schools of the organization to have achieved excellent international success. The fact that the organization's universities have not contributed in science and technology at the level of other universities clearly demonstrates that these schools are actually utilized by dominant global powers, and are nothing more than mere means to serve their secret ambitions. These schools have been given special importance in the national and international level, even though they have not been directing their resources into investment and development. These schools do not have any accomplishments at the university level and it is clear that FETÖ/PDY high schools and universities of the country do not have any considerable contributions. The youth have been guided towards these schools, and have been deceived by telling them that they are, "the *golden generation*", "*the expected youth*" and "*light cavalries*". This clearly demonstrates that in reality, the organization is not a local or national organization, rather it is a camouflaged disloyal network that was established by foreign powers, which has served them for fifty years.

A secret witness in the *Çatı İddainamesi* (Comprehensive Indictment) stated that, "*The first himmet meetings started to be held in 1983, the meetings were later on transformed into big events, people who had strong rhetoric and deep religious knowledge were selected as leaders in the meetings, these leaders' aims were to influence the participants, motivate them to get more contributions out of them.*" The fact that the witness who gave this information claimed that "*he met senior bureaucrats working in official offices in these community meetings*" proves that the organization had started to position its members in state positions well before the 1980's and continued long after that period.[38]

Furthermore, FETÖ/PDY voluntarily adopted the "moderate Islam" approach, which is one of the concepts produced by the "inter-religious dialogue process" developed by the World Council of the Churches[39] in collaboration with the Vatican, and has acted as a representative of the interreligious dialogue process in the Islamic world. Interfaith dialogue process, for FETÖ/PDY, is a new phase of the mission to *serve and cooperate with the global dominant powers.*[40]

The 1980's were the period when the "*chosen*" students of the organization were frequently directed to military high schools, police colleges and police academy. Since 1984, these chosen students have been continuously monitored and controlled by the members of the organization known as "*the Imam of the students*". The questions to be asked in the military high school, Police College and police school entrance exams were taken by the organization; their answers were given to the students to be memorized, by claiming that "*these were trial exams*" and that "*the older brothers saw some of these questions in their dreams*". Thus, the organization's students that prepared for such exams received high scores.[41]

Educating "*an extremely successful and moral student*" figure has been advertised extensively and has been used as a public relations material, which has been appreciated by most of the society. In addition, this acted as an "*auto defense*" function which the organization's opponents could not easily object towards. In this way, the organization was protected from all kinds of suspicion, criticism and attacks in advance by using this as an armor. With the recognition of the need for university preparatory courses, hundreds of preparatory course centers, such as the Fırat Education Center (FEM), were opened and these also drew attention just as much as the organization's schools.[42]

The system of Imams, which was implemented in the organization since the very beginning and was based on "*absolute obedience*", was extended to a hierarchical structure by extending it to include all provinces during this period. This system, which consists of the Imam of the province, the Imam of the town, the Imam of the district, the Imam of the neighborhood, the Imam of the school and the Imam of the house, evolved into a larger-scale organization system over time. In this period, "*The board of trustee's system*" was developed and the district trustees system was formed.

By this time *the Zaman newspaper*, became the most powerful tool and symbol for media division of the organization. This newspaper was established in Ankara on the 3rd of November 1986. In 1987, many of its employees were sacked and these were replaced by FETÖ/PDY's members. The newspaper was not only a means of sending Gülen's messages to the society, but also played an active role in spreading the so-called "*success stories*" of the organization. This was mainly done through promoting the FETÖ/PDY's schools.

Fetullah Gülen, in a meeting in November 1987, claimed that, "*They will give their votes to the Motherland Party (ANAP) in the early general elections of November 29 1987, because they were able to conduct the operations smoothly in the bureaucracy during the period of power (1983-1987), they were comfortable in this period and they had sympathizers in high official levels*"[43]

FETÖ/PDY, which grew rapidly, had started to act more like a corporation in the beginning of 1989 in order to sustain its increased and diversified needs. The organization later on started to operate as a major holding company to manage itself in the commercial and economic field. Sürat Yazılım, Sürat Teknoloji and Sürat Kargo are examples of companies established in this process. The main objectives of some of the companies established in this period, other than their apparent purposes, have emerged recently. For example, the Comprehensive Indictment (Çatı İddianamesi) states that, *"After securing governmental contracts, Sürat technology established infrastructure technology within ministries and public institutions, and it has backed up and archived all state data and confidential information."*[44]

Without doubt, one of the most important and sensational events of the nesting period was Gülen's visit to the Pope. Pope John Paul II's Encyclical *"Redemptoris Missio"* (Mission of the Redeemer), published in 1991 states that *"Inter-religious dialogue is a part of the Church's evangelizing mission... This mission, in fact, is addressed to those who do not know Christ and his Bible, and for the other religions. In Christ, God calls all peoples to himself and he wishes to share with them the fullness of his revelation and love."* Fetullah Gülen wrote a letter to Pope John Paul II on February 9, 1998 and used such phrases such as, *"We have gathered here to be a part of the Pontifical Council for Inter-religious Dialogue (PCID) initiated by the Holy Pope Paul VI. We wish to see the mission fulfilled."*[45]

Fetullah Gülen's Letter to Pope John Paul II

Dear Honorable Pope,

We have brought you the sincerest greetings from the people that are from the lands of the three great religions. These people know of our holy mission, which is to make the world a better place. We would like to thank you from the bottom of our hearts for taking the time for us, even though you had a very busy agenda.

We have gathered here to be a part of the Pontifical Council for Interreligious Dialogue (PCID) initiated by the Holy Pope Paul VI. We wish to see the mission fulfilled. It may seem presumptuous of us, but we have come to you to offer our most humble assistance to give our service to you for your very precious mission.

Islam has been a misunderstood religion and this situation is mainly the Muslims fault. A convenient effort in the right time can contribute to a significant reduction of this misunderstanding. The Muslim world will embrace the possibility of dialogue that will dissolve the false perception of Islam that has occurred over centuries.

Humanity, on the grounds that they present contradictory views, has sometimes denied religion in the name of science and science in the name of religion. All knowledge belongs to God and religion stems from God. So how can these two contradict? Our common efforts to promote interfaith dialogue to increase understanding and tolerance among people can have phenomenal results. In our own country, we have been in dialogue with the leaders of various Christian denominations. We would like to wish that this humbling effort not be wasted. Our aim is to establish a brotherhood through tolerance and understanding among the believers of these three great religions. We would like to come together and stand against those who are skeptical and have departed from the right way. We can act as barriers to stop them.

Last year, we organized a symposium on peace and dialogue between civilizations attended by famous international scientists. We would like to repeat such activities because we are encouraged from the success of our previous effort. We are currently in the process of organizing a conference in which we hope that the Vatican will be represented in the interreligious dialogue in order to strengthen the links between the devotees of the three major religions.

We do not claim to have new ideas. Again, please allow us to present a few offerings, to help you complete your noble mission. To honor the celebration of Christ's third millennium, we would like to suggest a number of events that include joint visits to some of the sacred sites in the Middle East, such as Antakya, Tarsus, Efes and Jerusalem. We would like to take this opportunity and repeat President Mr. Demirel's invitation to visit Turkey, and to show the sacred places in the country. The people of Anatolia are eagerly awaiting to show their hospitality and to greet you with enthusiasm. An invitation can be prepared, to visit Jerusalem together and engage in dialogue with Palestinian leaders. This visit may act as a great step towards the efforts of declaring this blessed city into an international region where Christians, Jews and Muslims can freely roam without any restrictions or even visas. We offer to start a series of conferences in various world capitals, the first of which can be in Washington, DC, with the cooperation of leaders from the three great religions. The second of this series can start with The Birth of Jesus's 2000th anniversary. A student exchange program will also be very useful. The education of these faithful young student will bring them closer, and they will create new bonds with one another. Within the framework of the student exchange program, a Theology school can be established in Harran, in the city of Urfa, known as the birthplace of the Prophet Abraham, who is recognized as the father of the three great religions. This can be done either by expanding the programs at Harran University or as an independent university with an extensive curriculum providing the needs of the three religions.

The suggested programs can be perceived as unachievable; but in fact they are not. There are two types of people in the world. Some try to adapt themselves to society. Others want to adapt society to their own values rather than adapting to society. The community owes all the progress to this second type of people. Praise the Lord for creating them."(Gülen / God's impotent servant/February 9, 1998)

In his letter to the Pope, Gülen made the following suggestions as if he were representing the entire Islamic world.[46]

1. To organize a conference to strengthen the links between the members of the three religions, where the Vatican is also represented.

2. To celebrate the third millennium of Christianity. For example; organizing visits to places considered sacred by Christianity such as Tarsus, Antakya, Efes and Jerusalem.

3. Visiting Jerusalem together with Palestinian leaders and having dialogue with them.

4. To organize a series of conferences with the participation of the three Abrahamic religious leaders.

5. To apply for an exchange programs among students from different religions and also open a theology school in Urfa, in the city that is identified with Abraham (pbuh).

Fetullah Gülen demonstrates some type of schizophrenia and personality disorder in his interreligious dialogues. For example, while FETÖ/PDY are against any Muslims who are not like themselves; i.e. they have a cold, exclusionary and alienating attitude towards them, towards the non-Muslims they are very tolerant and have a warm disposition. Thus, in total contradiction to the depictions in the 29th verse of chapter, al-Fath, the organization has instead been *"fierce against believers and compassionate against disbelievers"*. Moreover, Fetullah Gülen's dialogue with the non-Muslims was withheld from Muslim groups and always kept away from them. In fact, he has continuously shown his scorn for other Muslim groups, and in a very non-Muslim fashion he has plotted against these groups and has tried to silence them. In many Qur'anic verses[47], however, Almighty God forbade to abandon the believers, becoming friends with the disbelievers, the enemies of God, and the enemies of the Muslims.[48] Gülen has also blamed Muslims for all the evils of our time and shifted the responsibility only towards the Muslims.

While Islamophobia was rising in the West, rather than standing against this wave and guarding the Muslim's dignity as well as preserving the *Islamic Worlds honor*, he tried to appear sympathetic by using concepts such as tolerance and interreligious dialogue. He has also utilized the "*he Muslim figure that has been caricatured as the Devil*" and claimed that "*He has the Islamic way that would be appreciated very much*". Gülen thereby has looked for his dignity in the wrong places. Rather than defending the rights and dignity of the religion of Islam and The Islamic World that have been exploited over the centuries and are underestimated by the Western states, he has consistently criticized and denounced the Muslims. The interfaith dialogue that has been determined, announced and implemented solely by the Vatican, has actually been utilized to distort the Islamic religion. Fetullah Gülen who has been looking at the Turkish and Islamic World from a colonialist standpoint, has tried to position himself as a global actor by using this interfaith dialogue for his own benefit.[49]

After being in this interfaith dialogue for years, Fetullah Gülen has made these statements about the Crusades in a conversation which clearly shows the interfaith dialogue effects on Gülen and where he currently stands, "*It would not be very dangerous if the Crusaders invaded your country. Because there are clear red lines between you and them and they would not molest your wives or your daughters. They would not enter your sanctuaries. The Crusaders never acted like this.*"[50]

The interfaith dialogue activities increasingly continued in the following years. In the year 2000, an *interreligious dialogue* meeting was held in Harran which is a district of Şanlıurfa by the Journalists and Writers Foundation (*Gazetecil-*

er ve Yazarlar Vakfı). In order to spread the idea that Christianity as well as Islam is the true religion, a marriage ceremony was performed of a Christian male and a Muslim Women in front of a Mufti, Pastor and a Rabbi in this holy place of Prophet Abraham (pbuh). On 15th of April 2000, the Zaman Newspaper published news on this marriage under the heading, *"From Dialogue to Marriage"*. The Harran district of Şanlıurfa had been chosen especially for the location of the marriage. This land that has been inhabited by the Prophet Abraham (pbuh), and had the memory and legacy of the Prophet Abraham (pbuh) engraved within it was at this time under the danger of being erased, and transformed in to a place where the three Abrahamic religions come together and tried to resolve the differences between them by contradicting the religion of Islam.[51]

In fact, the *inter-religious dialogue* project that has took place between the years 1962-1965, is actually a project prepared in the II. Vatican Council[52] and its aim is to spread Christianity and to make all people familiar with Christianity or to bring them closer to Christian values. In fact, the idea of *interreligious dialogue* was initially developed by the Vatican based on Judaism. However, as a result of reactions and evaluations from Vatican churches and philosophers based on Christian theology, the concept of dialogue was extended to include Muslims, Hindus and Buddhists.[53]

In the document *Nostra Aetate* (In our time), which describes the inter-religious dialogue project, it is stated that the non-Christian religions should be seen as a preparation for the Bible. In fact, interreligious dialogue actually is the idea that the Church should adapt itself to the new era without damaging its essence, readjust itself to the changing conditions of the world, hence be able to spread its message across the world more effectively through new mediums. As a result, in the documents promoting the dialogue, it is stated that while establishing common relations with other religion members in the context of dialogue, values should be pursued; values that do not contradict with Christian core principles and beliefs can be agreed and compromised on.[54] Pope John Paul II. also stated that the dialogue with other religions was actually part of the Church's aim to spread the message of the Gospel, which is the main task of the Church.[55]

The main Muslim groups that oppose the "*interreligious dialogue*" claim that this type of interreligious dialogue is not a dialogue in the real sense. That is to say that this type of dialogue is more of an interpretation of the main mission of the Church adapted to the new conditions of our time. Moreover, the fact is that the issue of *interfaith dialogue* has been discussed in the Christian world for decades while the Islamic World have not had adequate preparation and discussion, which has led to a challenging situation. Fetullah Gülen has exploited this situation and has aligned himself with the theoreticians of the West's ideas and regarded their own calculations as his own, and acted accordingly. In summary, Fetullah Gülen basically took advantage of this situation by acting very rapidly. In addition, FETÖ/PDY's willingness to be a voluntary for this interreligious dialogue project has been met with serious suspicion. It makes one question from where this initiative arose and who gave this type of authority to Gülen, which also raises serious doubts of whether Gülen conducted these dialogues solely on good intentions. The argument presented above is now gaining strength which is the following: Fetullah Gülen is an ardent supporter, and an active member of the interfaith dialogue project. However, he has not been acting on any sincere religious and national concerns, but rather he is voluntarily become a tool for the numerous schemes that the Global Powers have created.[56]

Fetullah Gülen has promoted effortlessly the impression that the only organization in the Islamic World that understands and represents the concept "Moderate Islam" within the context of interreligious dialogue is FETÖ. He has claimed that he should be the only representative of the Islamic World in the interreligious dialogue field. His ambition later on presented itself as, *"What Vatican is to the Christian World, I am the equivalent of it for the Islamic World."*[57]

In order to realize the interreligious dialogue project that dates back to the 1960's, there was need for a *"so-called religious cleric"* in the Muslim World that could easily bend, and reshape himself. Fetullah Gülen had drawn attention from intelligence agencies and the deep state with his informant attitude during his time in the Alvarlı Madrasa. He worked on behalf of MİT when he was serving in the military, completed his military service early by using a falsified medical report, he took an active role in the establishment of Erzurum Anti-Communism Association upon USA's request, had an administrative role in community centers (*halkevleri*), attended as secret meeting in Vehbi Koç's house, where one of the invitees was the MİT Undersecretary of the time, and he also had several visits from foreign mission chiefs in Izmir. These all indicate that Gülen was selected as the person to realize the *interreligious dialogue's* goals. It can also be said that Fetullah Gülen's character of *"being a supreme leader"* has played a significant role in him being chosen for this mission. Considering that the FETÖ/PDY adapted these dialogue and toleration principles at the time it is possible that the organization might have tried to accustom Turkey to this interreligious dialogue idea.

Fetullah Gülen has audaciously claimed that he should be the only authority to represent the Muslim World on the stage of interreligious dialogue, and have acted accordingly. In addition, Fetullah Gülen's actions indicate the organization's efforts and aspirations to become a Global actor, and use this power to intensively oppress the government and the society. Furthermore, these interreligious dialogue efforts have opened major opportunities for the organization, and provided strong legitimacy for them within the Christian-Jewish community. As a matter of fact, the activities of the organization expanded rapidly after the declaration that FETÖ-PDY is a part of the interreligious dialogue processes. Support on a Global scale was provided to this organization after it was made known that it was a part of this project and this enabled it to open schools, associations, foundations, companies etc. in many countries abroad.[58]

It can be argued that using the notion of *"Abrahamic Religions"* within the framework of the interreligious dialogue project is a tool for steering Muslims to become part of the Vatican's mission. Moreover, by using this notion it may make it easier to revise the basic principles and values of Islam, and a common religion may be distinguished, which has similarities to contemporary Christian principles and values. Since Muslims have a great respect and love towards the Prophet Abraham (pbuh), his name was especially used in order to prevent any negative reactions. When a Muslim hears the name Abraham (pbuh), he automatically conceives this project in good terms.

After becoming a part of the interfaith dialogue project, the language and style used in the media body of FETÖ/PDY changed dramatically. For example, the general change in tone can be seen in Table 1.[59]

Table 1: Change of tone of FETÖ/PDY during the Interreligious Dialogue project.

Before taking an active role in the Interreligious Dialogue Project	After taking an active role in the Interreligious Dialogue Project
"A great shame for the Pope…" (23rd May 1991)	"A warm message from Vatican." (17th April 1996)
"PKK-Christian cooperation…" (25th February 1992)	"A reconciliation summit at Vatican." (09th February 1998)
"Christian Organizations movements towards Muslims is becoming concerning." (31st October 1991)	"Fetullah Gülen represents the Islamic world to the Christian world by discussing "Interreligious Dialogue" with Pope John Paul II for half an hour." (10th February 1998)
"The Patriarchate is planning a scheme." (18th June 1991)	"A message of tolerance from the Patriarchate." (19th February 1998)
"They are brainwashing the children they have contacted through dialogue, by giving them material assurances." (24th July 1992)	"President of The Association of Protestant Churches Relations with The Islamic World has made special statements to Zaman." (30th November 1998)
"An insidious trap by the Church: By appearing to be tolerant to Islamic values they are going to give lessons on Christianity" (9th June 1993)	"The first step of Dialogue; After Phanar Greek Patriarch Bartholomew completed his speech, he presented a gift to Fetullah Gülen." (2nd October 1996)

Furthermore, Gülen believes that having faith in God is sufficient for Faith. He has said that, saying *"There is no God but Allah"* is sufficient for him to embrace someone, even if the person does not add *"Muhammed is the messenger of God"* to complete the Declaration of Faith (Shahada). This has created excessive uproar in the Muslim public opinion. The Presidency of Religious Affairs has declared that the initiative of interreligious dialogue in unacceptable in Islam, by stating that, *"Proclamation of Faith cannot be fragmented by taking out Prophet Muhammed (pbuh). To be a true believer of Islam can only be achieved by acknowledging the Proclamation of Faith as a whole. That is to accept both God and his messenger Prophet Muhammed (pbuh)"*.[60]

Fetullah Gülen who claims that he meets regularly with Prophet Muhammed (pbuh) and receives information and instructions from him is supposedly expected to be the most committed to the Prophet Muhammed. Even Muslims that are not fully devoted to Islam find Gülen's affirmations *"unacceptable"*. Gülen's belief on this issue clearly indicates the kind of concessions he has had to make in order to obtain the approval and the support of global powers. Trying to remove Prophet Muhammed from the Proclamation of Faith is going too far, and it is mainly based upon Gülen's approach of not acting on any principles or not having any boundaries. He is delirious in his quest to achieve full authority and power. Such presumptuous attitudes of Gülen have been expressed by people that have been working with him for a long time.[61]

Within the context of interreligious dialogue activities, a meeting was held in Kasımiye Madrasah in Mardin between the dates of 13th -14th of May 2004, where priests and rabbis were also present. An *"as-Sirāt bridge"* was built symbolically, and the representatives of the three religions made speeches on the bridge. The same three representatives later on crossed over this symbolic bridge.[62]

It is noteworthy that FETÖ/PDY initiated a rapid expansion abroad during the period of *interreligious dialogue*. The organization, which actively took advantage of the international environment following the terrorist attacks in the USA on the 11th of September, developed serious connections with the Christian and Jewish religious leaders and the Western politicians and Statesmen through its interreligious dialogue efforts. Over time FETÖ/PDY's schools spread across all over the world.[63] Thus, the first of these schools were opened up in the Turkish republics. The organization tried to register itself as *"honorably"* representing Turkey even in countries where we as a nation do not even have foreign representation. The organization claimed to be *"a service and volunteers' movement that introduces Islam, spreads Islam, our culture, our language, our flag and our National Anthem even in the most remote African countries."* This enabled the organization to project an image that appealed to both religious and national people in the society. Teachers and students in those schools were motivated by these national and spiritual elements. Furthermore, in this period, students in the organization's foreign schools were brought together particularly with the Commander of the Turkish Armed Forces, high-ranking state officials, and high-ranking politicians. This was actually a systematic effort to show that the organization should not be considered as a *"threat"*, rather it was highly beneficial, and had many accomplishments. In one of the visits of the organization's top managers, İsmail Hakkı Karadayı, to the Commander of the Turkish Armed Forces of the time, the manager said that *"Fetullah Gülen recommends the building of schools instead of mosques"*. This statement clearly shows the organization as substandard and hypocritical.[64]

Following the dissolution of the Soviet Union, the first foreign school opened in Nakhchivan in 1992 and later on other schools were opened inside the country. In Azerbaijan and in the Central Asian countries, there was a need to fill the gap that emerged after years of being ruled under communism. The money that was saved by thousands of people from Anatolia was seized by the organization, under the name "*himmet*", to spread the message of Islam by opening new schools for the organization. So, FETÖ/PDY gave its school names of historical figures, and assumed the leading role in spreading the Turkish culture, and its moral values. In this way, it received support from several social actors but withheld its own secret agenda from them.[65] These schools did nothing more than to flatter the Turkish people and the country but the real benefits was for the USA. As a matter of fact, the main mission and purpose of FETÖ/PDY can be clearly seen by the CIA agent Graham Fuller's statements, "*thanks to these schools, we have brought an empty Islam to Central Asia*". Without spending a penny by the US, the US obtained functional bases without sacrificing anything and without taking any risks. The schools were basically bases for the US to conduct its own espionage activities and were full of CIA agents. It is also very important to note that the United States has almost no schools of their own in the countries where the organization has opened its schools.[66]

In 1994, Fetullah Gülen became the honorary President of the *Journalists and Writers Foundation* (Gazeteciler ve Yazarlar Vakfı), which was also founded the same year. The opening ceremony was considered remarkable in the media, and made the organization more recognized in both the National and the International field. Fetullah Gülen, using his honorary president title of the association had the opportunity to meet with the prime minister, other political party leaders, and leaders of religious groups and with leaders of minorities. This association acted as a spokesperson for Gülen. In the late

1990's, foundations such as the Abant Platform, the Medialog Platform, the Women's Platform, and the Intercultural Dialogue Platform were used as FETÖ/PDY's operational centers in the civil sector.[67]

In a video of Fetullah Gülen, which has been published frequently in the media, during an organization meeting he attended in 1995, he said to his followers, *"You shall put a thousand and in return only get one, what is important is to make them your captive, you should buy judges, prosecutors and lawyers. You should roam the capillaries of the state without them noticing until the right time comes."*[68] In accordance with his instructions, his followers who infiltrated the state started using code names in this time period. These codes, given by Fetullah Gülen himself, are considered to have been known only by a few people who were in Gülen's immediate circle. According to the witness statements in the Comprehensive Indictment, in 1995, upon the instruction of Fetullah Gülen, all of his followers serving in public office or in any place commenced gathering information, photographing, obtaining documents and information from public institutions, taking important copies of important information, and sending these documents to the administrators of the organization. It was also in this period when the organization started making blacklists of those that opposed FETÖ/PDY. Since then the archives in the state institutions were copied, and the organization began to create its own personal archive. Furthermore, the organization continued in this period to conduct its illegal activities such as, lifting exam questions, using falsified medical records, and interfering with examination juries. Fetullah Gülen positioned several of his followers in the Directorate General of Security and the Ministry of Justice. Considering that four hundred students who had graduated from the Police Academy in 1995, went to kiss the hand of Fetullah Gülen's, shows that the organization excelled rapidly in this time period.[69]

The organization also displayed a rapid economic growth during this period. "*Bank Asya*"[70] was founded on 24 October 1996. "*Işık Sigorta*" which was established in the same period, which is a subsidiary of Bank Asya fulfilled the need of "*conservative insurance*", and become a large and widespread insurance company. Conversely, shortly after Bank Asya was founded, another financial institution "Ihlas Finans" was confiscated by the Banking Regulation and Supervision Agency (BRSA). There are allegations that "Ihlas Finans" was confiscated to make room for Bank Asya.[71]

Fetullah Gülen continued to use the tactic of staying close and keeping strong relations to those in power. Immediately after the postmodern coup of 28th of February 1997, he wrote a letter that shows his commitment to Deputy Chief of the Turkish General Staff Çevik Bir and mentioned that making the intervention was a *very proper decision and that it was absolutely necessary*. In addition, he also pretended that upon a request he would in an instant transfer all of the organization's school to them.[72]

Fetullah Gülen's letter to the Deputy Chief of the Turkish General Staff Çevik Bir during the period of the 28th of February Coup

---

To Our Esteemed Deputy Chief of the Turkish General Staff

Dear Commander,

In recent years, my name has been associated with these schools, and this issue has been persistently resurfacing in the media. I consider the association of my name with these schools to be a grave

error. Please excuse and endure yours truly since I am taking your valuable time.

I choose the phrase "the association of my name with these schools is a grave error" on purpose. First of all, considering that even a military, political and administrative genius, like Atatürk himself, established a great state after taking over ruins used the following words "my humble body will become dirt one day. However, the Turkish Republic, will be everlasting." The great service that were given by the Turkish people during our Independence War in the name of the country, the nation, and its citizens can be considered true greatness. Therefore, appropriating someone who considers himself of not having a high a military, administrative or political capacity and having the sense that, "my humble body will become dirt one day" will be considered as seizing these people's love and enthusiasm in order to serve the country. That is why I said "associating my name with these schools is a grave error". I have repeated this countlessly, and believe that you have also heard this directly from me. As those who contribute to and manage the schools will admit, my relationship with these schools consist only as an incentive, an invitation, and nothing more. People may think of me highly in these terms, but in reality I am only serving the state and the country.

Dear Commander, as an honorable member of our heroic army and a commander of the highest rank, you are aware the nationalistic feelings that have highly developed in the cities of Kars, Erzurum and Ardahan, which have been frequently occupied by the enemies. Our country which entered World World I, fought the Turkish Independence War after the enemy occupation had taken place. As a man who has lived and grown up with great grief in the Eastern provinces in Turkey during the immediate aftermath of World War II, I have tried to channel my feelings of nationalism and service to my country in almost every place that I served as an official Religious Affairs officer and in the sermons that I gave in the mosque. At every opportunity, I tried to ignite the love of the nation and the state, in our people's hearts. I invited them to serve our Homeland without expecting anything in return from this World, nor in the Afterlife. The West opened itself to art and science after the Renaissance, and considering that one of the three greatest reasons we fell behind the great powers is our ignorance, poverty and disunion, I have always called upon the organization to educate the children, especially to enlighten their minds with positive sciences, to get rid of bigotries and superstitions, to work and to prosper, and to maintain our inner integrity in accordance with our state and laws.

Some of the people I have encouraged in this way, set up schools when our state allowed private schools to be set up, and they came together in different places and formed schools as if in a race, as you well know. These schools have represented our country with the education and success that they have achieved. They tried to open similar schools in the Turkic Republics after the collapse of the Soviet Union. Their schools main mission was to pave the way for our country to prosper, and to create lobbies on behalf of our country all over the world. They tried to establish and spread the Turkish friendliness everywhere they went.

These schools have operated entirely based upon the Turkish education system. If these schools conduct their operations against the Turkish Republics secular, independent and social structure, I will be the first to encourage these schools to be closed, even though I encouraged these school to be opened in the first place. If, as some have claimed, there is even one penny of support from enemy states or organizations from any country, I will end my own life which is already suffering from a serious ailment. Furthermore, **our state is able to take over these schools, which it already owns, at any time.** Since these schools already belongs to the state, it is foolish to think of such a thing. As a distinguished and honorable member of our glorious and heroic army that has undertaken the role of guarding the Republic of Turkey, you, the Deputy Chief of the Turkish General Staff can honor our schools and make an inspection anytime, anywhere and anyway you like.

I would like to apologize again for occupying your precious time, and wish you good fortune in the New Year. Please sir, accept my deepest respects.

Fetullah Gülen

In a short period, it has become clear that Fetullah Gülen and his organization, in fact, were the biggest victors of the 28th of February process in Turkey. Essentially Fetullah Gülen always positioned himself according to those in power.[73] In a book written by Latif Erdoğan, which is about Fetullah Gülen's life entitled "*My Small World*", claims that he said, "*March 12th was neither a revolution nor a coup*"[74] and praised the Commander of the Turkish Armed Forces during the time of Memduh Tağmaç.

The operation of "*Telekulak*" (wiretapping), which was carried out by FETÖ/PDY in 1999, led to an increase in the self-confidence of the organization, since it was considered a test of the organization in how much they excelled in their plots against a certain group. After the "*Operation Telekulak*"; the Chief of Ankara Directorate of Security Cevdet Saral, the The Chief of The Department of Intelligence under the Directorate General of Security Sabri Uzun, the Deputy Chief of Ankara Directorate of Security Osman Ak and eleven members of the police force including the above, were dismissed from office by Sadettin Tantan, who was at that time the head of the Ministry of Interior.[75] It was later on discovered that this operation was carried out against Chief of Ankara Directorate of Security Cevdet Saral and his team, who were investigating the FETÖ/PDY, and had prepared a report on the organization's real face.

During the *Telekulak operation*, information full of false data was leaked to the media related to the organization. The allegation that the above mentioned people wiretapped the top level officials of the state illegally was spread to form an environment where this group of people became distrusted. Later on the prosecutors of the organization were mobilized to remove these government officials from their positions by conducting investigations. Finally, the organization ensured that its own members replaced those government officials. The fact that the organization succeeded in such an operation immediately after the 28th of February is significant in terms of showing how much power the organization had gained.[76]

Fetullah Gülen went to the USA on the 22nd of March 1999 by using health problems as an excuse but he never received a treatment there. With Gülen's escape to the US, the discourse of the organization changed and more universal and global expressions began to be used. In this context, rather than using a nationalistic, statist rhetoric as previously used in Turkey; concepts on human rights discourse, globalization, and the notion of *mobile homeland* were used more frequently. The rhetoric of the organization changed to serve the global interests of the United States. Furthermore, in Turkey, important progress was made by the organization to position its own members in the state institutions it had previously infiltrated. The organization begun during this period to "externally manage" the seized institutions.[77]

During this period, the fifth floor of *FEM preparatory course center* in Altunizde was the host of many secret meetings held by Fetullah Gülen. Meetings took place here with the aim of managing and determining a strategy of the media outlets of the organization, such as Zaman and Samanyolu. In addition, it was also transformed into a *Tekke* (Sufi Lodge) where its members become "*enchanted*". For example, a witness stated that, "… *they had been taken to the building of the organization in Altunizade in 1998, and from there they had taken the elevator to the fifth floor. They were given the ranks of deputy sergeants. Supposedly the documents that indicated these ranks were believed to be like talismans because they were were prayed over (okunmuş) by Fetullah Gülen himself*."[78]

Fetullah Gülen's escape to the US on the grounds of his so-called health problems has been perceived by the organization as a grievance and *"emigration"* and thus it has been attempted to display it as a *"milestone"*. Essentially, this escape is a new phase for the organization's closer cooperation with global powers. Indeed, Fetullah Gülen in an interview in 1997, said, *"With the current state of the world, in this framework, America can control the whole world with its current position and power. Every activity that will be conducted around the world can be operated from here, and it can even be claimed that you will not be able to do anything in the world without being friendly to the USA, let alone getting their support. Now, if some voluntary organizations go under the name of integration with the world and open schools in different parts of the world, it is not possible for them to realize these projects if the USA is against it. America is still the steering wheel of the ship called the world."*[79] One of the reasons Fetullah Gülen used these words, is to show the organization's members the attitudes they must have in order for the safety and progress of the organization, and to show the importance of being in compliance with the USA. It can be said that Fetullah Gülen put forward the above statements in order to conceal the fact that he is an ardent servant and agent of the USA; in this way his attempt was to put an end to the hatred people -who were enchanted and in some ways even deified him- might have against the United States of America and bring them closer to it.

In 2000, the Chief Prosecutor of the State Security Court Nuh Mete Yüksel filed a lawsuit against Fetullah Gülen and his organization, under the name of *"Fetullahist Terrorist Organization"*. The prosecution was prompted by the following reason: *"To set up an organization with the aim of establishing a state order based on religious rules by changing the secular state structure"*. However, the public action carried out by this offense was within the scope of Law No. 4616[80] issued by Bülent Ecevit's coalition government and through this, Fetullah Gülen was cleared without being sentenced. The Law no. 4616 regulates the postponement of a final provision of crimes committed until the 23rd of April 1999. In particular, it has been argued that this date was specifically chosen with the initiative of Fetullahists for the protection of Gülen.[81]

A second case where Fetullah Gülen was sentenced was abolished by the amnesty law issued again by Bülent Ecevit, the prime minister of the period. During the same government period, Fetullah Gülen was rescued twice with postponement-amnesty regulations of the same Prime Minister Ecevit. For this reason, Fetullah Gülen later said, *"Bülent Ecevit will be the first person that he will intercede for in the afterlife"*. These are the reasons why Fetullah Gülen has also maintained a friendly and positive attitude towards Bülent Ecevit in the following years.[82]

Ever since it was founded, the FETÖ/PDY always sought to keep close to those who had authority, power and success. Therefore, in the general elections of 2002, the organization made an effort to appear like they were close to the AK Party, which won that year an undeniable victory. After infiltrating numerous state institutions in a thirty-year period, the FETÖ/PDY began to see their first serious results. The last phase of this infiltration process began by taking over such important institutions like the HSYK (The Council of Judges and Prosecutors), Yargıtay (The Court of Cassation) and TÜBİTAK (The Scientific and Technological Research Council of Turkey.) At the same time, this period was the time in which the economic and intelligence power of the organization excelled along with its human resources, and domestic and international networks. It also gained deep-seated clout in many fields in both the public and the private sector.

The results of the organization's investments that began in the 1970's finally started to rapidly present itself in the 1980's. As in the words of Gülen, "*The bird by expanding its wings widely*" spread like wildfire in the 1990's. In the 2000's the organization was ready for its "*golden generation*" to carry out its "*golden strike*". In this period, the organization continued its many public relations operations and to have a positive image in the public eye. In this context, the Turkish Olympics was organized for the first time in 2003, which continued on a regular basis. The Turkish Olympics was one of the universal activities of the organization where students from different parts of the world gathered and sang Turkish songs together that the Turkish society likes so much. These type of activities strengthened the virtuous perception of FETÖ/PDY, which was known as the "*Service Movement*". Again during this period, the organization developed its international connections through schools abroad and formed a giant network covering 160 countries. Particularly, relations with the United States were given more importance and the number of schools in this country increased rapidly. On the other hand, a great deal of money was spent to develop close relations with senior officials, and donations were made to election campaigns. For example, Ahmet Kara, which is the Imam that is responsible for the Kenyan region was among those invited to the presidential inauguration of Barack Obama. The invitation was made as a result of Ahmet Kara personally taking interest in Obama's relatives that reside in Kenya, accepting their children to the organization's schools free of charge, and establishing good relations with their families. This instruction is known to have been given by Fetullah Gülen personally.[83]

In this period, the organization took steps to institution-alize its power on a macro scale. In 2005, through the instruc-tion of Fetullah Gülen, the *Confederation of Businessmen and Industrialists of Turkey* (TUSKON) was established. This con-federation brought together businessmen that were members of the organization. In the following years, TUSKON became a giant structure which consisted of 7 federations and 211 af-filiated associations of these federations. As of 2014, the num-ber of businessmen and entrepreneurs as members reached 55,000.

The Offensive Period (2007-2017)

The FETÖ/PDY's attacks against the state order and the gov-ernment, contrary to what is believed, began in 2007. Ac-cording to the retired MİT Undersecretary Emre Taner, the organization's trinity of policemen-prosecutors-judges tried to control the state under certain circumstances, and the or-ganization that appeared until now to be docile, started to strike and carried out several operations[84] against the state. In the following section, the operations carried out directly by the organization or that have been contributed by them in way or another and that stand out in the public eye has been addressed.

The Assassination of Hrant Dink[85]

On the 19th of January 2007, Hrant Dink, the Editor-in-Chief of Agos Newspaper, was killed in front of the newspaper building in Şişli. In the aftermath, the relatives of the victim stated that some public officials had already been informed that the murder would be committed and that these public officials had not fulfilled their obligation to prevent the murder. They therefore filed a criminal complaint to the İstanbul Chief Public Prosecutors Office, claiming that the before mentioned public officials should be held responsible for the mishandling of the murder.

As a result of the investigation initiated by the Prosecutor's Office, the investigation numbered 2014/40810 on the 4th of December and the indictment numbered 2015/47335 were issued. According to the indictment; although Erhan Tuncel's duty as an assistant intelligence officer was terminated by Ramazan Akyürek, who was the Head of Intelligence Department on the 23rd of November 2006, this was not declared to him. The information related to the Hrant Dink assassination bill was obstructed, thus new details regarding the assassination was not transformed into the F/4 reports, and the information registration into official records were prevented. As a matter of fact, Erhan Tuncel stated in his statement dated 29th of November 2013 that even though 4 months prior to the Hrant Dink's assassination the information that a person named Ogün will conduct the assassination was received, information on the prevention of the assassination was not mentioned in the official correspondence.

Ramazan Akyurek unrelentingly concealed the information he had about the criminal network dealing with the assassination of Hrant Dink from the officers of the Istanbul Directorate General of Security. In addition, Ramazan Akyürek and Ali Fuat Yılmazer instructed the head of Trabzon Intelligence Branch Department Faruk Sarı not to give information relating to the assassination of Hrant Dink led by Yasin Hayal and his team to the officers of the Istanbul Provincial Directorate of Security.

Muhittin Zenit, who was an officer in the Bayburt Intelligence Branch Department, and some of his colleagues went to the Trabzon Intelligence Branch Department with the instructions of Ramazan Akyurek and Ali Fuat Yilmazer. Even though they weren't officially on duty they reorganized the official documents on the Hrant Dink assassination plan and destroyed some of the documents. In this context, the server and news report (F/4), which contained all the correspondence and media files in the Trabzon Intelligence Branch Directorate, were destroyed in order to hide the evidence of the crime. The meeting report (F/3) and the report containing the follow-up on Yasin Hayal dated 17th of January 2007 was hidden from the investigative authorities.

All the F/4 reports and intelligence related to the crime were conducted by the illegal unofficial C-5 office, which was established within the C Branch of the Directorate of the Intelligence Department. The requests for the expert witnesses were not provided by the Intelligence Department. A document dated 16th of February 2008, which was destroyed from the archive records of the department, was later found in the archive of the Trabzon Intelligence Branch Department. In addition, even though the phone line of Judge Erkan Çanak, who was the Chief of the Istanbul 14th Assize Court where the criminal proceedings were carried out, was registered in his name he was wiretapped under a fake profile whereby documents under the name Selman Büyükbuç were created with the claim that he was a member of a terrorist network. In this way, the judicial side of the investigation was kept under control.

Hacı Ali Hamurcu and Umit Denktaş were interviewed as witnesses by the public prosecutor Muammer Akkas, who conducted this investigation under the the matter of indictment. These interviewees later appealed to the Chief Public Prosecutor's Office on the basis that their previously statements had been given under duress and encouragement of Muammer Akkaş, the prosecutor of the investigation.

The perpetrator Ogün Samast, in the statement he gave at the Public Prosecutor's Office claimed that, "*a week before the assassination, Erhan Tuncel and Yasin Hayal told him that 'Ramazan Yürek and Ali Fuat Yılmazer are on their side, and they have nothing to worry about', and the day that he went to Trabzon from Istanbul for the assassination, Yasin Hayal told him 'you shouldn't be caught in Trabzon, but instead they will take you in Samsun, otherwise the Manager Ramazan might be discovered.'*" He further stated that after he had committed the assassination, he had suspected that the people who had followed him were police officers and informed Yasin Hayal of this matter on the phone. Yasin Hayal replied to him, "*do not fear them, they are with us*". According to the indictment report, the suspects Ramazan Akyürek, Ali Fuat Yilmazer and Coskun Çakar are the executives of the FETO/PDY's Directorate General of Security group and they used Hrant Dink's assassination as a tool for the organizations main objectives, such as Ergenekon and Balyoz. The case concerning the assassination of Hrant Dink is still continuing in the Istanbul 14th Assize Court.

The Ergenekon Davasi[86]

On the 12th of June 2007, an anonymous call was received on the 156 Gendarmerie Trabzon Provincial Command line. The anonymous call offered the following information, "There is a C-4 explosive and number of grenades located right next to an electric pole on the roof of a house located in the Ümraniye district of Istanbul." An operation was made to the above mentioned address and 27 grenades were seized.

As a result of the investigation a primary criminal indictment was prepared on the 25th of August 2008 under the charges Of managing an armed terrorist organization named Ergenekon, being a member of it, and trying to destroy the constitutional order, against the retired Brigadier General Veli Küçük, the Labor Party President Doğu Perinçek, the former President of Istanbul University Kemal Alemdaroğlu, and the Cumhuriyet newspaper owner and editor, İlhan Selçuk along with other 86 people, 46 of whom were detained.

The second Ergenekon indictment was accepted on the 25th of March 2009 with a total of 52 suspects, 37 of whom were detained and the third Ergenekon indictment was accepted by the court on the 5th of August 2009. Later on cases such as the action plan against the reactionary forces, the E-memorandum (*internet andıcı*), excavation of a criminal site in Şile, supplying arms to Alparslan Arslan who was the perpetrator of the attack on the Council of State, and the threat against the investigating prosecutor Zekeriya Öz were combined on the grounds that they were interlinked. In addition, the following cases such as the attack on the Council of State, the throwing of a grenade at the Cumhuriyet Newspaper headquarters, the throwing of a Molotov cocktail at the Cumhuriyet Newspaper headquarters, the assassination plot allegation of Fener Greek Orthodox Patriarchate Bartholomew, the two separate indictments on the assassination plot of the Sivas Armenian community leader Minas Durmazgüler, and the cases where the lawyer Yusuf Erikel and the publisher Hayri Bildik were subjects of the publicity known as the Ergenekon of Kayseri were merged with the Ergenekon case. As a result, a total of 23 indictments were merged and conducted under the *Ergenekon case file*. Thus, publicly known figures such as retired Generals Ilker Başbuğ, Mehmet Şener

Eruygur, Hurşit Tolon, Tuncer Kılınç, Kemal Yavuz, Hasan Iğsız, Mehmet Haberal, Mustafa Balbay, Tuncay Özkan and the former Head of Ankara Chamber of Commerce Sinan Aygün, became suspects under the same case.

Mustafa Balbay, Tuncay Özkan and Mehmet Haberal's requests for release, for their election as deputies were dismissed by the trial courts. Köksal Şengün, the chairman of the court, who opposed the decision, was later appointed as a regular judge to the Bolu province by the Council of Judges and Prosecutors of the time, while the judge Hasan Hüseyin Özese was appointed as the new chairman of the court.

The investigations and the prosecutions were based on statements of secret witness 9, under the code name *Deniz*, who stated that he did not want to remain anynoumous anymore. The testimony of the witness, taken under the code name Deniz, was actually a former administrator of the PKK named Şemdin Sakık. Moreover, the *secret witness* was actually a suspect in the case entitled Osman Yıldırım. In addition, these unlawful proceedings carried out in in the case accordance to the mission of FETÖ/PDY was examined in detail during the indictment dated 6th of June 2016 under the name of *"Fetullahist Parallel State Structuring Terrorist Organization"* by the Chief Public Prosecutor's Office of the Bureau of Investigation of Criminal Offenses committed against the Constitutional Order. Accordingly, the organizations Imam of the Directorate General of Security Osman Hilmi Özdil and the The Imam of National Intelligence Agency Murat Karabulut, were questioned during their entry and exit to the USA, and they were also body-searched. During the interrogation, the intelligence that was found with Osman Hilmi Özdil at the time, as well as the information on his computer, was copied.

It has been verified that the information and the documents sent by the US Federal Bureau of Investigation (FBI) were destroyed in the Directorate General of Security (EGM) and no records remain. However, as a result of the examinations carried out on the documents requested by the EGM from the FBI in January 2014 the following was revealed from the examination of said documents; it was discovered that the names of some people who were arrested in the Ergenekon case were in a hand written note. Even though an investigation process had not yet been started on these individuals, Osman Hilmi Özdil, who had no relation with the people mentioned as of the date of 18th of April 2007, had the names of these names in his personal notes that were seized from him. This indicated that the Ergenekon case was planned in advance, and was part of the strategic operation planned and implemented by the instruction of Fetullah Gülen and the administrators of the organization and that the instructions came into the country with couriers from abroad.

The Ergenekon operation was initiated by the FETÖ/ PDY in order to expose the so-called secret structure within the state. In this case, which occupied the public eye for many years, false evidence was used and people who are known to be absolutely innocent were slandered. Long indictments were prepared by deliberately using the method of copy-cut-paste. In the Ergenekon case, the reason for the accusation was not clearly understood at the time and in this atmosphere of turmoil major grievances took place; basically there was a plan to remove the people who opposed the organization within the TSK. For instance, the Ergenekon case was merged with the raid of the Zirve Bookstore in Malatya, and thereby the organization made it seem as though the Ergenekon was an armed terrorist organization by attributing the deaths of raid conducted in Malatya to Ergenekon. Moreover, although the FETÖ/PDY's agents in the Directorate General of Security knew that the journalist Hrant Dink was going to be killed beforehand, it was not prevented deliberately in order to create evidence for the Ergenekon case.

On the other hand, the attack on the Council of State was concealed by the Ergenekon case so that the aim of the assault and the real perpetrators would not be discovered. Nonetheless, a great deal of evidence has been submitted which demonstrates that the assault on the Council of State was known to the FETÖ/PDY members beforehand. The Directorate General of Security was subject to several comprehensive operations that were carried out through acts such as murders, assaults and lawsuits.

In the Ergenekon case, where a total of 23 different cases were combined, 275 defendants were tried and the defendants were punished with long-term imprisonment and aggravated life imprisonment with the decision of Istanbul 13th Assize Court by the case no: 2009/191 and the decision no: 2013/95. Due to long periods of detention in the proceedings, the defendants could only be released by an individual application to the Constitutional Court. The appeal of the case was conducted by the 16th Criminal Chamber of the Supreme Court of Appeals and the decision taken by the Istanbul 13th Assize Court was reversed on the 21st of April 2016.

The Balyoz Case[87]

The Balyoz case was prepared in order to take over strategically important Commands in the Turkish Armed Forces that had special importance in terms of the country's defense. Thus, the current commanders were discharged and the military personnel members of the organization were promoted. In news published by Taraf Newspaper on the 20th of January 2010, the public perception that the Turkish Armed Forces was planning a coup was created. This was according to two coup plot documents dated 2003 under the code names "*sheet*" and "*beard*" that was were seized, which stated that there will be a bomb attack in the Fatih and Beyazıt Mosques on Friday. The Istanbul Chief Public Prosecutor's Office launched an investigation based on these reports, and the journalist of the daily Taraf, Mehmet Baransu, handed in a suitcase full of documents, CDs and cassettes to the Chief Public Prosecutors Office on the 29th of January 2010.

The first TUBITAK report prepared from examining the CD/DVDs subject to investigation was handed over to the Istanbul Chief Public Prosecutor's Office on the 19th of February 2010. It was reported that the files on the CDs/DVDs were created in the year 2003 or pre 2003, and that no additional content was added to the CDs/DVDs. In the expert report prepared by the Military Prosecutors Office in the same period, it was revealed that 3 CD/DVDs sent from the Taraf newspaper appeared to have been created between the dates of 17-18 of August 2007. Furthermore, it was disclosed that the information on the dates of CDs/DVDs and computer were incorrect, and there were no documents relating to the investigation in the 1st Army Command computers. However, this report could not be found in the investigation file, so it was provided once again by the lawyers at the prosecution stage and submitted to the Chief Public Prosecutor's Office. The second TUBITAK report dated 16th of June 2010 stated similar findings as the first TUBITAK report. The indictment prepared by the Istanbul Chief Public Prosecutor's Office was accepted by the Istanbul 10th Assize Court and the case against 196 defendants in the Balyoz case started on the 16th of December 2010.

In the scope of the investigation carried out by the Istanbul Chief Public Prosecutor's Office and known to the public as the Prostitution – Espionage investigation, on 06 December 2010, a search was carried out at the Gölcük Naval Command Intelligence Branch. Numerous digital documents were seized in the search, which included several documents used as evidence in the Balyoz Case. The indictment prepared as of the 11th of November 2011, which was issued by the Istanbul Chief Public Prosecutor's Office on 143 defendants, was sent to the Istanbul 10th Assize Court with the request of merging the cases. After the admission of indictment, this was also combined with the Balyoz case as of 24th of December 2011.

On 19th of February 2011, the Istanbul Directorate of Security received a tip-off via email while the Balyoz Case was underway. This led to an investigation that resulted in a search warrant for the retired Intelligence Colonel Hakan Büyük residence that was in Eskişehir province. Based on the evidence obtained, the Istanbul Public Prosecutor's Office filed an indictment as of 16th of June 2011 on 28 defendants, and it was sent to the Istanbul 10th High Criminal Court with a request to combine this case with the Balyoz case.

The Istanbul 10th Assize Court issued an arrest warrant for 102 defendants on the 23rd of July 2010, just before the meeting of the Supreme Military Council. This decision was sent to the Turkish General Staff on the same day by fax. Thus, these defendants were prevented from being promoted. Furthermore, in the 14th hearing of the case on 11 February 2011, it was decided to arrest the defendants present at the hearing and to issue an arrest warrant for the detainees who were not present at the hearing. Throughout the trial, requests such as, the preparation of expert reports on the digital evidences of the case, listening to witnesses etc., were rejected by the court on the basis that they were unlawful.

The trial of the Balyoz case was completed on 21st of September 2012 at the end of its 118th session. According to the Article 147 and 61 of the Turkish Penal Code[88], decision of separation of the case was applied to by 3 defendants, a decision of dismissal was given to 2 defendants, 36 defendants were acquitted, 3 defendants were sentenced to 20 years in prison, 78 defendants were sentenced to 18 years in prison, 214 defendants were sentenced to 16 years in prison, 1 defendant was sentenced to 15 years in prison, 28 defendants were sentenced to 13 years and 4 months in prison, and 1 defendant was given a 6 year prison sentence on the basis of *"attempting to overthrow the government by force"*.

The 9th Criminal Chamber of the Court of Cassation decided to approve the conviction of 237 defendants with the case no: 2013/9110 and the decision no: 2013/12351 on the 9th of October 2013. It decided to approve the acquittal decision of 36 defendants and to reverse the conviction of 88 defendants on the grounds that they should not have been sentenced, or should be acquitted. In terms of the defendants' reversal decision of the Court of Cassation- as a result of the trial of Istanbul Anatolian 4th Assize Court- defendants that were accused of *"attempting to overthrow the government by force""* were acquitted on the proviso that they did not commit the crime. For some of the defendants, as a result of the evaluation of the evidence available, it was determined to acquit the defendants because of the fact that there were no reliable, conclusive and convincing evidence against their conviction in terms of the crime they were charged with.

Defendants and their lawyers that have been effected by

the decision of the approval of the 9th Criminal Chamber of the Court of Cassation filed a request for retrial to the Istanbul 10th Assize Court on the basis that the digital data used as evidences on their case was found to be false by the digital analysis report prepared by the TUBITAK officials on the 20th of January 2014. They also presented petitions containing allegations against the FETÖ/PDY for a retrial. The request for the renewal of the proceedings was rejected by the Istanbul 10th Assize Court on the 3rd of February 2014. Upon the individual application of some of the defendants to the Constitutional Court, the Constitutional Court decided on the 18th of June 2014 that the defendants' right to a fair trial had been violated, and that a sample of the decision was sent to the relevant court for retrial in order to eliminate this violation and the consequences. Following the closure of the Istanbul 10th Assize Court and the transfer of the case to the Istanbul Anatolian 4th Assize Court, the Istanbul Anatolian 4th Assize Court decided to renew the proceedings, to suspend the penalty of the convicts and to release them as of 19th of June 2014 based upon the additional decision. As a result of the trial; the now closed İstanbul 10th Assize Court's sentence decision on 21st of September 2012 was annulled, and the decision of the acquittal of the defendants was carried out on the 8th of June 2015.

The Istanbul Military Espionage Case[89]

According to the indictment of the Istanbul Chief Public Prosecutors Office dated 09.02.2011, a tip-off was sent to the Directorate of Security forces by e-mail on the 28th of April 2010 about a prostitution network under the leadership of three women, Vika, Dilara and Gül. This prostitution network was found to force women into prostitution and to contain girls under the age of 18. These girls were reported to be drug addicts. Within the scope of the investigation carried out, the phones used by suspects who were found to be in contact with this network were wiretapped. The investigation revealed that I.S. and Z.M, who were suspects in contact with this criminal network, were also military personnel. It was found out that especially I.S. was frequently supplied with girls from this network and his residence in Kadıköy was used for prostitution. There was also a claim that the suspect Z.M was reported to have had contact with another additional prostitution network. Furthermore, it was reported that the prostitute girls were treated medically by him, and even abortions were carried out by him of girls that fell pregnant.

On the 4th of August 2010, a tip-off was sent to the 155 police line. The tip-off stated that in the houses rented by a prostitution network, the Turkish Armed Forces, high-level commanders, officers and even students were engaging in activities with girls provided by this prostitution network. Within this network it was also stated that B.Ç, M.I, E.K, Y.S. and A.A were receiving girls from Vika and Nona Burdilli and that they operated 3 separate houses in the Kocaeli province for these purposes.

Some materials were confiscated by searching the residences of the above mentioned people. As a result of investigations on the documents and materials seized, the suspects, İ.S, Z.M., T.Z., M.S.A and Y.Ç. were found to be the managers of this network, which also conducted prostitution, blackmail and crime related activities. They also engaged in storing documents on the security of the state, conducting espionage activities, violating the privacy of life and the confidentiality of communication by illegally recording people's conversations and their personal data. Conversely, the suspects A.S.Ş., M.K., M.A., Ş.Y., F.C.Y., K.Y. and B.Ç. were claimed to have helped this network deliberately and willingly.

This criminal network established by the aforementioned suspects saved the personal data of nearly five thousand people by illegal means. It is claimed that the detailed information gathered about the thousands of people who work in different institutions can only be carried out by a criminal network with a significant hierarchical structure, that is well coordinated and have excelled in the distribution of roles among the members of the network, while attaining the utmost attention to confidentiality.

This criminal network has formed cellular structures within the state's most strategic institutions such as TSK, TÜBİTAK, HAVELSAN and Electrical Systems Command of the General Staff (*Genelkurmay Elektronik Sistemler Komutanlığı*). The network took its confidentiality very seriously; the network did not use telephones unless it was necessary. The members of the network mentioned in the above institutions were in close contact with each other, however, they did not recognize nor contact members of the network in different institutions. The organizational managers who are at the head of these cells are experts and active individuals in their fields; they send the decisions taken in line with the aims of the network to its members. The information, documents and materials they bring to them in the institutions they work for are also sent to Ibrahim Sezer, who allegedly was in charge of archiving this information.

Moreover, it has been reported that the members of the network created secret images and documents for the purpose of blackmail and espionage, the people that the organization planned to blackmail, such as the military personnel who served in important places, were provided with women for prostitution and issued them houses for such activities. They placed hidden camera devices in the above mentioned houses and blackmailed the military personnel to resign or retire. In some cases, they reported and ensured that an investigation was opened on the personnel whose upcoming promotions they wanted to prevent. They also did not hesitate to bribe in order to attain confidential documents located in strategic institutions. In particular, it is claimed that members of the network that were located in TUBİTAK, actively made an effort to stop, slow down or prevent projects conducted by TSK. The documents and projects attained through the networks espionage activities were planned to be sold to foreign countries. Also it has been claimed that in order to conduct their actions and activities in the institutions that they had infiltrated they actively tried to place their own members in these institutions. Thus, based on all the above allegations, a civil law suit was filed against the suspects.

As a result of the trial held in the Istanbul 11th Assize Court a number of defendants were sentenced on the 2nd of August 2012. Following the appeal of the decision, the 9th Criminal Chamber of the Court of Cassation approved the provision on 5th of December 2013 on the accusations for a number of defendants, reversed the sentenced for some of the defendants, and returned the case to the Istanbul 11th Assize Court. The Court finalized the provisions of the Court of Cassation. After the perpetrators made an individual application to the Constitutional Court, the Constitutional Courts decision numbered 2014/253 dated 9th of January 2015 was set, which stated that the perpetrators right to a fair trial had been violated, therefore the proceedings must be canceled, and the renewal of the proceedings must be conducted.

The decision based on the trials conducted in the Istanbul Anatolian 5th Assize Court dated 29th of January 2016 is in summary as follows; information relating to some of the wiretapping material were misquoted in the official records, the correction request were not taken into consideration, the digital materials were planted in the houses by the people that planned these operations, and no concrete and demonstrable evidences have been found concerning the allegation that the perpetrators were organized as cell structures. Although the alleged criminal network was asserted to act in great secrecy, identities and contact information of the accused perpetrators, who were mentioned as members of the network, were explicitly included in the digital materials. The fact that all digital data, including the archive of the network, was preserved in a bachelor pad used by many people is in contrast with any reasoning linked with a cover-up. There was also no concrete evidence that the members of the network have received anything for their interest from any domestic or foreign people or institutions. There was also vagueness regarding where and with whom the network conducted its operations, and which houses were used for prostitution. Regarding the persons or military personal who were the subject of the digital documents, none of them claimed that they were blackmailed, threatened or acquired any interests. The request of the perpetrators and their defenders, for the examination of the digital materials by experts, were denied. Any meta-data generated by the electronic signature indicating that the meta-data contained in the digital documents belonged to the perpetrators was not to be found in the case file. It was also not possible to determine that the meta-data contained in the evidence was created by the perpetrators, because the computers where the digital evidences situated were not confiscated in the first place. Also it was not technically possible to transfer confidential information about the projects developed by the TÜBİTAK for the TSK, and some of documents, which would directly affect the case for the perpetrators, were not put in the case file, and these documents were not made available to the perpetrators and their lawyers. There was basically only a tip-off sent from a counterfeit e-mail account from which the sender could not be identified, an inadvertently generated or a counterfeit communication tape, and digital data that could not be accepted as evidence that were substantial evidence in the case. Since there was no sufficient evidence against the perpetrators, who had never known each other and had no communication with each other, and had not engaged in prostitution or assisted in any activities related to prostitution, they were acquitted from the case.

Considering that cases such as the Poyrazköy, the Assassination plot of Admirals and Operation and the Cage Action Plan were all investigations that were initiated due to a tip-off that come from an e-mail, where the sender was unknown, and subsequent investigations on these cases that contained initially more serious accusations -including new found digital materials- were later on found to be falsified raises some major questions. When all this is taken into account, serious suspicions arise as to whether a specific network could have conducted all of these operations. In addition, considering the volume of the alleged criminal networks and the severity of the crimes they committed, it is not reasonable for such state institutions such as the National Intelligence Agency, the General Command of Gendarmerie and the Directorate General of Security's intelligence units to have not known of any information regarding the above mentioned network.

The Supposed Tevhid-Selam Jerusalem Army Terrorist Network[90]

Upon the decision to send a humanitarian aid ship (Mavi Marmara) by the Humanitarian Relief Foundation (IHH) on the 12th of April 2010 to Gaza, which had a blockade imposed on it by Israel, the investigation of the Tevhid-Selam Jerusalem Army Terrorist Network case was launched by the directives of FETÖ/PDY. The investigation was based on news dated the 10th of May 2010 on a website[91] about Nurettin Şirin who had been tried in the past for anti-Semitic crimes, insulting Turkic culture, the Turkish Republic and the institutions and organs of the state. The news stated that after being released from prison in 2004, he had been restoring his former staff into a team again and forming a new network. An investigation on the network was launched on the 12th of May 2010 without any prior examinations or serious research on Nurettin Şirin. The investigation was based on activities relating to Nurettin Şirin compiled from archive records. By the 7th of May 2010[92]the decision was taken on initiating the so-called corruption investigation case that formed the basis of the process extending from the 17 - 25 December judicial coup attempt. In this respect, it is vital to note that the FETÖ/PDY had already planned and implemented a comprehensive operation in order to expel the prime minister and some of the ministers on the absurd basis that the afore mentioned politicians were members of a terrorist network and that they were engaging in espionage activities on behalf of Iran.

Upon Emre Taner's leaving his position, Hakan Fidan was appointed as the Undersecretary of the National Intelligence Agency, and coordinated the project of national unity and brotherhood. Following this event, the scope of the investigation expanded and the Prime Minister, ministers, MİT

Undersecretary, counselors, bureaucrats, the president of the IHH Foundation, academics, journalists and writers, including many people were displayed as having close relations with Iran and the so-called Tevhid-Selam Jerusalem Army Terrorist Network.

At the same time, after a dispute between a woman named K.Y and her husband H.A.Y, a complaint was filed by the wife to the Istanbul Department of Anti-Terrorism unit under the Directorate General of Security. The statements she made during the complaint made on 4th of March 2011 and 6th of April 2011 were distorted in order to provide evidence for the above investigation and she was further deceived into signing these statements. In fact, the statements made later by her in the Istanbul Department of Anti-terrorism Directorate on the 26th of February 2014 and in the Istanbul Chief Public Prosecutor's Office on the 27th of February 2014 refute the earlier statements, "'...that her *husband H.A.Y. met with the MIT Undersecretary Hakan Fidan in his office, that he was an agent, that he was being paid because of his services, that her husband was a member of a network, and that a sketch of the Consulate General of Israel was located in her husband's computer' were not her statements. She also stated that her 4th of March 2011 dated statement had been distorted and were purely fictional. When she wanted to read the statements that the officials took record of, they told her, 'sister, do you not trust us? It will take too long.' She became self-conscious and went onto sign the statements. She also stated that she recently learned about the existence of the network called Tevhid-Selam from the media. After giving her statements on the issue, an official named Tank and other officials gave her a flash disk for her to bring the documents located in her husband computer. Because the flash disk did not work, she used her son's Mp3 player to transfer the files and delivered them to the Police Branch.*"[93]

During the investigation, decisions were taken to identify, listen and record the communication between 239 people, which included top politicians and bureaucrats, the monitoring of 78 people by technical means, and similar decisions were also made for 10 associations, foundations and addresses. The decision to monitor was extended for the cases above for a total of 2361 times. Conversely, as a result of a the examination of the CD sent from the Information Technologies and Communications Authority, it was found that the IP address 172.11.11.5 originated from Gastonia (United States) between the time period 2010-2014 and that some of the wiretapping activities were managed from the United States.[94] According to the report prepared by HSYK inspectors, the main reason for the wiretapping was to attain information that was of special importance to the state, considering the fact that the wiretapping and tracking was conducted on high level officials. As a matter of fact, it was determined that detailed information about the content of the meetings between Recep Tayyip Erdoğan and the Presidents, Prime Ministers, Ministers and senior bureaucrats of several countries should be recorded during the period when Recep Tayyip Erdoğan was the prime minister of Turkey.

An investigation was initiated with the claim of the existence of members of an armed terrorist network who were carrying out actions and activities on behalf of the network. In spite of the injunctions applied on hundreds of people over the past three years, not a single suspect testified on the issue, no procedural procedures were carried out and no arrest or detention was carried out. Therefore, instead of concluding the investigation, false witness statements, false tipoffs and intelligence correspondence were used as evidence and the wiretapping and tracking activity continued. In January 2014, an attempt was made to search the trucks belonging to the MİT in order to create a perception as if the MİT was providing weapons to Al Qaeda. Thus, there was an attempt to prove the arms element of the so-called network in order to prepare the ground for a possible operation in the future.

Following the abolition of the Chief Public Prosecutors Delegacy Office and The Prosecution Office's appointed by Article 10 of the Anti-Terror Law[95] pursuant to Law No. 6526 of the 21st of February 2014; it was decided by the public prosecutor that was assigned to conduct the investigation on the 21st of July 2014 that there was no evidence for the allegations against the 251 suspects who had been the subjects of the investigation and a decision for no prosecution was conferred. It was evident that they had not been involved in any activities related to terrorism and that there was no evidence of them establishing an armed terrorist network, to be members of the network, or to have conducted any such activities on behalf of the network.

The Theft of the 2010 KPSS Questions

After several news items were published in the written and visual media about some people who had sent exam questions, obtained illegally, from the Public Personnel Selection Examination (KPSS) to some other people via e-mail; the Yalvaç (Isparta) Chief Public Prosecutor's Office launched on the 31st of August 2010 an investigation into B. S., the person in question in the news. As a result of the evidence obtained in the investigation 5-14 days before, the exam questions of educational sciences, general skills and general culture on the exam were found located in B.S.'s hard disk. It seems 48 out of the 68 questions in the general culture section, 27 out of the 30 questions in the general ability Turkish section, and 25 out of the 30 questions in the general ability mathematics section overlapped. The booklets of the questions on the educational sciences and the general ability had been sent to thousands of candidates before the examination took place. However, in order to prevent suspicion in the case where all the candidates would have all of the same numbers of correct answers on the exam, some candidates were sent all of the questions, while some of them received only some of the questions. Experts upon investigating the question booklets of the candidates found that certain candidates did indeed receive the questions of the exam beforehand. It was also determined that 93 out of the 350 candidates who answered all the questions correctly were first degree relatives, 52 of them were residing in the same address or the same apartment, or the same complex or street. The Financial Crimes Investigation Board (MASAK) in its report dated October 02, 2014 stated that there was a suspicious money transfer between 2011-2013 between the organization's domestic and foreign organizations and those working in these areas. Following the cancellation of the exam, 1.175 out of 3.227 candidates, who achieved a high performance in the 10th of July 2010 dated KPSS exam's educational sciences section, did not take the KPSS exam dated 31st of October 2010. Considering that the initial KPSS exam was easier than the following KPSS exam, 1.999 out of 2.052 candidates (97.4%) who took the second exam receiving lower results seems contrary to the usual statistics.[96]

The Izmir Military Espionage Case[97]

In an e-mail tip-off sent to İzmir Directorate of Security on the 10th of August 2010 from an unknown source there was a message about a network which marketed young girls to rich people and high-level bureaucrats in return for money, and it also noted that the young girls were black mailed or controlled due to the network's ownership of inappropriate visual records of them.

The first indictment was prepared on the 6th of January 2013 and the second indictment was prepared on the 13th of February 2014, based on the digital materials and physical documents obtained in the searches conducted in various provinces within the scope of the investigation. According to the indictments, the defendants set up a network to commit crimes; obtained information on the security of the state and disclosed it, and recorded personal data and used it for a variety of purposes. Following the trial of the indictment by the Izmir 5th Assize Court, it was determined on the 26th of February 2016 that the search of digital materials and physical documents were unlawful and that these materials and documents could not be considered as evidence on the basis of case no: 2014/100 and the decision no: 2016/37. There was no indication of intelligence relating to the alleged crimes being exchanged or transferred over the internet. Furthermore, it was decided that the defendants could not be claimed to have committed the offenses since there was the lack of legal evidence, therefore the perpetrators were individually acquitted from the case.

The Assassination of Journalist Haydar Meriç

Haydar Meriç, a retired teacher and journalist living in Kırklareli, compiled important information about Fetullah Gülen's private life during the period when Fetullah Gülen was serving as a Kırklareli preacher during the 1960's. Haydar Meriç was planning to write a book about this, however, he disappeared on the 31st of May 2011. After an extensive search, on the 18th of June 2011 his body, which had been tied up and thrown into the sea, was found on the coast of Akça-koca (Düzce). It was only after two years that any hard information became obtainable through the crime investigation.[98]

It is now known that a team, which was a member of the FETÖ/PDY and was part of the Kırklareli Intelligence Department under the Directorate General of Security, received information that a book was intended to be written about Fetullah Gülen. Upon receiving this intelligence, Meriç's house and telephone started to be monitored on the charges that he was a member of DHKP-C (The Revolutionary People's Liberation Party/Front). Upon not obtaining any information through wiretapping about any preparation of a book, a team affiliated with the Ankara Intelligence Department under the Directorate General of Security came from Ankara and started a stakeout from a rented house in front of the house where Meriç was residing.

After not being able to obtain any information from surveillance they thought perhaps Meriç was carrying the information on him. In order to get this information from him they orchestrated an accident with a car and during the event stole his bag. However, no items of value related to a book were obtained from the material contained in the bag, still, whatever data found in his bag was copied without his permission.

When the teams from the Kırklareli Intelligence Department under the Directorate General of Security and the Intelligence Department under the Directorate General of Security could not obtain any information related to the "*book draft*", the intelligence teams mentioned above were asked to withdraw from the operation. At this point another separate team was sent from the Intelligence Department of the Directorate General of Security Intelligence Department. This team made a call to Haydar Meriç on the 1st of May 2011 around 01:00 a.m. from two telephone lines that were set up through two counterfeit ID's. The crime investigation shows that after this phone call Meriç left his home for the last time and was not seen or heard from again.

A police officer, who worked at the Edirne Director-ate of Security, obtained the information on Haydar Meriç's fate and decided to go to Ankara to share it with the Head of the Intelligence Department under the Directorate General of Security Engin Dinç rather than sharing this information with the Kırklareli Intelligence Department under the Direc-torate General of of Security and the Edirne Intelligence De-partment under the Directorate General of Security. He also shared this decision with his immediate circle. However, his intentions were noticed in short time by a team from the An-kara Intelligence Department under the Directorate Gener-al of Security. The police officer upon arrival to Ankara was met by two police chiefs and the police officer was taken to the Karşıyaka Cemetery in Yenimahalle district of Ankara. The police officer clearly received the message of the threat. Without contacting the Head of the Intelligence Department under the Directorate General of Security he returned to Ed-irne, and no progress was made in this criminal investigation until 2016.

However, the investigation was touched upon again at re-ceiving several tip-off of some of the police officers who were working in the intelligence departments of the Directorate General of Security, the Istanbul Directorate of Security, the Ankara Directorate of Security and the Kırklareli Director-ate of Security. Thus, these police officers were detained. It is known that at the same time the deputy police officer E.Ç., who was also an intelligence officer and was one of the detainees in police custody, was being tried for the 2011-2012 case of placing a listening device (wiretap) in the chambers of the Prime Minister's office and in the meeting rooms. Other suspects turned out to be part of the team that prepared the tape scandals of CHP Chariman Deniz Baykal, the MHP deputy chairman's and the members of the Board of Directors of MHP.[99] Furthermore, 6 out of 7 intelligence officers that came from Ankara and Istanbul from Kırklareli to monitor Meriç, were identified as users of the encrypted communication application known as Bylock.[100]

The Confession of Bylock's patent owner David Keynes

On the 28th of October, one of our commission members, Hüseyin Kocabıyık, called me, and said, *a person named David Keynes from the United States, who spoke Turkish very well, called me and David said that he would like to offer information about the application called Bylock. Hüseyin Kocabıyık told me that he would also like put us in touch.* I told him I could give him my number since he was directly involved with our research. He called me and explained why his name was associated with the Bylock application and because I believe that the faintest ink is more powerful than the strongest memory I made the following request, "can you send this information as an e-mail to me?" One day later I received the following email. I reported this phone call to the Istanbul and Ankara Chief Public Prosecutor's Office. I also informed the members of our Commission.

"Dear president, I am so sorry, but I have only now returned from work and the hospital to my home. I will through email offer you a brief summary of what I told you yesterday, along with the evidence I have.

Upon receiving a Green card, I went to the USA. I met with Atalay Candelen in Portland. He was studying in the Computer Engi-

neering field. In 2004-2005 or 2005-2006 we were roommates in a two-room flat for 9 months. There was also a flat of the FETÖ/PDY upstairs. We stayed in contact after he returned to Turkey. When I visited Turkey, I would bring his stuff that his sister in Portland bought for him. (Computer-Shoes etc.) As a habit from our time in America, when we returned to Turkey we would together watch movies or watch 3-4 episodes in a row of series that was popular in America at the time. Since his house in Ataköy was available, we would spend this leisure time there with our 3-4 friends. On the night of 7th of December 2013, we gathered at his house again to watch a series names Breaking Bad that was very popular in America at that time period. Before we started to watch the series, he told me that his credit card was being rejected when he tried to buy an Apple's developers licence because his Bank did not allow foreign transaction. He asked me if he could use my credit for the 99 dollars purchase. When I asked what it was for he mentioned the application (Bylock) that did not have a name given to it at that time. He said he would try to sell his program at the Silicon Valley, that was located in San Francisco, or at least introduce this application and try to acquire capital from the venture capitalists. When I told him not to get me in trouble with taxes, he said "since the application would be downloaded for free, a tax would not applicable in the USA." We did not speak until the mid-2015 after that. He said that his application was downloaded 600.000 time, and that if he sold the application for 3.99 dollars he would become a millionaire. He also said that the application had been downloaded even in Iran and Saudi Arabia. When I heard that one of the countries was Saudi Arabia, I said whether ISID used this application? I said 'Don't get me intro bureaucratic affairs with the FBI'. I did not hear about this application again until the morning of the 16th of July. When I asked him what Bylock was all about, he said that he gave the application to a couple of friends, and that they distributed it to each other. He also said something along the line that the application was not used in the coup. I was sure that he went to Germany that weekend. And later on he went to Portland USA and called me on August the 23rd or the 25th. Afterwards, he asked me if I could by him an Uber account in New

York, (Uber drivers make around 7.000-8.000 dollars in a month)
and I swore at him, closed the phone on him and blocked him.
He spoke to an accountant that we both know, and told him that
he did not have enough money to make calls, and that he would
return to Turkey around Eid ul-Adha. He had been investigated
before, but since the prosecutor had not requested his presence, he
more likely felt relaxed enought to plan to return to Turkey. In the
following e-mail, I will forward you the e-mails received from the
official Apple Store regarding Bylock.

Have a great day,

With my best regards..."

The phone calls of Meriç on the night of the event were
deleted from the records of the Presidency of Telecommunication and Communication (*Telekomünikasyon İletişim
Başkanlığı*). The security cameras belonging to public institutions or private individuals on the streets and roads leading to
the house were disconnected by cutting the cables, and therefore the cameras could not record during that night. It was
further claimed that the camera records showing the intelligence police officers who had been sent from the Intelligence
Branch Department under theDirectorate General of Security to enter the Kırklareli Directorate of Security could not be
found and that the MOBESE cameras in the entrance and exit of the city did not work and did not record that day.[101] The
members of the FETÖ/PDY were not able to leak any information outside their individual groups since "they only knew
the existence of the 3 cells that were in contact with them"[102]
The Istanbul Chief Public Prosecutor's Office launched an operation on the suspects on these grounds: to establish the existence of a terrorist network, to charge them for being members of a terrorist network, to charge them of murdering a
person, to charge them of violating confidentiality of com-

munication, to charge them of wiretapping conversations and recording, for obtaining personal data unlawfully, for forgery of official documents, for malpractice, for slander, for threatening behaviour and actions, for misleading the court, and for tampering with evidence.

The 7th of February MİT Crises (MİT Undersecretary Called in to Testify)

On the 7th of February 2012, the FETÖ/PDY organized an operation against the Undersecretary of MİT through its members in the judiciary, by using the Oslo negotiations as an excuse and taking advantage of Prime Minister Recep Tayyip Erdoğan's medical treatment period. This operation was the FETÖ/PDY's first major plot against the government in order to overthrow the Government of the Republic of Turkey. This was carried out by attempting to question and arrest the Undersecretary of MİT, the former Undersecretary of MİT, the former deputy undersecretary of the MİT and two other staff members.

The organization started the preparations for this plot by leaking confidential information about the Oslo Talks to the press in September 2011. In December 2011, MİT found the listening devices placed by the FETÖ/PDY in the office of Prime Minister Recep Tayyip Erdoğan's official residence and his place of residence in Ankara. Thereafter, the organization began to act more aggressive towards MİT, and in December 2011 the organization attempted to pass the blame and the responsibility of the Uludere attack, which was probably carried out by the pilots of the FETÖ/PDY in the Turkish Armed Forces, onto MİT. The final assault against the MİT for a favorable result was attempted on the 7th of February 2012.

The Undersecretary of MİT exhibited a strong resistance to this unlawful initiative and refused to appear to testify. In addition, a legal amendment[103] was passed that led to the failure of the organization's plot. It was later discovered that the organization's main target was the Prime Minister Recep Tayyip Erdoğan and the Republic of Turkey's government and not only the Undersecretary of MİT who was directly tied to the Prime Minister.

The retired MIT Undersecretary Emre Taner stated that the FETÖ/PDY changed its method clearly on the 7th of February 2012. The organization left behind it its disguise of benevolence, and abandoned its so-called democratic appearance. Thus, it quickly began its transformation into a new generation terrorist organization. The police-prosecutor-judge trio of this antagonistic movement, which was inherently unlawful, had attempted to bring its personnel to the top of the state, to the government and all the way into the top level of jurisdiction through the operation conducted against the MİT Undersecretaries and their staff. It also said that the MİT, which could not be sufficiently infiltrated by the organization, intended to undermine its plans entirely.[104] Whereas, the FETÖ/PDY's aim at that time was to prevent the peace process from progressing by disabling it through the arrest of the Undersecretary of the MİT.[105] Furthermore, through this investigation the aim was to disrupt the intelligence activities of the state by decipher the sources of the MİT and, thus to strengthen the terrorist organization PKK. As a matter of fact, the agents MİT had covertly placed within the PKK terrorist organization was disclosed by the FETÖ/PDY, and these people working on behalf of the Republic of Turkey, was callously tortured, and brutally murdered by the PKK.

The December 17-25 Judicial Coup Initiatives

In the December 17-25 operations the members of the armed FETÖ/PDY terrorist organization that were prosecutors and judges cooperated with the FETÖ/PDY members that were located in the Directorate General of Security and within the media. This was carried out in order t0 eliminate the Government of the Republic of Turkey through a judicial coup under the name of operation against bribery and corruption.

The Government through its intelligence understood the real intent of the organization and commenced to take some measures against the organization after the FETÖ/PDY conducted an operation against the Undersecretary of MİT on the 7th of December 2012. Within the framework of the measures taken, the closure of the preparatory course centers, which were the most important resource for supplying personnel to the organization led to an increase of criticism, defamation and slanders against the government in the media organs of the organization. All kinds of murky propaganda and disinformation was used to prevent the closure of the preparatory course centers of the organization. In order to prevent the realization of the the government's decision to close the preparatory course centers, the organization shortly before the local administrations elections of the 29th of March 2014 were held, it started to create a perception in the public eye that the AK Party was corrupt. The organization's first intention was to cause AK Party's defeat in the local elections, then to cause AK Party's defeat in a probable early general election and in this way remove the AK Party from power. Thus, a comprehensive judicial coup aimed at defeating and removing the AK Party from power was planned and put into practice.

A large number of people, including children of ministers, businessmen, bank managers, mayors and bureaucrats, were detained on the 17th of December 2013 through 3 separate investigation dossiers[106] that had no connection with each other. This was carried out under the name of bribery, and corruption operations were launched and several people were detained and several of those listed above were instantaneously arrested. The operations were conducted by the organization's members in the Judiciary Branch and the Directorate of Security. The FETÖ/PDY's leader Fetullah Gülen, responded to the statements made by the government representatives after the operations by swearing at them on the 21st of December 2013. The Government amended the judicial law enforcement[107] on the 21st of December 2013 after realizing the significance of the situation, especially after the 17th of December judicial coup attempt.

The violations of the judicial coup attempt, which was attempted by the prosecutors involved in the 17th of December investigation, were found documented in two separate investigative reports[108] prepared by the Chief Inspectorate of HSYK. According to the reports the following assessments were made about the public prosecutor Celal Kara; he did not examine the investigation files, which had a total of 3,419 pages of unrelated documents[109], he did not collect the evidences in favor of the suspects, restricted the rights of their defenses during the determination of the statements[110], he was unable to respond to the inquiries of public prosecutors, who were subsequently included in the investigation with regard to the investigative issues and who asked the law enforcement officers to respond, in this way, it was determined that the investigations were carried out in accordance with the verbal information obtained from the law enforcement officers. In addition, he sent the suspects to the court to be arrested without taking the signature of other public prosecutors[111] in the investigation, he did not register the suspects to UYAP (National Judiciary Informatics System), and he did not inform the Istanbul Chief Public Prosecutor Turan Çolakkadı at any stage of the investigation contradictory to the operating instructions of the Istanbul Chief Public Prosecutors Office.As a member of the FETÖ/PYD he attempted to eliminate the Republic of Turkey and to prevent it from exercising its functions, and he committed offenses that violated the honor and dignity of the profession. Moreover, he did not transfer the 2012/120653 numbered investigation files that contained information about the crimes attributed to the ministers of the Republic of Turkey to the private investigation office and kept the documents to himself, and even in the absence of a court decision he illegally recorded nearly a hundred telephone conversations[112] between the 61st Prime Minister of Turkish government Recep Tayyip Erdoğan, who has legislative immunity, and some of his ministers. He retained the records in the investigation file, and he incriminated some ministers[113] without having the proper authority to conduct an investigation. In order to create a negative perception in the public eye he ordered a cautionary judgement of the 60 suspects simultaneously within a different investigation[114], even though the investigation was not yet finalized, and that led to the deterioration of the economy and a loss by the Halk Bank due to these attempts to shape the public opinion. Moreover, although both investigations stated that a transfer of the investigations to other public prosecutors were not needed and a decision of non-prosecution was given, he gave several interviews to a newspaper[115] at different dates[116] to discredit the Prime Minister of the Republic of Turkey and the administrators by using sensational headlines[117] in the newspaper, all in order to charge the Republic of Turkey's Prime Minister Recep Tayyip Erdoğan with serious accusations. He insulted, defamed and slandered[118] Recep Tayyip Erdoğan through the press, and he was also clearly attacking his personal rights. Although there was no accusation against the Prime Minister Recep Tayyip Erdogan in the investigation file, he stated that the main aim of the 17th of December investigation was the Prime Minister Recep Tayyip Erdoğan, thereby contributing to an illegal action against the Government of Turkey. Moreover, later he admitted that they were conducting irregular processes by taking arbitrary decisions even though there was no evidence in the case file or in the summary of proceedings (*fezleke*) that indicated that Bilal Erdoğan committed a crime, since he had been trying to bring Bilal Erdoğan under suspicion by introducing unfeasible allegations against him.

Due to the afore mentioned reports, the following reasons became evident later about the public prosecutor Mehmet Yüzgeç. Even though the investigation was not yet finalized, 15 days after the investigation was submitted to him, he carried out an operation by using investigation files that had no connection between them[119], which led to certain individuals being detained and measures being implemented against them. He also did not inform the Istanbul Chief Public Prosecutor Turan Çolakkadı at any stage of the investigation, and as a member of FETÖ/PYD he attempted to prevent Republic of Turkey from exercising its functions and to destroy it, and he has also committed offenses that violate the honor and dignity of his profession. He also did not transfer the 2012/120653 numbered investigation files that contained information about the crimes attributed to the minister[120] of the Republic of Turkey to the private investigation office and kept the documents to himself. Even in the absence of a court decision he illegally recorded nearly seventy seven telephone conversations[121] of a minister of the Republic of Turkey, who has legislative immunity and retained the records in the investigation file. Moreover, he incriminated some ministers without having the proper authority by conducting an investigation in order to create a negative perception in the public eye. He ordered a cautionary judgement of the 24 suspects simultaneously with different investigations[122] even though the investigation was not yet finalized, and through this led the economy to deterioration because of the negative public opinion that occurred in the period.

In the same reports the following were stated about the Deputy Chief Public Prosecutor Zekeriya Öz: he did not inform the Istanbul Chief Public Prosecutor Turan Çolakkadı at any stage of the investigation[123]; he insisted on the permission of a hotel's extension to be covered up and for the same hotels unlicensed story to be accepted by the Fatih Municipality Mayor Mustafa Demir; he acted as a mediator to transfer a café named Rumeli Café, owned by the Fatih Municipality, to someone he knew, and after the completion of transference he requested the 51 square meter enclosed space to be expanded, although the a formal application was not made and the enclosed space was expanded to 600-700 square meters; the travel expenses, the total of 20.259,60 USD, that was spent on a vacation in Dubai between 17-21 October 2013 together with his family was paid by Akdeniz İnşaat Incorporated (Ali İbrahimoğlu is the owner of the company), which was being investigated by the Istanbul Chief Public Prosecutors Office[124]; he was found to be abroad at various dates[125] without permission; and he steered the Public Prosecutors Celal Kara and Mehmet Yüzgeç in the investigations numbered

2012/125043, 2012/120653 and 2013/24880. It is document-ed that he shared the following message on twitter on the 2nd of August 2015, "*If the PKK had been involved in the Gezi events the government would not be in office today. Because the PKK re-ceived orders from somewhere therefore they did not participate in the Gezi events. This issue was later expressed as a regret by the PKK. We are being governed by a temporary Prime Minister who does know that the Gezi Events has nothing to do with the Peace prOcesses.*" which indicates that he had the intention to over-throw the government. As a member of the FETÖ/PYD at-tempted to prevent Republic of Turkey from exercising its functions and to destroy it, and he committed offenses that violated the honor and dignity of his profession.

The Public Prosecutors Celal Kara and Mehmet Yüzgeç and the Istanbul Deputy Chief Prosecutor Zekeriya Öz were sentenced on the 12th of May 2015 by the 2nd Department of HSYK to be dismissed from their offices.

While the effects of these investigations, known as the 17th of December operations, continued, on the 23rd of December 2013, the public prosecutor of the FETÖ/PDY, Muammer Akkaş, started a second operation in order to further the per-ception of corruption. The Prime Minister Recep Tayyip Er-doğan's family members and the businessmen's who carried out projects of strategic importance for the country's econo-my such as the 3rd bridge and the 3rd airport were taken in-to custody along with several other people. The above men-tioned businessmen's total assets were confiscated.

After the operation, Muammer Akkaş, who was dis-missed from the investigation[126] for conducting an irregular investigation, issued a press statement in front of the Istan-bul Courthouse in Çağlayan and distributed leaflets alleging that he was prevented from doing his duty. On the 26th of December 2013, the Council of Judges and Prosecutors (HSYK) which was under the control of the FETÖ/PDY, issued a notice on their official website, that gave support to the judges and prosecutors who conducted the 17-25 December Judicial coup attempt.[127]

The judicial violations and irregularities made by the judges and prosecutors involved on the 25th of December investigation were documented by two separate investigative reports[128] prepared by the Chief Inspectorate of the Council of Judges and Prosecutors. Accordingly, the public prosecutor Muammer Akkaş did not attempt to conduct any investigation for evidence other than the phone calls in the investigation file no. 2012/656. It is also known that some of the decision request were made by law enforcement officers even though they were supposed to be carried out by the public prosecutor's office, Moreover, he did not examine the investigation documents consisting of a total of eleven folders whereby the decision for detainment, the decision to carry out a search and the decision of a temporary confiscation was implemented without any justification, merely by using rudimentary legal expressions. On top of that, the summary of proceedings and the tape recordings were not cross-checked. Thus, there were no tangible documents on the alleged transactions and tenders, people were detained in a rush without considering if they were mistreated, or if they could at all possibly have had the recourse to commit such a crime or whether bail should be set since they may not be flight cases. It was his duty to investigate whether or not there was strong evidence, and whether or not the crime had been committed. The alleged crime never took place but he still requested the confiscation of all the assets registered in the name of some of the suspects and at times these measures were requested in respect to the assets acquired prior to the alleged acts. Moreover, he requested the seizure of registered assets in the name of companies unlawfully, even though these legal persons, who have special legal personal privileges that cannot be suspects or perpetrators, and the suspects named were subject to technical and physical monitoring. Those suspects whose conversations were recorded were not registered in the UYAP. In fact, until the custody decision was given on the 25th of December 2013, "*unknown*" was written under the suspect section. Finally, he did not inform the Istanbul Chief Public Prosecutor Turan Çolakkadı at any stage of the investigation, and he did not send the investigation file to the authorized chief prosecutor. Thus, he hid information by giving evasive answers to the questions asked, he infringed the confidentiality of the investigation by sharing information and documents related to the investigation with the media, and he called together the members of the press and distributed leaflets with a notice under the name of press release in the Istanbul Palace of Justice A-1 Blok's entrance door that was used as an entrance and exit only to judges and public prosecutors. The notice released in the leaflet stated that, "*files relating to the investigation was taken from him without any justifiable reason. This was obstructing the investigation, the judiciary was clearly pressured through the Office of the Chief Public Prosecutor and through the judicial police, the evidences have been obscured, and the suspects were given the possibility to escape and obscure the evidence*". This was all false information[129], he conducted the investigation unauthorized, he also did not transfer the investigation files to the private investigation office, he wiretapped suspects without a court decision, in the absence of a court decision he illegally recorded nearly two hundred telephone conversations[130] between the 61st Prime Minister Recep Tayyip Erdoğan and some of his ministers who have legislative immunity and he retained the records in the investigation file, and he incriminated the 61st Prime Minister Recep Tayyip Erdoğan and some of the ministers[131] without having the proper authority to conduct an investigation. As a member of the FETÖ/PDY he left the country when it was in a challenging situation in the international arena and he attempted to discredit the country He attempted to display as if the government of the Republic of Turkey was helping the al-Qaeda terrorist organization, thereby making it look as if the country was responsible of the juridical aspect for the criminal activity in the international judicial organs. He attempted to prevent Republic of Turkey from exercising its functions and to destroy it, and he committed offenses that violated the honor and dignity of the profession. He also did not convert into transcript the audio conversation records of Former Deputy Chief Public Prosecutor Zekeriya Öz with O. A. (In the above mentioned tapes, Zekeriya Öz was requesting a coat and sunglasses from O.A. which was wiretapped on charges of establishing a criminal organization and engaging in collusive tendering.), therefore not fulfilling the obligation of notifying the 3rd Department of HSYK.

In the same reports the following was stated about the Judge Süleyman Karaçöl: In only 24 minutes he decided to confiscate all the assets registered on behalf of 7 actual persons and 2 legal entities without any prior examination of the investigation files; or determining if the assets were obtained from the crimes committed; or determining if there was a strong suspicion that the offense has been committed; and if the order to put a temporary injunction on the assets was necessary. As a member of the FETÖ/PDY he attempted to display as if the government of the Republic of Turkey was helping the al-Qaeda terrorist organization, thereby making it look like the country was responsible of the juridical aspect for the criminal activity playing out in the international arena. He attempted to prevent Republic of Turkey from exercising its functions and to destroy it, and he also committed offenses that violated the honor and dignity of his profession.

In the same reports the following were stated about Judge Menekşe Uyar; in the İstanbul Chief Public Prosecutors Office's[132] 2012/656 numbered investigation case file, even though crimes such as engaging in collusive tendering, establishing, managing, being a member of an organization, and engaging in bribery is not under the Turkish Civil Code's 10th clause, a decision was made to determine the communication of some suspects and monitor them by technical means, a decision prepared in the digital environment by officers of the Directorate General of Security regarding the determination of communication, and monitoring and recording by technical means was approved. Moreover, a decision was approved concerning the suspects; phone calls and e-mails be recorded starting from 15th of October 2013 and 18th of October 2013 retroactively with the intent to trace Republic of Turkey's Prime Minister Recep Tayyip Erdoğan's communications. Telephone numbers registered to M.V., Ş.K. and A.Ü. were also approved to be wiretapped without considering if there was a strong suspicion present on the above mentioned persons' registered telephone numbers. The above mentioned persons' registered telephone numbers communications were recorded. As a member of FETÖ/PDY, he left the country when it was in a difficult situation in the international arena and attempted to discredit the country, he attempted to display as if the government of the Republic of Turkey was helping the al-Qaeda terrorist organization, thereby making it look as if the country was responsible of the juridical aspect for the criminal activity in the international arena. He attempted to prevent Republic of Turkey from exercising its functions and to destroy it, and he also committed offenses that violated the honor and dignity of his profession. The Public Prosecutor Muammer Akkaş and Judges Süleyman Karaçöl and Menekşe Uyar were sentenced to be dismissed from their individual profession by the 2nd Department of HSYK.

The Initiative to Search the MİT Trucks[133]

A man who introduced himself as Tahir Kara called from a pay phone the Hatay Provincial Command of the Gendarmerie's 156 Gendarmerie line on the 1st of January 2014 at 15.29 and claimed that a terrorist network, whose name he did not disclose, was going to be transporting arms by a vehicle through Hatay's Reyhanlı, the Kırıkhan district and Gaziantep's Islahiye District to Kilis. He went onto provide the license plate number of the above mentioned vehicle. Sergeant M.M.A and Sergeant A.A who were sergeants in charge of the operation line located at the the Gendarmerie Public Order Station Command 156 Operation Centre in the Hatay Provincial Command notified the Security Units, other units of the Gendarmerie and Kırıkhan District Command of Gendarmerie about this information that was received.

Staff Sergeant I.D. who was stationed in the Kırıkhan District Command of the Gendarmerie called Y.A. the public prosecutor on duty and informed him about the tip-off received and the developments. I.D. prepared the search warrant transcript and went to the public prosecutor Y.A. but the Prosecutor Y. A. asserted that the incident was under the responsibility of the Adana Chief Public Prosecutor's Office, which was authorized under Article 10 of the Anti-Terror

Law. He went onto erase the phrase *"Kırıkhan"* on the search warrant transcript and changed it to *"Adana"*, and then sent the search warrant transcript to the Adana Chief Public Prosecutor's Office via fax.

Upon the search warrant being approved from the Adana Chief Public Prosecutor's Office, the head of the Kırıkhan Command of Gendarmerie K.A. went to the scene. He made the following statements; *"At the scene, there was the Kırıkkan District Chief Public Prosecutor Yaşar Kavalaoğlu, Branch Managers M.F., G.B., H.Ö from the Hatay Intelligence Department and a sergeant whom I did not know. The public prosecutor on duty Y.A. arrived at the scene later. The MİT personnel claimed that they were subject to a special law[134] and showed the relevant law articles that displayed that the search warrant did not apply to them. The public prosecutor on duty Y.A. called Public Prosecutor Özcan Şişman, whom was authorized by the Adana Anti-Terror law, and explained the situation to him. Özcan Şişman instructed them that 'this was not true, the truck must be towed to a safe place, they should not be influenced by anyone, and that they should not answer any phone calls even if a minister calls them'. However, attempts to search the truck were prevented by the MİT officials. It is reported that the Hatay Chief Public Prosecutor B.T. said to Yaşar Kavalaoğlu, "this operation is against the law, and the Adana Public Prosecutors Office is unauthorized for this action, therefore their instructions cannot be followed. In addition, if a search warrant issued by the court does not exist, then the search warrant issued by the authorized public prosecutor is unlawful since the situation does not create a problem because of a delay."* He also went onto say that the Public Persecutor's verbal instructions did not legally bind him, and he repeatedly warned that this would cause legal repercussions for him if he continued with this stance. Still, Yaşar Kavalcıoğlu went onto coordinate the security forces and stationed them in front of the truck, keeping the individuals and the vehicles under surveillance until the Adana authorized Public Prosecutor Özcan Şişman arrived at the scene. In the meantime, he responded to the Hatay Chief Public Prosecutor B.T.'s repeated warnings by saying, *"I will face the consequences"*. It is also recounted that there was a dispute between Yaşar Kavalcıoğlu and the MİT personnel to the point where Kavalcıoğlu went onto say, *"I am the ruler of this place now, and you are my slaves, everyone will do as I order.'*

By the time the Adana authorized Public Prosecutor Özcan Şişman arrived at the scene, the following order was sent by Hatay Governorship to K.Y; *"According to the law no. 2937, which the MİT officers are legally bound to, the personnel have special status and work directly under the authority of the Prime Ministry and therefore they cannot be detained within the scope of the legal procedures"*. Upon this order, all forces connected to the Kırıkhan District Command of Gendarmerie at the scene were ordered to withdraw to the District Headquarters of the Command of Gendarmerie. Meanwhile, the truck began to move again when Yaşar Kavalcıoğlu exclaimed, *"You cannot go anywhere, a crime is being committed here"* and ordered the stop of the truck. The departed truck was once again stopped by G.B. and M.F. who were stationed in the Hatay Intelligence Department. Following Yaşar Kavalcıoğlu's instructions they had followed the truck on their own vehicle and stopped it again. At this point, Özcan Şişman was contacted via cellphone by the MİT's legal counselor who stated, *"The truck belongs to MİT, according to the law no: 2937, the vehicle cannot be searched without an investigation permission, and therefore this is an illegal operation."* However, Özcan Şişman responded to the MİT counselor with the following, *"If you continue to speak in this way, you will be charged with attempt to obstruct the investigation."* Even though Özcan Şişman had never before participated in such search and determination procedures in similar investigations conducted earlier, he had personally come to the scene at 21.00 and instructed the Anti-Terror Branch team to take the MİT officials into custody. At this point the MİT personnel attempted to prevent the opening of the trailer of the truck by forming a line in front of the rear of the truck. They resolutely declared to Özcan Şişman, *"The opening of the trailer is a criminal offense; it can only be opened with the permission of the Prime Minister."* Nonetheless, Özcan Şişman requested the keys of the truck's trailer, and after the keys were denied to him, he gave instructions to locate a locksmith. By 22.00, due to the direct order coming from Hatay Governorship, all the Gendarmerie and the Police units left the scene. It was after that the personnel from the Hatay Intelligence Branch Command left the scene and the search of the truck ended up as a failed attempt.

Furthermore, reports have disclosed that the FETÖ/PDY members had already been informed in detail about another MİT planned shipment with trucks. According to the decision of the Ankara 13th Assize Court, within the scope of the above operation carried out by the organization, seven out of twenty-nine people whose phone calls were wiretapped were personnel involved in the shipments. Hence, the telephones that were used for the shipment information were also the phones that had been wiretapped. The transcript of MİT dated the 27th of March 2014 clearly stated that these people were deliberately interspersed with other defendants.

Due to wiretapping of these phones, the organization was informed as early as the 7th of January 2014 about the MİT planned shipment. It has been verified according to their assigned task departments that the wiretapping of the MİT personnel was conducted by the Ankara Command of Gendarmerie personnel lieutenant Hakan Gençer, the senior sergeant Gültekin Menge, the specialist sergeant Ahmet Yüksel and the specialist sergeant Cumali Katırcı.

Moreover, it has been verified that the arms loaded at the Esenboğa Airport were monitored by Hakan Gençer, Gültekin Menge and Cumali Katırcı until they arrived at Gölbaşı. Gülten Menge informed the Adana Provincial Command of Gendarmerie personnel first lieutenant Ö.K. that the MİT trucks were on their way, and informed him of their license plate numbers and other information on the 19th of January 2014 at 03.57 in the morning. Moreover, Ö.K., instead of informing the Prosecutor A.R. who was on duty that morning, informed the Prosecutor Aziz Takçı at 05.57, two hours later.

It has been disclosed that Gültekin Menge called the Adana Provincial regimental command of Gendarmerie's fixed line from a payphone located in an alley outside the field of view of the MOBESE camera that was located in the Etlik district of Ankara on the 19th Of January 2014 at 07.28 in the morning. He said the following, *"Three trucks are coming from Ankara, which are loaded with explosives to Adana. I'm giving their license plate numbers."* He gave an anonymous tip by giving the three trucks license plate numbers along with the courier vehicle's license plate number that was coming with the trucks, and said, *"Pal, these are loaded with explosives, the trucks are probably loaded with explosives, these trucks departed for Adana, and they departed from Ankara at 02.00-02.30, so they are about to arrive, in other words, they'll be there in 1-2 hours."*

Upon receiving the tip, the Adana Provincial Command of Gendarmerie officials applied for the approval request from the Adana Chief Public Prosecutors office in order to search the trucks at the Ceyhan Sirkeli tolls, and to seize the items found in the search. The request approval transcript was taken to the residence of Prosecutor Aziz Takçı, and then Prosecutor Takçı at 08.14 called the Adana Chief Public Prosecutor Deputy A.K., who was authorized under Article 10 of the Anti-Terror Law, about the information on the situation. However, on the day of the incident no one was on duty, and it was also known that the shipment trucks belonged to the MİT. The anonymous tip had only mentioned an *"explosive substance"* and had not referred to any terrorist network. Even though this was the case, on the search approval transcript a cautionary note was written with the following, *"May be related to the investigation file number 2014/2"*. Without explaining exactly why the search was urgent and what would be the drawback of such a delay, the search warrant transcript, which had *"Al-Qaeda terrorist organization"* and *"arms and ammunition"* inscriptions written on it, was approved. Thus, the ongoing investigation of the incident of the MİT trucks being stopped at Hatay Kırıkhan on the 1st of January established a correlation with the anonymous tip, and the investigation scope merged with the investigation that Prosecutor Takçı was conducting.

After getting the approval, a group of approximately 150 units of commandos, intelligence and technical personnel from the Adana Provincial Command of Gendarmerie went to Ceyhan Sirkeli tolls and took position. A jammer device was also brought by the armed forces to prevent MİT officials from communicating with their authorized personnel and institutions. On the 19th of January 2014 around 12.00, three trucks and a car was stopped, the MİT personnel were violently forcibly flatten to the ground, physically assaulted and handcuffed. During the search conducted in one of the trucks, some recordings were taken by the media structure of the organization and broadcasted very soon afterwards. After the public prosecutor arrived at the scene, even though it is not in his job description to participate in such search and determination procedures and during his active duty as a public prosecutor he had never done so in any of his previous investigations, he got inside the trucks and participated in determining what items were located in the trucks. He even went as far as to take photographs with his own personal cell phone and ordered the Gendarmerie units to also take some records. In addition, he ordered the physical examination report to be issued, the samples taken to be sent to the Ankara Gendarmerie Criminal Directorate Command and the experts' reports to be added to the investigation file.

When the news about the event began to appear in the press about half an hour after the vehicles were stopped, the Adana Governor H.A.C. and MİT authorities called Adana Provincial Gendarmerie commander Ö.Ç. and informed him that, *"The trucks were owned by MİT and cannot be searched without the permission of the Prime Minister".* Immediately after that an official letter was sent to identify the MİT officials and to release them.

The Gendarmerie personnel, who detained the trucks and the MİT personnel, released the MİT officers after inspecting the contents of the containers. In order to conduct detailed search, the gendarmerie personnel with the trucks departed from Sirkeli tolls around 12.50 to the Lieutenant General Recai Engin Barracks located in Adana Seyhan. The MİT officials, who followed the trucks, stopped the trucks at the Kürkçüler location of the TEM highway and managed to get the keys from their drivers. Upon this, Önder Kır, who was stationed in the Adana Provincial Gendarmerie Headquarters

Intelligence Branch, assaulted the MİT officers and took back the keys of one of the trucks and stationed the truck next to a private school.

While the MİT officials staying in the Kürkçüler district were warning the Gendarmerie personnel not to search the vehicles, the Adana Public Prosecutor Aziz Takçı arrived at the scene. He opened the trailer of one of the trucks and he ordered a sample to be taken from the searched items. By then, the Adana Provincial Police Commissioner C.Z. and Provincial Gendarmerie Commander Ö.Ç. arrived at the scene and Police Commissioner C.Z. declared that the *"search was unlawful"* and ensured the safety of the trucks with his security personnel team. Subsequently, the Adana Governor H.A.C. and MİT Adana Regional President arrived at the scene, and after their meeting with the Public Prosecutor Aziz Takçı, the delivery of the trucks to the MİT Regional Presidency was ensured.

The official identities of the intelligence officers, who did not have any judicial duties and worked in the Ankara and the Adana Provincial Command of Gendarmerie, were kept concealed. The other provincial[135] security forces on the Ankara-Adana route were not informed regarding the stopping of the trucks even though the officers in Ankara were physically following the trucks since their departure from Esenboğa Airport and there were opportunities to stop the trucks at any time before exiting the boundaries of Ankara. It is clear that Adana was specifically chosen for the trucks to be stopped. Some news agencies and newspaper reporters were even called to the Ceyhan Sirkeli tolls before the vehicles were stopped. The members of the press were allowed to take images immediately while the trucks were stopped and searched. These images taken were released to the press, without any opportunity given to the authorized state institutions to intervene in this operation even though they knew that the vehicles were within the scope of the legal activity of the National Intelligence Agency. All the actions stated above indicate that the operations main objective was to display to the world, on national and international platforms, as if the Republic of Turkey was a country that *"supported terrorism"* through the National Intelligence Agency. Thereby, the nation would be left in a difficult position, it would be discredited, and would have legal and criminal liability before the international judicial bodies.

Prior to the operation of stop and search of the MİT trucks, a comprehensive perception propaganda operation had been carried out in certain media structures affiliated with the organization in order to shape the national and international public opinion. In this context, the investigation of the so-called Jerusalem Army Terrorist network, which was initiated by the organization's members in the judiciary, was extensively covered in news bulletins and discussion programs. In the column entitled *"Who is supporting Al-Nusra?"* in the Taraf Newspaper written by Emre (Emrullah) Uslu, who is a manager in the organization, claimed that Al-Nusra was being supported by MİT. In a news article published in the newspaper Zaman on the 27th of September 2013 and in the TV series entitled Şefkat Tepe on Samanyolu television on the 28th of September 2013 the following phrases were used, *"Turkey will be introduced as one of the countries that support terrorism. Turkey will be reported as it has been assisting networks that have been accepted as illegal networks across the globe. Operations will be conducted to shape the perceptions that Turkey was supporting Al-Qaeda and the other terrorist networks, thus Turkey will become isolated in the international field."*

Emre (Emrullah) Uslu, who wrote a column entitled *"Disengaging from Al-Qaeda"* in Today's Zaman Newspaper on the 6th of October 2013 claimed that *"Turkey was turning a blind eye to the Al-Qaeda militants that were crossing the border into Syria from Turkey, that MİT was assisting these groups, and that even some non-governmental organizations were acting as an intermediary for MİT's assistance to Al-Qaeda."* In the series Şevkat Tepe broadcasted on the 12th of October 2013 such phrases as *"We have successfully displayed that Western antagonism and cooperation with radical religious groups is conducted, and we must continue"* were found. In the column entitled, *"Why was the news on MİT leaked, what will happen next?"*, published in the Taraf Newspaper on the 24th of October 2013 by Emre (Emrullah) Uslu, it was stated, *"The Westerns have serious misgivings about whether Al-Qaeda's activities were coordinated through Turkey, and that Turkey would be isolated because of MİT's extracurricular activities, and even that Turkey would be displayed as one of the countries that supports terrorism."*

In the series Şevkat Tepe broadcasted on the 11th of January 2014 the following phrases were used, *"On the one hand, we are infiltrating the country as the capillaries of the country, and on the other hand, we are increasing the massacre occurring in Syria with the money we receive. In spite of everything, our strategy will consist of fear, panic, kidnapping, and 'tırlatma' [The word 'tır' means 'truck' in Turkish. The word 'tırlatma' means 'to be out of one's mind, to lose it']. If everything ends up converging with the 'MİT' then the events will be at an end."* On the 14th of January 2014, within the scope of the Al-Qaeda investigation conducted by Van Provincial Security Anti-Terror Branch Directorate units where Serdar Bayraktutan was a Branch Manager, the IHH Foundations office[136] in Kilis were searched and the computers in their office were seized and after this operation, media outlets that were connected to the organization made the claim that MİT was supporting Al-Qaeda through IHH.

In Emre (Emrullah) Uslu's column entitled "*Al-Qaeda, IHH, Truck etc.*" published in the Taraf newspaper on the 15th of January 2014, he claimed that "*The raid of the IHH offices conducted within the scope of the operations on Al-Qaeda raised some concerns again regarding if Turkey was assisting Al-Qaeda.*" The column also stated that Turkey was assisting Al-Qaeda, especially through its intelligence agencies. Moreover, he wrote that Heysem Topalca, who was the owner of the mortar warheads seized in Adana, was an intelligence officer. He argued that Heysem Topalca was taken into custody but not arrested and that IHH organized a ceremony for sending five humanitarian aid supplies from Ankara to Syria in the previous weeks. From that he concluded that there were three trucks in the ceremony area and only one truck was stopped by the Gendarmerie, but MİT did not let the Gendarmerie search the truck and that truck, which was not searched, was linked with the IHH Foundation.

Furthermore, he wrote in the column entitled "*Are the trucks being captured by the Aydınlıkçı (The Light Brigade) units in the MİT*" published in the Taraf Newspaper on the 22nd of January 2014, "*The arms were going to Al-Qaeda, and there were several measures that could have been taken to prevent the stopping of the trucks, however these measures were deliberately not taken. Thus, they wanted the trucks to be captured in the first place -at first they loaded the arms in the trucks and then they made a tip-off- by claiming that parallel prosecutors are capturing us would bring the organization and Erdoğan come to face to face.*" The column also claimed that there was an *Aydınlıkçı* unit that infiltrated MİT, this unit made sure the arms were captured, thus preventing the arms being sent against Assad. All these remarks above were aimed mainly to remove the focus on the FETÖ/PDY, which actually carried out the operations.

The Istanbul Illicit Evacuation Initiative

The suspects' request for release was first of all refused. These were suspects who had been detained for a large number of offenses by the Istanbul Public Prosecutor's Office of Terror and Organized Crime Investigation Bureau's investigation files, consisting of a total of 594 folder known publicly as the "July 22, Espionage, the illegal listening, the December 17-25 plot, the Tevhid-Selam Plot, the Tahşiye group plot and the parallel structure investigation by the Directorate of Security. It was the day after on the 19th of April 2015 that Fetullah Gülen asked the FETÖ/PYD judges on active duty to release the detainees through the cryptic order *"Mukaddes Çile ve İnfak Kahramanları"* (spiritual trial and benevolent people, which was masqueraded under the name of religious sermon in the form of a prayer. The defendants of some of the suspects gave 51 petitions dated the 20th of April 2015 to the Istanbul 29th Criminal Court of First Instance Judge Metin Özçelik in violation of the routine application regarding the refusal of all Criminal Courts of Peace Judges and the requests for the release of the suspects.

Although the above mentioned judge was unauthorized for the court in which he served, he registered the petitions on the system in secret the next day after all the staff had left. In addition, although the examinations could not be completed electronically due to lack of access over UYAP due to the restriction decision, the physical investigation files were not present, all the Criminal Courts of Peace Judges gave a negative review, there were only petitions and their attachments submitted by the suspects defendants; the judge made a decision on the 24th of April 2015, accepted the refusal of all the Criminal Courts of Peace Judges' request made by the suspects defendants and assigned the FETÖ/PYD member Judge Mustafa Başer of the Istanbul 32nd Criminal Court of First Instance, whose on-duty ended by 17.00, to look into the release requests of the investigated suspects.

Judge Mustafa Başer who was appointment unlawfully by the 29th Criminal Court of First Instance Judge Metin Özçelik used his power based on this and ruled the release of the 63 suspects detained by giving generalized seven assessments that were basically the same reasoning that were given on Saturday the 25th of April 2015.[137] The Judge made this decision without initially receiving the investigation files, which consisted of 594 folders, without examining the investigation files, and without making any individual inquiry into each suspect in terms of their crimes and evidence submitted. This clearly shows that an extraordinary effort had been made on that weekend to issue the release order. After this incident occurred the Council of Judges and Prosecutors gathered and decided to dismiss those Judges from the profession who had made this unlawful pronouncement.

The Cosmic Room Incident

It is known that some personnel from the Ankara Regional Mobilization Directorate of the General Staff was monitored by the communication control measures and that this technical monitoring was conducted within the scope of the Ergenekon terrorist network allegation. In order to provide certain public support, an assassination attempt was made against the State Minister and the Deputy Prime Minister of the time, Bülent Arınç, which was in both written and visual media utilized as sensationalism. The purpose was to strengthen the accusation, fake evidences were created, and some documents and notes were assigned special meaning incompatible with reality and thus the investigation was taken out of its normal course of events, which is exactly what happened; the number of soldiers included in the investigation was expanded and the control measures of the communication were illegally applied.[138]

The search and seizure procedures were carried out in unlawful ways in cosmic rooms (state vaults) 11 and 16, which contain information and documents that are state secrets; although these operations were carried out by a tip-off based on false information. This tip-off was put forward in the case of the defense without prior proper examination and it was prepared without objectivity, and prepared biasedly in accordance with the law enforcement reports. These search and seizure procedures were carried out even though there were reasonable doubt in this situation and documents containing some of the information and documents of the state were also illegally obtained.

A person named Ünal Tatar, whose position was that of an expert, was dismissed from TÜBİTAK because of the fact that the information, documents and data relating to the publicly known cases such as the Balyoz, the Military Espionage, the Poyrazköy, the Ergenekon and the Oda TV expert reports were all prepared by him through bias and prejudice. Although he did not have any authority and duty in the investigation file, he examined and received a digital image file of the investigation files, and in this way, it was ensured that unauthorized persons were informed about the state's confidential information and documents.[139]

According to the Criminal Procedure Law[140] , the confidential subjects relating to the state are not allowed to be examined even in the investigation stage; however in this case information and documents on the Republic of Turkey in terms of the quality of internal and external security of the state, were illegally seized and disclosed by the Judges and Public Prosecutors for the purpose of political and military espionage. During the investigation process, decisions in unlawful ways were taken in order to ascertain the communications, to find out about persons who had shared these ideas, their critical reviews, and the information relating to the evaluations about the organization, which was of no interest and had no connection with the pertained investigation. Moreover, excessive protective measures were taken to protect the organization.[141]

The Initiatives for Strategic Politics

The FETÖ/PDY interjected themselves with political parties in order to attempt to design their political sphere. They did this through creating plots, conspiracies and traps based on the intelligence information they have seized. The name of the organization became almost synonymous with the cassette scandals and it was considered the main suspect in all of these instances.

The incident, which the organization had the most impact on within the political sphere, is considered to be the cassette operation, which resulted in the resignation of CHP Chairman Deniz Baykal from the party leadership. Another incident, which is seen as the intervention of FETÖ/PDY in the political sphere, is the disclosure of the private life recordings of 10 senior executives in the MHP to the media on the 21st of May 2011. After this incident nine of the above mentioned executives withdrew from the MHP and withdrew as deputy candidates. One of the mentioned people above was expelled from the party. A case has been opened, and is ongoing, on the suspicion that these actions against the privacy of the private life of these persons were carried out by the FETÖ/PDY.

In the first stage of the organization it infiltrated its members into all the institutions of the state in order to take over the administration. In the second stage, the organization became a major economic power.[142] In time the organization wanted to reach such a level of power that no would would dare to stand against it.[143] Thus, when the organization felt strong enough it started to intervene in politics and tried to control the leaders of the political parties.

The interventions of the organization in politics can be summarized as follows; the organization tries to seize the management of political parties provincial and district offices (*il ve ilçe teşkilatı*) and if possible the headquarters of the parties. If it is not possible, they resort to placing members of the organization in the managerial levels. Again the organization resorts to placing its members to the municipal and provincial councils, making them deputies, placing its members in the municipal and provincial commissions, contacting with the elected political party representatives for the interest of the organization, making these representatives members of the organization, steering the government and political party policies, having a say on the decision making processes, discrediting political persons or the institutions that oppose the organization, degrading persons by broadcasting demeaning propaganda against them, using intimidation, coercion, suppressing other through fear mongering, using threat, and finally incapacitating or forcing someone to resign. The organization carried out its political policy intervention activities through the Imams who were responsible for the political figures. The execution of these plans was made by mobilizing the intelligence members who had seized the intelligence units of the security.

The campaign launched by the organization, regarding the CHP Chairman Deniz Baykal and the MHP senior executives, right before the general election of 2011 severely deteriorated the natural course of politics. It has been established that Fetullah Gülen sent the following message himself to his members: *"Hereafter the inside of CHP and MHP will become frantic. The head of CHP and MHP, as well as the people that are around them, are of foreign kind. They are not the children of this land."*[144]

The political interventions conducted by the organization, especially the listening to the CHP and the MHP headquarters and obtaining political secrets, the illegal monitoring of the offices and managers of the political parties, recordings of audio and images/videos, with a remarkable timing, and the voice and image/video recordings were all shared with the public right before the general elections. It was alleged that the CHP Chairman Deniz Baykal was informed before the above mentioned cassettes were published and broadcasted in the media; he even, it was argued, tried to be influenced by mentioning of a *"Varan-1"*, *"Varan-2"* and *"Varan-3"* recording. The decision to listen into the targeted political figures was made in order to fabricate a false view that they had connections with crime and terrorist networks. The administrative procedures to do all this was accomplished by specifying a fake name or identity information and an incorrect residence address. For example, A.G., an advisor to the CHP Chairman Deniz Baykal, was listened to under a false number, and as if he was a member of a terrorist network.[145]

The illegal listening, tracking, voice and video recordings about the managers and their representatives of political parties were made in such a way that the perpetrator was never known and for this specifically foreign Internet service providers and programs were used. The same method was used for the publicizing the audio and video recordings. Thus, the parties in question were prevented from entering the elections due to the discrediting of their administrators and deputies, and the parties were left in a difficult position in front of their voters and these parties were knocked out of their original political course.

These interventions' aimed at managing people and institutions operating in the political arena from a single center. It could both destroy the pluralist politics and affect the political decision making and the implementation process and cause the elimination of openness and transparency in the political sphere. The political structures, which take their legitimacy and power from the public, faced now the danger of being controlled by external powerful forces.

According to a specific plan after the December 17-25 attempts, whose aim was to destroying the government by the organization and to imprison many statesmen, especially Prime Minister Recep Tayyip Erdoğan, the deputies and mayors who were members of the association and the administrators in the AK Party offices began to resign gradually. The main aim here was to create the impression that the AK Party, which was in power, had a dissolution, and that the process of the dissolution of the Refah Party and the True Path Party (DYP) in the February 28 process started within the AK Party. Within the scope of this plan, ten deputies including İdris Naim Şahin, Hakan Şükür, Hasan Hami Yıldırım and İdris Bal were made to resign from the AK Party periodically. With the perception management conducted by media outlets of the organization, the aim was to create the false view and expectation that about seventy of the AK Party deputies would resign and thus the government would fall as a result.

The ongoing propaganda against the AK Party and the government increased after the December 17-25 events by the FETÖ/PDY. In addition, in an attempt to create a perception that Prime Minister Recep Tayyip Erdoğan and members of the government had carried out the largest corruption feat in the history of the Republic, the organization tried to reduce the public support for the AK Party. Moreover, it tried to gather opposition parties against the AK Party on a single front. To this end, the organization collaborated with many opposition parties, particularly the Republican People's Party (CHP) and the People's Democratic Party (HDP).

During the local elections held on the 30th of March 2014 it carried out an intense propaganda effort against the AK Party to get the lowest possible vote, but it was not successful. AK Party's votes in this election, instead of falling, its local election results in 2014 were 45.60% which indicated a 7.21% increase from the local elections in 2009.

The FETÖ/PDY, who supported Ekmeleddin İhsanoğlu, one of the candidates against AK Party Chairman and Prime Minister Recep Tayyip Erdoğan in the presidential elections held on August 20 2014 for the purpose of determining the 12th president, declared nearly a mobilization in order to prevent Prime Minister Recep Tayyip Erdoğan winning. However, despite all their efforts, Prime Minister Erdoğan could not be prevented from winning the election in the first round.

The FETÖ/PDY implemented the same strategy in the parliamentary general elections held on the 7th of June and 1st of November 2015 and made a great effort for the Peoples'

Democratic Party (HDP) to pass the threshold. As a matter of fact, Ekrem Dumanlı, the chief editor of the Zaman Newspaper, visited Diyarbakır metropolitan municipality on the 11th of April 2015 with his accompanying people[146] and visited them secretly by entering from the backdoors of Diyarbakır metropolitan municipality and conducted a 40 minute meeting with the municipal administrators. At that time, some writers of the period such as Nazlı Ilıcak, Şahin Alpay, Seyfettin Gürsel, Ali Yurttagül, Ali Bulaç, and Ahmet Turan Alkan made statements to support the HDP in the elections.[147]

At the same time, the Democratic Society Congress (DTK) Co-President Ahmet Türk and the Peace and Democracy Party (BDP) Deputy Chairman Nazmi Gür had a meeting with Gülen in Pennsylvania and Ekrem Dumanlı confirmed this meeting.

The FETÖ/PDY tried to ensure that no party could reach a majority in the Turkish Grand National Assembly after the parliamentary elections held on the 7th of June. They also made a great effort to establish a coalition government between CHP, MHP and HDP. However, they were not successful in their goal. The FETÖ/PDY continued its attempts to intervene in politics in the early elections. For example, the Cihan News Agency, which is affiliated with the organization, called for an open support to the HDP before the parliamentary general elections that were held on the 1st of November 2015. The media outlets associated with the organization increased the criticism of the government's actions in this period. Still, the AK Party came first with 49.48% of the votes in the parliamentary elections held on the 1st of November 2015.

It is known that Selahattin Demirtaş stated that *"Injustice was done to FETÖ"* and requested them to support HDP on the 34th Abant Platform organized on the 30th of January 2016.

Furthermore, Alaaddin Korkutata, the president of Diyar-bakır Entrepreneur Businessmen Association, who is affiliated with FETÖ/PDY, participated in the ceremony of laying the foundation of the dormitory of 272 girls commissioned by Diyarbakır Metropolitan Municipality.[148]

The organization has taken up all kinds of ways to reach its goal of designing their strategy for the political sphere of Turkey. In this process, much slander, crime allegations, and widespread murky propaganda campaigns were carried out such as establishing networks to commit crime, mutah marriages, spying, theft, bribery and even black magic; against politicians, senior bureaucrats and especially the members of the council of ministers.

ADMINISTRATIVE STRUCTUREOF THE FETÖ/PDY

The FETÖ/PDY, just like any other religious community, was expected to be on good terms with its country, state and fellow men. However, instead it considered the state and all other communities in the society as rivals and opposition. It worked just like an intelligence agency, and utilized *"code names, specific channels of communication and money coming from unknown sources."* All the administrators of the organization, first and foremost Fetullah Gülen, avoided coming to Turkey, despite the fact that state officers invited them on many occasions. They administered the activities of the organization from abroad. They took advantage of all kinds of unethical and illegal means to eliminate their rivals. With representatives of foreign missions, they held gatherings with hidden agendas. They made use of weapons and whenever they felt it was needed, they got in contact with terrorist organizations, and supported them by all means. All these activities count as evidence demonstrating that this structure is a well-established terrorist organization. Certainly, in order for an organization to be considered as a terrorist organization, it must have a purpose that is legally considered as a *"crime,"* it must pursue illegal activities to realize this purpose;

it must have a secret structure of organization, secret methods of communication, gunmen and members with clandestine identities.[149]

It is now well known that FETÖ/PDY has a hierarchical structure, similar to a military institution. This structure, led by Fetullah Gülen, functions under the control of administrators who are individually called "*Imam.*" In the FETÖ/PDY organization, an *Imam* at any rank must be obeyed unconditionally, and the orders given by the superior may not be questioned by the subordinate. The first thing that is taught to students, who lived in houses and dormitories administered by the organization, is to "*obey the Imam.*" The Imams administering houses and dormitories gave sermons about the necessity of obeying the Imam almost every month. The youth educated in this system, adopted the attitude of unconditional obedience, and when they occupied the position of the administration (*Imam*), they maintained the same manners.

Fetullah Gülen, who is the founder and the leader of the organization is considered to be a great Muslim scholar and spiritual figure, "*who does not make any mistake, or err, who can think of that which may not be thought by other people, and is the Mahdi [in traditional Islam a messianic deliverer at the end of time] who knows everything.*" This impression is supported by the enlargement of the organization, and the power and success that it acquired in socio-economical areas inside Turkey and abroad. Members of the organization believe that Fetullah Gülen has direct contact with God (Allah) and the Prophet Muhammad (pbuh) and that he receives all orders and instructions instantaneously from them. Consequently, Gülen's orders and instructions cannot be questioned, or be subject to negotiation, at all. The effect of such a high rank allocated to Gülen is reflected in the Imams who act on Gülen's behalf at all levels of the hierarchical structure. It is for this reason is believed that all of Gülen's Imams are in a position to carry out the decisions taken by him. Thus, objection against an Imam, no matter at what rank he is, means to object to Gülen himself. Furthermore, objection against Gülen means opposing God and the Prophet. Similarly, obedience to an Imam means obedience to Gülen, and hence to God and to the Prophet. All thoughts opposing the decisions of Gülen and of those who receive orders, inspiration and encouragement from Gülen were therefore suppressed immediately and harshly. They did not tolerate even the slightest emergence of alternative ideas. Indeed, FETÖ/PDY has been practicing an order of "*dictatorship*" which for many years they accused President Recep Tayyip Erdoğan of doing. It is evident that they have no tolerance at all.

With such overall characteristics, the FETÖ/PDY established its organization in two spheres, i.e., inside Turkey and abroad. The establishment in all two spheres has a complicated structure with a legal and an illegal dimension as well as a vertical and a horizontal dimension. The vertical organization consists of a hierarchical order of strongly connected units. The horizontal organization is made out of cells, which maintain secrecy and confidentiality measures at the highest level. Fetullah Gülen, considered as the 'Imam of the cosmos', is elevated above all the organization, like a throne (*Arş*); and he is seen as being beyond the hierarchy.

The Throne of Fetullah Gülen[150]

Members of the FETÖ/PDY believe that Fetullah Gülen governs the cosmos by orders that he receives from God. Hence Fetullah Gülen's instructions cannot be questioned and they are spiritually at an inscrutable level, beyond the limits of reason. Fetullah Gülen is the unique authority and leader controlling the whole organization. He is supposed to be even *"not bound by what he says and what he writes."* This is the result of the fact that Fetullah Gülen does not consider himself to be bound by moral, legal and religious rules, which consist of divine commands. Based on this conception, Gülen gives priority to his organization with regard to the state order, and considers himself above all these institutions. By his followers it is not flawed if he acts contrary to what he says, if he changes his statements, if he abolishes any prohibition, or if he commands new prohibitions. Since he is in constant consultation with the spiritual realm, he even has the authority to change the religious rules. As such he is accepted as the *Mahdi*. Gülen, who is at the zenith point of this belief system, considers his community to be high above the state authority. Accordingly, he has attempted to dominate the constitutional order of the state and to govern it behind the scenes.

In the FETÖ/PDY organization, any act of thinking that may imply to question the decision made by the leader, or any action or attitude with a similar implication, is harshly suppressed. The instructions given by Fetullah Gülen and other administrators within the organization are taken as sacred instructions and implemented accordingly. The administrators of the organization, first and foremost Fetullah Gülen himself, appear to be really modest people when they address people outside of their organization. However, when it comes to their behavior within their organization, they assume an absolute authoritative and suppressive attitude.

All activities are carried out by the instructions given by the 'Imam of the Cosmos' in the organization with a strict hierarchical order. Since there is no authorized person to represent him or to function as his assistant, he is the single authority to decide on so many divergent activities of the organization. These activities may include, for example, investments and activities concerning money and capital flow that may be carried out within Turkey or abroad, funding certain lobbying activities, gifts to be presented to foreign statesmen, the political messages that shall be communicated to the public, the political positions in any given context, the topics and ideas that will be spoken or written through the media apparatus, organization of meetings with foreign officials, and deciding on issues related to the collaboration with secret service agencies and terrorist organizations. He had the authority to shape major policies, activities related to them and controlling the actual implementation of these activities. Although he claims to be in asylum and leading a life of seclusion, he seems to be an administrator of an organization which takes care of all kinds of worldly affairs, in some sense he acts, behaves and appears like a leader of the mafia. Despites all the errors so far, he kept provoking his organization against the state authority, and taking a definite political side. He openly challenged the Government of the Turkish Republic, and secretly collaborated with countries that were hostile to Turkey. Moreover, he tried to acquire private information about the people and state secrets.

The Domestic Side of the Organization[151]

The Vertical Organization

Since the companies and nongovernmental organizations, which are the legal aspect of the FETÖ/PDY organization, are discussed in a separate section further on in detail under the heading "*Financial Structure of the FETÖ/PDY*", they will not be elaborated on in this section. It has been verified that the illegal aspect of the organization is to be found within the hierarchical structure that has seven ranks. These ranks in the order from the highest to the lowest are as follows: Trustee of Turkey (*Türkiye Mütevellisi*), Imam of Turkey, regional Imams, provincial Imams (*il imamları*), district Imams *(ilçe imamları)*, Local Imams (*mahalle imamları*) and household Imams (*ev imamları*). Furthermore, as part of the domestic organization, there is a group of administrators, called "*Specialists*" (*Husûsîler*), who are directly linked to Fetullah Gülen. The Specialists were in charge of the critical state offices concerning the security of the country, such as the General Directorate of Security Affairs, the National Intelligence Organization, the Turkish Armed Forces and all judicial institutions such as the Constitutional Court (*Anayasa Mahkemesi*), the Court of Cassation (*Yargıtay*) and the Council of State (*Danıştay*). (See, figure 1)

The Throne of Fetullah Gülen	
Trustee of Turkey	The Specialists
Imam of Turkey	Security (*Emniyet*)
Regional Imams	MİT
Provincial Imams	TSK
District Imams	Jurisdiction
Neighborhood Imams	
Household Imams	

Figure 1: General scheme of domestic organizational structure of the FETÖ/PDY organization.

With regard to the geographical-local organization, they established their organization in five regions around Turkey. The regions and the provinces in those regions are shown in Table 2 and Map 3.

Table 2: The FETÖ/PDY's domestic organization (regions and connected provinces)

Region	Connected Provinces
Istanbul	Bilecik, Bolu, Bursa, Düzce, Edirne, Eskişehir, Kırklareli, Kocaeli, Sakarya, Tekirdağ, Yalova, and Zonguldak.
Izmir	Afyonkarahisar, Antalya, Aydın, Balıkesir, Burdur, Çanakkale, Denizli, Karaman, Kütahya, Manisa, Mersin, Muğla, and Uşak.
Ankara	Aksaray, Amasya, Bartın, Çankırı, Çorum, Isparta, Karabük, Kastamonu, Kayseri, Kırıkkale, Kırşehir, Konya, Nevşehir, Niğde, Samsun, Sinop, Sivas, Tokat, and Yozgat.
Gaziantep	Adana, Adıyaman, Batman, Bingöl, Bitlis, Diyarbakır, Elazığ, Hatay, Kahramanmaraş, Kilis, Malatya, Osmaniye, Siirt, Şanlıurfa, Şırnak, and Tunceli.
Erzurum	Ağrı, Ardahan, Artvin, Bayburt, Erzincan, Giresun, Gümüşhane, Hakkari, Iğdır, Kars, Muş, Ordu, Rize, Trabzon, and Van.

The FETÖ/PDY organization acquired a gigantic size by exploiting the sincere feelings of the people, who did not know most of the time about the illegal activities of the organization and who loved it and its administrators for the sake of God. Although the organization grew by exploiting large masses of population by all means, the true foundation and faithful mass of the FETÖ/PDY is made up by people who worked either in the public institutions, the private sector, or in the nongovernmental organizations. These were people who knew about the main intention of the organization i.e. 'to seize the state' and who attended the religious conversation (*sohbet*) inside the organization and regularly paid their affiliation fee (*aidat*). These people included counselor students (*rehber öğrenciler*) who were placed in publicly administered dormitories and public schools,[152] teacher aides (*belletmenler*),[153] major counselors (*serrehberler*),[154] household, neighborhood (mahalle), localities (semt), towns (belde), districts, and student Imams,[155] and *abis* (like lieutenants of a cult or organization, lit. older brothers, singular *abi*, plural *abis*) and *ablas* (like lieutenants of a cult or organization, lit. older sisters, singular *abla*, plural *ablas*) administering the religious conversation groups.

The operational administrators are the main people behind the spread of the ideology of the organization and who coordinate the operations of the organization in practice. The medium and high level administrators of the organization are those who have a position in governmental offices, and people that work at a private sector, and at nongovernmental organizations. This group includes the Imams of larger districts / provinces, Imams of small cities, groups of guidance (*irşat ekipleri*) and *abis* and *ablas* who are in charge of special religious conversation groups.

A group with a higher rank in the hierarchy consists of the administrators, who inspect the operational activities carried out by the organization, who control lower-level administrators by protecting them from being exposed and appraises their loyalty. These administrators are in charge of identifying any possible antagonists and are in charge of eliminating them when it is needed. They are in charge of transferring the special instructions, which they received from their superiors, to the administrators of the operational units, and the implementation of these instructions. The administrators belonging to this group are appointed by Fetullah Gülen directly. They are selected from among his people, who are affiliated with the organization since their childhood, who have demonstrated their loyalty and obedience to the organization. This group of administrators includes the Imams of municipalities, the regional/ state Imams, the Imams of some minor counties, the Imams of some public institutions, nongovernmental organizations and professional organizations, and inspectors with special authorities (*murakıp*).

There are also Imams who govern and administer the accomplishment of the strategic activities identified by Fetullah Gülen. These make up the strategic high ranking administrators. These are selected from among the most faithful disciples (*murit*) and are appointed personally by Fetullah Gülen. They work under the immediate command of Fetullah Gülen. This group include Imams of continents and continental regions,[156] Imams of countries, Imams of certain groups, such as Alevites and Gypsies, Imams of important international institutions, Imams of specifically important non-governmental organizations, political activities, athletic clubs, and last but not least the Imams of certain sectors that are important for the organization, such as Imams of Bank Asya, Kaynak Holding, and Samanyolu Broadcasting Group (*Samanyolu Yayın Grubu*).

The FETÖ/PDY made sure to appoint Imams to public institutions paralleling the administrators of those institutions. The members of the organization working in those institutions were required to obey not only the orders and instructions of the official administrators of those institutions but to those of the Imam appointed by the organization. This parallel structure inserted into all public institutions is called *"circles of state"* (*devair-i devlet*).

There is another group that had the responsibility of nomination, promotion and withdrawal of the administrators of strategically important units and the administrators of the important operational units. Fetullah Gülen directly appointed members of this group choosing them from among those whom he trusted and in their work, they were in direct contact with him. However, *"Specialists"* (*Hususîler*), which included Imams, who are responsible for critical public institutions including security, jurisdiction, armed Forces (*Silahh Kuvvetler*) and MİT is known to have an equal rank to that group.

The *Specialists* were indispensable for the FETÖ/PDY to reach its goals. The units of *Specialists* are considered to be built up with private service units; a cell type structuring. They are the agents which carry out all the critical operations. This is why all their operations are carried out in outmost secrecy and all the members of these units use code names and encrypted programs of communication, so that they can protect themselves from being found out.

At the top of the hierarchical structure, there are the Imam of Turkey, the Imam of *Specialists* and the Imam of the Trustees of Turkey. Furthermore, the general staff (*kurmay heyeti*) which is the special advisory board of Fetullah Gülen, is included in this group. Some of the administrators, who have the highest position in the FETÖ/PDY, are as follows: Abdullah Aymaz, İrfan Yılmaz, İsmet Aksoy, Mehmet Ali Şengül, Mehmet Erdoğan Tüzün, Mustafa Yeşil, Naci Tosun, Reşit Haylamaz, Sadık Kesmeci, Şerif Ali Tekalan, Mustafa

Özcan (Imam of Turkey).[157] It is known that the office of the Imam of Turkey was established after Fetullah Gülen escaped to America in 1999. It has a special status within the organization. Although formally, Fetullah Gülen does not have a deputy or an assistant, the Imam of Turkey has the most authoritative position after Gülen.

The Horizontal Organization

Horizontally, the FETÖ/PDY is organized with a structure of chain-units bound to Imams. To ensure the secrecy and to increase the flexibility of the organization, each unit is made up of cell type structures. Cells are either student apartments, or religious conversation groups. These are the smallest units, which consist of five-six people administered by an *abi* or and *abla*. The Imam/*abi*/*abla* of each cell is also a member of a higher level cell. Members of the cells carry out only the instructions given to them. This is why each member of a cell knows only what he/she carries out, but does not know that what he/she does is a part of a greater and illegal activity. Even if he/she finds out later on that the end result is a criminal activity, he/she cannot change anything, because he/she participated in the accomplishment of the end result.

The household Imams or *abis*/*ablas* are highly important people, since they are the one who uphold the organization's connection to the ordinary people and who maintain the dynamism of its grassroots. This is why they were chosen from among the people who are most faithful to the organization, who are highly articulate, hardworking and presentable. The organization is also known to have been very careful about the suitability of the material conditions of the *abis*/ *ablas* of the religious instructions and how that impacted upon their religious conversation groups.

The formation of the organization starts as a student house or a religious conversation group in a public institution. In time, when the number of students increases, they establish new student houses. Similarly, when members of a religious conversation group increases, they form new religious conversation groups. In some neighborhoods, one could find tens of student houses, and in some public institutions, one could find hundreds of such religious conversation groups. Just as student houses were the smallest units (cell) of the organization in social life, the religious conversation groups were its smallest units in the political, bureaucratic and economic life.

In both student houses and religious conversation group meetings, they viewed video records of the sermons (*vaaz*) by Fetullah Gülen. They also read texts together from Gülen's own books, and through this they thought that they achieved religious instruction. The religious conversation was led by the Imam of the house, the *abi/abla* of the religious conversation group, or by a major counselor (*serrehber*); an invited Imam or a guest could also lead the religious instruction. Moreover, they used to visit houses of people who were not actually a member of the organization but who had sympathies with it and supported it. During these visits, they held religious conversation programs; for example, they formed groups to recite the whole of the Qur'an. Nevertheless, it is well known that *abis, ablas* and the household Imams of the organization were far from having the proper schooling to know how to recite the Qur'an according to the proper recitation rules (*Ilm al-Qirâ'a*).

The religious conversation groups that consisted of

wealthy people preferred to use video sermons by Fetullah Gülen, which were especially prepared for them. Before inviting people to a religious conversation group, they carefully scrutinized and classified them. They classified them according to their economic conditions and the amount of donation they gave to the organization. The decision determining, who will be invited to which of the religious conversation group, was made in accordance with the economic conditions of the individual person. Those who donated large amounts of money or quite expensive real estate received significant gifts by Fetullah Gülen. Some of them had a chance to be received by him personally and to receive the gifts in person from him. They also organized tours abroad for the wealthy people, and they were taken to visit aid stations, as well as the schools of the organization and other institutions abroad. By these organizations, they wanted to give the impression that they are providing education for the destitute students. They related the activities of the *Kimse Yok Mu Derneği* (Is there Anyone who may Help: a charity institution run by the FETÖ/PDY) with much exaggeration; in a sense they were playing with the heartstrings of the wealthy people. That is how they made a number of wealthy people give high amounts of donation at their return to Turkey from such a tour.

The Organization in Strategic Public Institutions[158]

Although the objective of the organization was to seize all public institutions, they gave priority to institutions of security and jurisdiction and therefore tried to take hold of the armed forces and the civil administration (*mülkî idare*). Thus, inside the organization any effort to take hold of these institutions was called, 'important services' (*Mühim Hizmetler*), and they appointed authorized Imams to govern activities in all of these areas.

Necip Hablemitoğlu, in his book, *Köstebek (Mole)*, published in 2008, described the aim of the organization as follows: "*to infiltrate the strategic institutions of the state and ultimately seize the state by stringently hiding their true identity (taki-yye) and by establishing an organization that does not openly confront the state structure.*"

They question why the organization paid such special attention to some public institutions is answered by Hanefi Avcı, a retired Director of Security Office, in his book *Haliçte Yaşayan Simonlar: Dün Devlet Bugün Cemaat (Simons of the Golden Horn: The State in the Past, the Community in the Present)*, published in 2010, as follows: "*Those who want to collect information from all around the country and those who want to track activities of whomsoever they want, must at first, take hold of the Office of Security and Intelligence (Emniyet İstihbarat Dairesi). They can do this by controlling MİT (National Intelligence Agency). However, this institution cannot sanction anything further than such actions. Therefore, if they want to carry out judicial proceedings about the institutions and persons of whom they are collecting information, they have to also be influential in the Security Department for Fighting against Smuggling and Organized Crimes. If they want to not only collect information and carry out judicial proceedings, but also carry out judicial proceedings about any state officer, military officer and about those who are protected by laws, then they have to be influential on the attorneys and judges working at specially authorized courts. Thus we see that in recent years such a plan was carried out inside Turkey.*"

The Security Agency

Necip Hablemitoğlu, in his book *Köstebek*, describes the infiltration of the organization into the security agency as follows:

"Fetullahists placed their members successfully within the security agency as a result of their efforts to obtain "balance" against the TSK (Turkish Armed Forces). They frequently expressed their vision, to encourage [the members], that in the future the state would be seized, the system would be totally changed and finally an alternative structure of armed forces would be used against the TSK. The centers where the Fetullahist members of the security agency got together and were educated are called "barracks of light," and their members within the security agency are called, with a general designation, "armies of light."

The Security agency is one of the institutions where the organization started to place their members as staff at first. This activity of placing their members in the security agency was carried out under the control of an Imam who was considered to have a position higher than that of the Minister of the Internal Affairs and it was carried out in all strategic units of the agency. To insure the staffing in the agency, they appointed special Imams to the Police Vocational Schools, to the Police College, the Police Academy, and to the specific departments at the General Directorate of Security Affairs, such as the Intelligence Department, the department of Fighting against Terrorism, and the department for Fighting against Smuggling and Organized Crimes. They worked very hard to place their members into the staff of the agency at the headquarters as well as at the provincial branches. In this process, they motivated specifically selected youth since the middle school years to enroll into the police schools, the Police College and the Police Academy. Thus, over time they were able to take control of all of the crucial positions.

The Organization increased its efforts to infiltrate the public institutions during the 1980's. When the university graduates were given the opportunity to enroll in the Police College and Police Academy starting during the 1986-1987 educational period; they started increasingly to place members of the organization into these institutions. In the same year, a group of students—almost all of whom were members of the organization—graduated from the program within a nine-month education period. They took the office with the title of "*special class.*" This situation made it easy for them to staff multitudes of their own people in the security agency. The "*special class*" program continued until 1991.

Since the 1990's, the General Directorate of Security Affairs came under the control of FETÖ/PDY rapidly, because of two factors. On the one hand, the organization dominated the schools which provided education for the members of the security agency. Moreover, those who got educated in those schools were accepted into the agency directly. Within the Law Enforcement Agency (*Emniyet Teşkilatı*), they first took control of the personnel department. By using the authority of this department, they were able to rapidly control the strategic positions at the headquarters and, as well, the provincial branches of the agency. By the privileges of these units, they gave priority to their members to attend certain training courses and educational programs abroad. Consequently, they made their members more qualified and preferable than other members of the agency and thus acquired the power to eliminate those that did not belong to their group. Almost all of the members of the Law Enforcement Agency, who occupied a medium or a higher position and who were arrested after the July 15 military coup attempt, are people who were placed in the Police College or Police Academy during this period.

Mehmet Kılıçlar, a former General Director of Security Affairs, stated that 65-70 out of all eighty-one provincial security directors until 2011 were members of the organization and that when he was in the service, this number was as high as 75. In a similar statement, former chief of the Office of Security and Intelligence (*Emniyet İstihbarat Dairesi*), and General Directory of Security Affairs, Sabri Uzun, confirmed that almost all of the students enrolled at the Police College were members of the FETÖ/PDY, and that almost all of the personnel hired by the security agency between 2007-2013 years belonged to the organization. He held that in no other country could something like this happen whereby the staff who would try to seize the state was in fact hired by the hands of the state itself. Celalettin Lekesiz, a former General Director of Security Affairs, stated that out of seven thousand personnel working at the Office of Security and Intelligence, six thousands five hundred were members of the organization. The Former Minister of the Internal Affairs, Efkan Âlâ stated that *in the operational units and intelligence department of the security agency, more than 90% of the directors* belonged to the organization.

The first report to identify and examine the attempts of the organization to place staff in the security agency was prepared in 1991 by Dr. Ahmet Dündar, a chief police inspector, and police inspector İzzet sezgin Şenel. In this report, they called the organization "*Students of Illegal Fetullah Hoca.*" They stated that this illegal organization got organized in educational institutions, especially institutions such as the Police Academy, the Police College and the police schools. They said that those students who did not become a member of the organization, and those who cancelled their membership to it were threatened, dismissed through denigration and inflicted upon through a disciplinary action. They also stated that the Fetullahist superiors forged documents of slander indicating that those students had committed a crime. For example, it is stated that these superiors somehow got into contact with more or less half of the students at the Ankara Police College, and they systematically continued their effort to assimilate them. However, the report was silenced and made ineffective by the operations of the organization.

The fact that the organization did what it could to place its members in the security agency was revealed by Ünal Erkan, the General Director of the Security Affairs, in the same year (1991). He discovered an illegal activity by students whereby through drawing lots they were trying to identify the places where the new police officers should start working. Erkan was given a notice stating that "*selected students who were members of the organization and who were going to graduate from the Police Academy were going to be appointed to the intelligence, personnel, and communication departments of the Security Agency (Emniyet) and police schools.*" He immediately discovered and stopped the drawing lots ceremony of the students and found out that there were two different bags for drawing lots. Students who were affiliated with the organization would draw their lots from one bag, in which there were placement tickets for the intelligence and personnel departments, the Police College and similar strategic important offices; other students would, on the the hand, draw their lots from the second bag, which included placement tickets for police stations and other commonplace departments.

In addition to these testimonials, correspondences in that

period inside the different units of the General Directorate of Security Affairs indicate that the illegal activities of the organization were being identified at that period. However, as the number of the members of the organization increased, towards the end of the 1990's, they published books and reports expressing positive evaluations about the organization. For example, one may cite Ali Fuat Yılmazer's book, *Islamda Mezhepler, Tarikat ve Dini Akımlar*, which was published by the Office of the Security Intelligence, General Directorate of Security Affairs, in 1996 to clear Fetullah Gülen and his organization. A similar work is the booklet published by the same office in July 1998.

Educational Institutions

The organization's aim was to annex the educational system, as Fetullah Gülen's instruction to his organization, *"assume offices in the national education, by whatever way you can,"* indicates. For this reason, they appointed the Imam of national education, who was considered to have a higher position than the formal minister of the national education. They also appointed specific Imams to important units of the educational system. The organization started running preparatory course centers (*dershane*), schools, study centers (*etüt merkezleri*), student dormitories and student houses all around the country. They also systematically oriented an important amount of students, who were preparing for the university placement exam, to prefer faculties of education. In a short period of time, the majority of the students enrolled in the faculties of education turned out to be students who got educated in the schools, preparatory course centers and study centers run by the organization, and students who lived in the houses or dormitories run by the organization. When these students graduated from faculties of education and took up positions in schools, members of the organization occupied a significant part of the teaching positions. Consequently, they started extensively to propagate in schools for the organization.

One of the areas where the organization focused most at was the higher education. This is because it was imperative for a person to have a university degree to be employed at any of the significant bureaucratic offices; and the high school teachers and the academic staff who educate the future generations were also obliged to have university degrees. This is why, on the one hand, the organization established new universities of its own, and infiltrated the state universities, on the other. It made those universities "liberated regions" by intensely placing its members into them. The situation became so appalling that it became impossible for those who were not members of the organization to be placed in these universities. This activity of placing people in key positions at universities made it possible for the organization to propagate itself to the wider student populace and also to receive huge amounts of money through the corporations operating in universities, at techno parks, technology research and development institutions, and through the tenders initiated by the universities. The Imam who was in control of all the higher educational institutions and the other Imams, who assumed the responsibility for individual universities, led and administered all of these operations for the organization.

The organization also appointed Imams who were in charge of important higher educational and scientific research institutions, such as for TÜBİTAK, Turkish Academy of Sciences, Public Administration Institute for Turkey and the Middle East and ÖSYM. A significant activity of staffing especially in TÜBİTAK and ÖSYM was carried out. By virtue of the fact that they infiltrated ÖSYM, they were able to steal exam questions and to place masses of their members in public institutions in such a way that they were able to occupy their target institutions.

Jurisdiction[159]

The FETÖ/PDY paid special attention to the judiciary system, including higher judiciary institutions, such as the Constitutional Court, the Council of Judges and Public Prosecutors, the Court of Cassation, the Council of State, the Military Court of Cassation, and the Supreme Military Administrative Court, as well as various other departments such as the Justice Academy of Turkey, the regional and provincial administrative courts, the appeal courts, the courts of justice and the tax courts. It instituted specific offices of Imams to be in charge of each of these institutions. The Imam of the Jurisdiction was considered to be more authoritative than the minister of the justice, and his orders and instructions were given priority over those of the minister.

Intending to place its members into the judiciary system, the organization established a well-designed system directing students from the high school period onward. According to this system, students who were talented in Turkish-mathematic division, were directed to law schools and judiciary vocational schools. Some of the students who graduated from these schools were again directed to pursue an academic carrier, hence to take up a position of assistance, some of them were directed to take the exams to become a judge or a prosecutor, some of them were directed to pursue a career in the courts as an officer, some of them were directed to become a lawyer—so that they could control the Bars, and some of them were directed to be even wardens—so as to be able to even control the final aspects of the judiciary process.

In the process of infiltrating the public institutions, including universities, the members of the organization committed many illegal activities, such as stealing exam questions, favoritism, and seizing offices at public institutions by forged court decisions. As they took control of the judiciary departments and security agency, they completed the triangle of police-prosecutor-judge and thus the period of conspiracies, taking people into custody, detentions and law-suits based on fake evidence began. At one point the prosecutors began to sign the documents—such as precepts, instructions, and bills of indictment—prepared by law enforcement officers who were members of the organization without even reading them. The judges who were members of the organization, issued verdicts without listening to some of the witnesses and without properly hearing the defense of the suspects.

After the constitutional referendum on the 12th of September 2010, the Council of Judges and Public Prosecutors (HSYK) was formed anew. In this process, the organization took all the positions which were decided on the basis of elections within the HSYK. And then the organization took action to take over the Court of Cassation and the Council of State. Ahmet Hamsici, former deputy chairman of the HSYK, in his publicly reported statement, summarized what happened as follows: *"In the year 2010, after the members of the HSYK was identified, they asked us to make preparations, because the minister of justice, Sadullah Ergin, and undersecretary, Ahmet Kahraman 'were preparing to make a new law, and accordingly at least 50 members to the Council of State (Damştay) and 150 members to the Court of Cassation (Yargıtay) would be elected.'... In the elections to select members of the Court of Cassation, 107 candidates out of 108 candidates designated by the Fetullah Gülen community were elected. Moreover, in the elections to select the members of the Council of State all the candidates designated by that community were elected."*

The organization got the majority of members in the Court of Cassation through the support of their members in the HSYK. Consequently, it became so powerful that in many criminal divisions it could approve of any verdict it wanted, or it could change any verdict with which it was not happy. Kerim Tosun, a former member of HSYK, in his statement was quoted in the media providing the following information: *"People who were members of the Fetullah Gülen community were distributed in the chambers in such a way that they had the majority of the members in the 4th and 18th of the Civil Chambers and in the 4th 5th 8th 9th 11th 14th and 15th of the Criminal Departments. These departments were vital for the community. After Nazım Kaynak became the president of the Court of Cassation, division of labor among the department of the Court of Cassation was changed, and it was the organization itself that was behind this change of the division of labor. By this new division of labor among the departments, the important cases for the community, such as Balyoz, Şike, Hipnoz, Kurdoğlu, were given to the responsibility of the departments where the community was strong."*

Mustafa Özçelik, a member of the HSYK, described the situation as it was reported by the media in short as following: *"The establishment among the members of the Court of Cassation was divided into two: civil and criminal departments. Each group had an abi (older brother), and the community dictated to the members of the groups which candidates they had to support in the elections of the Court of Cassation. No one who was not supported by the Gülen community was elected as the president of a department. When the community did not support a definite candidate for the presidency of a department, members of the community voted in such a way that the election got stuck."*

The HSYK, the Office of the Inspection Board was used as an instrument to investigate the judges and prosecutors, whom the organization choose as its target, on the basis of tip-off petitions (*ihbar*) without any name or signature on them. These people were given unfair (*haksız*), disciplinary penalties; they were denied any promotion or taking up important positions. Their performance improvement and appraisal forms were unfairly filled with lower grades and negative evaluations. Moreover, certain crimes and misdemeanors, which might damage their family relations, were attributed to them and their private lives became subject to heavy intervention. In contrast to this, when the members of the organization carried out activities and transactions contrary to laws, they were either not prosecuted, or those who were prosecuted were cleared, one way or another.

Although in many activities of the organization, they paid strict attention to working in secrecy and hiding their true identity (*takiyye*), in the elections for the positions at the Council of Judges and Public Prosecutors in 2014, because of the importance of that election, the FETÖ/ PDY members were known to have made visits to courts, visited homes and organized dinners in all provinces and districts while taking the risk of revealing their true identity. The tried to influence judges and prosecutors who were not members of the organization by offering certain gifts. Before the election, the organization identified its own members by the secret communication network, which they had created. It calculated probable number of votes that would go to purported independent candidates for the membership of the Council of Judges and Public Prosecutors.

Since the administrators of the organization thought that different groups had equal chances in the election, they did not want to risk the results of the elections. Thus, in order to insure that the candidates, majority of whom belonged to their organization, vote in the election, they instructed, via their encrypted communication system, their members who just finished their internship and were preparing to draw their lots. Those members of the organization did not, in fact, have the right to vote and take office. However, following the instruction given by the organization, they by-passed the Secretariat of the Supreme Council of the Judges and Public Prosecutors, they applied to vote in the elections using illegal documents that they obtained from the inspection judges within the Council. Members of the organization lost in the election with a minor variance. If their fraud had not been noticed, they would certainly have won the election. Their plan was ruined due to a tip-off communicated by the Supreme Electoral Council to the Council of Judges and Public Prosecutors.

After they lost the election, members of the FETÖ/PDY got together and started a systematic campaign, with the support of certain media outlets, to discredit the decisions of the new members of the Council of Judges and Public Prosecutors concerning judges and prosecutors affiliated with the organization. Members of the organization who were elected to the Court of Cassation and the Council of State supported this campaign in collaboration with other members of the organization by leaking information to them.

By the acknowledgement of witnesses, it is understood that after they lost the election to the HSYK, the organization increased the precautions inside the organization. Especially, from 2015 onward, number of the participants in the religious conversation groups was diminished to 2-3 persons, and the range of communication was fixed to the lowest level. In the middle of 2015, the encrypted communication program *ByLock* began to be used. They kept indoctrinating and warning members of the organization. They confirmed that although things might be getting worse for FETÖ/PDY, they would get it in order very soon; they claimed that it was getting closer to the end of the world, and at this time one should keep in mind that people are in a process of major test, and that those who loose in such a test would truly be thwarted.

We may summarize the operations of the organization and its illegal practices in the judiciary system as following:

1. To steal questions in the exams designed for the members of the judiciary institutions, to move together as a group, take over critical positions in the judiciary system and establish an illegal hierarchical structure contrary to the official bureaucratic hierarchy.

2. To manipulate and use the time period of education and internship by dominating the administration of the Justice Academy, to favor the judges and prosecutors affiliated with the organization in all activities related to their profession including their candidacy for various positions, and assist them to receive language education by organizing domestic and international programs for them to improve their professional and personal skills. Furthermore, due to its members working at law schools, the organization also provided its members with titles of master and Ph.D. unjustly.

3. To target those officers in the judiciary system, who did not submit to the interests and benefits of FETÖ/PDY, to put a blot on their career by imposing a disciplinary punishment based on fake reports of investigation, thus prevent

their promotion, to obtain information about them using illegal means, to fabricate crimes and evidence, to smear, to file law suits against them without a firm basis, to threaten by violating their presumption of innocence, to limit the freedom of people for many years, by putting them in prison without even stating their charges, to perjure, to violate the right of defense and fair trial, to maltreat and torture in prisons, to push detainees and prisoners into committing suicide, to murder and to make it look like a suicide, to erase the evidence of crimes, and to decide these cases in the law suits counter to the sufferer.

4. To abuse, in the judiciary processes, national and spiritual values, such as the homeland, the nation, the Turkish language, the religion of Islam, the mosque, the call to ritual prayer, the ritual prayer and to abuse all the prophets and our noble prophet first and foremost, the Muslim scholars and the respected religious figures.

5. To monitor all the law suits which were important for the organization by the appointed members of the organization to each and every court, and to make sure that the court rulings were issued in favor of the organization.

The people who were tried via false lawsuits and were sentenced were in for another major shock. They lost their credibility, family order, acquired psychological disorders and psychiatric health problems because of the dark propaganda that were broadcasted by the media channels of the organization for days and even for weeks. The police-prosecutor-judge triangle established by the organization turned into a devil's triangle with addition of the corrections officers (*cezaevi görevlileri*) and their media team.

The Civil Administration[160]

One of the places where the organization heavily placed its members secretly was in the civil administration. The organization had its members placed comprehensively across in the various offices such as the office of the governor (*vali*), the office of the district governor, the office of the deputy governor, the office of the undersecretary (*müsteşar*), the office of the deputy undersecretaries, the office of the general directorate, the office of the chairs of departments, the office of the branch directorates (*şube müdürleri*) and in the offices of the ministry of interior affaires. It was the Imam positioned in the civil administration by the organization who directed all the attempts of their staff placed in the civil administration and all other operations carried out by them in these offices. Under the office of the Imam of the civil administration, there were Imams of the units who were in charge of organizing activities regarding the major departments of the civil administration. The organization gave priority to the work in the metropolises, and the governors of almost all the metropolises, especially that of Istanbul, and the district governors of major districts were appointed from among the members of the organization. That is how the organization carried out, with ease, its illegal activities in the most important metropolises and the districts of the country. Due to the organization's success in occupying positions at the civil administration, the office of the Imam of the civil administration was handpicked out of the *specialists*.

The Turkish Armed Forces

Ahmet Keleş, who once belonged to the core staff of the organization and later on left the organization, explained in his book, *FETÖ'nün Günah Priamidi (FETÖ's Pyramid of Sin)* how the organization placed its members within the Turkish Armed Forces as follows: *"After the 1980 military coup, Gülen decided earnestly to place the organization's members in the military because he came to the decision that no matter how effectively he placed his members of the organization in the state offices, the army had the capability to carry out a military coup at any time and procure the government under its own control. Therefore, placing his people within the military was even more important than placing them in the state offices. Certainly, if his men were positioned in the military offices, it would not only prevent possible military coups, but also military coups may be carried out when needed. The strategy was to primarily educate talented students with high IQ's with the aim of placing them in the military. These students were not sent to the schools of the organization and were required not to take part in the preparatory course centers of the organization. Their families would be told to make sure not to portray themselves as being religious... Their mothers and sisters would not wear headscarves...They would subscribe to newspapers such as Hürriyet and Cumhuriyet... They would even take walk in the promenades in the city holding either the Cumhuriyet or the Hürriyet newspaper in their hands. These students, who applied to the military high schools, were carefully prepared for the student selection oral exams in order to be able to face any perplexing questions. After all these preliminary preparations, when the candidate student was accepted into the school, a special 'Abi' was assigned to take care of him, and would instruct him in the ways to conduct himself in his new environment. They used to say that all other members of the Hizmet (Service) / organization used to envy these individuals and expected that these would be the great commanders of the future. Those students themselves were indoctrinated into believing that they were prominent persons. They were identified with great names from the past, for example they would say, 'you will be like Khâlid b. Walîd... and you will be like Hamza, the uncle of the prophet...' They used to receive special greetings and prayers from Gülen...and then gifts..."*[161]

According to Necip Hablemitoğlu, it was quite difficult at first for the Fetullahists to infiltrate the Turkish Armed Forces. However, they did not give up in their efforts.[162] Thus, for the organization the Turkish Armed Forces became one of the most important state institutions to be targeted for annexation. This was based upon the fact that the history of the Turkish Republic demonstrates that the Turkish Armed Forces are the only power that can carry out military coups and take over the government with arms.

A newspaper columnist, Hüseyin Gülerce, explained the method of infiltration of the organization into the Turkish Armed Forces as follows: *"Fetullah Gülen's earnest plot to occupy the military emerged in 1985... They identified intelligent students with high IQ's*[163] *in the rural parts and in the districts of Anatolia... They provided these students with excellent education, in groups of two or three people. When they took exams, these youths chose either to enroll in the Police Academy, or in the cadet schools, or in the military high schools, even though these youths would have been able to enter the Bosphorus University, the department of Computer Engineering, or even METU, the department of Business Administration due to their quite high marks in their exams. Obviously, the highly intelligent students within these schools easily surpassed the other students, and the Armed Forces took advantage of these superior students. These students received such a robust education that any person in charge of selecting students would feel obliged to not select any other students over these students."*[164]

The fact that Fetullah Gülen supported the military coups and that he flattered the coup plotters through the organization's media indicates how much importance he gave to the role of the Armed Forces. This is why the organization appointed an Imam to be in charge of all the Armed Forces, just as it did in the case of other important institutions. Under the authority of this Imam, it also appointed imams who were in charge of the service commands, the commands of Gendarmerie, the command of the Coast Guard, the military high schools, the cadet schools, the war academies and the sergeant prep schools. According to the organization the Imam of the armed forces is credited with a position higher than that of the Commander of the Turkish Armed Forces and that of the Minister of the National Defense. He was in charge of all the operations took place within the Turkish Armed Forces.

In 1982, the organization put together a special class consisting of students that had graduated from civilian regular high schools. What's more, they took advantage of this when majority of the students making up this class obtained the rank of general in their careers. Almost all of these were found to have participated in the military coup attempt on the 15th of July 2016. A newspaper columnist, Yavuz Selim Demirdağ, stated in this context that *"In 1980's it was discovered that hundred and thirty-six students enrolled in the Kuleli Askerî Lisesi (Kuleli Military High School) regularly visited the houses run by the organization. Eighty-six out of hundred and thirty-six students were discarded from the school, but the rest were exonerated. Eleven of the generals who joined the 15th of July coup attempt were among those who were exonerated back then."*[165]

With the organization lifting state exam questions in 1986, almost half of the students who took the exams to enroll in the military high schools answered all their questions correctly in the Turkish language exam. When this was noticed, some of the students who answered all the questions correctly were rejected from those schools, but some of them continued their education. Students in this group graduated in 1994 from the cadet school, and the quantity of military offices that came out of this group was higher than all the previous annual records of the TSK. The appropriate people in charge knew that there were some illegal actions behind this result and investigation were carried out in some cases, but no clear-cut result was achieved.[166] Later on, as a precaution to this kind of results, they decided that the exam to place students in military high schools must be carried out by the ÖSYM. However, since the organization had already taken over many offices within the ÖSYM the members of the organization increasingly continued to be enrolled in the military schools.[167]

Fikri Işık, a former Minister of National Defense, confirmed in an interview the following facts about the exams to place students in military high schools. Between the years 2000-2007, 1598 of the students who obtained the right to enroll into the military high schools studied the first year of the secondary school outside the formal educational institutions; they simply took the exams to be placed in the military high schools, without taking either the SBS[168] exam or the TEOG[169] exam. Between the years 2000-2014, students achieved really high scores in the placement exams for military high schools, for example, once 419 students answered either all, or almost all, the questions correctly, and in another year, 700 students reached an incredible high score in the exam. When in 2014, the system of exams for the military school was changed to ÖSYM, first, only two students got full scores, and in 2016 only 6 students had such a high score.[170]

Whenever the organization discovered a health problem with any of the student it wanted to place in the military high schools or cadet schools, they overcame this impediment by issuing fake reports of good health through members of the organization who worked at GATA. The period between the years 2007-2013 was the time when the Armed Forces removed the highest numbers of students from the military schools. The reason for why these students were rejected was based upon their affiliation with some religious communities, of course, these were other than Gülen's organization, and they were rejected because they wanted to perform religious acts of worship in accordance with their beliefs. They were rejected from the military with the accusation that they did "backward-ist activities" (*irticâî faaliyet*). In the same period, none of the students who were affiliated with the FETÖ/ PDY, that introduced itself as a "religious community," was rejected from the Armed Forces. The number of students rejected from the military, during these six years, exceeds the numbers of students ever rejected from the military throughout the history of the Turkish Republic.[171]

As of 2008, in order to fill up the empty positions quickly in the military schools with the members of the organization, the cadet schools began accepting students that graduated from civilian high schools. From that time onwards the proportion of the students who graduated from military high schools and enrolled in the cadet schools got lower and lower, and the proportion of students who graduated from civilian high schools and enrolled in cadet schools rapidly increased. That is how the organization was able to place its specially educated students to cadet schools directly. Moreover, the required level of exam score was lowered to insure that the organization's staff was placed in the cadet schools. Thus, members of the organization were positioned into the military schools *en masse*, and in a short period, it became the dominant power inside the military schools.[172]

Following the intimidation and discrimination policies of the organization against students who graduated from military schools but were not affiliated with the organization, the number of such students in cadet schools gradually decreased. Due to the intentional policies of positively discriminating the graduates of civilian high schools, this group of students became the majority in a short period of time. To counter students who wanted to continue their education in these schools despite all the coercion, the members of the organization working at GATA or other military health institutions took action and issued reports contrary to facts, so that these students were rejected from the military schools.[173] By the year 2012 nobody, who was not a disciple of Gülen (*şakirt*), was able to enroll in the military schools.[174]

In the year 2006, the General Staff, in the Office of the Military Prosecutor started a prosecution against the placing of Fetullahists in the military. Although it continued for many years it did not yield any definite result. In this prosecution, instead of exposing the illegal staff placement in the TSK, the Office of the Military Prosecutor collected news reports from different sources of the media and tried to silence those who produced those news reports by using the power of TSK. In this prosecution, nobody was interrogated as a suspect and nobody was subject to a disciplinary investigation on the basis of the illegal staffing by the organization.[175] In the Turkish Grand National Assembly, a commission was formed in 2013 to investigate claims of systematic torture and persecution against the students graduated from military high schools. However, no definite result was achieved by the commission.

The major methods applied in this process by FETÖ/ PDY, which took control of the placement of students in schools, and the promotion and the appointment of staff into offices in the TSK were as follows:[176]

1. To eliminate those who are not members of the organization, by intervening in the process of enrollment into all kinds of military educational institutions, especially military high schools and cadet schools.

2. To force students of military high schools and cadet schools, who were not members of the organization, to quit by systematic demoralization and discouragement.

3. To remove commanders and teachers at the military educational institutions by appointing them to other services and to replace them by the members of the organization.

4. To appoint members of the organization to permanent services abroad that in some way is understood as a promotion for a military officer.

5. To place many members of the organization in the War Colleges, whose staff makes the foundation of the TSK, by either stealing the exam questions or by implementing subjective criteria to select the students.

6. To mislead administrators in the ranks of command by sending anonymous complaint petitions.

7. To help the members of the organization to get promoted more rapidly by changing the criteria concerning registry (*sicil*), promotion and appointment.

8. To depict commanding officers, who are not members of the organization, as covetously by manipulating the performance criteria and indicators determined by inspection and evaluation offices.

9. To carry out operations to destroy the reputation of the

personnel whom they chose as their target, by abusing the authority of their members in the army and military jurisdiction.

10. To issue misleading documents in the personnel security investigations of the TSK personnel by collaborating FETÖ/PDY members in the intelligence services.

The organization did not only try to reach its goal of placing its members in the Armed Forces through military schools, but it also took over the judicial justice and filed many conspiracy lawsuits (*kumpas davası*). Thus, it had many active personnel of higher ranks arrested, and it appointed to their position new staff who were members of the organization. The conspiracy lawsuits filed by the organization,[177] were presented as *"efforts to remove the military domination over the civil politics and to prevent military coups."* Hence, they got widespread public support. Members of the organization hid their true intention, and by the elimination of military personnel, the FETÖ/PDY staffing in the Turkish Armed Force reached quite an alarming level. Kemalettin Özdemir, one of the former members of the organization, stated that in the TSK at least 60% of the personnel were members of the FETÖ/PDY. In addition to the criminal prosecutions, through disciplinary investigations, the registries of those who were not members of the organization were stained, their promotions were prevented; and to the offices that they might have reached if they had gotten their promotion, members of the organization were appointed. Işık Koşaner, a retired Commander of the Turkish Armed Forces, stated that the organization eliminated important personnel of the Turkish Armed Forces and provided offices for its members through fake documents and false information produced by the organization.[178]

The military intervention carried out by the TSK, on the 28th of February 1997, which is commonly referred to as the *"postmodern coup"* made the whole conservative part of population obliged to support the organization, and contributed to the staffing of the organization in the Armed Forces.[179] Antidemocratic attempts during the process of the 28th of February [military coup] were approved by the media outlets. These media outlets broadcasted programs that intended to overthrow the civil government.[180] In fact, Fetullah Gülen supported this coup, and made efforts to get closer to the military and turn this close relationship into an opportunity to place his members into the military. As a result of this effort, the Commander of the Turkish Armed Forces of that period, four star general İsmail Hakkı Karadayı, received the administrators of the FETÖ/PDY in 1995 in his office. He took care of the students who attended the visit with them and he gave advice to the students, shook their hands and had his photograph taken together with them and presented them with gifts.[181] The same person, however, made vigorous efforts to overthrow the legal government of that time under the name of *"fighting against backwardism"* (*irticayla mücadele*). Moreover, Fetullah Gülen, sent a letter to the deputy chief Commander of the Turkish Armed Forces Çevik Bir, immediately after the 28th of February 1997. In that letter, Gülen confirmed that he supported the coup.[182] (See, Table 4)

Indeed, Nedim Şener, a journalist, confirmed as well that Fetullah Gülen was part of the 28th of February military coup.[183] The youth, whose parents were conservative religious people, who were faithful to their state with no political intent were removed from the military, and these recently emptied positions were filled up by members of the FETÖ/PDY.[184] On this issue, statements of the retired Commanders of the Turkish Armed Forces are quite interesting. Hilmi Özkök, a retired Commander of the Turkish Armed Forces, said: *"among those whom we removed back then, there were generally Nurcular and similar people but not members of the FETÖ."* Similarly, İlker Başbuğ, a retired Commander of the Turkish Armed Forces, said: *"It seems that those guys used us to discard members of another community, who was rival to their own community."*[185] Moreover, Prof. Dr. Nevzat Tarhan stated that back then Fetullahists skillfully used psychological operations.[186]

Members of the FETÖ/PDY hid themselves during the 28th of February military coup as a precaution or with the intention to hide their true identity. Consequently, they insured their place in the TSK, they even got stronger and secure. They collaborated with the 28th of February junta and they even made use of them, in such a way that they were able to have all the nationalist conservative commissioned officers and noncommissioned officers-whom they might have considered as possible impediments before the military coup, which they planned to carry out themselves in the future—removed from the military.

Other methods that were used by the organization against people who were affiliated with the TSK but were not members of the organization were intimidation, lying, defaming, making up fake evidence, perjuring, illegally recording their video and audio, manipulating, blackmailing, rejecting their right of fair trial and similar immoral methods. Since 2008, the organization featured news reports about the personnel who they chose as its target on the internet sites under its control. In these news reports the private lives of the relevant military personnel was denigrated. Including some high ranking commissioned officers (*subaylar*), many military personnel were subject to mistreatment by such news reports in such a way that their family life and psychological condition were damaged. The members of the organization acted collectively and followed well laid definite plans. Due to their appalling persecutions and coercions many people were compelled to retire, or resign from their positions. In fact, the complaint part that is generally included in the survey forms that are filled by retired personnel at their instance of retirement was concealed from the command level. The retired personnel were systematically denied the opportunity of providing the command level with information.[187]

As the organization in time took control of the military jurisdiction, no prosecution concerning the organization produced any tangible result. As the organization took over many strategical positions in the Armed Forces, some of the commissioned officers in the military establishment were kept under control through threats and blackmail, some other were kept under control via sympathetic relations or simply qualms about their future. Thus, they could not make any movement or objection against the demands of the organization. Some others were compelled to obey the organization by assisting them with their civil affairs, and others assisted or due to being offered a position, or any other bribe. All the colonels who were members of the organization were promoted to the position of general between the years 2013-2015.[188]

The Attorney general, Zafer Dur, who worked at the Office of Izmir Chief Public Prosecutor, filed an indictment concerning the financial support for FETÖ/PDY, and this indictment was accepted by the court. In this indictment, it is stated that the FETÖ/PDY had 150 members at the position of general, 10 thousand members at the position of commissioned officer and 12 thousand members at the position of non-commissioned officer. Back then in TSK, there were 358 generals and admirals, 39 thousand 468 commissioned officers and 97 thousands 145 non-commissioned officers in total. Given this information, it is clear that the amount of FETÖ/PDY members inside the military had reached a frightening level.[189]

One of the reasons why FETÖ/PDY expanded so quickly and was able to infiltrate its staff in the military like cancerous cells is that the organization was able to exploit the efforts to improve the TSK for their own benefit. Furthermore, members of the organization were appointed to strategically important positions with lower duty risks, such as the department of personnel, the adjutancy, the office of the private secretary, the military assistance and the department of close protection officers. These positions aided the members of the organization to get quickly promoted in the military bureaucracy. The Members of the organization also insured quick promotion of their friends by manipulating certain criteria of promotion in the TSK, such as being able to show "*outstanding success*" and "*early promotion based on graduate education.*"[190]

After the period of December 17-25, military personnel of the FETÖ/PDY were removed from many state institutions. However, the situation of the members of the organization, who were nested away in the TSK, and who were able to control the high firepower weapons of military, could not be scrutinized at all. The critical offices at the command level, in the TSK, such as the military assistants of the President of the Republic, including the presidential guard regiment, the adjutancy, and the Office of the Private Secretary were filled by members of the FETÖ/PDY and an important number of bodyguards consisted of its members. Certainly, it is reasonable to assume that when this kind of personnel is appointed, they are closely investigated according to the data provided by the intelligence agencies, in addition to the specific institutional criteria of investigation in the TSK. Hence, despite such rigorous investigation, if the members of the FETÖ/ PDY filled the critical offices extensively, this shows how influential the organization was within the intelligence agencies.[191]

The National Intelligence Agency (Milli Istihbarat Teşkilati)

One may say that Fetullah Gülen's connection to the Intelligence Agencies goes back to 1960's. Fetullah Gülen was, most likely, noticed by the intelligence agencies and the structure, labeled "*deep state*" (*derin devlet*), because of his tip-off while he was at the Alvarlı Medresesi (*Alvarli Madrasa*). One may include the following as evidence proving that Fetullah Gülen had strong connections with MİT as well as foreign intelligence agencies for a long time: his ability to falsify his age, making him older, on official papers through dubious methods; his work as an informant during his military service; his active role in the establishment of the Erzurum branch of the Society for Fighting Against Communism; his attendance at a secret meeting in 1971 in Vehbi Koç's house at the request of the USA, which was attended by a number of officials including Fuat Doğu, the undersecretary of the MİT back then, certain officers of the TSK, Kasım Gülek and Yaşar Tunagür, the deputy chair of the Presidency of Religious Affairs (Diyanet İşleri Başkanlığı) at that time;[192] and that he was frequently visited by foreign chiefs of mission (yabancı misyon şefleri) during 1970's. Moreover, Fetullah Gülen's following statement indicates how much he and his organization emphasized on the subject of counter-intelligence: "*one should always be well above the opposition with regards to collecting infor-*

mation."[193] Necip Hablemitoğlu explained the interest of the FETÖ/PDY in the intelligence services as follows: *"By infiltrating into the intelligence agencies (istihbarat birimleri), the Fetullahists insured that they know beforehand any operation that could be carried out against them, and thus could prevent such operations and could even start a counter operation. This situation provides them not only with the option of defense but also with the option of an offensive attack."*[194]

Since Fetullah Gülen considered intelligence quite important, the organization appointed an Imam who was in charge of the MİT and they established a significant organization within it. Murat Karabulut, whose code name was Doctor Sinan, served as the Imam in charge of MİT for a long time. Later on, Harun Doğan was appointed to this position. Determining exactly how and to what extent the organization placed its members into MİT is difficult because of the special structure of the MİT as an intelligence agency. There were members of the FETÖ/PDY who were transferred to the National Intelligence Organization from other public institutions, such as the Security Agency and the Department of Telecommunication (*Telekomünikasyon İletişim Başkanlığı*).[195] Due to the organization's strong interest in the MİT, the organization was able to engage in fraudulent operations in 2009, first in the MİT Erzincan Regional Unit, and then in the Diyarbakır and Batman Units. Furthermore, the organization on the 7th of February 2012 went as far as to attempt to arrest the Undersecretary of the MİT.

The Organization Abroad[196]

The FETÖ/PDY organized itself abroad based upon continents, subcontinent, and nation-states, and for each such unit, it appointed an Imam. It is Fetullah Gülen who decided in which country they would have activities by consulting with the secret service agencies of global powers, and the decision was made first and foremost of the USA. The organization would enter the country where they would like to be active by providing certain sympathetic services such as education, health and humanitarian aid. At the same time, they established strong relations with politicians, state officers, academics and businessmen. They prepared yearly reports of their activities in that country which they would present to Fetullah Gülen and receive instructions about what to do next. When they were encountered with a problem in any country, they demanded help primarily from certain dominant global forces, and from their supporters both in Turkey, as well as in other countries.

Table 3: Countries abroad where FETÖ/PDY established its Organization

Continent-Subcontinent	Country
Asia	Afghanistan, Azerbaijan, Bangladesh, China, South Korea, Georgia, Irak, Israel, Japan, Qatar, Kazakhstan, Kyrgyzstan, Kuwait Lebanon, Mongolia, Nepal, Pakistan, Saudi Arabia, Tajikistan, Oman, Jordan, Yemen
Australia, Southeastern Asia	Australia, Indonesia, The Philippines, Hong Kong-Taiwan, Laos, Malaysia, Papua New Guinea, Singapore, Sri Lanka, Vietnam, New Zealand.

Europe	Germany, Albania, Austria, Belgium, Belarus-Latvia, Bosnia and Herzegovina, Czech Republic, Denmark, Estonia, Finland, France, Croatia, Netherland, England, Ireland, Spain, Sweden, Switzerland, Italy, Kosovo, Lithuania, Hungary, Macedonia, Moldova, Poland, Portuguese, Romania, Serbia, Slovakia, Slovenia, Ukraine.
North America	United States of America, Dominican Republic, Canada, Mexico
South America	Argentine, Brazil, Colombia, Chile, Venezuela
Africa	Angola, Benin, Algeria, Djibouti, Ethiopia, Morocco, Gabon, Ghana, Republic of South Africa, Kenya, Libya, Malawi, Egypt, Mozambique, Niger, Nigeria, Rwanda, Senegal, Sudan, Tanzania, Tunisia

The organization divided the globe into six parts on the basis of continents. These are Asia, Australia, Southeastern Asia, Europe, North America, South America and Africa (see, tables 3 and 4). By the year 2017, it acquired the structure of a complicated and atrocious organization which carried out activities in the *"religion-politics-money"* triangle, in 170 countries/ regions / states / autonomous republics. As documented by the intelligence services, FETÖ/PDY carried out its activities abroad by affiliated institutions, which included 520 corporations. These corporations governed 767 schools, preparatory course centers, schools, study centers (see, table 4), 216 hospitals, 269 foundations, 327 associations and 206 media institutions.

Table 4: Numerical distribution of FETÖ/PDY's educational institutions abroad

Continent / Subcontinent	Number of Schools
Africa	63
Asia	222
Europe	150
South America	7
North America	315
Australia, Southeastern Asia	10
TOTAL	767

The organization has been continuing its activities in the USA where Fetullah Gülen currently lives, especially in the states of New Jersey, Pennsylvania and Texas. It maintains its activities also in cities where Turks are densely populated, such as in Houston, Nashville, Chicago, Pittsburg, Columbus, Washington D.C. and Boston. In the schools run by the organization in this country, more than 60 thousand students are enrolled; approximately 5 thousand personnel are employed. The organization earns approximately 500 million US $ yearly. Although it varies from one country to another, one may also discern a pattern in the names of their schools. The organization commonly calls its schools by certain names, such as Horizon, Light, Rainbow, and Harmony. Their schools cover quite different areas of education, ranging from kindergarten to university education. The organization also runs many educational courses in the preparatory course centers and study centers. The essentials of these agencies abroad and the schools run by these agencies are taken care of by the agencies in Turkey until those agencies abroad develop enough to become self-sufficient. For this reason, for each of the agency found in such countries a provincial Imam is held accountable. Their requirements are taken care of by the board of trustees affiliated with the office of the provincial Imam. Certain companies provide financial aid through the board of trustees to these agencies. In turn, the organization assists these companies to get into contact with companies in other countries in order to compete in bids for projects and to invest in those countries. Thus the financial aid provided by such companies is compensated back to these companies in one way or another by the agencies located in those countries. The organization rapidly grew in the Turkic Republics, the Middle East, North Africa and central Asia by manipulating the positive feelings people in these regions have towards Turkey and the Turkish people based on a historical, cultural, and religious affinity.

The FETÖ/PDY's establishment of an extensive network of agencies provided the organization with strong foreign connections. Consequently, the organization acquired more foreign support and powerful strategic skills. It is known that in all the important meetings of the organization within the USA, representatives of the secret services attended; and the organization carefully, with utmost secrecy, carried out the instructions given by these secret services. In fact, Paul L. Williams, the former advisor to the FBI, provided the following information on this issue: *"Fetullah Gülen applied to the court in 2007 to obtain permanent residence permit. In November*

2007, his application was rejected by the USA Citizenship and Immigration Services, on the suspicion that 'Gülen had a financial and political connection with the CIA.' Later on the FBI informed the court stating that 'this man is dangerous; they should not keep him in the country and send him back.' However, Graham Fuller, a CIA agent, informed the Judge of the trial that 'this man should not be allowed to leave USA, because he was quite an important person.' This is how Fetullah Gülen obtained permanent residence permit. There is a CIA agent in every school run by Gülen's organization in central Asia. CIA helped Fetullah Gülen to make a fortune of billions of dollars. This money is mostly earned through drug trafficking in Afghanistan. There is an immediate connection between the CIA, which controls the drug trafficking in Turkey, the Gladio and Fetullah Gülen."

Wayne Madsenise, a journalist and research-author, stated the following: "*I personally found out that Fetullah Gülen was quite helpful to CIA in the wars of Kosovo and Bosnia. In order for Fetullah Gülen to obtain his permanent residence permit, Graham Fuller, Turkey Desk chief of CIA, Morton Abromowitz, former USA ambassador to Ankara, and George Fidas, director of the analysis department of CIA, stood as his guarantors.*" Moreover, Bishop Alexander Karloutsos from the Office of the Greek-Orthodox Archbishop, which is located in New York, sent a letter to the court in favor of Gülen and spoke highly of him.

Prof. Dr. Aleksandr Dugin, the leader of the Eurasian Movement in Russia, stated the following in this context: "*The schools affiliated with Fetullah Gülen constitute a communication network that serves the plans of geopolitical lobby of NATO. Having figured this fact out, Russia closed down these schools. These schools functioned like centers of foreign secret services. Instead of functioning as institutions to teach religion, culture and language, they instilled in them NATO's vision. Russian secret ser-*

vice had reliable information and documents about these schools, otherwise these schools would not have been closed down. This decision was taken in a meeting where personnel from the office of the president and national security administers attended."

Prof. Dr. Asghar Fardi, of Tehran University has the following statement in this regard: *"USA wants to give the impression to people that there are two types of Islam. The first type is the Iranian model. This model of Islam is that after producing an atomic bomb it intends to wipe Israel of the earth. The second model of Islam is established on moderation and dialogue as it is exemplified by Gülen's speeches and in the schools affiliated with him. Fetullah Gülen, the leader of the second model of Islam, lives in USA. He collaborates with the US authorities in the Middle Eastern project. The second model was used as a means against the first model. They want to give the impression that the true model of Islam is in central Asia. Gülen community uses exotic names, such as light, milky way, moon, sky and heaven. The message in such unreachable and heavenly names is to suppress human beings as small, powerless and weak creatures. None of these events happened randomly."*

Their Methods to Recruit Members[197]

Fetullah Gülen mentioned in his sermons and s the goal of educating the (so-called) *golden generation*, who uphold tolerance, who are faithful to their motherland and nation, who would appropriate good character traits and who would be successful. This goal received strong support from the Turkish people partly because of the socio-economic conditions of the people and consequently FETÖ/ PDY's power increased within the society.

Fetullah Gülen recruited, at first, members to his organization from his own sympathizers from people around him. Especially those students, who studied under his tutelage when he worked as a teacher in Qur'an teaching courses, made up the first generation of staff of the organization. Although at the beginning, Gülen used *Risale-i Nur Collection*, written by Said Nursi (*Risale-i Nur Külliyatı*) as his study material, later on he used books either written by himself or on his behalf.

Fetullah Gülen's so-called *golden generation*, which he sometimes referred to as "*the long awaited generation, the cavalry of light, the generation of the Qur'an, the lover of the Real, and the cavalry of the dawn*" was educated in houses which he called "*light houses*" in dormitories, preparatory course centers, study centers, schools, universities, affiliated corporations, camps and religious sermons; and then these people were made into militants.

The effort of the organization to recruit members was accelerated when it started running dormitories. Fetullah Gülen established student dormitories and placed intelligent but poor students into these dormitories. He made benevolent people take care of their needs and thus he started educating the core personnel of the organization. Those students were given certain responsibility under supervision, and their works and leadership capabilities were scrutinized. They were supervised under a certain *abi* or *abla*, and this strong hegemony of the *abi/abla* continued throughout their life.

The *abis* and *ablas* played quite an important role in finding new members for the organization and in maintaining their relations with the organization. These *abis* and *ablas* understood human psychology and the way to establish connections with people very well. They displayed a profile of being mature and helpful human beings. They communicated with people outside of the organization in schools, preparatory course centers, in houses or religious conversation sessions. Even if people outside of the organization tried to keep a distance, they tried hard to maintain their communication with them. When *abis/ablas* held religious conversations, they carefully examined especially people's material needs and they tried to help them by all means, so that those students got closely tied to them with the appreciation of their assistance. A student, who was invited to the house, to the religious conversation meetings and other sorts of meetings carried out by the organization, got acquainted with the ideology of the organization after a certain time. After students were connected to the organization by special attention, gifts, compliments and elevation from their disadvantages, they were instructed *"to hide their true identity (takiyye)"* in the name of *"precaution."* Thus, the innocent youth of Anatolia, those young minds, in the spring of their life, full of feelings, and carefree were manipulated and made into some kind of mindless automatons through sob stories and surreal tales. At that point, any course of life other than the one drawn by Fetullah Gülen seemed harmful to them. When these youths reached their appropriate levels, they became, as Gülen himself said, *"Soldiers who are ready to cross over the seas of blood and pus."*

In accordance with the expansionist strategy, each student was held responsible to find new members to the organization. In this way, as Gülen stated, *"Each student brought in"* to the organization *"functions the way a stone thrown into water produces circles around the point where it falls into the water."* Supposedly, these students assumed the mission of protecting the faith of the youth. They, first, identified themselves as the inheritors of the companions of the Prophet. When FETÖ/PDY became international, they perceived themselves as the "veterans of the *Akıncı* units" ["*akıncı* units," were part of the Ottoman army located at the borders], fulfilling *"this sacred mission"* at the global level. When the ideas like, interreligious dialogue and the concepts such as Abrahamic religions became popular, they turned into *"world citizens"* whose aspiration was to live in a friendly, brotherly and tolerant environment altogether with the members of the heavenly religions. In this process, while religious and nationalist feelings declined, globalist discourses were adopted.

Mass of students, from all different levels of education, were included as targets to recruit as new members of the organization. The organization modified and modernized, according to its own needs, the *devşirme* system [recruiting members for a definite establishment], which had been previously used in Turkish history. In addition to other factors, the socio-economic conditions were taken advantage of in their agenda to acquire new members. They shrewdly used to their advantage different conditions, such as, domestic violence within the family, economic hardships, communication problems within the family, insufficient religious knowledge i.e. religious illiteracy, and the fact that families were not able to provide sufficient educational conditions for their children. In fact, the highly intelligent and talented children of poor families, children who could not get a proper education and even decent nourishment, was one of the most fertile ground for the *"devşirme"* system. These children received form the organization the proper attention and care that they could not get from their families and their social environment. These students were recruited to the FETÖ/PDY, because members of the organization offered them attractive opportunities with familiar religious references. These students mostly consisted of middle and high school students who got affiliated either on their own, or by the guidance of their families with the organization due to various reasons, such as being able to realize their ideal to be a good Muslim who serves people for the sake of God, to insure that they have social network and status, to have better opportunity of employment either in the private or in the public sector, and to insure a better living condition in the future. Hence, these students lived in dormitories, or houses, run by the organization, and got their education in its preparatory course centers, schools and study centers.

When a student was invited to a *light house* (*ışık evi*) for the first time, he was simply asked about his studies, and was offered food. Later on, he/she would be asked about the profession of the parents, income level of the family, if his/her father drank alcohol, performed ritual prayers and if his/her mother wore the headscarf. In later stages of conversations, they would speak to students about the worldly life, sins, paradise, hell etc. They would lend the students books by Fetullah Gülen and ask them to summarize what they had understood by reading these books. Finally, the student would be convinced that Fetullah Gülen is a sacred person, and that to be a Muslim and to live according to Islam, in the given context, require one to follow the instructions of Gülen.

A senior student would administer a light house, as the *"Imam/ Abi of the house,"* which usually provided accommodation for five students. They charged fees to students for the expenses of the house according to their financial conditions, and they paid for the expenses of these houses, such as rent and food expenses by the fees they collected from such students and the charity money collected from benevolent businessmen. Students who visited light houses were educated by the instructions of the *abi/abla* observing the hierarchical order according to the rules of the organization. It would be ingrained into these students to serve the cause of Fetullah Gülen with a feeling of an unconditional submission. In these houses, students were also recruited to the organization via some kind of brain-washing activity- they called it via a *"program,"* in which they used to read Fetullah Gülen's books and watch records of his religious conversations. Light houses were presented as decent places, where the successful, morally upright and pious youth lived. These houses were active under the control of neighborhood Imams.

While the light houses served the students as accommodation, the religious conversation houses (*sohbet evleri*) functioned as places where they held certain meetings, religious conversations, and carried out divergent activities under the name of a course. In these houses, bachelor members of the organization lived and they had an Imam to direct them. In these houses, three-five people lived; and these people would be normally of the same profession and working in the public sector. The commands issued by the higher offices of the organization were delivered to the people and units, who would carry them out via these houses. Those who had some sympathy with the organization would be put into connection with people living in these houses and convinced over time about the outlook of the organization.

Since the organization focused on the educational institutions and dormitories, to produce the *golden generation*, the larger masses of people in the country had a positive impression about the organization, they saw it as an innocent enterprise of providing service to the society. The vacant areas and missing elements in the educational system was cunningly used to the advantage of the organization. It accepted students belonging to different parts of the society whether they were sympathetic or not to the organization. In fact, even parents with a leftist political standpoint sent their kids to the preparatory course centers and other educational institutions run by FETÖ/PDY supposing that they would help their children succeed in their exams that were required to enroll into various further higher educational institutions. In some places, people felt compelled to enroll their children to these preparatory course centers of the organization, because there were no other institutions available to prepare their children for these state exams.

Perhaps it was the preparatory course centers that played the most vital role in maintain the existence of the organization. The preparatory course centers were fertile resources in term of both human and financial resources. They functioned as means to recruit members coming from all different segments of the society to the organization. They also functioned as fertile sources of income because of the higher rates for such courses. The preparatory course centers were also places where they sold books, stationary material and products of printing companies affiliated with the organization. Another reason that made the preparatory course centers important and indispensable was that they were like centers of gathering secret information. They collected and archived information about all the students enrolled in the preparatory course centers, information about the financial conditions of their families, their lifestyle and the impression they had about the organization.

The preparatory course centers also provided temporary job opportunities for the members of the organization, when they graduated. Unlike other religious communities, the FETÖ/PDY did not leave its members alone when they had completed their undergraduate education. It employed them in their preparatory course centers and thus provided them with socio-economic security. The preparatory course centers served as a basis to infiltrate the state bureaucracy, because in these preparatory course centers they dealt with the exam questions stolen by the organization before the students actually took the exam. The study centers also had a function similar to the preparatory course centers.

The schools established by the organization were considered as the gate to a wonderful career by all the different groups within the society, because students enrolled in those schools obtained noteworthy achievements in the national and the international contests, the science Olympics and the university entrance exams. Fetullah Gülen himself asked all the relevant people, *"please do not present the schools as being affiliated with us."* Thus he wanted to hide the connection of those schools with the organization and, in fact, wanted to prevent the visibility of the organization itself.

In these schools, they did not immediately try to recruit students enrolled in the preparatory course centers or schools to the organization. First, they took time to determine the personal properties, behaviors, family conditions, the level of success and relation to religious values of any student. After collecting relevant information about a student on these issues, they approached him/her accordingly. They paid special attention to students who were successful in their courses and had a promising capacity to the effect that they could achieve important works for the organization in the future, who could be staffed in strategic public institutions. When they felt appropriate, they even expunged their name from the registry of the schools of the organization as a precaution not to expose them.

The parents had their children involved with houses, dormitories, schools and preparatory course centers of FETÖ/

PDY not only with the expectation of quality education but also with the expectation that their children would acquire good moral properties. However, the organization took advantage of the confidence which people had in it. Hence the organization educated the children of this land in such a way that they could realize the hidden agenda of the organization instead of educating them so that they could be *beneficial to the motherland and the nation*. The 15th of July military coup attempt by the organization shows how these people affiliated with the organization were terrorized and were in time turned into militants, becoming like wild animals, in such a way that they were able to kill their own people without any compassion or regret.

The expansion strategy of the organization abroad can be summarized as follows: It began its activities at first, in the name of establishing schools, in Turkic Republics, which were called, *"geography of the heart."* It was well received by the state administration as well as by the people, and hence it obtained legitimacy in those countries. Afterwards, it infiltrated into those countries, which were different in religious or national identities, under the guise of providing *"very successful education."* It was quite an efficient and decisive strategy. After opening the schools abroad and organizing the Turkish Language Olympics (*Türkçe Olimpiyatları*), which was simply a fiction, the prestigious position of the organization domestically reached a new peak, and the network of its sympathizers exceedingly expanded.

For those who attended the Turkish Language Olympics, it was quite flattering to see students brought from countries where the organization had its schools, to see how these students displayed their skills as they were dressed in their colorful national costumes, and to see students of different nations and colors speak Turkish and sing Turkish songs. However, one of the people who hosted a session in a Turkish Language Olympics program stated that he was asked *"not to ask questions to foreign students, because they had those students simply memorize certain things, and if they were asked anything that they did not memorize, they could not answer it."*

Certain benevolent business men wanted to give fellowship to students who were enrolled in the schools, outside the country, of the organization if those students selected Turkish as their foreign language. First year, the organization allowed this nominally but afterwards, it prevented this initiative on the grounds that *"there was no sufficient demand to learn Turkish."* Many people who visited the schools of the organization abroad inquired and asked questions on this issue. However, all of them got the stereotypical answer, "there was *no demand to learn Turkish."* It is highly doubtful that nobody wanted to learn Turkish in any of the school established in so many countries from around the world. To the contrary, majority of the countries involved is known to have deep historical and cultural connections to Turkey, and thus their citizens hold Turkey and Turks in high esteem.

If this structure, which imagines itself to be the *"people of service"* (*hizmet ehli*) and wants to give the impression that the mission for which they struggle is a *"movement of service"* (*hizmet haraketi*), were sincere in their claim to serve Turkey and the world of Islam, then they would do their best to increase the demand to learn Turkish in those schools. Since the FETÖ/PDY was a movement of treachery rooted abroad, the administrators of this organization would never allow anything that would benefit Turkey, and in fact they did not do so. In fact, there was a larger hand in play, dominant global force, behind these traitors.

The organization placed the students, whom it wanted to place as staff into the public institutions, which were strategically important for the organization, into special houses and provided specific and comprehensive education concerning these institutions. The exam questions for acceptance to these public institutions (*kamu sınavlarının soruları*) were stolen by the members of the organization, and they made these students memorize the answers to these questions. That is how these students got very high results in those exams. This whole process was carried out under the control of specially appointed Imams. These Imams and students were placed in special houses and all relevant attendants were given code names so that the disclosure of their identity could be prevented. These young people were assisted to succeed in the oral exams by the members of the organization who were nested in higher positions of the public institutions. Thus, these youths would in time advance, in such proportion that they would be able to commit all kinds of crimes which might be demanded by the organization.

The organization did not cut its ties to the members who were staffed into public institutions. It maintained it relations to them through *abis/ablas* who worked in those public institutions. It continued to benefit from its members after they were placed in those institutions by recruiting new members, in collecting financial support by donations [under the name *himmet*] and by monthly payments, and also in paving the way for the activities of the organization in the public as well as in the private sector.

The FETÖ/PDY applied the following methods to increase the number of its members by taking advantage of its power in the public bureaucracy and politics:

1. Suggesting that members of the organization would be

better Muslims, be more useful to their country and nation, and that supporting the organization would be rewarded by God.

2. Promising that they would get promoted to higher and better positions.

3. Promising that their income would increase.

4. Insuring that they would keep their current job.

5. Promising that they would be protected against the coercion, loathe and marginalization of others.

6. Keeping them in the organization by threats and blackmails.

7. Forcing them to commit a crime at first and thus making them obligated to the organization.

The FETÖ/PDY practiced all types of fraud in order to place its members who did not satisfy the requirements, such as issuing counterfeit diplomas, forged health certificates and similar false documents.

The following methods were used by the organization to recruit members form among the workers in private sectors:

1. Suggesting that members of the organization would be better Muslims, be more useful to their country and nation, and that supporting the organization would be rewarded by God.

2. Promising that they would benefit more from the mutual support within and have protection from the organization.

3. Promising that their number of customers would increase, and they would have more business opportunities

with the corporations that are affiliated with the organization.

4. Threatening that if they did not get affiliated with the organization, they would be excluded from the business life and they would come across some type of subjugation.

5. Placing an embargo on them, threatening and blackmailing them, making the transactions of resisting corporations checked by using their connection in public institutions and thus compelling them to pay heavy fines.

The Secrecy in the Activities of the Organization: Precautions and Clandestine Operations

The structure of the the FETÖ/PDY organization was configured with a *"binary character"* (*ikili karakter*) in accordance with Fetullah Gülen's *"binary language."* This binary structure consisted of the *"visible"* and the *"invisible"* networks. Visible networks included educational activities, non-governmental and professional organizations, and media outlets, local, national and international corporations. In the invisible networks, however, there seems to have been a ghost-like structure that included a hidden hierarchy and operation. Since the organization was established with the major goal of taking the state over the basic principle efficient in this ghost-like structure was to act with precaution, and to hide their true identity through clandestine behavior.[198]

This secret structure, who infiltrated primarily the judiciary, the military and the security institutions as well as all other governmental institutions (*devlet organları*), turned out to be a structure analogous to the formal governmental hierarchy. Members of the organization made their identity in the visible networks, boasted of being members of the service movement (*hizmet hareketi*). In the invisible networks, that is, within the parallel government structuring (*paralel devlet yapılanması*), they preferred to conceal themselves until they fully got control of the state. The pangs of conscience caused by this duplicitous situation was tried to be explained away by using certain concepts like, *Mahdi, Messiah, Darulharb* [place of war], and *Dajjal* [Antichrist] by Fetullah Gülen and other prominent figures of the organization. Members of the organization were given the good news that they would be greatly rewarded in this world as well in the hereafter. Thus, Islamic beliefs were manipulated into tools in order to shroud their true identity for the sake of achieving the goals of the organization.

Since its beginning, the FETÖ/PDY had displayed not the character of a religious community, but the character of a secret organization which intended to infiltrate its people as staff in the state bureaucracy. Moreover, it tried with every means to achieve this goal. This is why it specifically emphasized being such a crypto-organization. Fetullah Gülen's following statement has been the basis of the efforts of the organization in this regard: "*It is vital for our future to go far away without leaving any trace, to stroll through their arteries and if we want to come back, we must be able to come back without being harmed, without making them feel us. In order to go towards the future, discover the vital points of the system.*"[199]

For this reason, the organization started with the educational institutions and started running schools, preparatory course centers, and study centers. Additionally, it selected young minds to place them into the public bureaucratic offices. It brainwashed them through emotive messages and conversation from the *Abis* and *Ablas* in the houses called *light houses* run by the organization. It made all these students uniform in thought and action, submissive to the organization. Thus, they were instructed like *militants*, they were taught the ways of how to operate in a clandestine state by hiding their identity in the public institutions in which they would be placed. Furthermore, they were programmed in such a way that they would without a moment hesitation take action when the time came; which they did. The following statement by Fetullah Gülen indicates that the organization placed its members into state offices with the goal of taking over the constitutional order. Thus he said: *"It is necessary that we act quite solemnly (temkinli) and with precaution," "any step taken would be untimely, if we take it before having all the power on our side in all the constitutional institutions,"* and *"you must wait until we become strong enough to carry the world on our shoulders."*[200] These instructions personally given by Gülen himself indicate that for him the state offices were of vital importance, as well as that staffing of the people of the organization in the bureaucracy was the strategy followed by the organization to take the constitutional order over.

In order not to be discovered, members of the organization at times pretended to be against Fetullah Gülen, they made against him and the organization gross insulting statements. This was the result of the fact that the organization had a multifaceted structure with hidden goals, multi-identity, and quite changeable positions and approaches. The FETÖ/PDY was like a clandestine network or a gang of criminals, which *"considered all means to reach the goal to be permissible."* It observed commonly a cell-type structure, using encrypted communication programs and code names, and operated as a global agent with connections to foreign intelligence agencies. Due to the cell-type structure, which was adopted by the organization, when the identity of a member, or a unit, was uncovered, new members were appointed or that unit was eliminated and new one was established.[201]

Hence, *takiyye* (hiding one's true identity) meant that they were able to hide their true identity and provide false information whenever they were confronted with a danger that threatened their life or a property. It was considered to be a concession (*kolayhk*), allowing that which is not acceptable under normal conditions and its meaning may be traced back to certain verses in the Holy Qur'an.[202] However, it is considered in Islam to be a more praiseworthy behavior if one does not hide one's true identity and prefers the difficult option when one faces oppression. In the Sunnite conception of Islam (*ehl-i sünnet*), only under extreme necessary conditions, *takiyye* (hiding one's true identity) is allowed. Contrary to this, the FETÖ/PDY followed a conception of *takiyye* that specifically has historically belonged to the "*Safawid Shi'a*" group. This kind of conception of *takiyye* is very open and is meant specifically to save only oneself. The organization took advantage of such a conception on all occasions.[203] Since the grassroots of the organization would be suspicious about, hesitant and even repudiate this kind of *takiyye*, the organization preferred to use the term "*tedbir*" (precaution) instead of *takiyye*.

In fact, the FETÖ/PDY, which was supposed to have adopted the Sunnite (*ehl-i sünnet*) Islamic creed, implemented a *takiyye* conception which was far more advanced than the Shi'ite conception, and thus applied all kinds of deception, duplicity and ploys etc. Members of the organization always hid their true intentions and considered many things to be permissible (*mubah*) for the sake of reaching their goals. On the one hand, Fetullah Gülen said that "In Islam, there is no place for *takiyye*. The *takiyye* that is adopted by the Shi'ites cannot have any Islamic foundation."[204] On the other hand, he made comments that indicated that he held the *takiyye* attitude in high esteem.

The organization considered the teaching of *takiyye* as a protective shield. According to witness reports, it even provided instruction to its members teaching how to apply *takiyye*, and it also had a booklet prepared with such a purpose. In those reports, the following information is provided in this regard: "*(a certain scholar) taught how to apply takiyye... in these courses certain fatwas were issued. For example, the Kemalist, secular, non-religious state structure exhibits the place of war (darül-harp) conditions. Because of the oppression applied by the state, Islamic rules cannot be observed properly. This is why in our time, not only military personnel, but also civilian people are not required to perform the Friday ritual prayer, following the practice of the Prophet who could not perform the Friday ritual prayer in the first time. In those courses, casual references to the Qur'an and prophetic traditions were made to justify takiyye as a permissible action. An alternative conception of religious rules were taught based on a seventeen page book, called Kevser.*[205] *According to this book, one could perform minor ritual ablution in restrooms, one could perform ritual prayer by eye movements imitating the regular movements, one could perform daily ritual prayers altogether at once (cem edilmesi), one could perform ritual prayers in one's bed by way of imitation, altogether at once. If one feels necessary, it would be permissible to drink alcoholic beverage, to gamble, to participate in parties that may include religiously illegitimate activities, to watch porn movies and to have sexual intercourse with the permission of an Abi.*"[206]

Similarly, in the witness reports, it is stated that they received an instruction as following: "*take the headscarves of your wives of, let them have their hair open. We are going to pay for their expenses for lipstick and hairdresser.*" Thus the organization asked the members to practice precaution, and also "*instructed that they must perform daily ritual prayers altogether at once, they must keep it absolutely secret so that nobody knows about it, that those who do not follow the instruction would be excluded, and that they would be closely inspecting if the instructions were obeyed or not.*"[207] Since the beginning, members of the organization displayed a devious and secretive attitude in the name of being precautious and moderate (*temkinli*). They neither appeared as they were, nor did they act as they appeared. Especially at strategic ranks of bureaucracy, they displayed a different identity and thus succeeded in hiding themselves for so many years. In this regard, the attitudes expressing the true intention and goal of the organization were considered as "*betrayal.*"

All practices of the organization concerning *takiyye*, precaution (*tedbir*) and other ways of hiding the identity can be traced back to the following statement of Fetullah Gülen: "*Survival (bekâ) of the hizmet (service) is the survival of the Muslim community (ümmet), this is why for the survival of the hizmet, things that are forbidden (haram) by religion are lawful (helal).*" It is claimed that Fetullah Gülen, by conversing (*görüşerek*) with the Prophet in the realm of wakefulness, (*yakaza alemi*),[208] received the permission to transform forbidden things into lawful things.[209] Based on this belief, members of the FETÖ/PDY considered all kinds of instructions given either directly by Gülen, or by administers, who were called *abi/abla*, as if they are "*God's commands.*" They obeyed unconditionally those instructions without questioning them, even though those instructions were contrary to Islamic principles. They thought that "*there must be wisdom behind them, a wisdom that is incomprehensible to us.*"

To insure the establishment and maintenance of the order

within the organization, members of the organization were taught from their first day onward to adopt the attitude of submission. They were taught that all what they did on behalf of the organization have a sacred purpose, and thus the instructions they received were not open to deliberation. This belief was established in them in such a firm manner that no member had any right to question the instructions given to him/her, and they would consider any attempt to question them as *"objection," "disobedience,"* and even *"rebellion."* Moreover, the organization would take measures against such an action by the mechanism of the *"warning-threatening-blackmailing-slap of compassion."* When needed it would even cut the ties of this person to the organization and put him/ her in seclusion.

The fact is that there were people who did not see anything erroneous in carrying out religiously forbidden actions on the basis of Fetullah Gülen's statements, whom they think have a special connection to God. It indicates how the organization adopted a binary language. There are so many examples of insincere sayings and behaviors in the 40 years period of Gülen's life that Said Alpsoy, who once worked with Gülen, wrote a book called *"A Man of Contradictions."*[210] Alpsoy exposed Gülen's incoherencies by giving many examples.

As *takiyye* was practiced in Turkey and abroad frequently, in a sense, it turned out to be a regular behavior. Administrators of the FETÖ/PDY claimed in Turkey that they *"had no ties to Sufism."* However, when they reached the West, especially USA, they realized how Mevlana Jalal al-Din Rumi was respected by them. Thus they published English translation of the third volume of *"Kalbin Zümrüt Tepelerinde,"* a collection of the writings of Fetullah Gülen, with the title, *"Su-*

fism." They also instituted an internet site with the name *Rumi Forum.*

While Fetullah Gülen frequently manipulated and took advantage of referring to the name of the Prophet, statements transmitted from him and his respectable practices; when he engaged in activities of dialogue with the outside world he instead endeavored to omit the name of our Prophet from the *Word of Unity.* Similarly, while he pointed out Abu Zarr as an exemplary figure while he was in the process of establishing the organization; when the organization got larger he appealed to Mu'awiya's political strategies to recruit new members to the organization.

When he addressed the public opinion in the West, or the secular-modern parts of the domestic population, he used discourses of modernism, post-Islamism and interfaith dialogue, while when he wanted to satisfy the spiritual feelings of conservative Muslims, he displayed traditional religious attitudes. While he declared in the public programs broadcasted by the media outlets of the organization that the organization was not a religious movement, people who were considered to be the spokesperson of the organization confirmed to the grassroots of the organization that those public messages were declared due to *takiyye.*[211]

In the same vein, when the general staff in the military who were members of the organization had meeting with Israeli and American officers as a result of their deeper network of relations, they were able to say to them that *"they use Islam against their own grassroots as part of takiyye."* In the organization which had a gigantic mechanism of lies, *takiyye* was used like a multi-functional handy device.[212] Consequently, on the one hand, Fetullah Gülen, the leader of the organization, gave messages of tolerance, peace, and brotherhood for decades; while on the other hand, he did not hesitate to have hundreds of people killed by directing, on the first occasion he got, tanks, war aircrafts and military helicopters against the people.

Arranged Marriages

The FETÖ/PDY established a system that insured the marriage of its members with each other, so that the organization could preserve and fortify their affiliation to the organization. The organization also used the method of *strategic marriages* to infiltrate into the families that were influential in the state bureaucracy, politics and the business world. It placed into those families either brides or bridegrooms so that it could have a grip in their arena (*kıskaca almış*). Furthermore, by these arranged marriages (*katalog evlilikleri*), the organization made it almost impossible for its young members to get out of it. Accordingly, those who got married to someone who was outside of the organization were either placed at a distance, or removed from the organization, so that the secrets of the organization could be protected from being deciphered.

Since the early 1990's, women began to assume more active roles in the organization. Similar to the case of male members, in order to make sure that the female members (*şakirdeler*)—who were educated in the light houses, who lived in dormitories run by the organization, who continued their education by the scholarships provided by the organization, and who got offered a position by the organization—engaged in arranged marriages, and they cataloged all their personal properties in specifically designed forms. Their marriage to someone outside the organization was definitely forbidden. Activities concerning marriage were organized by the "provincial *Abla*" and the "*Abla* of marriage." Their husbands had a similar duty concerning the male members of the organization: to design the special forms and to catalog personal properties of the male members. In this cataloging activity, male and female members were classified according to their occupation. The catalogues that were designed according to the provinces and districts would be finalized by the approval of the provincial Imam.

The following is a news report published at an internet site of the Hürriyet Newspaper on the topic of arranged marriage [based on catalogued information]: "The *FETÖ interfered even with the family life of the personnel whom it placed in public institutions and establishments, and it decided who should marry whom. Members of the organization could marry only people whom Abis or Ablas would suggest and approve. A certain catalogue that included information about unmarried members, such as photographs, information about hometown, height, weight, religious sensitivity etc., would be shown to the marriage candidates and they would make their choice. And sometimes they had female students intentionally marry a man whom they wanted to recruit to the organization. Divorce was also subject to the approval of the Cemaat.*" An eyewitness stated the following in his testimony (*ifadesinde*): The person (x) told me, 'We heard that you are getting married,' and asked, 'who is the girl, does she have ties with the hizmet, is she a member of it?' I told him, her name and that she graduated from a faculty of theology and from an Imam-Hatip high school. Then (x) and another person together with him said by asking me, 'O brother what are you doing? We are saying that you should be precautious, you are getting married to a graduate of a faculty of theology.' And then he asked 'Will she take the headscarf off?' ... then he continued with a milder tone 'OK, if the person you want to get married to will take her headscarf off, then you can marry her, we do not want to lose you.'"[213]

The Illegal and Immoral Methods of Eliminating People

Members of the the FETÖ/PDY resolutely used many illegal and immoral methods against those who did not show complete submission to them. It did not matter whether they were raised within or outside of the organization as long as they were considered to be an obstacle against the interests of the organization. They even considered these unethical methods to be permissible, even meritorious (*sevap*), and a kind of a ritual act, carried out for the sake of the *hizmet*. Moreover, they closely tracked certain people, collected private data on them, and then they adapted that data through ruses, cons and frame ups (*montajlama*) in order to intimidate and blackmail them. Through such ways, they were often successful in preventing the promotion of blameless people in their office, in having such people expelled from their offices, or even incarcerated. By applying such methods, they fabricated many cases where there was unwarranted suffering, and they caused the loss of profession, reputation, freedom and even the life of countless individuals.

Although the FETÖ/PDY introduced itself to the society as a religious community, it did not see at all anything wrong with violating the Islamic religious principle that "*private life is confidential.*" They did not observe the religious prohibitions in this regard. In fact, in the Holy Qur'an in chapter Hujurât in verse twelve these kinds of activities are prohibited.[214] The private life of a person includes affairs concerning an individual, his/her family and his/her possessions as long as there is nothing harmful to their life or any outsiders. The responsibility of such affairs included in the private life is between the person and God, whether those actions are meritorious or sinful is left for the person to resolve. The principle that must be followed is not to expose the sinful acts committed by a person in his/her private life, but to guide that person with good intentions in such a way so that he/she gets to do away with carrying such actions again. In this process of guidance, it is essential to respect the reputation of the person in public. While all the religious communities respected this rule and paid relevant attention to it, the FETÖ/PDY poked into the private life of others with malicious intent. It tracked people, illegally listened into their conversations, filmed them through video recording (*görüntülerini kaydetme*), ensnared them through well-planned plots, slandered (*iftira atmak*) them in public when it suited their agenda, threatened and blackmailed them by using their closest relatives (*en yakınları üzerinden*), and even went as far as ruthless murder, as in the case of the news reporter Haydar Meriç. None of these crimes have ever been committed by any other religious community. It feels like that the FETÖ/PDY even surpassed, through its methods, the infamous Hasan Sabbah's[215] network of crimes.

Unnamed witnesses have confirmed that in order for the lawsuit filed against Gülen by Nuh Mete Yüksel to remain inconclusive and to be able to pronounce Gülen free of such crimes, "*the judge, prosecutor and all other officers related to the investigation were sought to be silenced by intimidation, blackmail and bribe; that they conspired against (kumpas kurmak) Nuh Mete Yüksel, that a girl who lived in one of the houses of hizmet was convinced by an Imam of the house to play a role in this context, and that security officers secretly recorded the events by placing cameras and other recording devices.*"[216]

The methods that were used against those who did not belong to the organization varied depending on the profession, family life, personal weaknesses and social status of the person in question. One may include the following in the illegal methods applied by the organization in the public sector: assailment, blocking promotions, keeping others away from important assignments, inflicting disciplinary punishments that may lead to the termination from the profession, altering the place of work (*tayin edilmesi*) of someone without their knowledge or personal request, arranging for some individuals to be given challenging and severe jobs, especially in the military service or in the rural regions where the risk of a shootout was very very high,[217] cancelling the reward of a person who was entitled, and preventing some individuals from being able to travel abroad for education. The purpose of applying these methods was either to compel the person in target to submit to the organization or to pacify him/her and push them aside. Even if a person who was a target of this kinds of slanders knew their origin, he/she were not able to resist for long, and thus would either apply for retirement, or resign, or act in accordance with what was dictated by the organization.

The means utilized in applying these methods included numerous ways. These were such as filing a disciplinary investigation or a lawsuit, on the basis of tip-off petitions (*ihbar*), or e-mails, without any name or signature on them. The publishing of defaming and humiliating news reports on internet sites that were maintained on the internet servers located abroad, so that one could not identify the true agent behind such publications. The organizing of campaigns to discredit people by the media outlets run by the organization based on those news reports published on those internet sites. Furthermore, carrying out searches illegally, placing fake evidence into areas of search, modifying the data that were found it the areas of the search, issuing fake reports, deleting official records (*kayıtlar*), violating the right to have a fair trial, giving false testimony, slandering, conspiring and plotting, illegal bugging and monitoring (*takip etmek*), blackmailing by means of the collected data, bribing, and keeping records of such activities (*fişleme yapmak*). Last but not least, compelling people to commit criminal activities and leaking the secret information about the lawsuits and suspects to the media.

The FETÖ/PDY obtained and applied these methods and the relevant means thereof, by using either the members of the organization or those people who either feared or wanted to ingratiate themselves with the organization or by collaborating with the agents affiliated with secret services of foreign countries. In some cases, innocent people unknowingly became part of the conspiracies, plots and games of the organization. No matter, what method or means were used, the reputation of persons and families were irreparably destroyed, secret information belonging to the state institutions was disclosed, and state secrets were offered to other countries.

The first step of all these illegal and immoral methods applied by the FETÖ/PDY was the manipulation of public perception. The major methods used to manipulate the public perception were as follows:

1. Spreading gossip about individuals or institutions, publishing some information and documents, highlighting, exaggerating, distorting and spreading the material at hand.

2. Frightening, punishing or rewarding in order to keep other people—on a given case—silent. By these means individuals would be either kept silent on that issue or be forced to support the organization.

3. Defaming those who resisted the formation of public perception in the way they wanted by using illegal and unethical methods.

4. Taking over the intra-office mechanisms through which information is conveyed, providing huge amount of

information coming from various sources in a premeditated way and supporting all these activities—in some way—by the approval of their adherents within that office.

It has been noted that cases of manipulating public perception increased during the period of appointing people to certain offices, updating registries and giving promotions. In these periods, the following major steps were taken:[218]

1. The first step: identification of the target person/institution that should be discredited, and identification of the office, which has the high-ranking position over the case of this person/institution.

2. The second step: collecting information about the person/institution that is intended to be discredited.

3. The third step: preparing the office to decide on this issue and making the public opinion ready in order to manipulate its perception.

4. The fourth step: starting an information bombardment via social media, strengthening the attacks by the inclusion of printed and visual media, activating a mechanism of gossip by the members of the organization, and taking the attack to the level of social relations.

5. The last step: engaging in certain pitfalls and conspiracy activities to insure that the office to decide on the issue decides as it wants and as soon as possible.

THE ABUSE OF RELIGIOUS VALUES

Fetullah Gülen was presented as a great religious scholar because of his successful rhetoric, the efforts of the people gathered around him and because of the operations of the domestic and international intelligence services (*istihbarat teşkilatı*). In fact, he was not probably even as knowledgeable as an average Imam in religious matters since the traditional religious education he was able to acquire during the middle of the twentieth century was rather precarious and superficial. The mysterious sense of loyalty (*bağlılık*) which he generated in the members of the organization provided Gülen with an authority to radically transform the conception of religion of the people who were affiliated with him. This is why members of the FETÖ/PDY believed that Gülen had direct contact with the Prophet Muhammad and God. Consequently, they considered his statements high above the sayings of all other people. In a book on Gülen, he is reported to have said, "*God told me that 'certainly, I have created the universe for the sake of Muhammad. But I have been maintaining it for your sake'...*"[219] Indeed, according to the Holy Qur'an, God, the almighty, gave messages either through revelation (*vahiy*) or inspiration (*ilham*) to His chosen prophet, to Mary, to the mother of prophet Moses (pbuh) and to the disciples (*Havarîler*).[220] There is no evidence that God spoke directly to any other human being other than these highly regarded figures.

In some of his sermons,[221] Gülen stated that *"The Prophet strolled through the members of his community and inspected them."* For example, in his sermon delivered on June 03, 1990, Gülen stated that *"One of the hands of the Prophet was on the Prophet's noble companions and the other was on Gülen's community."* He said that the Prophet indicated Gülen's community as his own *"companions."* The most striking example of the abuse and manipulation of the status of the Prophet is that in a television series, *Şefkat Tepe (Mountain of Mercy)* broadcasted on a television channel of the organization, they represented the Prophet as a beam of light, as if he was mounted on a track.[222]

Probably the most obvious misuse of Gülen, of religious matters, is the claim of being the *Mahdi* and being the *Messiah*. Although he did not explicitly say it, he produced within the people loyal to him such a perception of himself that when they began to call him by such labels he condoned it. He did not reject the claims of such dreams and the rumors spread among his followers. Instead of rectifying the claims that he was a *Mahdi* or *Messiah* based on these perceptions and the stories retold by his followers, he preferred to take advantage of such an impression left on his followers. In a sense, he consciously contributed to the establishment of this perception. This attitude of Gülen contributed to the development of the perception that he was the expected *Mahdi* and *Messiah* among the members of the FETÖ/PDY. In fact, Gülen implied in his speeches, delivered in places where many people attended, that he was *Jesus the Messiah*. He tried to create a hallowed personality for himself by stating that *Jesus the Messiah* was going to arise out of Izmir, that Izmir had the property of the "*the beautiful city*", which is mentioned in the Qur'an,[223] that *Jesus the Messiah* (pbuh) had three major properties, one of them was to give sermons, that *the Messiah* would not be descending from heaven, to the contrary he was going to come to this world as an offspring of parents, that he was going to speak eloquently just as Gülen himself spoke eloquently, and that *Jesus the Messiah* (pbuh) in fact visited Izmir once. Moreover, he strengthened the perception about himself among the members of the organization by supporting it with numerological calculations known as *Hurufilik* [i.e. assignment of numerical values to letters] and onomancy (*Cifr*).[224] Members of the organization already believed, based on the works of Bediuzzaman Said Nursi, that *the office of Mahdi* had three stages; the first stage was realized by Bediuzzaman they said, Fetullah Gülen was at the second stage, and the third stage was going to be realized by Fetullah Gülen as well.

Ilhan Karagöz, a judge working at the Istanbul 18th Criminal Court of First Instances (18. Asliye Ceza Mahkemesi) issued a court decision just before the 15th of July coup attempt. It is quite a noteworthy document showing how Gülen's followers strongly believed that he was the Mahdi and that they had a special role in this context as followers of the Mahdi: "*Now we announce from here that Fetullah Gülen, respectable hoca (hocaefendi) is the person who is descended from the family of the Prophet Muhammad Mustafa (pbuh). He is the elected person whose coming was foretold by the Prophet, as we have traced the reports from Ali [the fourth Caliph] and from the books of Abdulkadir Geylani, who was descendent from the family of the Prophet. The following information is recorded in the sources: while Abu Bakr, Umar, Uthman and Ali were caliphs of the Prophet, the Mahdi (pbuh) is a special man who is going to lead humanity to the true path and who is going to eliminate falsehood distinctly and specifi-*

cally (özel). Although he will display certain extraordinary acts and miracles, many people will be waiting for him when he will arise, and they will give allegiance to him immediately. He will immediately start restoring the human conditions. Since he has all the kinds of freedom to act, since he will know how to act and how to guide people, he will arise (huruç) as the caliph of God... The stick of the prophet Moses will arise and accompany Fetullah hoca. Later on, prophet Jesus (pbuh) will arise and perform a ritual prayer behind the Mahdi (pbuh) and follow his guidance. But at a later stage, the Mahdi (pbuh) will perform a ritual prayer behind the prophet Jesus (pbuh). .... [The judge continues] Thus, I suppose by making this decision, I happen to be the Cehcah, who was mentioned in the book of the office of Mahdi..."

Another element that one sees continually in the FETÖ/PDY is the arts of *Hurufilik* and onomancy (*Cifr*). Fetullah Gülen claimed that letters have their own secrets, and discussing certain expressions in sacred texts, he deduced certain dates. From these he came up with some predictions and made his followers believe these predictions and deceived them. However, in Islam we all know that only God knows that which is hidden (*gayb*). No human being other than the prophets, whom God entrusted with specific knowledge, can offer such information about what shall take place in the future.

Instead, Gülen replaced the Qur'an and the Prophetic traditions with himself as the absolute authority in deciding or understanding all religious rules. He utilized the perception of people around him as a protective shield for himself. They thought that God protected him. On this basis, he convinced his followers that all that he was saying was absolute true. Since his followers believed that Gülen represented "*the truth*" (*hakk*) and that in order to reach happiness in this world as well as in the hereafter, one must submit to him, they accepted unquestionably all what he said.

Another important manifestation of Gülen's faulty conception of religion is the fact that he manipulated and abused, even damaged, the status of certain Islamic concepts, such as the Imam, the preacher (*vaiz*), the respected hoca (*hocaefendi*), the *cemaat* (community), the *hizmet* (service) and *Himmet* (monetary donations and charity actions). The meaning of these concepts, which were frequently used by the FETÖ/PDY in describing their activities were altered, and even drained of any true meaning. They were used in such a different sense that these concepts have today begun to have negative connotations. This is why Muslims in Turkey are hesitant in using these concepts.

The organization started something like a holy war against those whom it considered as enemies. It distorted the meaning of the Prophetic tradition, which says, "War is trickery," and did not see anything wrong in adopting unethical methods and means for its cause. In fact, Islam forbids a person to deceive another under normal situations.[225] Only in the case of war is it permitted that one utilize certain ruses, war strategies and, if needed, offer false information.[226] We must underline that this permission is valid only under war conditions and only against the enemy. However, Muslims are not allowed such actions against each other. This warped understanding adopted by the organization destroyed in its students, whom it educated, the sense of unity of the Muslim *Ummah*, and transformed them into slaves (*kapı kulu*) that were programmed simply to implement orders of Fetullah Gülen. These characteristics are reminiscent of the treacherous squads of the Assassins (*Haşhaşî*) found in our history.[227]

Another method the organization frequently manipulated to direct its own members, as well as other people, was to appeal to dream interpretation. According to such dream-claims, one was able to see the Prophet in his/her dream and receive definite instructions from him immediately. They believed that in the dreams that either Gülen or the Abis/Ablas had, the Prophet himself instructed them on many definite issues, such as donating a piece of land (*arsa bağışlanması*), instituting a certain school, tweeting on certain occasions and identifying which political party will be supported in elections.

Although Gülen argued that dreams do not count as evidence in religious matters and one may not organize one's practical life according to dreams, he used his own dreams and those of his followers as reliable evidence for action, and he led his people as he wanted by those dreams. His approach thus acquired a status whereby he could direct his follower and communicate specific messages via dreams. Nevertheless, in Islam it is clear that dreams that include messages that are contrary to that which is taught by the Qur'an and by the Prophetic tradition have no affirmative value at all, and those that are not contrary to that which is taught by the sources of Islam are still never binding. Moreover, if a person describes a dream, which he/she in fact did not have, that action by the Prophet has been labeled as "the gravest lie."[228]

The divine illumination (*keşf*) and miraculous events (*keramet*) that are used by the organization to influence its members are off course not binding either. Indeed, Imam Rabbani considered such divine illumination and inspiration to be similar to rational legal decisions (*içtihat*), and argued that just as rational legal decisions are conceivable to be accurate or inaccurate, so are those two open to both possibilities. Furthermore, it is clear that Gülen formed an unsound 'theolo-

gy', which leaves his statements and practices beyond sound religious knowledge. Yet he looked for a basis of justification for his actions in the Islamic religious sciences such as the Qur'anic exegesis, the Prophetic traditions, the life of the Prophet and the Islamic law. He has implemented the conviction that he has; which is that there is *"wisdom"* behind everything that he does. Thus, in this way emerged the cult of the personality of Gülen, and in turn, this cult provided a means for the members of the organization to be conceited against all other Muslims. They became a people that believed they could simply take everything. Just as their leadership due to a belief in a divinely elected person, and as someone representing the divine will and the 'project of future', they considered everything lawful for themselves, including a military coup.

The FETÖ/PDY paid strict attention not to have any conflict with different groups within the society except with the conservative parts thereof. Similarly, around the world, it was quite careful not to have any conflict with people other than the Muslims. For example, in their projects of *"Interreligious Dialog"* and *"Abrahamic Religions,"* they displayed quite a tolerant attitude towards the Christians and the Jews, developing close relations, while displaying quite a detached, exclusivist, and marginalizing attitude towards Muslims outside their own group. They withheld from Muslim groups the kind of dialogue that they offered to the Christians and the Jews and they always kept other Muslims at a distance.

To justify the process of dialogue with the Christians and the Jews, they manipulated the Chapter Âl-Imrân, verse 64;[229] they consciously highlighted only the first part of the word of testimony, [i.e., saying that "there is no god, other than God"]. In fact, in some of his sermons, Gülen said, *"I have great respect for anybody who says Lâ ilahâ illallah [i.e., there is no god, other than God].*" And his statement caused his followers to think that for Gülen, Jews and Christians cannot be considered as "unbelievers." Thus it was argued that in order for a person to be a Muslim, it would be sufficient to pronounce the first part of the word of testimony, "*Lâ ilâha illallah,*" and that those who do not acknowledge that Muhammad (pbuh) is a prophet could also go to paradise.

As it is well-known, the essence and foundation of Islamic religion is to pronounce the statement of testimony as an expression of one's sincere belief, "*I bear witness that there is no god other than God and that Muhammad (pbuh) is His servant and Messenger.*" The "*Lâ ilâha illallah*" part of the word of testimony indicates the unity of God, and the "*Muhammadun Rasulullah*" part indicates approval of that Muhammad is a messenger and of all the divinely determined principles that he brought to us from God, the almighty. It is similar to a rejection of Islamic beliefs, if one separates the two halves of the words of the testimony, which is the foundation of the religion of Islam, in order to implement the hidden agenda of the organization and to make most out of any given occasion.

THE METHODS OF COMMUNICATION
AND CORRESPONDENCE

The main purpose of the methods of communication and correspondence used by the FETÖ/PDY is to collect the information that is useful for the interests of the organization and to use them in the most efficient way for the benefit of the organization. This is why the FETÖ/PDY functioned as if it was an intelligence service. According to Necip Hablemitoğlu, *"Fetullahists are a group that owns a private intelligence service. This illegal organization took advantage of facilities of the stately intelligence agencies and obtained their secret information. It has an archive containing material that indicates discrepancies of its opponents, politicians who were its targets, journalists, crime bosses, state officers, bureaucrats, scholars, military personnel and members of other professions. This material includes various visual and auditory records, analysis of these records, pictures, official documents and even personal notes that may be used to blackmail people. Moreover, it has been found that the specialization of this organization lies in issuing fake documents about those rival people whom they could not buy with money or were unable to intimidate. In the same manner, Fetullahists abused the intelligence ser-*

vice to eliminate corporations that competed with its own corpora-
tions. In this regard, it is said that competing corporations were mis-
leadingly investigated based on information concerning smuggling,
and the effects of these investigations were highly destructive. The
same strategy was applied in the case of rival foundations, associa-
tions and individuals. This organization played, at the same time,
an important role in internalizing, pacifying or discarding the ri-
vals, and placing its supporters in vital positions."[230]

It is noteworthy that the FETÖ/PDY, which had activities
all around the world, developed methods of correspondence
specific to different interests that it developed. The following
are the methods of correspondence used by the members of
the organization:[231]

1. Face to face meeting: the primary way of communication is to have a face to face meeting. In cases of emergency, if
there is a person, or an issue, of whom they had to talk about,
they definitely would make a face to face meeting. For example, the 15th of July military coup attempt was planned in a
face to face meeting in an apartment in Ankara.[232]

2. Cons concerning cellular phones and GSM numbers:
The mobile phone numbers that were used by the organization are such that the true owner of those numbers cannot be identified by looking for the customer information,
because either they are registered by the name of other people, or by the name of a company controlled by the organization, or by the name of people who live outside Turkey.
Such phone numbers were used especially by the members of
the organization who carried out confidential duties. Those
who used these kinds of phone numbers were given a new
GSM number, approximately every three months. With the
change of the GSM numbers, their cellular phones were also changed. Critical issues were never discussed with them

on the phone. In the last period, however, communication within the organization was carried out via phones and internet "*messaging*." Members of the organization would not pronounce their names while corresponding as a precaution, but they would address each other as "*Abi*" or "*Hocam*" (master). Imam of provinces and districts would, generally, use "*code*" names.

3. Internet programs, social media and encrypted software: Software programs that facilitated correspondence via internet, which were encrypted and not expensive, such as *Skype, Tango, Kakao, Talk, Viber, Line, WhatsApp* etc. were used in correspondence. Encrypted special software, such as *Acrobits, Softphone, Bylock* and *Eagle*[233] were also commonly used. Among these, especially, *Bylock* software program was used by *hundred-thousands* of people and secret meetings and operations of the organization were coordinated via this program. When MİT decrypted *ByLock,* the organization moved to *Eagle*[234] a more complicated program. During the 15th of July military coup attempt, they communicated through groups formed in the *WhatsApp* program.

4. Encrypted IP line: Especially in its schools abroad, they used encrypted IP pones by means of rentable lines.

5. Live courier: Using a live courier was preferred, especially when the organization carried out the most critical operations. Ergenekon investigations were secretly started by the Imams of security and intelligence who received commands via live couriers and who delivered them to Turkey. The suspects who administered the organization are known to have gone abroad frequently, especially, to the USA. For example, Âdil Öksüz, who is supposed to have been the Imam of the Air Forces, went abroad 109 times between the years 2002-2016.

6. Giving instructions via media: the organization called its members up via the media outlets controlled by the organization, and it moved its grassroots base in this way. They frequently used media outlets to communicate the news to all cells-structures and to all staff of the organization. The secret messages hidden in the religious conversations and sermons of Fetullah Gülen were communicated in this way. For example, that Fetullah Gülen delivered a speech in a light olive green colored garment was considered to be "*the secret code of the military coup*."

7. The meetings of the organization: cell-structures of the organization carried out periodical meetings such as religious conversations, lectures, consultations and board meetings. Thus, they had the opportunity to decide planned activities of the organization and to exchange information in these face to face meetings. Almost all groups regularly would get together on certain days of the week. Only members of the cell-structure could attend the meetings of the organization. And members of a definite cell-structure could attend only the meeting of their own cell-structure; no matter how faithful they were members of a definite cell-structure could not attend meetings of other cell-structures. In accordance with the general principle of the organization, everybody should know only what it should know, not more than that. In this way, to prevent being discovered, members of each cell-structure could know only his/her colleagues. When extraordinary events arose, these meeting would be held either in the house of the abi/abla or in a place he/she designated. In such cases, the time and place of meetings would be communicated by coded expressions such as "*come to me*," "*let's have tea*," and "*let's go to watch the game*." The purpose of the meetings of the organization was not religious at all. It rather pretended to or-

ganize religious conversations with the purpose of insuring the solidarity among members, commissioning certain duties to cell-structures, and establishing a discipline inside the organization and communicating instructions to lower units. At first, the instructions were written by those who were responsible to carry out those instructions and when those instructions were carried out, they would destroy those notes. When he was in Turkey, Fetullah Gülen used to hold meetings with Imams of provinces and institutions regularly every month. After he escaped to the USA, he still kept holding these meetings regularly on a threemonth basis. The instructions given directly by Gülen himself were delivered by authorized Imams to lower units via meetings that were labeled "confidential".

Other than these, it has been observed that the members of the FETÖ/PDY paid attention to the following issues in their meetings and gatherings concerning their organizational activities:[235]

1. Meetings were usually held at the weekends and in places that did not belong to the organization.

2. People who attended the meetings would pretend to be like leftist people.

3. They were extremely careful against the possibility that someone might be following them.

4. They would not use GSM, unless it was necessary, they would normally communicate by using payphones.

5. If they had to use GSM, they would communicate via encrypted software programs.

6. They used code names.

In the media outlets run by the organization, the organization used an iron hand in a velvet glove i.e. hard power covered with soft power. It produced certain advertisements and communicated certain subliminal messages so that it could compel the government to give up certain policies that disturbed the organization. For example, in the movie advertised in the Zaman newspaper, "*This Time is the Time of brotherhood*" (*Zaman Kardeşlik Zamanı*), it communicated the message, "*we are all around Turkey, we are the people, you cannot defeat us.*"[236]

In one of these advertisements, a person who looked like Fetullah Gülen and a young man with a military uniform were pictured next to each other, and there it said "*there is another possibility*" ("*bir ihtimal daha var*"). The message was a threat of a military coup. With the same purpose, on the cover of the *Sızıntı Journal* published in May 2016, there was a person with a military uniform opening a door to a nice garden. The message of the picture was taken to be that they would carry out a military coup and this would lead to the "*good*" days from the perspective of the organization.[237]

They produced an advertorial movie for the Zaman newspaper, nine months and ten days before the 15th of July military coup attempt. In the advertorial movie, one hears sirens first and then one sees a baby smiling. They seem to be giving the message that they were in a state of emergency, and then they entered into a process without return.[238]

Ekrem Dumanlı, who was the chief editor of the Zaman Newspaper, in a television program which he attended on the 1st of September 2015,[239] referring to the President of the Republic, who was directly elected by people said in a patronizing manner: "*He should leave without resistance otherwise he will have to leave.*" This statement does not simply indicate violation of one's limits, insolence and disrespecting the will of the nation, but also indicates how much self-confidence and arrogance the FETÖ/PDY carried.

The organization conveyed subliminal messages in cinema films that the organization produced. For example, in the movie *Kelebek (Butterfly)*, they showed members of the cemaat i.e. members of Sufi orders to be on the same side with George Bush, a former president of the USA, on the issue of terror organizations. For them, al-Qaida and Taliban solely bear the responsibility of terror. In this case, the USA is innocent and oppressed. As such the film makes propaganda for an American moderate Islam.[240]

Another example is the movie called, *Eşrefpaşahlar* (Those Who Come from Ashrafpasha), which features an idealist Imam as its main character. He is called in the film "*Hoca*" (master). This Hoca almost never visited a mosque, but he is presented as an eager religious official, who wants to change the inhabitants of the neighborhood. There are subtle messages indicating that the Hoca in the movie in fact represents Fetullah Gülen.[241] At the end of the movie, in the section where they offer their thanks, at the top one sees the expression "*To him.*" This pronoun "him" is also taken as a reference to Gülen.[242] It is also interesting that there is no reference to the prophet Muhammad (pbuh) either in the movie *Kelebek*, or in the movie Eşrefpaşalılar.

In another movie, *Selâm* (Peace) which informs us about a story of *Hizmet* (service), a message of dialogue is given by all the scenes showing churches, crosses, and a Christian funeral ceremony. Imam Adem's following words, who attended the funeral ceremony of Irina Radovich, offers a clear notion about the message of the film: *"O my Imam (hocam)", in the movie, 'The Message', there is quite a telling scene. The king of Abyssinia drew a line on the ground and said 'the difference be-*

tween you and us is like this, no more than that.' Thus, is the difference between Irina Radovich and us, I cannot cross over this line." When these words were pronounced, the crescent and the cross were shown, in the movie, next to each other.[243]

In the television series, *Şefkat Tepe* (*Mountain of Mercy*) which was broadcast on a television channel of the organization, they represented the Prophet as beam of light, as if he mounted on a track. This deeply embarrassed the people. Furthermore, the operation against the MHP (Nationalist Movement Party) through a video recording, and the removal of Zekeriya Öz, a former public prosecutor, from the office were featured in episodes 120 and 121 of the series.

THE FETÖ/PDY'S FINANCIAL STRUCTURE

Sources of Income

The most visible difference of the FETÖ/PDY from other religious communities with regard to financial conditions is this: while other religious communities wanted to finance their activities, concerning teaching religion to people, education, cooperation and solidarity, the FETÖ/PDY pulled itself away from this kind of spiritual causes. It evolved into a free market player, in a sense it turned into a profit-oriented corporation or a holding, into an agent which engaged in international business, and carried out transactions abroad in foreign markets to make money. The sources of income of the organization, which had quite an expansion and complicated financial structure, are as follows:[244]

1. Income that is acquired from public sector and civil servants:

a. Having public tenders been given to companies that are affiliated with the organization on the basis of fraudulent specifications.

b. Finding out the amount of tender bids that would be offered by rival companies, through illegal means, and making sure that companies affiliated with the organization would offer the lower amounts of tender bids.

c. By using information obtained via intelligence activities, compelling rival companies to leave the tenders that they won, or compelling them to pay some share to the organization.

d. By carrying out certain judicial or administrative proceedings concerning the rival companies, ensuring that companies affiliated with the organization become dominant.

e. Leaking secret information about the plans of public institutions concerning financing and investment to the affiliated companies.

f. Transferring public lands to foundations, associations or educational institutions that are affiliated with the organization without any charge.

g. Having the change of development plans done by municipalities in a way suitable for the benefit of foundations, associations or companies affiliated with the organization.

h. With the help of the members of the organization, who were employed at Turkish Cooperation and Coordination Agency, obtaining some commission on behalf of the organization for helping Turkish business men to establish foreign connections.

i. Doing favor for companies affiliated with the organization in delivering the public funds of donation, support and encouragement.

j. Contribution from monthly salaries and rewards received by civil servants.

k. Confiscating the amount of "promotion" payment that should have been paid to members of the organization; this promotion payment given by the contracted banks to the civil servants because they get their monthly payment from these banks on the basis of a contract with the relevant public institution.

l. Compelling members of the organization, who were placed in public institutions, to donate their first monthly salary to the organization.

2. Contributions from the income of the affiliated corporations between 20-50%.

3. Incomes acquired from businessmen.

a. Commissions taken from businessmen in return to finalizing their judicial and administrative issues in favor of them.

b. Protection money taken from businessmen through threats and blackmail, based on their audio and video records documenting certain weaknesses in their private life.

c. Commissions taken from businessmen in return for helping them establishing certain business connections.

4. Incomes acquired from Non-Profit Organizations:

a. Membership fees taken from affiliated confederations, federations, unities, associations and foundations

b. Money collected from people by means of affiliated charity agencies

c. Benefits obtained by taking over the administration of the chambers of commerce, and making decisions about the market values in favor of the non-profit organizations affiliated with the organization when public institutions purchased services.

5. Incomes that are collected under the guise of voluntary activities:

a. Money collected from businessmen, companies and tradesmen before the *Eid al-Fitr* (Feast of Sacrifice) by promising them they will sacrifice an animal(s) for their religious duty.

b. Money collected in provinces and districts by establishing advisory boards consisting of businessmen and collecting money that might be given as annual alms tax (*Zakat*), Fitr charity, plain charity, *Himmet* (donation) and charity for scholarship.

6. Payments collected from students who got educated in schools, preparatory course centers, or other educational institutions affiliated with the organization and from students who live in dormitories run by the organization, inside Turkey or abroad.

7. Payments collected for subscribing to newspapers, journals and other printed material as well as other media outlets that are affiliated with the organization.

Economic Activities

The organization started its economic activities in the educational sector. It started running schools, preparatory course centers and dormitories. In time, it established printing houses to serve the educational sector, and then it got engaged in the paper production business, since printing houses needed paper. To sell the products, it established book shops. It also established companies producing uniforms, special school cloths and furnishing materials, since these were part of the school life. After establishing printing houses, the organization established a cargo company to transport the printed material and books. It continued establishing its own companies in relevant sectors, so that it would not need to buy products and services from others. After a while, it established Bank Asya to finance the economic and commercial activities of its own members. Later on, it started its enterprise in the health sector, so that its members would not need to buy health services from others, and it would be able to provide these services to its members.

It has been confirmed that the economic power of the organization in Turkey and around the world reached one hundred and fifty billion US dollars.[245] The economic power of the organization played an important role in affecting not only the general public, but also many educated, intellectual people and even its opponents.[246] The number of corporations that financially supported the organization is approximately ten thousands. These corporations may be divided into three groups:[247]

1. Affiliated corporations: these are the corporations that were established and operated at first for the use of income for the organization. They were developed by the use of the financial source of the organization. In turn, they provided immediate material support for the organization. Bank Asya and Kaynak Holding are two examples of this group.

2. Linked corporations: some of the corporations in this group were established by the capital of the organization, some of them came under the control of the organization and some of them were wealthy corporations which provided the organization with extensive material support. Koza İpek Holding is a good example of this group.

3. Financial provision corporations: These are the corporations, the founding capital of which did not belong to the organization and they were not under the control of the organization. But these corporations provided the organization with material sources.

The organization promoted the manipulation of public perception to support corporations that may be classified under one of these groups. It was claimed by them that it is not religiously permissible to buy the products and services of other corporations, when those products and services were available through one of these corporations. It was taught that the products that were produced by the affiliated, linked and financial provision corporations were religiously lawful and the products of the rival corporations are doubtful whether they are religiously lawful or not. These claims were first imposed at the grassroots of the organization and via media outlets to the whole society. Dubious or illegal provisions that are found in the corporations affiliated, or linked, to the organization, or financial provision corporations may be summarized as follows:[248]

1. These corporations are usually family corporations and majority of the members of the family are members of the FETÖ/PDY and had an active responsibility in the organization.

2. Almost all of the corporations were engaged in the sectors of education and consulting, in addition to their area of specialization.

3. All the corporations got the membership to the same associations and foundations and gave donations to the same institutions.

4. These corporations frequently changed their names.

5. Since the shares frequently transferred, the partnership structures (*ortaklık yapısı*) are complicated and ambiguous. In the case of many corporations, the formal owner of the corporation and its real owner are different people. Almost all corporations were administered by the high ranking administrators of the organization.

6. Certain people who were not in fact partners of corporations were registered formally as partners of the corporation, or even its owners. This was called "*depository partnership*" method.

7. After the December 17-25 process, there was evidence of an increase in attempts to change the name, principal agreement, transfer of shares and hiding the activities of corporations.

8. These corporations were also used as places of human resources for the organization.

9. Transfer of human resources among these corporations was well above the average market rates - all these corporations benefited from the same human resources repository.

10. Those who established the organization or who had a prominent position in it also had active roles in the administration of these corporations.

11. Goods and services were purchased from these corporations, i.e., affiliated and linked corporations and financial provision corporations. These corporations focused their business in areas which were closely connected to each other, so that they were able to monopolize certain business sectors.

12. Due to the special efforts of the members of the organization who were employed in public institutions, these cor-

porations were able to sell vast amounts of goods and services to public institutions.

13. To make sure that these corporations paid a lesser amount of tax, they applied special transfer rates for supplying goods and services among them.

14. Dividend payment to shareholders was either very small or did not take place all. The profits were transferred to other institutions of the organization.

15. Vast amounts of money were transferred to the schools abroad run by the organization.

16. An important part of the monthly salary of the personnel was appropriated and used to finance certain operations of the organization.

17. Money collected by the organization through illegal methods was legitimized via these corporations. Hence there was a concentrated money flow, the source of which is unknown, to these corporations.

18. Their activities were carried out not according to the free market economy, but with the purpose of providing financial support to the operations of the organization.

Here is a list of some of the affiliated and linked corporations, financial provision corporations, non-profit organizations, labor unions and media outlets:[249]

1. Holdings: Kaynak Holding, Koza-İpek Holding, Akfa Holding, Naksan Holding, Boydak Holding, ...

2. Corporations (education, consultation, cargo, logistic, printing, publishing, insurance etc.): Asır, Atlantik, Başkent, Bedir, Coşku, Çağ, Çağlayan, Doruk, Elmas, Firdevs, Galaxy, Gonca, Gökkuşağı, Güvender, Işık, Mavera, Memba, Mizan,

Sema, Söğüt, Sürat, Şahika, Şelale, Toros, Ufuk, Zafer, Zambak, Zümrüt, ...

3. Preparatory course centers: Anafen (213 branches), Analitik, Coşku, Değer, Dijital, Dilfem, FEM (280 branches), İhtiyaç, Körfez (126 branches), Maltepe, ...

4. Bank: Asya Katılım Bankası A.Ş. (Bank Asya).

5. Schools: Alparslan, Bahar, Bakış, Betül, Birlik, Burç, Çağlayan, Delta, Dicle, Fatih, Feza, Fırat, Gonca, Gönül, Gülen, Hoşgörü, Huzur, İkbal, İstikbal, Kılıçarslan, Nil, Nilüfer, Özcan, Sahil, Sema, Samanyolu, Serhat, Sümbül, Toros, Ufuk, Üftade, Ümran, Yamanlar, Yavuz Selim, Yıldız, Zümrüt, ...

6. Hospitals and medical centers: Ailemiz, Akpol, Altınova, Anadolu, Bahar, Baran, Burç, Doğa, Fatih, Gümüşiğne, Harran, İstanbul, Kurtuluş, Nurlu, Primer, Rentıp, Sincan, Şifa, Turgut Özal, Ufuk, Uzmanlar, ...

7. Dormitories: Acar, Ati, Ay, Baran, Berk, Çağlayan, Derya, Erdem, Feza, Fecir, Helezon, Işık, İffet, İlkbahar, Kamer, Kampüs, Kardelen, Keykubat, Koza, Melikşah, Mimar Sinan, Muradiye, Paye, Ramiz Bey, Samanyolu, Şafak, Şems, Tomurcuk, Tuna, Yağanbaba, Yasemin, Yıldız, Zerafet, ...

8. Media outlets (newspaper, journal, radio and television channels): Akademik Araştırmalar, Aksiyon, Asya Pasifik, Bisiklet Çocuk, Bugün, Burç FM, Cihan Haber Ajansı, Dialog Avrasya, Eko Life, Gonca, Gül Yaprağı, Kanaltürk, Mehtap TV, Meydan, Millet, Muhabir Haber Ajansı, Nokta, Özgür Düşünce, Samanyolu TV, Samanyolu Avrupa TV, Samanyolu US, S Haber, SEM Haber Ajansı, Sızıntı, Taraf, The Fountain, Today's Zaman, Yağmur, Yeni Ümit, Yumurcak,

Zaman, and Zirve. Moreover, 11 television channels, 20 radio channels, 36 local newspapers and six movies that were shown at national level.

9. Foundations (123 units): Akdeniz, Akyazılı, Anadolu, Başarı, Battalgazi, Boydak, Burç, Çukurova, Derya, Feza, Gaye, Gazeteciler ve Yazarlar, Gevher Sultan, Güvenilir Gıdalar, Hatuniye, İpek, Kafkas, Kaynak, Koza İpek, Körfez, Memurlar, Merve, Nil, Okyanus, Pamukçu, Ramiz, Serhat, Sipahi, Sistem, Şeyhzade Selim, Tanrıverdi, Turgut Özal, Türkiye Öğretmenler, Türkiye Tabipler, Uludağ, ...

10. Associations (902 units): Ahenk Uluslararası Öğrenci, Aktif Çalışanlar, Anadolu Alevi, Anadolu Alevi Bektaşi, Anadolu İşadamları ve Sanayicileri, Gelişen Sanayici ve İşadamları, Hür Sanayici ve İşadamları, Kimse Yok Mu, Sağlık ve Eğitim, Sivil Toplum Akademisi, Süleymaniye, Tüm Memur İşçi Dayanışma, Tüm Teknik Çalışan Elemanlar, Uluslararası Türkçe Öğretim Derneği (Türkçeder), Türkiye İşadamları ve Sanayicileri Konfederasyonu-TUSKON (TUSKON included 7 federations, 211 associations and more than 55 thousands of member.), ...

11. Universities: Canik Başarı (Samsun), Fatih (Istanbul), Gediz (Izmir), Hamdullah Emin Paşa (Alanya), İpek (Ankara), Izmir, Kanuni (Adana), Melikşah (Kayseri), Mevlana (Konya), Murat Hüdavendigar (Istanbul), Orhangazi (Bursa), Selahaddin Eyyubi (Diyarbakır), Süleymanşah (Istanbul), Şifa (Izmir), Turgut Özal (Ankara), Uluslararası Antalya, and Zirve (Gaziantep).

12. Labor unions: (2 confederations, 19 labor unions): Aktif Eğitim-Sen, Pak Deniz İş, Pak Eğitim İş, Pak Enerji İş, Pak Finans İş, Pak Gıda İş, Pak Maden İş, Pak Metal İş, Pak Taşıma İş, Pak Toprak İş, Ufuk Bayındır-Sen, Ufuk Büro-Sen,

Ufuk Enerji-Sen, Ufuk Haber-Sen, Ufuk Kültür-Sen, Ufuk Sağlık-Sen, Ufuk Tarım Orman-Sen, Ufuk Ulaştırma-Sen, and Ufuk Yerel-Sen.

The foundations that were identified to be affiliated with the organization and hence were closed down by legislative decrees possessed 10.604.643 Turkish Lira in cash, real estate that was worth 648.208.676 Turkish Lira and assets that were worth 36.821.429 Turkish Lira. The total number of real estates of the organization was 1531. Moreover, 1310 associations were closed down because of their affiliation with the organization. These associations had 11.901 female and 57.005 male members. The total number amounts to 68.816. They also had 81 means of transportation and 178 building sites and buildings.[250]

The General Directorate of Security Affairs and the Department for Fighting against Smuggling and Organized Crimes prepared a report about the acquittal of the illegal income of the Fetullahist Terror Organization, dated 07 March, 2016 with the document number 40226. According to this report, "...*associations and foundations (affiliated with the organization)*" were used "*to acquit the illegal income of the organization.*" When all of this data is taken into account and processed, one may easily declare that the FETÖ/PDY had become an international "*holding organization*" with millions of partners, which carried out activities almost in all countries around the world. They carried out so many clandestine and questionable activities, and as an organization it seems to have dimensions of which all is still not exactly known.

The Koza-İpek Group is a noteworthy example with regard to the questionable economic activities of the organization. The Koza-İpek Group, once, was about to go bankrupt. Interestingly, since the year 2004, it turned around its business and grew increasingly annually. All the corporations included in the Koza-İpek Group reached very high income levels, the sources of which could not be identified at first sight. However, deeper investigations showed that their corporations were supported by an unrelated source. This source was supporting the corporations of the Koza-İpek Group with the money collected by the organization. It has been verified and confirmed that the *Himmet* money was transferred to the Koza-İpek Group and its corporations. Moreover, it is evident that they entered into their accounts that they had acquired this money through their gold mining operations and thus the money was considered as legal income of these corporations. It has also been confirmed that the Eti Mining Corporation (Eti Madenleri, once a public corporation which specialized in mining) was privatized with a much lower price than its real value and it was bought up by the Koza-İpek Group. It has also been verified that the former owner of the Kanaltürk television channel had to sell his channel to the Koza-İpek Group because he was pressured by an investigation and lawsuit. Furthermore, they transferred money, the source of which was unidentified, abroad by using the accounts of corporations included in the Koza-İpek Group. They also transferred the income obtained from the joint stock companies to the organization acting as if it was donated to it by the stock holders. Finally, it has been verified that the television channels called Bugün (Today) and Yaşam (Life) and its newspapers were administered by the organization, and that the university that was established by the Koza-İpek Group was allocated to the organization.[251]

In this regard, many transactions contrary to normally accepted banking procedures were identified within the activities of the Asya Katılım Bankası (Asya Participation

Bank). For example, illegal incomes were deposited in many accounts and thus incorporated into the system. This provided high amounts of credit to institutions run by the organization and these credit loans were paid back by *Himmet* and donations, which were illegal income. The Asya Katılım Bankası also got tax identification number for fifteen institutions abroad, which were affiliated with the organization, and provided them with the amount of 115.136.829,07 Turkish Lira for financial support. These credit loans were paid back by third parties by high amounts of cash payment deposits although those who made the payment did not have any connection to these institutions such as participation or administration. Furthermore, the bank provided credit to certain people without having any information about who would be paying the loan back.[252]

Himmet: Community Tax

One of the most important sources of income of the organization was the "*Himmet*." It is a "community tax" in a sense. Through this, members of the organization had to pay a type of protection money under the label of *Himmet*. According to the statement of an anonymous witness included in the *Çatı iddianamesi* (Comprehensive Indictment), "*In 1983, they started holding Himmet meetings, in the course of time, such activities turned out to be extensive organizations. To influence participants in these organizations, they had people with good rhetorical skills and with comprehensive religious knowledge give sermons. These people encouraged participants to give more money.*"[253]

The organization made the "*Himmet*" come directly from the salaries of its members, such that those who were infiltrated into the state bureaucracy had to give, for the first time, all of their first monthly salary. Later if they were bachelors they had to pay 20% of their monthly salary, 10% of it if they were married and if they had three or more children, then they had to pay 5% of their monthly salary. In addition to this fee, their payment to the organization increased because of their mandatory subscription to the newspapers and journals published by the organization and other similar responsibilities. Those members who did not want to pay *Himmet* were documented and after inspection of their situation, they would be subject to the *"mercy of slap"* (that is the wrath of the community). Thus, *Himmet* definitely turned out to be very much like a protection racket.[254]

It is known that the *Himmet* programs targeted businessmen and a vast amount of money was collected and to insure such high amounts they were unscrupulous. They even deceived people with flagrant lies such as, *"I saw our Prophet in this room."*[255]

The focus of the *Himmet* programs was to push people into a race of donation by announcing the amount donated by each person in the group. It is stated that in a *Himmet* meeting, a high ranking administer of the FETÖ/PDY would give an engaging speech at first and make the participants enter a spiritual and emotional flurry. Then the participants were asked to pronounce the amount of donation they would like to make. At this point, first certain members who were instructed previously by the organization would come up and playing their role they would promise to donate certain high amounts of wealth. Upon hearing these high amounts, other members became motivated to promise to donate ten-twenty times more than what they planned before attending the *Himmet* meeting.[256] In order to insure donations, they would have people immediately sign an invoice (*senet*). In cases when people could not pay the promised donations, the promised amount were obtained (*tahsil etmek*) by legal procedures (on the bases of decisions made by the members of the organization in jurisdiction through a strong-arm tactic).[257]

Although collecting money by these methods is clearly forbidden according to relevant legislation,[258] those who donated money kept silent, since they feared adverse consequences of any legal procedures as the organization dominated the legal arena. Thus, this *Himmet* oppression continued for many years. Those who paid the *Himmet* that they promised on time were provided with all kinds of convenience in the public institutions that were controlled by the organization. They had the motto, "*Take away from the hostile state, deposit into the Himmet,*" encouraging the members to weaken the state, which was considered as an enemy, and the revenues obtained in this way made an important sources of income for the organization.

Witnesses have stated frequently that many businessmen, who were afraid of the shadowy face of the organization, could not carry out their business without paying this protection racket. Businessmen who wanted certain approvals that should have been carried out in public institutions, or who did not want to be struggling with problems that might be coming from judiciary and security departments, were forced to pay extortionate amounts of donation. Those businessmen, who rejected to donate to the organization, were subject to extraordinary harassments, and they were punished by falsified reports, investigations, police supervisions, detentions and character assassination campaigns carried out via media. Another murky side of the *Himmet* tyranny of the organization was that certain businessmen, who were validly being prosecuted in the legal courts, were able to bribe themselves out of such prosecutions due to the high amounts of donation they made to the organization. Moreover, those businessmen who offered high amounts of donations to the organization were generously treated in return by attaining any public bids.[259]

Out of all the income acquired by *Himmet* in Turkey, 15% was always sent to Fetullah Gülen as "*the share of sacred Hoca.*"[260] When they collected the *Himmet*, they never told the donors that they were going to give certain amount directly to Gülen. It is only Fetullah Gülen, who knew how and for what purpose this money was being utilized. None of the members of the organization, no matter their rank, were allowed to scrutinize this matter.

The Imam of the organization, who was in charge of the financial affairs of the organization, had the authority to decide where and how to spend the money collected as *Himmet*. The surplus money was used for operations related to the organization via companies with shared capital under the control of the organization, such as Bank Asya, Kaynak Holding and İpek-Koza. The *Himmet* money was used as capital to fund the establishment of commercial enterprises (e.g., the television channels, new agencies, the schools, the preparatory course centers, the bank, the publishing houses, and the printing houses owned by the organization.

The Compulsory Subscription Practice

In addition to *Himmet*, another source of income of the organization was the compulsory subscription payment, which was charged in return for the products and services provided by the press affiliated with organization. In addition to members of the FETÖ/PDY, hundred-thousands of people were compelled to subscribe to the newspapers and journals, such as Zaman, Bugün, Sızıntı, Aksiyon and Yeni Ümit, published by corporations affiliated with the organization. More often, they simply charged the subscription payment without even delivering those products. It was impossible to work at a corporation affiliated by the organization without subscription to these products. The mock exams at the preparatory course centers were done only with the condition that they would subscribe to these products and the ÖSYM exam questions were either selected out of these mock exams or the majority of questions included in the ÖSYM exams were added in the mock exams. Thus the organization acquired money, insured placement of its members to public institutions by the Civil Servants Election Exam (*Kamu Personel Seçme Sınavı*), got more students by publicizing its preparatory course centers and its newspapers got bigger shares from the public advertisements in newspapers since their sales figure were quite high.

Boards of Trustees and Treasurers

All the illegal units within the organization had a treasurer and a board representative (*mütevelli sorumlusu*). And all these were connected to the Turkey Board (*Türkiye Mütevellisi*).[261] Additionally, under every office of the provincial Imam, there was a board of trustees. Such boards mostly consisted of businessmen and tradesmen. They were responsible for the activities that would be held within that province as well as for the provision of financial sources for the activities within the country that was placed under the supervision of their province. In this regard, these boards carried out the activities such as collection of *Himmet* and other financial incomes, organization of *Himmet*, settling tenders etc. In districts, similar boards with similar structures and functions were instituted. The financial income that was collected by the boards of trustees would be handed over to the treasury units connected either to the Imam of a province or a district depending on the circumstances.[262]

Members of the boards of trustees would make a camp program, under the coordination of the Imam of a province at least once a year. In these camp programs, they were taught how to apply certain methods to increase collection of the amount of money, i.e. addressing the religious sensitivities of the society and thus getting *Himmet*, annual alms tax (*Zakat*), payment for the ritual sacrifice and scholarship. They would confirm that they would be rewarded in the hereafter with paradise in return for collecting this money. Members of the board of trustees would be accepted as members of the non-profit organizations. It was the *Abis* of the religious conversation who determined who would become the member of which organization. Moreover, members of board of trustees were also responsible to take care of the material need of the light house.

They collected from people financial aids and as well as similar aids, all under the names of Himmet, scholarship, annual alms tax, donation of ritual sacrifice and the like, by saying that these donations would be used to satisfy the needs of the needy, poor people, students, children who lost one of their parents or both. However, these collected donations were not spent in areas, which were designated in the Qur'an as stated above, rather they were used as capital for commercial activities. Or they ended up as the personal wealth of the administrators of the organization, or were donated to lobbies abroad, or were donated for the election campaigns of politicians in the USA or in other globally dominant counties. Or they were used to pay as a fee or as a bribe to newspaper columnists, program hosts, media affiliated people and politicians in return for supporting Gülen and members of the organization in their articles or columns or programs and criticizing the AK Party government and the President of the Republic, Recep Tayyip Erdoğan. These sources were also used to pay for the expenses of the mansion where Gülen lived, to pay the monthly salaries of the Imams who were members of the organization and the like. Whereas, in order for the annual alms tax to be religiously valid, it must be spent in areas that were specified in the chapter al-Tawba, verse sixty,[263] and if it is spent in a different area as mentioned above it is not religiously acceptable.

THE FETÖ/PDY AS AN ARMED TERRORIST ORGANIZATION AND ITS COOPERATION WITH TERRORIST ORGANIZATIONS[264]

The FETÖ/PDY was described as a *"Parallel Government Structure"* (*"Paralel Devlet Yapılanması - PDY"*) for the first time in the MGK press release (MGK bildirisi) dated 30th October 2014. In the National Security Policy Document, it was included in *"illegal structures with a legal appearance"* (*legal görünümlü illegal yapılar*), and was called a *"Parallel Government Structure,"* and described as *"an illegal hierarchical structure with a legal appearance."* As a result of these decisions, the General Command of Gendarmerie included the FETÖ/PDY in the list of terrorist organizations, on 8th of January, 2016 with the approval of the command level.

They filed a lawsuit against seventy-three administers of the organization, including Fetullah Gülen, as the person who established and led the FETÖ/PDY, with the following accusations: establishing and leading a terrorist organization, attempting to remove the Government of the Turkish Republic or to eliminate its functionality, engaging in political and military spying, illegally taking over properties, aggravated fraud, forgery of official documents, laundering properties that were obtained by criminal activities, recording personal data by illegal means and handing over these data to a third person. Additionally, in the justification of the Ergenekon lawsuit that was decided in Erzincan, on 16th of June 2016, it was stated that the FETÖ/PDY must be treated "*as an armed terrorist organization*," and that the FETÖ/PDY is an armed terrorist organization legally certified by the decision of the Kırşehir High Criminal Court.

The strongest evidence indicating that the FETÖ/PDY is an armed terrorist organization is its bloody military coup attempt on the 15th of July 2016. It was the bloodiest and the most brutal of all the military coup attempts by armed forces throughout the history of the Turkish Republic. During this military coup attempt 249 of our citizens were cruelly killed, and 2193 of our citizens were injured and all became qualified to be entitled 'veterans.' Throughout the history of the Turkish Republic, it was the first time that fighter aircrafts, attack helicopters and thanks fired at civilian people; and the Veteran National Assembly was attacked for the first time.

As examples of crimes committed by the FETÖ/PDY before the 15th of July military coup attempt, one may cite murders of Hrant Dink and Haydar Meriç, two journalists. Indeed, the fact that this organization continued its efforts to place it people as staff in the Turkish Armed Forces and the General Directorate of Security Affairs indicates how the organization was interested in arms and armed action.

The FETÖ/PDY's affects may also be traced to the fact that Turkey's fight against terrorism lasted this long. It has been verified that the FETÖ/PDY, which was at first considered as an illegal organization with a legal appearance, then as an armed terrorist organization, had a multi-dimensional cooperation with terrorist organizations through its members in the public and private sectors as well as through foreign secret services.

Around the world, no terrorist organization moves on its own, but rather they carry out their activities with the support of powerful states. Experts on security and intelligence agencies stated that the support behind the FETÖ/PDY comes from the United States of America and Israel. Among the evidence that indicates such a connection are the following facts: Fetullah Gülen has not been extradited to Turkey by the USA, despite all the insistence of Turkey. Members of the FETÖ/PDY greatly love Israel, and they defend Israel every time, despite all the tragedies suffered in the land of Palestine. Even when the event of Mavi Marmara ship happened, they supported Israel not the Turkish side, and described the event as a *"rebellion against legal authority."* They referred to Israel as the *"friendly land in the south,"* and they applauded Israeli politicians on many occasions. Additionally, the fact that Germany turned out to be a kind of shelter for the members of the FETÖ/PDY indicates that this country also strongly supports it.

Terrorist organizations collaborate or make terrorist attacks with other terrorist organizations when it is in their interest or according to the instructions of the states behind them. In the same vein, the FETÖ/PDY collaborated with PKK, ISIS and DHKP-C on many occasions. It provided them with intelligence data; it misled the operations against these organizations and thus prevented conclusive attacks. It revealed the identity of the MİT agents who infiltrated into these organizations and had those agents killed. It supplied them with logistical means, and supported them on the media with their propaganda. It manipulated the perception of people by creating an impression that higher ranking bureaucrats and commanders worked in collaboration with the so-called political wing of the terrorist organizations. Its members infiltrated into the masses that got together in open spaces for their democratic rights, and they provoked both the masses and the security forces. For example, when the 15th of July military coup attempt was being carried out, it was observed that some members of the FETÖ/PDY came to the civilian masses warned them saying *"soldiers are going to fire at you,"* and then went to those soldiers and encouraged them by saying *"fire, fire!"*[265]

The FETÖ/PDY acted according to the interests of foreign powers and carried out all kinds of manipulations and betrayals in order for the resolution process to fail. For example, in the event of Habur, on the one hand, they pushed families to go to Habur saying that *"your children are coming down from the mountains,"* and, on the other hand, they provoked the people who gathered in Harbur and caused the created an atmosphere of resentment.

When they dug ditches in certain cities in Western and Southwestern Anatolia regions, they placed explosives and stocked weapons and military supplies (*mühimmat*). There were two members of the FETÖ/PDY as Directors of Security in these regions. Atilla Uğur, a retired colonel stated the following regarding the relationship between FETÖ and PKK: *"If one and the same hand established you [both], then this hand has made you collaborate, or will make you. Both Abdullah Öcalan and Fetullah Gülen are simply accessories. They are simply puppets used by America and England. In his book, 'Imrah Notlan' (Notes from Imrah), published in Germany, ten months ago, Öcalan said: 'I am the one who can understand Fetullah Hoca best, because they are our strategic partner in the Middle East.' One day after the bloody rebellion, one of the administrators of the FETÖ* in Europe made a phone call to Kandil via satellite connection and said: 'please help us, carry out brutal demonstrations.' Upon this request, a person—as far as I could identify from the voice—probably Cemil Bayık responded and said: 'We are going to do what it takes. If there are friends of yours with difficult conditions, they can take refuge in one of our units in Europe'."[266] Moreover, it was Abdullah Öcalan who used the "parallel government structure" for the first time. He said, in 1999, "The authority that brought me here took Fetullah Gülen away."[267] Furthermore, it was discovered that the prosecutors and judges, who were removed from the profession, and were arrested after the 15th of July coup attempt because of their affiliation with the FETÖ/PDY, handled the lawsuits regarding KCK. Again policemen who were members of the FETÖ/PDY had important role in leaking information about the Oslo meetings.

Immediately after the general parliamentary election on the 7th of 2015, Turkey was in a period of uncertainty. Then KCK announced on the 11th of July that it ended the de-conflict period, and on the 14th of July Bese Hozat, a high ranking administers of KCK, announced that they started the war of the people in the Özgür Gündem newspaper. After that time, terrorist activities of PKK began to increase. It stopped its terrorist activities only immediately before the 15th of July military coup attempt.[268]

A communication between Fehmi Atalay the so-called responsible person (sorumlusu) of PKK/KCK for Media Defense Areas Headquarters (Medya Savunma Alanları Karargâhı) and Fatih Özden, the so-called responsible person for Cilo Region (Eyalet) took place on the 19th of July 2016. In this communication, it was stated that they sent a message to those who would like to leave the military, to surrender to the PKK organization with the guaranty that they would be taken to whatever region they would like to go; and that two armed people who attended the military coup attempt passed to the north of Iraq with their arms from the Hakkari-Uludere region.

On the other hand, by the efforts to uncover the activities of the terrorist organization ISIS in our country, they found the following line of connections: security forces arrested Muhammad Sulayman, an ISIS terrorist who was a Syrian citizen with the code name Abu Haydar. He was arrested in Şanlıurfa on the 8th of July 2016. When they searched through the apartment where he lived, they found many weapons and military supplies. During the preliminary interrogation, it was clarified that Muhammad Sulayman got information about explosives from someone who was known as Elvan Yüzbaşı, with the reference of Hüseyin İpek. Elvan Yüzbaşı was, in fact, İrfan Çetinkaya, a Gendarmerie Senior Master Sergeant, an officer at the Şanlıurfa Provincial Command of Gendarmerie, Directorate of Intelligence Agency Branch. After the military coup attempt on the 15th of July he was taken into custody on the 28th of July 2016 with the accusation of being involved with the FETÖ/PDY activities in Şanlıurfa. Later on, he was arrested and discarded from the army. Additionally, the intelligence agency obtained information that 12 military and 8 civilian and 30 security personnel, who participated in the FETÖ/PDY's military coup attempt, tried to go to regions under the control of ISIS, in Syria, with the help of the smugglers who had activities in that region from the Akçakoyunlu village, Oğuzeli district of Gaziantep, because they did not want to be detected by security forces in the country. If these runaway members of the organization were able to cross the border, a delegation from ISIS was waiting for them on the other side of the border.

THE MILITARY COUP ATTEMPT THAT WAS CARRIED OUT BY THE FETÖ/PDY ON THE 15TH OF JULY 2016

The Chronology of the Important Events Before the Coup Attempt

The FETÖ/PDY, which seems to have been established by the foreign powers, carried out a coup attempt against the Government of the Turkish Republic and the President, who was directly elected by the people, on the 15th of July 2016. There are important reasons why this exact date was chosen for this attempt. For example, in the Turkish Grand National Assembly, *The Law of Council of State* and *the Law about Modifications in Certain Laws*[269] were accepted on this date. By these laws, fundamental changes in judiciary system were introduced. The following are included among these changes: ending the office terms of the members of Court of Cassation and Council of State, allowing only presidents, vice presidents of these institutions, chief prosecutors and department administers to continue their work; decreasing the number of departments as well as the number of members in both Court of Cassation and Council of State; decreasing the number of departments in Court of Cassation from 46 to 24 and the number of members from 516 to 200; decreasing the number departments in Council of State from 17 to 10 and the number of members from 195 to 90.[270]

When these laws came into effect it was clear that the members of the FETÖ/PDY, who were placed in the higher judicial offices, were going to be eliminated. And this would have un-repairable consequences for the organization. If the 15th of July 2016 coup attempt had been successful, the FETÖ/PDY was not going to be affected, since its members would continue to be at their office. Thus, these laws were approved by the President on the 23rd of July 2016 after the military coup attempt was prevented, and it was published on the same day in the Official Gazette (Resmi Gazete).[271]

In the meeting of the National Security Council, on the 26th of May 2016, it was emphasized that the FETÖ/PDY *"was a terrorist organization threatening the national security."*[272] Furthermore, in the press there appeared news reports stating that during the Supreme Military Council (YAŞ), which was planning to meet between 01-04 August, members of the FETÖ/PDY who had infiltrated the Turkish Armed Forces were going to be eliminated (*tasfiye*).[273] It was going to be a powerful, quick and sharp strike at the FETÖ/PDY in order to eliminate its members from the army, which it had spent tens of years to accrue.

When the FETÖ/PDY decided on the timing of the coup attempt, it chose a critical date determined by taking many variables into account, such as fighting against terrorism, which was carried out by TSK and other state departments, security of the borders, foreign developments, festivals-holidays, appointment of new states officers and changing their work places, preparation for the YAŞ meeting, international and regional issues, sensitive and problematic foreign affairs, and the change of administration in the governing party and in some of the parties of the opposition. It might be said that the date of the coup attempt was finalized, when they understood that the members of the FETÖ/PDY were going to be eliminated from the military by the YAŞ meeting, and when some soldiers, including members of the FETÖ/PDY, became subject to investigations just a few weeks before the coup attempt.[274] In order to fully understand the meaning of the timing of the coup attempt, it will be useful to remember some of the events that happened during a few years before the coup attempt:[275]

29 January 2009: The Prime minister Recep Tayyip Erdoğan criticized Israeli policies [towards Palestine] in the Davos Summit in the session focusing on, "Gaza and the Peace in the Middle East," to which Shimon Peres, the President of Israel, Ban Ki Moon, the Secretary General of the United Nations, and Amr Musa, the Secretary General of the Arab League, attended in addition to Erdoğan. This session was identified with Erdoğan's saying, "one minute." This assertion of Erdoğan got wide spread positive reaction at both national and international levels. But some groups started an international campaign against Erdoğan. The FETÖ/PDY was disturbed by this assertion of Erdoğan and strengthened its ties with Israel.

31 May 2010: Israeli forces attacked the ship named Mavi Marmara that carried humanitarian aid to Palestine on international waters. Nine volunteers, peace loving people, travelling in the ship were killed by Israeli soldiers. Many people in the ship were injured. The leader of the FETÖ/PDY made announcements stating that Israel was justified in its activities.[276]

07 February 2012: Sadrettin Sarıkaya, Istanbul Specially Authorized Prosecutor, called Hakan Fidan, Undersecretary of MİT, to testify.

07 May 2013: Demonstrations, which were called "*Gezi Olayları*" (*Gezi Events*), began, when the construction equipment entered into Gezi Park, as part of the Taksim pedestrianization project. Eight people lost their lives in the events that occurred around the country, and one policeman was martyred. The demonstrations, which ended in July, caused considerable losses in the national economy. The FETÖ/PDY adopted an attitude supportive of these events.

03 July 2013: Nabi Avcı, then the Minister of National Education, announced that "*preparatory course centers would be closed down.*" In the middle of November, a lot of discussions about the outline of the Ministry of National Education in how to close the preparatory course centers took place. The Zaman Newspaper captioned , "Strong Blow against Education" (14 November, 2013) and "Such a Law Could not be Applied even during the Military Coup Period" (15 November, 2013).[277] Thus, the FETÖ/PDY started to maintain its campaign against the Government in a more offensive way.

17 December 2013: An operation by the decree of Celal Kara and Mehmet Yüzgeç, two public prosecutors takes place. Eighty-nine people were taken into custody; twenty-six people were arrested. This operation was coordinated by Zekeriya Öz, the Istanbul deputy public prosecutor. And people who were taken into custody were accused of "*bribery, abusing the official authority, collusive tendering and smuggling.*" It was understood that the true target of the operation was Prime Minister Recep Tayyip Erdoğan, his relatives and colleagues. This was how the FETÖ/PDY started the strongest attack against the Government and the President of the Republic.

25 December 2013: Public Prosecutor Muammer Akkaş carried out an investigation on 96 people. The accusations he raised against them included "*establishing an organi-*

zation to commit crimes, administering that organization and collusive tendering and bribery." The Prosecutor Akkaş prepared a list of people to be taken into custody, which included forty-one businessmen. He also had the court issue a decision to confiscate the properties of some businessmen. Akkaş also signed a document calling Bilal Erdoğan, son of Prime Minister Erdoğan, to testify, describing him as a suspect. However, the Istanbul Provincial Directorate of Security Affairs did not carry out the suspicious instructions of Prosecutor Akkaş. This operation was like the continuation of the operation that was carried out on the 17th of December. It was also carried out by the FETÖ/PDY but it was unsuccessful.

01 January 2014: A trailer truck and a passenger car belonging to the MİT were illegally stopped by officers working at Hatay Provincial Command of Gendarmerie in Kırıkhan (Hatay), by the instructions of public prosecutors, Yaşar Kavalcıoğlu and Özcan Şişman. They wanted to search the trailer truck. This attempt that was carried out by the FETÖ/PDY did not succeed.

19 January 2014: Three trailer trucks and a passenger car was illegally stopped by officers working at Hatay Provincial Command of Gendarmerie in Kırıkhan (Hatay), by the instructions of the public prosecutor Aziz Takçı. They were searched through and the information about this event was leaked to the media. In this operation, which was carried out by the FETÖ/PDY, the objective was to display Turkey "*as a country which supports terrorism,*" and put it in a difficult situation and under international pressure.

06 March 2014: The assize courts , which were established by the Anti-Terror Law, article 10,[278] were eliminated. Thus, the hegemony of the FETÖ/PDY in this area of jurisdiction was inflicted a heavy blow.

March 30, 2014: General elections for local administrations were held. The FETÖ/PDY decided to support the most powerful candidate in every election district against the candidate of AK Party where AK Party was powerful so that it would receive the least possible result in the elections. It also started the campaign to defame the government. In the elections, AK Party got 45.60% of the votes and had the highest number of votes. Thus, the efforts of the FETÖ/PDY failed to a great extent.

August 10, 2014: The Presidential election was held. Recep Tayyip Erdoğan was elected as the 12th President of the Turkish Republic in the first round, since he received 51.79% of the valid votes.[279] In this election, the FETÖ/PDY supported Ekmeleddin İhsanoğlu, who was presented by some oppositions parties as the "joint candidate."

October 06-07, 2014: After ISIS surrounded the Kobani (Ayn-al-Arab) district in Syria, HDP called people out to the street.[280] Due to these calls to the streets, some incidents took place in 35 cities. During these incidents 2 policemen were martyred and 31 citizens died, whereas 221 citizens and 136 policemen were injured, 1113 buildings were damaged and 1177 motorcycles were rendered unusable.[281] The FETÖ/PDY displayed a confrontational attitude upon these incidents and vehemently made efforts to damage the public order.

October 12, 2014: An election for the membership to the Higher Council of Judges and Prosecutors was held. The candidates who were supported by the FETÖ/PDY were able to get only two seats out of ten.

December 14, 2014: By an investigation pursued by Hasan Yılmaz, one of the prosecutors in the Office of Istanbul Chief

Public Prosecutor, Department of Terror and Organized Crimes, a number of people were taken into custody such as Ekrem Dumanlı, Editor in Chief of Zaman Newspaper, Hidayet Karaca, Chief of the Samanyolu Broadcasting Group, and Tufan Ergüder, a former chief of the Istanbul Branch of Fighting against Terror. Hidayet Karaca and Tufan Ergüder were both arrested, whereas Ekrem Dumanlı was released by the court pending a trial.

June 07, 2015: General parliamentary election for the 25th period was held. According to the official results announced by the Supreme Electoral Council, Adalet ve Kalkınma Partisi (Justice and Development Party) got 258 seats, Cumhuriyet Halk Partisi (Republican People's Party) got 132 seats, Milliyetçi Hareket Partisi (Nationalist Movement Party) got 80 seats, and Halkların Demokratik Partisi (Peoples' Democratic Party) also got 80 seats in the parliament. The FETÖ/PDY decided to support the most powerful party to oppose the AK Party in the regions where AK Party was more powerful than others. Furthermore, some of the members of the organization were participating in the election as independent candidates. But none of them were elected.

July 13, 2015: The Constitutional Court cancelled, by a majority of votes, the relevant articles of the law that required that private preparatory course centers should be closed down.

August 10, 2015: Zekeriya Öz and Celal Kara, two members of the FETÖ/PDY fled to Georgia through the Sarp border gate in Artvin.

August 24, 2015: President of the Republic, Recep Tayyip Erdoğan's decision to renew the election of the Turkish Grand National Assembly was published in the Official Gazette.

October 26, 2015: A trustee was appointed for the Koza İpek Group.

November 01, 2015: The general parliamentary election for the 26th period was held. The FETÖ/PDY decided to support the most powerful party as opposed to AK Party in regions of election where AK Party was more powerful than others. However, AK Party got 317 seats in the parliament, and 49.50% of the votes. Cumhuriyet Halk Partisi got 134 seat (25.32% of the votes), Halkların Demokratik Partisi got 59 seat (10.76% of the votes) and Milliyetçi Hareket Partisi got 40 seat (11.90% of the votes).[282]

November 24, 2015: A Russian Su-24 model fighter aircraft was shot down by the Turkish Air Force, on the grounds that it had violated the borders of Turkey at the Turkish-Syrian border. Still, suspicions emerged whether this incident was carried out by the FETÖ/PDY to sever the Turkish-Russian relations.

March 04, 2016: A trustee was appointed to the Zaman Newspaper.

The Chronology of the Coup Attempt

It is perhaps suitable to take the tip-off communicated to the MİT before the coup attempt as the starting point to relate the chronology of events in the process of defeating the military coup attempt that was carried out by the FETÖ/PDY on Friday, the 15th of July 2016. This is because this tip-off was one of the most important elements that helped defeat the military coup attempt. This tip-off included the claim that there would be an attempt to assassinate the Undersecretary of the MİT. This event was like a warning sign indicating that some major illegal developments within the nation state were emerging, given the fact that a group of soldiers belonging to the Armed Forces attempted to assassinate the Undersecretary of the MİT/ This to take place in a bureaucratic environment where state institutions were supposed to work in harmony in a country like Turkey, which had a tradition of state management going back thousands of years. Upon this tip-off, the Commander of the Turkish Armed Forces met the Undersecretary of the MİT to examine the probability of the tip-off and he also sent an ordinance to the force commands and inspectors to certain military units. These safety measures were adequate to make the coup attempters fall into a state of panic. The coup attempters were organized under the name 'Council of Peace in the Country'. Certain events that took place during the coup attempt has brought to light, that, in fact, they planned to start the military coup at 03:00 a.m., on Saturday, the 16th of July, 2016. However, due to the initiative of the Commander of the Turkish Armed Forces, they got into panic and decided to start the military coup 6 hours before the planned time. Thus, they started it at 20: 30 p.m. on the Friday 15th of July 2016.[283]

When a mobilization started in the military at that time, at first, many people could not make sense of what was going on. Especially citizens who lived in Ankara could not make sense of why certain military aircrafts flew at such a low altitude. In Istanbul, when people saw that the bridges on the Bosporus was blocked, they thought it was a terrorist attack. Many people thought that a foreign country had attacked Turkey. Only a small number of people considered the possibility that it could be a military coup. The incidents that took place during the following hours revealed that the Turkish Republic was confronting one of the most brutal coup attempts in its history.

The coup attempt that was initiated by the FETÖ/PDY was eliminated before long due to the tenacity and determination of, first and foremost, the President of the Republic, followed by all other administrators of the state offices, the mobilization of the Turkish people to be willing to protect the democratic constitutional system, the resistance of the security officers, and by the fact that majority of the members of the TSK resisted the coup attempters. The coup attempt was put under control all around the country approximately within sixteen hours. The chronology of events that took place from the beginning of the coup attempt on Friday, the 15th of July 2016, until Saturday, the 16th of July 2016 when the coup attempt was totally put down may be summarized as follows below.[284]

The Events and Developments of Friday, July 15, 2016

Although the coup attempt started in the evening, the first bits of tip-off information were received around the noon time. And the events thereafter changed the whole course and the final stage of the coup attempt.

14:45: A pilot with the rank of corporal who was an attendant at the Army Aviation School Command came to MİT and gave the tip-off saying that "*at 03:00 a.m. three helicopters are going to attack the house of the MİT Undersecretary, and they are going to kidnap him.*"

15:05: They interrogated the pilot squadron leader, who had a position at the Army Aviation School Command.

16:03: Deputy Undersecretary of MİT went to the Office of the Commander of the Turkish Armed Forces to discuss the obtained information.

16:30: The Undersecretary of MİT went to the Office of the Commander of the Turkish Armed Forces and provided the Deputy Commander of the Turkish Armed Forces with detailed information about the tip-off.

18:00: The Commander of the Turkish Armed Forces, Four-star General Hulusi Akar, the Land Forces Commander, Four-star General Salih Zeki Çolak, the MİT Undersecretary Hakan Fidan and the Deputy Commander of the Turkish Armed Forces, Four-star General Yaşar Güler attended a meeting at the headquarters of the Turkish Armed Forces Command. They discussed the measures that must be implemented.

18:30: The office of the Commander of the Turkish Armed Forces sent an order to all units commanding *"the airspace all around the country is closed down for all flights, no military aircraft should be allowed to take off and no military vehicle should be allowed to leave the military quarters."*

19:06: The order of General Staff Operation Centre (*Genelkurmay Harekat Merkezi*) stating that *"All flights operated by the Armed Forces should be cancelled and aircrafts that are flying should land immediately"* was delivered by the Air Operations Centre in Ankara to the Air Forces Commander.

19:20: Air Operations Centre in Eskişehir delivered the precept of the General Staff Operation Centre to all units.

20:22: The MİT Undersecretary left the Office of the Commander of the Turkish Armed Forces.

21:00: The Commander of the Turkish Armed Forces, the Four-star general Hulusi Akar and the Deputy Commander of the Turkish Armed Forces, the Four-star General Yaşar Güler were taken hostage by the coup attempters.

21:05: Following the order of the Office the Commander of the Turkish Armed Forces, 36 aircrafts belonging to the Turkish Armed Forces landed.

21:15: The Commander of the Land Forces, the Four-star General, Salih Zeki Çolak and the Executive Officer of the Land Forces, Four-star General, İhsan Uyar, both of whom were invited in a underhand way to the Office of the Commander of the Turkish Armed Forces, were taken hostage.

21:30: The Coup attempters released certain self-styled orders, "*identify people in charge of headquarters*" and "*warning for preparation and transferring units*."

21: 30: The main building of the headquarters of the General Command of Gendarmerie was seized by 85 coup attempting soldiers.

21:30: When the noise of gunshots coming from the General Staff Headquarters was heard, security officers called the General Staff Headquarters and informed them that, "*there were military exercises going on.*" Then Ankara Provincial Security Director Mahmut Karaaslan called Ankara Provost Marshal and asked if there were any military exercises going on. The Provost Marshal stated that "*There is no military exercise; I have no knowledge about that.*"

21:30: A deputy director, who was in charge, of Istanbul Provincial Directorate of Security, called Istanbul Provincial Security Director, Mustafa Çalışkan, and stated that "*some military authority called them and stated that they had declared martial law (sıkıyönetim ilan etmek), and asked them to submit to and to cooperate with them.*"

21:35: The vehicle that was driven towards the Beylerbeyi district carried certain people of protocol; it was stopped by the coup attempters. They broke its glasses and slapped the officers. The event was reported by the Chief of the Prime Ministry Center for Protection () to the Prime Minister Binali Yıldırım.

21:35: The personnel guarding personnel who worked at the Prime Ministry's building in Kızılay area reported that noise of gunshot was heard from the General Staff Headquarters. Then authorized personnel working at the General Administration of Security Affairs called the authorized personnel working at the Armed Forces Centre for Command Control and Operations. The answer they got was that "tactical *immediate intervention squads were carrying out military exercises.*"

21:45: Prime Minister Binali Yıldırım, who went from his work office located at Istanbul, Dolmabahçe, to his house located at Istanbul, Tuzla district, started to closely track the events unfolding.

21:45: When some aircrafts flew at a low level over Ankara, authorized personnel working at the General Administration of Security Affairs called the authorized personnel working at the Armed Forces Centre for Command Control and Operations. They responded by saying that "*they did not know why F-16 aircrafts were flying so low. Since the Operations Centre was underground, they did not hear the noise of the aircrafts.*"

21:45: The connection to the General Commander of Gendarmerie was lost. Galip Mendi, the General Commander of Gendarmerie, was deceived by Mustafa Yılmaz, the infantry lieutenant colonel, an adjutant, who told him, Mustafa Yılmaz said to Galip Mendi, "*My Commander is waiting for you in the General Staff Headquarters, Office of the Deputy, together with the Commander of the Turkish Armed Forces,*" and escorted him to the car where he abducted him by force. Galip Mendi was taken to the 4th Main Jet Base Command (*4. Ana Jet Üs Komutanlığı*) in Ankara, Akıncı district. He was taken into custody there, together with the Training and Doctrine Commander of Land Forces, Four-star General Kâmil Başoğlu, who was kidnapped from his home.

22:00: They fired on people from a military helicopter. The coup plotting soldiers took over the General Staff Headquarters and TRT Head Office.

22:00: The Bosporus and Fatih Sultan Mehmet Bridges were closed to traffic on a one-way by the coup plotting soldiers.

Photo 1: The Bosporus Bridge under the invasion and attack of the coup plotters[285] and the patriots who resisted against the coup attempt[286]

22:00: The MHP leader Devlet Bahçeli called Binali Yıldırım and said "MHP will never approve of the coup. We fully support the government and democracy."[287]

22:00: At the Çankaya Office of the Prime Ministry, a committee of coordination were formed and relevant personnel were called to the Office of the Prime Minister immediately.

22:03: The MİT Undersecretary Hakan Fidan communicated with the Administer of the Office Guarding the President of the Republic and asked if they had any preparation for a possible attack.

22:05: Commander of Ankara Garrison, Metin Gürak was taken hostage in the General Staff Headquarters.

22:05: The so-called *"Instructions of Martial Law"* issued by the Office of the General Staff was declared by coup plotters.

22:15: A crisis management center was formed in the General Directorate of Security Affairs, which was coordinated by the General Director of Security Affairs, Ankara Governor and Ankara Provincial Security Director. After the meeting held by them, they sent instructions to be implemented to the governors of all provinces. Instructions to be followed included the following issues:

> The Presidential Complex, the Turkish Grand National Assembly, the Prime Ministry, the Office of the General Staff, the Ministry of Internal Affairs, the MİT, the TRT, the buildings of the Security Directorates and other strategically important buildings will be surrounded, nobody will be allowed to enter these buildings.

> The officers may fire their weapons if they feel that they have to.

> All personal employed by the General Directorate of Security Affairs, including those who were on sick leave, must attend to their office immediately.

> All armories all around Turkey should be opened, and long barreled weapons should be given to the police officers and they should resist by using these weapons.

The commanders of gendarmerie and other military units in provinces will be contacted and it will be explained to them with foregone conclusion that if the armed forces leave their military barracks for the streets, all police officers will respond with their weapons. Moreover, if they support the coup attempt, they will be held responsible for the possible terrible consequences.

All police officers around Turkey will be called to attend their office, even if they are on leave or on sick leave.

No police officer shall surrender to coup attempters, and shall not under any circumstance hand over their weapons to them.

In order to prevent tanks reaching the squares in the cities, major roads shall be blocked by parking wreckers, first and foremost, and other larger vehicles. They must, as much as possible, be prevented from approaching the city centers.

If some officers submit to the coup attempt, they must immediately be taken into custody.

22:20: The 8th Main Jet Base Command, in Diyarbakır, declared that it will not observe the ban of flight ordered by the General Staff.

22:22: Ankara Provincial Commander of Gendarmerie, Ferdi Korkmaz was seized (*esir alındı*) by the coup attempters.

22:25: The Air Force Commander, Abidin Ünal ordered the commanders in Akıncı, who was in charge at the 4th Main Jet Base Command, that they should stop flights going above Ankara. However, the commander of the base refused to obey this order.

22:31: At the main gate of the Beştepe Headquarters of the General Command of Gendarmerie, the police forces for special operations together with the Gendarmerie teams for special operations fell into direct combat with the coup plotters.

22:38: The coup plotters started air strikes on the campus of the MİT at Yenimahalle. Airstrikes continued until 06: 30 in the morning.

22:40: A tactical command place (TKY) was established near the Hisarcıklıoğlu Mosque which was located nearby the Beştepe Headquarter of the General Command of Gendarmerie.

22:45: In the Presidency of Religious Affairs, they formed an emergency crisis management commission.

22:56: All officers in the governors' offices and in Provincial Directorates of Security were alerted against what was going on. The Ankara Provincial Governor was instructed to increase security safety measures around the strategically important buildings, especially TBMM, the Presidential Complex, the Çankaya Office of the Prime Ministry and its Kızılay building, and the TRT building. The Ankara Provincial Governor was instructed to stop the internet connection, electricity, water supply and telephone services to the buildings of the General Staff, Force Commands and military bases. Furthermore, the General Command of Gendarmerie was prevented from having access to HTS registry.[288]

23:00: All on leave permissions were cancelled in the General Directorate of Security Affairs. All personnel were asked to assume their duty in their office immediately and they were instructed to *"open up armories all around Turkey, and to give long barreled weapons to the police officers, so that they should start resisting against the coup plotters."*

23:00: The Bursa Provincial Regiment Commander, Yurakul Akkuş, who was a FETÖ/PDY member, was taken into custody by Bursa Regional Commander of Gendarmerie. Yurdakul Akkuş had the coup plan, which included the so-called martial law commanders of 81 provinces. All offices of governors and provincial security directorates were informed about these people and they began to take these people into custody.

23:00: When it was discovered that the Air Operations Centre in Ankara was under the control of coup plotters, they declared that the orders on behalf of the Air Force Commander were going to be released not from Ankara bases, but from the Air Operations Centre in Eskişehir.

23:03: Anadolu Agency reported that *"a small group made a coup attempt in the General Staff."*

23:05: Prime Minister Binali Yıldırım was broadcasted live on a television channel[289]. He stated that "there is a *brutal rebellion attempt in process, this attempt will not be allowed to succeed, those who are engaged in his attempt shall pay severely for it."*[290]

23:08: The General Directorate of Security Affairs, and the Presidency of Aviation Department, which was located in Gölbaşı, was bombed by the coup plotters. Seven officers were martyred.

23:14: The General Director of Security Affairs, Celalettin Lekesiz got into contact with the Mayor of Ankara Metropolitan Municipality. They decided to block the main roads with construction equipment and trucks, so that they could prevent the military vehicles from entering the city.

23:30: The Secretary General of the Presidency of the Republic, Fahri Kasırga was captured by the coup plotting soldiers who were registered in the Regiment of Presidential Guard (*Cumhurbaşkanlığı Muhafız Alayı*).

23:35: The CHP Chairman Kemal Kılıçdaroğlu declared that *"this country suffered a lot from coups. We do not want the go* *through similar difficulties. We will protect the Republic and our democracy."*[291]

23:42: The Office of Istanbul Chief Public Prosecutor started an investigation about the coup attempt.

23:43: The coup plotters fired directly at people in Taksim Square.

Photo 2: Patriots resisting soldiers who attempted the coup d'état at the Taksim Square[292]

23:45: The First Army Commander, The Aegean Army Commander and the Third Army Commander broadcasted on live television that they are against the coup.

23:50: Prime Minister Yıldırım began his journey from his house in Istanbul, Tuzla, to Ankara using the land route.

23:50: Some of the provincial headquarters of AK Party were attacked by the coup plotters.

The Events and Developments that Happened on Saturday, the 16ᵗʰ of July 2016

By the first minutes of Saturday, the 16ᵗʰ of July it became quite clear that the coup attempt was carried out by the Fetullahist Terrorist Organization (FETÖ/PDY).

00:00: Representatives of security departments declared that *"A group of junior officers who are members of the Fetullahist Terrorist Organization/Parallel Government Structure, tried to carry out a military rebellion."*

00:03: The coup plotters made an air strike at the General Directorate of Security Affairs, the Turkish Police Special Operations Department, which is located in Gölbaşı. 44 personnel, 38 of which were members of the special operations department, died at that air strike.

Photo 3: Turkish Police Special Operations Department bombed by the coup plotters.²⁹³

00:10: The coup plotters seized the Commander of the Air forces, the Four-star general Abidin Ünal and other Four-star Generals who were together with him, in Istanbul, Moda.

00:13: The coup plotters, who occupied TRT, had the declaration of the coup read live on television.

00:13: By the instruction of the Presidency of Religious Affairs, Imams began to recite the *Sala* [a call consisting of religious praises and prayers recited from the mosques on special occasions, such as religiously important days or nights and before funeral ceremonies] from mosques in all provinces.

00:18: The Prime Ministry Coordination Center released information to the international press for the first time.

00:20: TÜRKSAT, the Satellite Communications and Cable Television Operations Company stopped TRT's broadcast.

00:28: The President of the Republic, Erdoğan contacted a television channel[294] who live broadcasted the following statement where he asked people to gather at city squares and airports: *"This evening, a group within the Armed Forces and affiliated with the known structure (malum yapı) started a rebellious movement against the unity, solidarity and integrity of the country. I, as the President of the Republic of my country, would like to undoubtedly say this. I would like to invite all members of the party, of which I am the founder, and all the people who make up the national will to come out at the squares of cities. And I would like to say that we are going to be together with our people, hand in hand, at the squares, and we are going to teach an appropriate lesson to those who carried out this rebellion. Turkey is not a country to be knocked down. It is not a country to be governed from Pennsylvania."[295]*

Photo 4: The President of the Republic, Erdoğan, calls people to resist the coup plotters.[296]

The story of a brutal betrayal: whoever called you out to the streets, let him take care of your treatment.

We live in Gölbaşı. When the Special Operations (the General Directorate of Security Affairs, the Turkish Police Special Operations Department) was bombed, my husband and I thought that we must go out (to the squares). We thought that *we are more than 60 years old, let us be sacrificed for this homeland.* So we said goodbye to our daughter, we performed our minor ablution and we went out. In fact, we did not know what to do, where to go. Then we went towards the Eskişehir road. We were quick. Then we saw a group of people in front of the General Command of Gendarmerie. They put on their waistcoats and began targeting, with guns and pistols at hands, at a helicopter. There was a tank further ahead. I said to the soldier on the tank, with an endearing tone: *"O my son, you are like our kid, I am like your aunty, like your mom. Don't do this, please come down, don't commit a crime."* Then immediately from the right side, somebody said: *"Hey soldier! Shoot these dishonest people, follow my command to shoot, shoot these dishonest people."* Then we were cross fired by them and also by the helicopter from above. I do not remember, how I fell down. I regained consciousness on the ground. I could not move at all. I was shot at my arm. My arm was quite painful, I felt terrible pain. My husband was with me. He called the 112, medical emergency line, and 155 police emergency line. Nobody answered. Then he called friends to come and help us. Then there appeared two people whom we did not know. They helped us get in a van. I suppose we were 12 injured people. They took us to the Turgut Özal University Hospital,[297] which was located nearby. However, the personnel at the hospital did not accept us and reacted saying: "*Whoever called you out to the streets, let him take care of your treatment.*"

Note: this is a summary of the statement of Mine Özer, a veteran of the 15th of July, given to the Commission.

00:30: By the instruction of the Minister of Energy and Natural Resources, Berat Albayrak and the Minister of Internal Affairs, Efkan Âlâ, Governor of Ankara Mehmet Kılıçlar called the district governor of Gölbaşı and asked him to take as many people as possible police officers and gendarmeries, and to go to TÜRKSAT, to get that place under control so that television broadcasting would continue without interruption.

00:35: Küçükçekmece Chief Public Prosecutor, Ali Doğan declared that "*he had started an investigation about the coup plotting soldiers and they should be taken in custody wherever they are found.*"

00:40: Coup plotter made an airstrike on the region where the Presidential Complex is located.

00:48: The patriots started resisting the coup attempt by climbing up on the tanks in Vatan Street in Istanbul and in front of the General Staff building in Ankara.

00:51: The First Army Commander, and the Four-star General, Ümit Dündar, contacted a private television channel and broadcasted live the following statement: "*This movement is a* *movement carried out by a small group, it is not supported by the TSK. Together with the respectable governor and security units, we are implementing required safeguards. There is nothing to worry about."[298]*

00:57: The Minister of Justice, Bekir Bozdağ declared that *"There is not a government who shall take its fedora and flee away. First they will have to tread over our dead bodies. To eradicate our democracy, they will have to execute us by shooting, every one of us, one after the other. The government is fully efficient with all its units. We are going to do everything that can be done within legal boundaries against these people. We are going to take all safety measures."[299]*

01:00: The Air Operations Centre, in Ankara, was made inactive.

01:01: The coup plotters started an attack strike from the air and from the land to seize the Ankara Provincial Directorate of Security. They killed and martyred 5 police officers and injured 133 other police personnel. Both civilian citizens and police officers resisted against this attack, and they prevented the Ankara Provincial Directorate of Security from being seized by the coup plotters.

Photo 5: The Ankara Provincial Directorate of Security under air strike from soldiers acting on behalf of coup plotters[300]

01: 10: The coup plotters made an airstrike on the Gölbaşı facilities of the TÜRKSAT. During the airstrike, two officers were martyred and two officers were injured.

Photo 6: The coup plotters attack the TURKSAT (Satellite Communications and Cable Television Operations Company).[301]

01:05: The President of the Republic, Recep Tayyip Erdoğan took a helicopter from Marmaris to go to Dalaman Airport.

You are witnessing a special historical moment

In the evening when the coup attempt took place a military rebellion was mentioned. I went to the villa where the President of the Republic resides. I went there to reinforce my support and to ask if he required anything. When he saw me, he invited me in. He said, *"Come in and sit by the table."* Then he said, *"Look, you are witnessing an important historical moment."* At that time, Mr. Hasan, Mr. Muhsin and Mr. Berat kept bringing telephone machines. He spoke on the phone, one after the other. Then he made a press release to the invited press agents. However, this press release was not publicized. Then they brought a new report that TRT had been occupied by the coup plotters. I remember how the President of the Republic strived at that juncture, and it was at that time that they also established connections to television channels either via internet or via FaceTime. There is a detail at this juncture of the story that I would like to particularly relate with emphasis. I saw and heard two police officers on duty saying goodbye to each other with a hug and speaking together they said, *"They are coming here, we will be martyred but we will not submit, our President of the Republic."* Then Mr. President of the Republic turned towards me and asked, *"Serkan, where can we go by boat?"* I had already thought about that; where we could go and where we could not. So I said to him *"Sir, we can go to Dalaman."* He asked, *"How long does it take?"* I said, *"Approximately forty-five minutes."* Then I said, *"We will pass by the Aksaz base."* He then asked, *"Where else can we go?"* I answered, *"Sir, there are islands around, but no other place."* Then he said to me, *"What shall we do with islands, Serkan? I am asking how I can go to Istanbul."* Finally, he decided to go by helicopter. Indeed, there was no other way. There was no place to go by a boat or a car. So he said, *"O my son, whatever shall happen, shall happen. Either this work becomes good for Turkey; otherwise, I have already put on my kefen (shroud)."* Afterwards, the helicopter departed from the runway towards the Dalaman Airport without the lights turned on intentionally due to security concerns.

Note: This is a summary of the statement given by Serkan Yazıcı, who is the owner of the hotel where the President of the Republic, Recep Tayyip Erdoğan, stayed during his vacation in Marmaris.[302]

01:28: The Commander of the Turkish Naval Forces (*Deniz Kuvvetleri*), the Four-star Admiral Bülent Bostanoğlu stated, *"As the command level (komuta kademesi), we do not assent to this coup attempt at all."*

01:30: The President of the Republic Recep Tayyip Erdoğan arrived at Dalaman Airport by helicopter.

01:39: Members of the Turkish Grand National Assembly affiliated with four political parties began gathering in the Turkish Grand National Assembly upon the request of the TBMM speaker.

01:40: Citizens and members of the security department prevented the coup plotters, who came arrived with a tank to gate number 5 of the Prime Ministry Çankaya Office, from entering the office.

01:43: The TC-ATA airplane, which carried the President of the Republic, Recep Tayyip Erdoğan, departed from Dalaman Airport. The airplane used a passenger airplane code (THY 8456) with dimmed lights as a defense mechanism so it could be kept undetected from the fighter jets that were under the control of the coup plotters.

01:45: The coup plotters carried out an air strike on the MİT Headquarters located in the Beşiktaş area.

01:45: The HDP co-leader Selahattin Demirtaş stated, *"We support the democratic politics."*[303]

01:50: The Ministry of Foreign Affairs sent a memorandum about the coup attempt to the foreign delegations, and requested that they do not take any proclamation as official state announcement or facts as long as they do not come from the Ministry of Foreign Affairs.

01:52: Prime Minister Yıldırım made the following announcement: *"Those who shoot and employ bullets and bombs on the institutions with the jets above are identical to the members of this terrorist organization. Such an activity can never have been carried out by a junior officer or a soldier who loyally serves the* *glorious flag of the Armed Forces. Such an activity is a terrible offense to our soldiers whom our Republic and nation are so grateful towards since they have been fighting a bitter struggle in the Southeastern region. Today is the day to support (sahip çıkma) democracy, the country and the nation. I would like to thank my nation. Turkey is standing up, Turkey is on the streets. These plunderers will not be given the opportunity to do what they want.*[304]

01:54: On the Vatan Street, in Istanbul, the police units took into custody a colonel and three soldiers.

01:54: Sixty-one coup plotting soldiers who wanted to occupy the Riot Police Branch Administration in Istanbul Bayrampaşa were neutralized by the police force.

01:55: The Minister of Labor and Social Security, Süleyman Soylu, made the following statement: "*We are in the TBMM right now. Nobody should worry. The government is functioning appropriately. The TBMM is functioning by the book. Our President of the Republic and the Prime Minister are carrying out their duties.*"[305]

02:00: The Ankara Provincial Command of Gendarmerie was liberated from the coup plotters and they sent a message of command to all units of gendarmerie stating that they must not pay attention to the messages sent by the coup plotters.

02:05: The coup plotting soldiers, who were members of the FETÖ/PDY, began in larger numbers to be neutralized, arrested and taken into custody.

02:16: The Coup plotting Brigadier General Semih Terzi, who tried to take over the Command of the Special Forces that is connected to the General Staff, was killed by Ömer Halisdemir, the adjutant of the Commander of the Special Forces, Major General Zekai Aksakallı. However, in the ensuing battle Ömer Halisdemir was shot and martyred by the coup plotting soldiers.

02:26: Thirteen soldiers—three of whom had specific ranks—attempted to enter the Presidential Complex forcefully and were captured.

02:30: The coup plotting soldiers who tried to seize the General Directorate of Security Affairs by the air operations were driven away.

02:30: When the Police Units for Special Operations were informed that the President of the Republic, Recep Tayyip Erdoğan, was on his way to Istanbul, they liberated the tower of Atatürk Airport.

03:00: The TRT Head Office was liberated from the coup plotters by an intervention coordinated by Süleyman Soylu, the Minister of Labor and Social Security. TRT commences its regular course of broadcasting.

02:37: Prime Minister Yıldırım made the following statement: *"I would like to convey my deepest gratitude to our citizens, and express my sincere thanks to our political parties. Everybody joined together under democracy, the unity of the people and the survival of the nation."*[306]

02:38: The coup plotters carried out an air strike at the crowd that got together in the square between the General Staff Office and the Turkish Grand National Assembly.

02:42 - 02:50: The coup plotters made three further air strikes three times at the Turkish Grand National Assembly. During these strikes approximately 100 members of the National Assembly were present. Some parts of the Assembly building were heavily damaged. Still, İsmail Kahraman, the speaker of the Assembly, and the other members of the parliament continued their work in its bunker.

Photo 7: The Turkish Grand National Assembly is attacked for the first time in its history.[307]

02:43 - 02:55: Prime Minister Yıldırım made the following statement: *"All commanders of our army are on active duty. Commanders belonging to the lower level command are also on active duty. Our nation asserted itself in order to to eliminate this tribulation. We are on active duty as well. God willing, we are going to eliminate this tribulation. Let our nation be unperturbed. Those who shot and employed bullets and bombs on the institutions with the fighter jets above are identical to the members of this terrorist organization; it is as if they are their extension. Such an activity can never have been carried out by a junior officer or a soldier who loyally serves the glorious flag of the Armed Forces."*[308]

03:00: The Türk Telekom building located in Ankara, Ulus district, was liberated from the coup plotters. In this operation twenty-nine coup plotting soldiers were arrested and taken into custody.

03:10: With the intention of seizing the hotel where the President of the Republic, Erdoğan, was staying, a group of thirty-four coup plotters that included SAT[309] and SAS,[310] landed from air at Marmaris. During the fight in the hotel, two police officers were martyred and eight of them were injured.

03:20: The TC-ATA Airplane which carried the President of the Republic, Erdoğan, landed at Istanbul Atatürk Airport.

04:00: The Office of Ankara Chief Public Prosecutor issued a decision to take into custody the judiciary officers who were connected to the FETÖ/PDY that attempted to carry out a coup and the soldiers who were members of the *Yurtta Sulh Konseyi* (The Council of Peace in the Homeland).

04:17: The President of the Republic, Erdoğan, made a statement at Atatürk Airport saying, "*There is no power above the nation. This is a movement of upheaval, a betrayal, a betrayal to the homeland. They will pay heavily for it.*"[311]

04:40: Prime Minister Yıldırım gave the following instruction to the Air Defense Commander: all the aircrafts that were used in the coup plot must be compelled to land, and those that do not land must be shot down (*düşürmek*). He instructed the Deputy Commander of Combatant Air Force and the Commander of Combined Air Operations Centers to shoot down all the aircrafts that left the Akıncı Base. Furthermore, he instructed the Commander of the 4th Main Jet Base to bomb the Akıncı Base.

04:53: The fighter jets began taking off from the air bases in order to force the landing of aircrafts controlled by the coup plotters.

06:00: The Office of Gölbaşı Chief Public Prosecutor opened an investigation on the coup attempt.

06:18: From the coup plotters fighter jets two bombs were dropped at the bridge crossing nearby the Headquarters of the General Command of Gendarmerie and at the side of the Millet Mosque within the area of the Presidential Complex. Many citizens lost their life through this air strike.

Photo 8: Coup plotters bomb the intersection in front of the Presidential Palace turning many of the patriotic citizens into martyrs.[312]

06:30: All the roads leading to the Çankaya Mansion, which was cordoned off, and to the Official Residence of Prime Ministry were blocked by the security forces.

06:30: The military helicopter that was used by the coup plotters to bomb TÜRKSAT was shot down in Gölbaşı.

06:34: The road between the Air Force Command and the General Staff headquarters was blocked in both ways by the earthmoving trucks, which belonged to the Ankara Metropolitan Municipality.

06:40: During the battles that took place throughout the night at Bosporus Bridge, 34 citizens were martyred, two of which were police officers, and 165 people were injured. After the unyielding resistance of the people and the security forces, the coup plotters, approximately 50 soldiers, began surrendering at the Bosporus Bridge.

06:46: The President of the Republic Erdoğan stated, "*I also address Pennsylvania. Your betrayal toward this state and to this nation has gone far enough. If you think you have enough courage come back to your homeland. You will not be able to cause any further disorder in this country from there.*"[313]

06:52: Prime Minister Yıldırım declared that the First Army Commander, Four-star General, Ümit Dündar was appointed as the Commander of the Turkish Armed Forces.

07:10: 336 people who were members of the FETÖ/PDY were taken into custody.

07:28: The Third Army Operations Executive Officer Brigadier General Ekrem Çağlar was taken into custody in Erzincan.

07:33: The coup plotters who wanted to enter Sabiha Gökçen Airport with tanks were neutralized, and their tanks were commandeered.

07:40: The Gendarmerie and the security forces carried out an operation on the Army Aviation School located in Ankara, İncirlik. The coup plotters fled through helicopters to the 4th Main Jet Base located in Ankara, Akıncı.

07:41: A tank was driven out of the Headquarters of the General Staff and it fired at the trucks that were parked on the road to block the road against the coup plotters.

07:48: 5 Four-star Generals and 29 colonels, who participated in the coup attempt, were suspended.

08:00: The last aircraft controlled by the coup plotters was shot down.

08:04: The Istanbul Harbiye Officer's Club and the TRT Istanbul Radio were secured by the security forces.

08: 10: The Headquarters of the General Command of Gendarmerie, which was located in Beştepe, was reclaimed from the coup plotters. Approximately 1500 soldiers were taken into custody.

08:17: In Izmir the Executive Officer of the Aegean Army Command Major General Memduh Hakbilen was taken into custody.

08:30: The Bosporus Bridge was completely cleared of the coup plotters and regular traffic was permitted again.[314]

08:48: The Commander of the Turkish Armed Forces, Hulusi Akar was rescued by an operation to the 4th Main Jet Base located in Ankara, Akıncı. He was brought to the Prime Ministry, Çankaya Office.

09:00: 39 military officers, who served at the General Command of Gendarmerie, and whose participation in the coup attempt was confirmed, were removed from their positions by the Minister of Internal Affairs Efkan Âlâ.

09:00: Presidency of Religious Affairs decided to have *Sala* recitation from the mosques for a week.

09: 26: The Higher Council of Judges and Prosecutors met to discuss the heaviest disciplinary penalties that might be applicable to the judges and prosecutors who were members of the FETÖ/PDY.

09:33: In Istanbul, 80 students of Kuleli Military High school, who attacked the police, were taken into custody.

09:40: Approximately 200 private and noncommissioned soldiers came out of the General Staff building without bearing arms and surrendered to the security forces.

09:46: A legal prosecution was filed about the former Air Force Commander Akın Öztürk and Army Training and Doctrine Command (EDOK), Communication and Support Education Commander Lieutenant General Metin İyidil, with the charge of *treachery against the homeland.*

09:56: Fatih Sultan Mehmet Bridge is totally open to traffic.

09:56: As a result of the investigations concerning the coup attempt 1563 military personnel across Turkey were taken into custody.

09:58: It was decided that all judges and prosecutors across Turkey, who were on leave must cancel their period of leave, and assume their duty immediately. The judiciary recess was cancelled.

10:07: 933 private soldiers, noncommissioned soldiers, military officers and military personnel surrendered to the security forces.

10:15: Bingöl 49th Commando Brigade Commander Brigadier General Yunus Kotaman and Bolu the 2th Commando Brigade Commander Brigadier General İsmail Güneşer were both taken into custody.

10:30: Approximately 100 military officers, who worked in the 2th Army Command—which actively participated in the coup attempt—located in Malayta, surrendered.

10:34: Noncommissioned officers and commissioned officers who worked in the General Staff and who were kept under lock and with tied hands because they did not participate in the coup attempt were released.

10:59: The Minister of Internal Affairs, Efkan Âlâ removed the Commander of Coast Guard, Rear Admiral Hakan Üstem, from his office.

11:00: Istanbul Governor, Vasip Şahin declared that activities concerning the coup attempt were now totally crushed.

11:05: Prime Minister Binali Yıldırım began his work to suppress the coup attempt from the Prime Ministry, Çankaya Office.

12:04: The Police Forces for Special Operations launched an operation on the central building of the General Command of Gendarmerie headquarters, and they took more or less 200 soldiers into custody.

12:15 - 12:55: Prime Minister Yıldırım released a statement and said: *"This rebellion is suppressed. We have 161 martyrs overall, and at this moment we have 440 injured people. At this time, we have in custody 2839 soldiers who participated in this contemptible rebellion. These soldiers included ordinary soldiers as well as soldiers of different military ranks."*[315]

Photo 9: Prime Minister Yıldırım announces that the coup-attempt has been completely overpowered.[316]

12:57: Major General Suat Murat Semiz the Commander of the 1th Main Jet Base Dursun Pak and JFAC[317] Commander Brigadier General Recep Ünal are both taken into custody.

14:37: HSYK General Board decided to cancel the membership of five board members whom the Office of Ankara

Chief Public Prosecutor decided to take into custody. HSYK 2. Department laid off 2745 judges from their office.

15:03: 5 members of the Council of State, who were also FETÖ/PDY members, were taken into custody.

15:26: 10 members of the Council of State on whom there was an arrest warrant as a result of the investigation regarding the coup attempt were arrested and taken into custody.

15:30: A rescue took place of the Air Force Commander Four-star General Akın Ünal and other Four-star Generals who were all held captive in the 4th Main Jet Base Command in Ankara Akıncı.

16:08: The Office of Ankara Chief Public Prosecutor issued a decision to take into custody 140 members of the Court of Cassation and 48 members of the Council of State with the charge of "*being a member of a terrorist organization.*"

17:00: Turkish Grand National Assembly held an emergency meeting.

Photo 10: Turkish Grand National Assembly holds an emergency session after the coup attempt.[318]

17:10: Speaker of the Turkish Grand National Assembly, İsmail Kahraman, gave a speech to the members of the National Assembly during an emergency meeting held due to the coup attempt.

17:25: Prime Minister Binali Yıldırım gave a speech to the members of the National Assembly during an emergency meeting held due to the coup attempt.

17:45: The four political parties that have representatives in the TBMM released a joint declaration and condemnation of the coup attempt.

20:02: Alparslan Altan, a member of the Constitutional Court, was taken into custody.

20:50: A successful rescue takes place of General Commander of Gendarmerie Galip Mendi who was held hostage at the 4th Main Jet Base, in Ankara, Akıncı district.

21:09: Erdal Tezcan, member of the Constitutional Court, was taken into custody.

21:57: Office of Ankara Chief Public Prosecutor sent a transcript to all assize courts, and offices of chief public prosecution. It requested that *"they should take into custody and start an investigation about the total of 2745 judges and prosecutors, who worked in either judicial justice or administrative justice, and who were considered to be affiliated with the same organization."*

The Assassination Attempt Against President Recep Tayyip Erdoğan

A team of 39 heavily armed soldiers, who were a part of the task force of the Combat Search and Rescue (MAK), appointed by the coup plotters departed from Çiğli 2. Main Jet Base with 2 Cougar type helicopters and 1 Skorsky type helicopter around 02.00[319] and arrived at Marmaris around 03.10 in order to assassinate President Recep Tayyip Erdoğan, who was at that time to be found in the Marmaris district of Muğla.

Even before that President Erdoğan left for the heliport,

which was ten minutes away by road from the hotel, where he was staying in Marmaris. With the intention to reach Dalaman Airport, there was a helicopter waiting for him to take him to İzmir Adnan Menderes Airport. The helicopter took off with dimmed lights to avoid detection. In order to maintain its identity hidden, the TC-ATA aircraft taking President Recep Tayyip Erdoğan to his final destination Istanbul took first off from İzmir Adnan Menderes Airport with the code number THY-3451 as if it were a passenger airliner, and landed at 00.40 in Dalaman Airport. Again, in order to keep its identity hidden the same aircraft departed to Istanbul at 01.43 with code number 8456.[320]

After President Erdogan's departure from the hotel by helicopter, the military helicopters fired directly at the area where the hotel was located, and masked and heavily armed soldiers descended near the hotel.[321] Police officers were dispatched to the region following calls made by the hotel authorities. Police officer Nedim Cengiz Eker and Presidency security man Mehmet Çetin were martyred and 8 other people were wounded in the clashes that lasted until the morning. After learning that President Erdoğan had left the hotel and realizing that the course of the coup attempt was changing, the assassination teams left the hotel and fled to the forest area of İçmeler.

After the coup attempt, the captain and pilot of the TC-ATA plane that brought President Erdoğan from Dalaman Airport to İstanbul Atatürk Airport got in touch with the Atatürk Airport Air Traffic Control Tower controller and landed at the airport without being caught out by the P-16 planes that were under the control of the coup plotters. The controller, reporting the status of the F-16 airplanes minute by minute, directed the aircraft to the "*3-5 left*" numbered runway so that the aircraft would not be caught out by the F-16s and would be able to park swiftly after landing.[322]

President Recep Tayyip Erdoğan arrived at Atatürk Airport at 03.20 on Saturday on the 16th of July. Erdoğan held a press conference where he gave a determined decisive message to fight against the coup plotters and began to manage the process from Istanbul.

Suppressing the Coup Attempt
President Recep Tayyip Erdoğan's Leadership

After the December 17-25 coup attempt, President Recep Tayyip Erdoğan considered the fight against FETÖ/PDY in terms of the legality of the state as *"a matter of life and death"*. He engaged them with determination, and especially in the Judiciary, Security and the Media organs, a significant portion of the organization's members were dismissed from their positions and this resulted in organization running out of its economic resources, and this situation played a vital role in the prevention of the success of the coup.

For example, after the December 17-25 judicial coup attempt, 35 thousand people working in the police force were taken from the operational units and assigned to other institutions and units. Some of them were later retired, and some of them were expelled from the profession. After the December 17-25 judicial coup attempt, 848 operations were carried out in the country, 5.742 people were taken into custody in these operations, 1.554 of them were in the police force, while the remaining 4.188 were among other professions and 1.465 of them were arrested. In addition, 649 holdings, companies, foundations, associations, private schools, preparatory course centers, dormitories, private hospitals and similar institutions were subject to operations until the 15th of July 2016, and 609 of them were assigned to trustees, 38 of them were confiscated, and 2 of them were banned to either transfer or to sell their companies. Moreover, 850 fuel stations, which were thought to be providing finance and support to the organization, were audited and 268 of them were officially taken action against. Again in the framework of the fight against the FETÖ/PDY, operations were conducted against 1.426 special education institutions operating in 80 provinces. These operations played a very important role in preventing the 15th of July coup attempt.[323]

With the policies implemented during the period of Prime Minister Recep Tayyip Erdoğan, the power and influence of the Armed Forces on politics had been largely eliminated. On the 15th of July, the perception that was formed at all levels of society against any type of military tutelage ensured that all political parties were against the coup attempt. In this period, the transformation of the bureaucracy and the fact that the different segments of society had developed a different perceptive became highly effective in shaping the public sector and creating opposition to the coup attempt. Again in this period, the strengthening of the middle class and the increasing self-confidence of the conservative people were effective in the struggle of the people against the coup plotters. In addition, the AK Party's April 27 e-memorandum, the Gezi Park incidents, the stopping of the MIT trucks and the success of struggling with political crises such as the December period 17-25 became vitally important aspects in preventing the coup.

Moreover, the transformation, diversification and the developments in communication technology of the media during President Recep Tayyip Erdoğan's prime ministry made it difficult for the coup plotters. During the 1980 military coup period, only the state television TRT was actively broadcasting. Therefore, at that time the seizure of the TRT was sufficient to control television broadcasting. The commanders of that period had largely been successful in controlling the media by cooperating with the executives of the so-called "*cartel media*". During the periods when the AK Party government was ruling, a significant transformation in the radio, television, newspaper and magazine sectors, which are considered as *traditional media*, took place, as well as extraordinary developments occurred especially in the field of internet broadcasting and social media due to the strengthening of the communication infrastructure of the country. This situation made it difficult to keep everything under control because of the diversification in the media. For this reason, the coup plotters' attempts to seize the media during the 15th of July coup attempt failed.

Without any pre-planning or preparation, just President Recep Tayyip Erdogan's phone connection to a television station[324] to invite the people to the streets was sufficient, and people flocked to the streets confronting a very well-planned coup and were successful in suppressing the coup attempt in a very short period time. This was an example of a struggle for democracy that the world had never seen before.

President Recep Tayyip Erdoğan took all kinds of risks coming to Atatürk Airport, even at the cost of his life, and joined the public to fight against the coup and the coup plotters. In addition to being a great source of morale for the people and the security forces, this contributed to the defeat of the coup by causing panic, demoralization, disbanding and the sense of capitulation that arose in the coup plotters.

President Recep Tayyip Erdoğan's support and leadership

during the suppression of the coup attempt strengthened the re-sistance of our people, politicians and state institutions against the coup and ensured a national stance. President Recep Tayyip Erdoğan motivating the public by connecting to television chan-nels, challenging the coup plotters, putting his life at the fore-front, then arriving in Istanbul and taking over the resistance movement against the coup plotters; it can be said that him lead-ing this process from the beginning to the finish is the most im-portant event of Turkish Republic's recent history.

Following the prevention of the coup attempt, President Recep Tayyip Erdoğan thanked the people on Tuesday the 19th of July 2016 and thanked all the institutions and organi-zations that contributed to the suppression of the coup.

President Recep Tayyip Erdoğan's speech in which he thanked the public.

"My Precious nation,

Turkey, on the 15th of July 2016 beginning around 22.00 faced a coup attempt that lasted until noon the next day.

This coup attempt initiated by a group of members of the Fetul-lahist Terrorist Organization, from various classes and ranks, that acted independent from the chain of command of the Turkish Armed Forces, had limited effects, but because of the power of the weapons they had on hand, reached dangerous levels.

We immediately acted in the face of these developments. We gave instructions to our units and took steps to stop the coup attempt. We invited all those who love our nation, country, homeland, to come out to public squares and embrace the state and democracy. Despite receiving several threats and being subject to danger we immediately set off to Istanbul and together with our nation, we demonstrated our determined stance against the coup plotters.

The attempts of a bunch of criminals that do not receive their orders from their military commanders and do not serve the nation and the state, but instead have surrendered their will to the leader of the Fetullahist Terrorist Organization, have failed in the face of the will of the nation and the determination of the state with all its institutions.

Our nation, which has been suffering because of not being able to do anything about Menderes and his associates in the 1960 Coup and the youth in 1960's that were sent to the gallows because of the "one from the right-wing, one from the leftwing" ideology, has finally said 'stop' to this type of thinking on the 15th of July 2016.

For the first time in our country's history, an attempted military coup was prevented by the nation itself. Turkey's commitment to democracy and the rule of law was demonstrated not to be only in name, but it showed the world that it is a country where these values are even realized at the expense of the lives of its citizens. No democracy, no rule of law; will allow the existence of the military, the judge, the prosecutor, the police, and the bureaucrat, who take orders from an outside organization structure rather than within the institutional hierarchy. There will no longer be the slightest compassion, the smallest tolerance, for those who support the Fetullahist Terrorist Organization and other terrorist organizations. For us, the survival of our nation and our state comes before everything. Without making concessions from the principles of democracy and the rule of law, we will fight and struggle with all the terrorist organizations and structures that threaten the future of our nation and our state.

There is no alternative to a system that has guaranteed the fundamental rights and freedom, democracy and the rule of the law in Turkey, and there is also no other way to go. There is only the need to build up the country; strengthen, develop, increase its welfare, and fortify its defense, to develop its education system, health system, justice system and to strengthen its infrastructure. My only aim is to build this visionary Turkey as the first President of the Republic of Turkey who has come to power directly from the peoples vote.

As President, we will continue our way with determination to reach our 2023 objectives, with the support of our Parliament, our government, our political parties, our civil society organizations, along with everyone else who supports Turkey."

President Recep Tayyip Erdoğan called Speaker of the Grand National Assembly of Turkey, CHP leader Kemal Kılıçdaroğlu and MHP Chairman Devlet Bahçeli on Saturday the 16th of July to thank the Grand National Assembly of Turkey and the political parties' contribution to the suppression of the FETÖ/PDY coup attempt.

President Recep Tayyip Erdoğan invited CHP leader Kemal Kılıçdaroğlu, MHP Chairman Devlet Bahceli and AK Party Chairman Binali Yildirim to the Presidential Complex to thank them for their determined approach towards the coup attempt and to evaluate the latest developments and to receive suggestions from them. The following statements were made from the Presidency after the meeting on the 25th of July; *"actions that will be taken for the freedom, security and prosperity of our nation, the implementation of the state of emergency, security measures, and the works on the constitution and economic policies were evaluated. Turkey will fight against terrorist organizations such as FETÖ and PKK, which are trying to take over and destroy the state, with determination. The necessity of taking the essential measures to prevent similar incidents such as the 15th of July coup attempt was dwelled on. The investigation of the 15th of July coup attempt and the OHAL process will be carried out meticulously. The importance of cooperation of all political parties in this matter was emphasized and there was a consensus on the effective use of political dialogue mechanisms to produce solutions to our common problems."*

Photo 11: Evaluation meeting held at the Presidential Complex after the coup attempt.[325]

Following the 15th of July coup attempt, President Recep Tayyip Erdoğan, as an indication of the spirit of unity and solidarity in politics, gave up the lawsuits against the CHP leader Kemal Kılıçdaroğlu and the MHP President Devlet Bahceli. The CHP leader Kemal Kılıçdaroğlu also withdrew his lawsuits and complaints against President Recep Tayyip Erdoğan.

The Determination of Prime Minister Binali Yildirim

Prime Minister Binali Yildirim's struggle against the suppression of the coup attempt played a significant role in the course of the coup attempt. Prime Minister Binali Yıldırım's statements at 23:00 revealed the determination of the public authorities against the coup plotterss when he said, *"My citizens shall know that no actions will be allowed to harm the democracy. We are faced with a possible insurrection. Obviously, some people in the military are acting unlawfully out of the chain of command. This insurrection attempt is initiated only within a group in the ar-*

my. This initiative will not be allowed. Those who do this will pay the heaviest price. There will be no compromise in democracy. Necessary actions will be taken even if we are faced with death as a result."

As a matter of fact, the Prime Minister departed from Istanbul to Ankara using the highway and chose different routes to avoid the coup plotters. Nevertheless, he was the target of the bullets of the coup plotters along the way, but with absolute determination, he arrived in Ankara and started to coordinate the resistance against the coup plotters from the capital.

On the 16th of July 2016 at 17:00 speaking at the Grand National Assembly of Turkey's extraordinary meeting, Prime Minister Binali Yıldırım emphasized the following points in the following summary: *"I commemorate, with great gratitude, our martyrs who have preserved the independence of the nation with their blessed blood, the people who flocked to the streets and stood as heroes in front of tanks to protect the honor of the nation last night. I salute them all with respect, and with gratitude from the Grand Assembly. I call upon the families of those heroes; do not greave because they have achieved the greatest level after the prophets. These heroes were your children until yesterday, but today they have become the children of the nation. Their names will live as long as the Republic of Turkey exits. I salute my wounded brothers; I wish them a speedy recovery.*

I am proud to be the son of such a nation. I would like to thank our President, our Commander-in-Chief, Recep Tayyip Erdoğan, for him taking such a robust stance. I would like to thank the political party leaders, media representatives, NGOs, our imams who read Salas and the brothers/sisters who were praying for us on their prayer rugs.

I would like to thank my fellow citizens who took their flags and flocked to the streets, and the nations that are our friends and brothers. You came to the Grand National Assembly of Turkey by overcoming the barricades, the tanks, the bullets and stood tall and said, 'democracy or death' last night. You have shown an exemplary stance amongst the world democracies. While the nation was defending its independence, you embraced the democracy and the national will here in the Grand National Assembly of Turkey. With this attitude, this Supreme Council made history once again. You have changed the history of Turkey. Today is a milestone."

Prime Minister Binali Yıldırım exchanged views with the CHP leader Kemal Kılıçdaroğlu and MHP Chairman Devlet Bahçeli at the Çankaya Mansion on the social and political consensus regarding the post-coup process on Tuesday the 19th of July 2016.

Photo 12: Evaluation meeting held at Çankaya Mansion after the coup attempt.[326]

Prime Minister Binali Yıldırım, CHP leader Kemal Kılıçdaroğlu and MHP Chairman Devlet Bahçeli attended the funeral prayer and stood side by side in Ankara Kocatape Mosque; for Infantry Officer Colonel Sait Ertürk, Artillery Officer Senior Chief Sergeant Bülent Aydın, Police Officer Fırat Bulut, Police Officer Muhammet Oğuz Kılınç, Chief Police Officer Cüneyt Bursa, Police Officer Hüseyin Kalkan, Police Officer Köksal Taşaltı and Deputy Commissioner Kübra Doğanay.

Attitude of Ismail Kahraman, the President of the Grand National Assembly of Turkey, the Council's Common Position and the Perspectives of the Political Parties

Shortly after the beginning of the coup attempt, the President of the Grand National Assembly of Turkey, İsmail Kahraman, came to the parliament, and decided to convene the General Assembly to demonstrate its determined stance against the coup attempt. As a result of Kahraman's attempts, some ministers and members of the AK Party, CHP and MHP deputies and the Assembly staff came to the Parliament. İsmail Kahraman took his seat at the general assembly and instructed the AK Party group deputy chairman Mehmet Muş, CHP group deputy chairman Özgür Özel and MHP group deputy chairman Erkan Akçay to sit next to him. Thus, the message, *'we are one, and defending the homeland and democracy together'* was sent to the coup plotters. İsmail Kahraman, who opened the General Assembly, stressed that the coup will be disallowed by stating, *'Our experience with democracy goes back many years, our democracy has been settled and rooted. The coup attempt is doomed to fail.'*[327]

İsmail Kahraman continued to work with deputies in the Assembly until the coup attempt was beat off in the morning. He clearly stated how the nation and its deputies were determined to fight against the coup plotters. To emphasize the overall stance against the coup attempt conducted by the FETÖ/PDY he made the following statement, *"The coup has been defeated and democracy has won. This unity and integrity will* soon eliminate the evil sides of the coup. Hopefully, we will soon be treating these wounds. Those who have ill intentions inside and outside the country will be disappointed." President of the Assembly, İsmail Kahraman, ended the session by calling for an extraordinary meeting on Saturday the 16th of July 2016.[328]

At the extraordinary meeting held in the Assembly on the 16th of July 2016 at 17:00, the President of the Assembly İsmail Kahraman received a standing ovation for reading the ten continents of the Independence March. The joint text agreed by the four parties was also read by the İsmail Kahraman in the General Assembly.

The joint statement released against the coup plotters by the four political parties that have representatives in the Grand National Assembly of Turkey.

"We, as the parties of AKP, CHP, HDP and MHP condemn the attacks against the Assembly and the coup attempts which started on the night of 15th of July and were defused in the morning of the 16th of July; against our people, the national will and especially against the deputies who are representatives of our nation.

Our nation stood against the coup and the bloody coup attempt was prevented. This glorious nation which protected the Republic of Turkey and its institutions at the expense of their lives deserve all praise and the appreciation eminently. We are grateful to the martyrs who gave their lives for this cause and we will never forget our heroes. The Grand National Assembly of Turkey has proved that this is a parliament worthy of our nation once again, by performing its task which has been authorized by the people, while bombs and bullets were fired at it. Our assembly proved its dignity against the coup by showing great courage and acting as a single heart and one body.

The determination of the Assembly against the coup attempt is extremely valuable for the further development of democracy. Ev-

*eryone should know that in the future as today, any action taken
in order to harm our nation, the national will or the Veteran Assembly, will face the strongest force of the Assembly's willpower.
The Grand National Assembly of Turkey will continue to reflect
the unshakable faith in the nation's democracy. It will be written
in history that all political party groups in our assembly had a
common stance towards the coup attempt and they stood against
the coup attempt with one common language. The Assembly is active and the attack against the people's assembly, the nation and its
sovereignty will be punished according to law severely. The most
concrete proof that nothing will be the same in Turkey is also the
joint statement. Even though we have different opinions as four
parties, we are all standing together alongside with all of our deputies, national organizations, all of our offices and protecting the
nation's will and we will continue to do this forever. Our nation
should be assured.*

*We ask our people to stay away from violent acts that exceed the
limits of the democratic reactions and to stay away from any acts
that may badly represent our country. We remember our martyrs
with respect, gratitude and compassion. We wish a speedy recovery for our wounded and we wish our nation a swift recovery. We
salute all friendly and brotherly countries that have stood with us
and have sent us their messages of support."*

The decisive attitude of the political institution with the
ruling and opposition groups determined joint stance against
the coup completely eradicated the basis of the legitimacy of
the coup plotters memorandum and increased the resistance
of the people.[329]

The first and strongest support to the government against
the coup attempt came from MHP Chairman Devlet Bahceli. Devlet Bahçeli, by calling the Prime Minister Yıldırım and
saying that *the coup is unacceptable, and that they are standing
side by side with the government of Turkey,* clearly demonstrat-

ed their stance against the coup attempt. Bahçeli in his speech to the Assembly, which had gathered on extraordinary terms on Saturday the 16th of July, briefly touched upon these issues in the following summary:

"I express my gratitude to every citizen. Last night there was an attempt to eliminate our democracy through a coup attempt. The nation's will was clearly attacked. A handful of enemy collaborators that had infiltrated the honorable Turkish army have come to light. A rare betrayal in our history has occurred through the perpetrators and those related. Please pay attention to this overwhelming issue; The Veteran Assembly was bombed by air. The bombing of the Grand National Assembly of Turkey is a betrayal that appalls us all. This inglorious upheaval has not only targeted the elected government, but the entire Turkish nation. The corrupt group and its proxies' aim was to drag our country into chaos by playing their last card.

What happened last night is actually a treacherous terrorist attack. This attack was carried out by a small group of Turkish soldiers who had been recruited, deceived or overzealous. This deep plot was repelled with faith. The era of savior officers ended long time ago. The common future of the Turkish Nation is law and democracy. No band of criminals, parallel structure, terrorist organization, or source of violence will be able to pierce this platform."

After Devlet Bahçeli Kemal Kılıçardaroğlu made a statement to the public that he was against the coup and the coup plotters, CHP leader Kemal Kılıçdaroğlu in his speech to the Assembly, which had gathered on extraordinary terms on Saturday the 16th of July briefly touched upon these issues in the following summary: *"We openly condemn the attack on our democracy yesterday. The event has created a deep sorrow in all of us. This process united us on a common ground which we should have in politics been on from the beginning. However, we will continue to say this verbally but we will also say it with our hearts. Yesterday, our people went to the public squares and practiced their right to resist the coup. For example, we have seen how legitimate the right to resist is in cases where democracy is being destroyed by the coup or when the law is violated. There is no better example than this. This parliament will defend democracy until the end. This parliament will defend the Republic's values until the end. There is a historical responsibility for this assembly. We have to expand the front in the context of freedom.*

A self-criticism of every party has become a historical necessity due to this coup attempt. It is the duty of the parliament to oppose any coup. We must never accept the tutelage on democracy. Since the national will is very valuable, any tutelage over democracy must not be accepted regardless of the authority, position or rank it's based on. Whoever goes over the limits of the constitution and law must definitely pay the price.

İdris Baluken, the Group Deputy Chairman on behalf of the People's Democratic Party (HDP), who condemned the coup attempt, summarized the following points in his speech[330]: "*We strongly condemn this anti-democratic coup and the massacre attacks that took place on the 15th of July without any 'but, however and nevertheless'. Our attitude towards parliament and the will of the people has been clear and principled. Unfortunately, 161 civilians have lost their lives due to the reckless attack of this initiative. Even this picture shows the danger of democracy in our country. Such attacks will never succeed. Those who make such types of attacks and those who want to plot a coup against the public should know that Turkey never did lend credence to these people and will never do so in the future.*

The coup-attempt last night, the bombing of the parliament, the massacre of hundreds of people in the middle of the streets exceeded a typical military coup; and we are indeed facing a complicated plan that aims for chaos. I would like to emphasize that it is the political will of all of the 78 million people that is targeted in this respect."

Bekir Bozdağ, the Minister of Justice, following statements during the bombing from the air and addressing the Speaker of the Assembly İsmail Kahraman had a profound effect on the public; "*We are here even if you hurl bombs at us. Whatever you do, we will be here. We will make you give an account of all the transgression you have carried out against the public, and you will be taken to court*", and "*The assembly should not be closed, what we are going to do is to die here*".[331] At the same time, AK Party group deputy chairman Mehmet Muş, CHP group deputy chairman Özgür Özel and MHP group deputy chairman Erkan Akçay, as well as many other deputies, made decisive speeches against the coup attempt.[332]

Other Important Events that Occurred During the Overpowering of the Coup Attempt[333]

The people of Kazan District, who learned that the planes bombing many places in Ankara took off from the 4th Main Jet Base in Akıncı, flocked to the base in the district and the coup plotters soldiers in the base opened fire on the people. Some of citizens were martyred and many of them were injured.

Police teams were placed on the roads in case the senior state officials came to Ankara and about 15 thousand people were directed to the Esenboğa Airport in Ankara.

2,000 special police officers from the Eastern and Southeastern provinces, 4,500 special operations police candidates who would graduate soon, and 7,800 police from the surrounding provinces were directed to Ankara.

The passports of the persons whose names were mentioned in the seized coup plans, the FETÖ/PDY judiciary members and other persons that had connections with the FETÖ/PDY were canceled in case they tried to escape abroad.

Police officers stopped and neutralized 80 coup soldiers that were stationed in Polatlı 58thArtillery Brigade departed to Ankara with armored vehicles and missile launching platforms near the district of Temelli.

A Whatsapp group, where 104 members were found communicating, was identified on the cellphone of a colonel who was captured while travelling in a tank towards Vatan Avenue. Very vital information about the coup attempt was identified in these Whatsapp messages.

On the night of the 15th of July, eight military transport airplanes that took off without permission from the 12th Air Main Base Transport Command in Kayseri Erkilet landed in Malatya Erhaç's 7th Main Jet Base early in the morning. It was discovered that the aircraft carried 39 high ranked officers, aircraft technicians, armed sergeants and ammunition. It was later discovered that the purpose of these people was to load the F-4E 2020 type warplanes with bombs and missiles and thus start the second wave of the coup attempt.[334]

Fortunately, the second wave of the coup attempt was prevented by the civilian fire brigade and the search and rescue teams, called the ARFF at Malatya Erhaç Air Base. They carried this out by placing their vehicles on the runway and barring the bomber aircrafts from taking off.

Some of the Public Institutions that Was Effective in Suppressing the Coup Attempt[335]

The Directorate General of Security, the Turkish Armed Forces, the General Command of Gendarmerie, the National Intelligence Agency and the Judicial organs, particularly the Council of Judges and Prosecutors at the time played an important role in the suppression of the coup attempt. Police officers working in the Directorate General of Security, soldiers in the Turkish Armed Forces who love the homeland and the nation, governors, mayors, municipal employees, judiciary members, and several institutions' selfless struggle also contributed to this cause.

The failure of the coup attempt is also mainly a result of the FETÖ/PDY's own ineffectiveness and miscalculation in forming a perception where they thought they were going to achieve their mission. However, in reality they were unable to achieve the necessary capability, because the majority of the Turkish Armed Forces, particularly the senior commanders, resisted the coup attempt. Moreover, the coup plotters were unable to exploit the elite units of the Turkish Armed Forces and the majority of the strike force. Using inadequate forces led the coup plotters to make major inaccurate strategies, and their smaller units were easily besieged and neutralized by civilians and law enforcement. The fact that the coup plotters could not manipulate or maneuver the First Army Commander, who was in charge of the greatest strike force of the land forces - the First Army, that the coup plotters were unable to seize the Special Forces Command; and that the killing of a prominent member[336] of the coup plotters demoralized the movement, all led to the withdrawal of the coup supporters, and prevented the coup plotters using their initially limited military capacity that they did have control over.

Furthermore, establishing a crises center coded *"emergency"* under the command of the Directorate General of Security during the first hours of the coup attempt (15 July 2016 around 22.15) that resisted the coup attempt played a significant role. In this context, the mandate that was sent to all the provincial police headquarters ensured that safety measures were taken around the Presidential Complex, the Grand National Assembly of Turkey, the Prime Ministry, the Ministry of Interior, the MİT, the TRT and the Directorate General of Security buildings and all other critical buildings; and that access to these areas was prohibited. In order to prevent the tanks taking control of the public squares, towing vehicles and heavy vehicles were used to close off as many roads as possible. All arsenals were opened and the long-barreled weapons were distributed to the personnel. All personnel that were on leave were requested back on duty. A total of 7,800 police from the surrounding provinces were transferred to Ankara and a total of 1,729 special operations police were sent to Istanbul. The 10 armored tactical vehicles ordered by the Directorate General of Security, which had not yet been delivered, were delivered from the supplier company and sent to Ankara. The Commanders of Gendarmerie and other Military Units Commands were contacted, and informed that the all police units were ordered to act, if the military units went out on the streets.

On the other hand, the Special Operations Policemen were deployed and the fuel pump and the storage tank at the 4th Main Jet Base in Ankara Akıncı were rendered ineffective and attempts were made to prevent the landing and departure of fighter planes. Police teams were placed on roads in order to assist senior state officials in case they had to come to Ankara. Thousands of citizens were directed to the Esenboğa Airport and the 4th Main Jet Base in Akıncı and the air traffic control towers safety in the Esenboğa Airport were ensured. In addition, by contacting the friendly elements in the Turkish General Staff; airways, runways and heliport areas arranged to be used during war time were ascertained and proper measures were taken accordingly. The use of air travel in Uşak, Kütahya, Afyonkarahisar and Sivrihisar were disallowed.

On the night of 15th of July, a coup document that contained information regarding the appointment of Commanders to the 81 provinces for the so-called martial law, was found on a Bursa Provincial Gendarmerie Commander. These names were swiftly sent to the 81 Provincial Governorates and Police Commands, and these people were taken into custody. The gendarmerie personnel who were in this list were also dismissed from their duties on the same night by the Interior Minister, passports of the judiciary members and other persons that had connections with the coup plotters were promptly cancelled. All of the warships in Gölcük and Aksaz that were assigned to participate in the coup and had left the harbor were persuaded to return. Out of all the warships that departed, only 2 of the warships did not return.

The General Command of Gendarmerie officials on Friday 15th of July at various times made anti-coup statements at private television channels[337]. Using the signature block of the Commander of the Turkish Gendarmerie Forces Army, General Galip Mendi, "...*the gendarmerie troops shall not comply with the unlawful orders and instructions (directives from the so-called martial law). All supervisors and commanders are responsible and authorized to take any measures within the legal framework against this situation...*" orders were given to the affiliated units, and the message regarding the return from leave was requested for the ranked officers. Furthermore, there were difficulties in sending the message by the Operations Center and the Communication Center of the Land Forces Command. In response using the signature block of Commander of the Turkish Land Forces Army General Salih Zeki Çolak the same message was sent to all units through the Operations Center of the Ankara Provincial Command of Gendarmerie. Moreover, a joint operation was initiated by the Gendarmerie Special Operations and Police Special Operations units that started from 01.00 on the 16th of July 2016 in order to neutralize the coup plotters who occupied the military quarters of the General Command of Gendarmerie in Beştepe. The military quarters were seized and gotten under control at 08.10 on Saturday the 16th of July. An important part of the coup plotters who attempted to assassinate President Recep Tayyip Erdoğan in the Marmaris district of Muğla, were captured by a successful operation of the İzmir Bornova 2nd Gendarmerie Commando Brigade Command.

The National Intelligence Agency also played an important role in the suppression of the coup attempt. A pilot major that was stationed at the Land Aviation School Command came to the MİT and gave a tip-off that, "*Three helicopters would attack the MİT Undersecretary's house at 03:00 am and the Undersecretary would be kidnapped.*" After this person was cross-examined, the Deputy Undersecretary of the MİT went to the General Staff to evaluate the information obtained. Subsequently, a meeting was held with the participation of the MİT Undersecretary, Commander of the Turkish Armed Forces, the Commander of the Turkish Land Forces and the Deputy Commander of the Turkish Armed Forces to evaluate and decide what measures needed to be taken.

After the start of the coup attempt, all the personnel of the agency were put on full alert. With the first attack of coup plotters, the MİT Headquarters in Ankara and all the regional units throughout the country were ordered to resist and "*not allow any coup members into the MİT's compounds and to conduct the necessary cooperation with the local administrative authorities and security forces*". Moreover, they were given the order to fire at will if attacked. Helicopter attacks carried out at the Headquarters and the Istanbul Regional Presidency of MİT was immediately responded to with light weapons due to the afore mentioned 'fire at will' order. The descent of the coup plotters helicopter to capture the MİT Undersecretary was prevented with strong resistance by the Agency staff. The attempt of the coup plotters to enter the Kars Regional Presidency by tank was also prevented by the resistance of the MİT personnel.

It should also be noted that the judicial organs also played a strong role in overcoming the coup attempt. For example, the Istanbul Chief Public Prosecutor's Office launched an investigation into the coup plotters in the early hours of the coup attempt, and the Chief Public Prosecutor of Küçükçekmece, Ali Doğan, stated that the soldiers who had participated in the coup attempt *would be arrested on sight*. The Ankara Chief Public Prosecutor's Office also decided to detain the judicial members of the terrorist organization FETÖ/PDY in connection with the attempted coup, including the generals, admirals, commissioned officers, sergeants, officers and petty officers of the so-called 'Peace at Home Council'. A total of 1,374 military personnel were detained within twelve hours of the coup attempt. Council of Judges and Prosecutors requested the judges and prosecutors on leave, to come back to offices and begin their active duty, and the judicial recess was cancelled. HSYK General Assembly decided to dismiss the membership of five HSYK members in line with the detention decision of Ankara Chief Public Prosecutor's Office and the 2nd Office of HSYK dismissed 2,745 judges. Members of FETÖ/PDY on the Council of State were taken into custody. 140 Court of Cassation members and 48 Council of State members were charged with being a member of a terrorist organization by the Ankara Chief Public Prosecutor's Office and a decision to take the members into custody was passed. The members of the Constitutional Court, Alparslan Altan and Erdal Tercan, were also taken into custody. Ankara Public Prosecutor's Office, sent a transcript to the Heavy Penal Republic Chief Public Prosecutors Office that requested that an investigation be opened against a total of 2,745 judges and prosecutors that were in the administrative and judicial justice, which were also *"assessed as being members of the same organization"*, and that these judges and prosecutors should be taken into custody.

Head of the Religious Affairs Presidency of the time, Prof. Dr. Mehmet Görmez gave instructions to all muftis to recite *Salas* from the 85,000 mosques throughout the country. Thereby the *Sala* started to be recited from the mosques throughout the country. In addition, President Recep Tayyip Erdoğan's invitation to the public to gather in public squares was announced by the religious staff from the minarets after each *Sala* was recited.

The Diyanet TV and Diyanet Radio kept giving encouraging messages against the coup throughout the night during their broadcasts. The broadcasting of the Diyanet TV was changed and the invitation of President Recep Tayyip Erdoğan, the instructions of the Head of Religious Affairs Presidency, Mehmet Görmez, against the coup attempt and; and the Qur'an recitals (chapter al-Fath) were displayed without interruption in order to stand against the coup attempt to protect the democracy. The Head of Religious Affairs Presidency, Mehmet Görmez, gave telephone messages to the public during the night by being connected to the live broadcasts of various TV channels.

The recital of *Salas* in the mosque's strengthened the spiritual emotion in the people, which led to the revival spirit of freedom of the public. Thus, the public felt that the country and nation entered into a new national struggle. The people, whose national and spiritual feelings were fired up, flocked to and surrounded the public squares, avenues, airports and military bases, and clinged together as if they were a unified wall. Despite the attacks of military planes, helicopters and tanks, which resulted in 249 martyrs and more than 2 thousand wounded people, the struggle of our people at the expense of the coup is a rare event in world history.

On the night of the 15th of July 2016, municipalities also played an important role in the struggle of our nation against the coup plotters. The personnel of the municipalities in many cities, mainly in Ankara and Istanbul, worked together with the police forces and acted in a coordinated manner to take the necessary measures, especially in the provinces and districts, where the coup plotters were active. They also directed our people to the places where the people were most needed, and made great efforts to close the entrances of the transportation roads and military facilities used by the coup plotters. This was done by constructing barricades from construction machinery and heavy vehicles that belonged to the municipalities. Thus, the coup plotters trying to come from the surrounding cities, especially to Istanbul and Ankara, were prevented from entering these cities. In addition, millions of citizens reacting to the coup attempt prevented the coup plotters from moving in the city by filling the public squares and main arteries in coordination with the municipalities.

Democracy and Martyrs Rally

On the 7th of August 2016 in Istanbul *"The Democracy and Martyrs Rally"* was organized where approximately 5 million people attended. In attendance at the rally were President Recep Tayyip Erdoğan, the Speaker of the Grand National Assembly of Turkey İsmail Kahraman, Prime Minister Binali Yıldırım, the 11th President of Turkey, Abdullah Gül, former Prime Minister Ahmet Davutoğlu, CHP Chairman Kemal Kılıçdaroğlu, MHP Chairman Devlet Bahçeli and the Commander of the Turkish Armed Forces, Hulusi Akar.

Photo 13: The Democracy and Martyrs Rally in Yenikapı, Istanbul.[338]

The MHP leader Devlet Bahceli, who made the first speech at the rally, emphasized the following: *"On the 15th of July they carried out the project which would have led us all into disaster; they waited for us to draw our last breath. The 15th of July was to be a new massacre. A terrorist in Pennsylvania, where he has taken refuge and is camouflaged as a scholar and religious preacher, gave the 'order to shoot' through his murderous organization where he indulges in profanity, hate speech, and fits of fury. The Turkish nation is aware of the global scenario. This homeland will not fall by the so-called sermons of a couple of terrorists. This religious preacher who sold his soul to Satan, this evil traitor (voyvoda) that appears as a Muslim, has reached a new peak with this treachery, with his hostility to Turks and Turkey, and has set a new record in corruption and hypocrisy. The 15th of July FETÖ coup attempt was a new attempt of those that were defeated in Kosovo 627 years ago. It is the revival of those that were crushed 620 years ago in Niğbolu. It is the counter-operation of those that we assumed to have been choked from the blood that they had poured 572 years ago in Varna, 563 years ago in Istanbul and 490 years ago in Mohaç."[339]*

The CHP leader Kemal Kılıçdaroğlu briefly mentioned the following points in his speech at the rally: *"This is the bloodiest coup attempt in the history of our Republic. We have 240 martyrs, and we have buried our 240 lions. We will not forget them and they will not be forgotten, they are the heroes of democracy. The terrorist organization FETÖ was found nested in the army. The FETÖ terrorist organization was found nested within the judiciary. If a judge decides not by conscience, but through an authority sitting in Pennsylvania, that judge is not a judge, that court is not a court. We need to have self-criticism in our politics. We need a noble reconciliation. We must base the system of merit in the construction of the state. We must protect democracy in every situation. We must eliminate obstacles that are affecting the nation's will. We must protect the founding values of the Republic. We should contribute to the strengthening of our democracy in the future."[340]*

In his speech at the rally, Prime Minister Binali Yıldırım underlined the following points[341]: *"The President of the Republic, the Commander-in-Chief invited the nation to the public squares. Salas were recited, the call to prayers echoed in Turkey from end to end. In Istanbul, Ankara, İzmir and in the 81 provinces of this noble nation people said the following together: 'Rather than live in dishonor over the soil, we will sleep under the ground in honor, we will become martyrs, and we will become veterans. This nation, which wrote an epic during the Independence War in Çanakkale, wrote the epic of the 15th of July in the same spirit. The 15th of July is the second Independence War.*

We will strengthen our reconciliation and cooperation. We will move Turkey towards its 2023 targets, with our nation, our political parties, and civil society. These were the traitors that were coming between the Kurds and the Turks. We will clear these bastards away between the Kurds and the Turks. If we stay together there is no obstacle we cannot overcome. If we stand together and become Turkey, there is no problem we cannot overcome together. We will take this terrorist organization's members into account for our fallen martyrs and veterans.

Everyone should be assured that FETO [a derogatory term for the leader of the Fetullahist Terrorist Organization], the leader of the organization, who made the night of the 15th of July ominous for our nation, will be brought to Turkey and account for his actions. Do not feel ill at ease. I thank all of you for saving this nation from the greatest danger of the last century. Any coup that does not kill us will make us stronger."

In his speech, the President of the Grand National Assembly of Turkey, İsmail Kahraman underlined the following points: *"We endured a very difficult situation together. We resisted the evil forces that wanted to set our nation against one another and we won. Our nation gave a well-deserved response to the agents and traitors that have infiltrated our nations' institutions, and were elevated through the preparatory course centers and schools that they have opened. Our Grand National Assembly of Turkey is the only parliament that has the title 'veteran' in the world. Following the start of the coup attempt on the night of 15th of July, the Grand National Assembly of Turkey was opened even though it was not a working day, and it stayed open throughout the night. The next day we had an extraordinary meeting and we issued a joint statement signed by the four parties. The parties declared to the world that they were on side of democracy. For the second time, our Assembly deserves to have the title veteran."*[342]

President Recep Tayyip Erdoğan, who made the final speech at the Democracy and Martyrs Rally, said the following briefly[343]: "*Our brothers and sisters who filled the streets on the night of the 15th of July played a role in protecting our democracy and freedom. We as a population of 79 million should all feel blessed. Every city that was exposed to the coup attempt should feel blessed. The people leaving aside all their differences and staying together that come from all sorts of origins, which fascinated the watching world, should feel blessed. You know very well how this nation's homeland would have benefitted others if this coup attempt had been successful.*

Photo 14: President Recep Tayyip Erdoğan greeting the public at the Democracy and Martyrs Rally in Yenikapı.[344]

This nation is not like any other nation. The same faith of the nation, which opened the doors of Anatolia thousand years ago in Malazgirt, stood against the coup plotters on the 15th of July. We fought with the same belief on the 15th of July as we fought to our last drop of blood in Çanakkale.

The 15th of July demonstrates that this country is not only strong against political, economic and diplomatic attacks, but also against military sabotage; that it will not fall to pieces and that it will not derail. That night our enemies were rubbing their hands together waiting for the collapse of Turkey, but they woke up the next day in grief, realizing that their plans had become much more difficult to implement. This image we are displaying right now, people from all sorts of backgrounds coming together, has upset and frustrated our enemies as much as the morning of the 16th of July.

This image is the declaration that Turkey will achieve its 2023 goals. This image is the manifestation and the proof that unity, togetherness, and brotherhood is much more than a wish and slogan, in fact these all can be a reality. This image is the declaration and proof of the price we are willing to pay for people that even set an eye on merely a single stone in this 1000-year-old homeland. This image is the proof and proclamation that Turkey will reach its 2023 goals. Do you know what we do after this? It's time to go beyond the level of contemporary civilizations.

We're going to go in solidarity. We will love one another not for offices-positions, nor money, we will love one another only for God. Our Republic's founder, Gazi Mustafa Kemal, said the following in the dark days when most of the country, particularly Istanbul and Ankara, was under enemy occupation: "Our nation is so great, let us not fear. It will not accept bondage and degradation. However, it is necessary to bring it together and ask, 'O nation, would you accept captivity and degradation?' I know what the nation's answer will be."

Now I am asking the same question again. I am asking the same question as Gazi, 96 years later in Yenikapı Square. O nation, would you accept captivity and degradation? (The people and the rally gave the answer 'no' in unison.) This is the point. No one can bring bondage to this nation.

We must put politics, media, and the business world that was designed by the illegitimate power of the organization back on its natural course. We should give all the opportunities back to the people that the organization obtained by exploiting their religious sensitivity, compassion, kindness and feelings of cooperation of the people in the country. No one should worry about the dormitories, schools, and houses being closed. Both the relevant institutions of our state, as well as non-governmental organizations serving in the same field, will fill this gap much better and more.

We need to give opportunities back to the original owners, our state and nation, which the organization obtained by using our country's name and reputation abroad. Our government has taken important steps in all these fields with the authority that it attained after the announcement of the state of emergency, and continues to do so."

THE STATUS OF THE MEDIA

The media organs, which were under the control of the FETÖ/PDY, attempted to create such an atmosphere so that the society would be better disposed towards a coup. The media carried out this function in a planned way. For this purpose, fabricated news and excessive and unfounded criticism were made. While trying to shake the trust in democratic institutions, they tried to create the perception as if the country was caught up in a swamp of corruption, unlawfulness and international isolation. Moreover, they created an image where it seemed the country was going to face terrible dangers such as civil war and even partition in the immediate future. They tried to make the public feel that, "*it did not matter who came to power, as long as the present government left.*"

The media attacks, which increased during the process of the wiretapping activity of the organization and the closure of preparatory course centers, reached their highest level with the 17 and 25 December coup attempt. Frequently repeated concepts such as "*theft*" and "*corruption*" were carried out in the international field with the illegal operations conducted against the MİT trucks. Thus, this intervention demonstrates a false image that they created in the international are-na where it seemed Turkey was assisting ISIS. In addition, the FETÖ/PDY pushed the privacy limits of state and politi-cians by gathering illegally recorded telephone conversations. All the rants and messages regarding an '*indirect coup*" made through the written, visual and social media, was in fact car-ried out in order to produce a strong public response against the elected President and the government. All kinds of illicit and illegal methods were used in order to, so to speak, appre-hend the elected President and his government.

Since the last months of 2015, messages that evoked a coup were sent by the social media accounts belonging to some members of FETÖ/PDY. For example, one of the pop-ular names of the organization, Emre Uslu, which was a jour-nalist, gave the response "*July 2016*" on the 14th of September 2015 from his twitter account, to the question that someone asked, when will he return to Turkey from USA. Again, Uslu, gave a clear time frame by tweeting the following on the 14th of March 2016, "*Twitter followers who want to pay for my ticket please get a ticket from DC to Istanbul between the dates 22nd of July - 12th of August. You know my e-mail.*" A person who is thought to belong to the same organization, but who cannot be iden-tified, without doubt sent the following tweet on the 16th of June 2016, "Friday the 15th of July *2016, a military coup in Tur-key. Favorite this tweet, my intelligence is solid.*" Tuncay Opçin, one of the leading names of FETÖ/PDY, sent the following tweet on the 14th of July 2016 "*They will catch them in their beds, and hang them at dawn*". Another twitter user that was a mem-ber of the organization tweeted, "*You say July, I say coup. The TSK will stage a coup in July.*"[345]

Although the public was confused with the unusual situa-tions experienced at the night of the 15th of July with the Bosphorus Bridge being shut down by soldiers, gunshots heard in Ankara, and jets making a sortie while flying at low altitudes in both cities; they still did not think of a possibility of a coup attempt. This is despite all of the FETÖ/PDY members' activities in the social media platforms. Although in the beginning the series of events were not defined as "coup", the sharing of such events in large numbers and analysis and reasoning within the social media led to the rumors that this was perhaps a *"coup attempt"*. The first official explanation of the extraordinary developments was made by Prime Minister Binali Yildirim at around 23:00 on some television channels[346]. Prime Minister Yıldırım stated that this desperate incident was an unlawful uprising carried out by parts of the Turkish Armed Forces that was not coordinated within the chain of command and that those who made this attempt would pay the severest price.

In the TRT channel, which was occupied by a group of coup soldiers, a coup manifesto was read out at 00.13 by an illegal group which called itself 'Peace at Home Council'. Thus, it became evident that the coup attempt was being carried out by members of the FETÖ/PDY, who were nested in the Turkish Armed Forces and by some military personnel who were supporting them. Immediately after the coup manifesto was read out, President Recep Tayyip Erdoğan contacted a private television channel[347] and on the air, live, at 00.28 he invited the people to the public squares and the airports. Moreover, he stated that he would also be in the public square and said that the coup plotters will learn an essential lesson.

Other television and radio channels, web sites and social media platforms began broadcasting on the coup attempt; security experts, sociologists, academics, politicians and civilians also joined live broadcasts and gave instant information.

Thus by adopting a particular attitude against the coup the resistance of the people was encouraged. In addition, in particular Anadolu Agency along with Ihlas News Agency and Doğan News Agency made great efforts to inform the public correctly and to resist the coup.

Facing this situation, the coup plotters who wanted to stop the television, radio and internet broadcasts attacked TÜRKSAT, but they did not achieve their aims. In order to avoid being monitored by the security units, the coup plotters started to communicate with each other by setting up groups in an end-to-end cryptic social media platforms.[348] With this method, it was discovered that the coup plotters created an operation center through social media, and their messages indicated that they focused on the how to prevent information reaching the public from the media and the measures to be taken to prevent the mosques reciting *Salas.* For example, the organizations' raids on mosques, cutting electricity lines of the places where the call to prayer were being recited through a central system, arranging raids on private television channels, and attempts to disable transmitters in Çamlıca and similar hills can be considered as such attempts. As a matter of fact, in order to prevent the broadcasts of CNN Türk TV, the Doğan Media Center was raided, and an attempt was made to land soldiers by helicopters at A Haber and Sabah newspapers headquarters.

In the first hours of the coup attempt news claims and messages that supported the coup attempt such as, "*the army has seized the power*" were sent through social media accounts and media organs that were involved with the organization. For example, Can Erzincan television channel published video archive images that propagated the idea that the government was harming the country in the early hours of the coup attempt. However, after recognizing in the following hours that the coup attempt would not be successful, the TV channel changed its position and portrayed the whole event as "*an attempt from an unidentified source.*"

Messages were also sent from social media accounts that belonged to the organization in order to influence the public. After President Recep Tayyip Erdoğan invited the public to go outside and into the streets, Twitter and Facebook accounts tried to persuade the public to stay at their homes instead of going out in the streets. Messages such as, "*The coup leaders are fully in control and resistance will only result in more bloodshed*" were sent to break the resistance, which was the biggest obstacle against the coup attempt. Messages full of manipulation were shared more frequently in order to demoralize the public and to decrease the support of the national will.

The resistance of our citizens and law enforcement officials that put their life on the line trying to prevent the coup attempt were insulted by messages from social media accounts that belong to the FETÖ/PDY members and they tried to spread the rumor that President Recep Tayyip Erdoğan had requested asylum in Germany. On some of the social media accounts, the coup attempt was openly supported and President Erdoğan and other politicians, who were fighting against the coup attempt, were insulted. On some social accounts, crueller expressions such as "*Our soldiers shoot them; be more relentless towards them*" were used and instilled in the coup plotters soldiers. As a matter of fact, according to the Digital Mediums Analysis of the Coup Attempt (*Darbe Girişimi Dijital Mecralar Analizi*) between the 15th of July and the 19th of July, 50.5 million Turkish messages were shared on

Twitter and about 8 percent of them supported the coup implicitly or openly.[349]

Moreover, many lies were fabricated on the social media accounts of the organizations' members and baseless photographs that were taken out of context were used to make false accusations. For example, a photograph of a military vehicle that happened in 2006 was spread as "*A Turkish soldier cut at the throat*". Similarly, various photographs from Korea, Egypt and Morocco were used in social media to manipulate information.

The messages from a Whatsapp group called "*We are Peace at Home*" (*Yurtta Sulh Biziz*) created by soldiers that were members of the FETÖ/PDY indicated that the chain of command, which forms the basis of the military profession, had been broken and that the superiors were taking orders from their subordinates. For instance, a Major named Mehmet Murat Çelebioğlu gave orders to a colonel that was at a higher rank then him. This situation is a clear reflection of the warped structure that the organization operates within. This afore mentioned Whatsapp group exposed who gave support to the coup plotters and who resisted it within the Armed Forces. In addition, it also revealed the violent tendencies of the coup plotters.

On the one hand, with the understanding that the coup attempt will fail, the media organs under the control of FETÖ/PDY and social media accounts belonging to the members of the organization started to spread the message and information that "*This was actually all staged by President Erdoğan*". Whereas, on the other hand, an effort was made to spread the news that the coup attempt could not have been administered by the FETÖ/PDY, and for this purpose, a video condemning the coup attempt by Fetullah Gülen was circulated through the social media.

The western media ignored the bloody coup attempt that targeted the democratic system in Turkey and made an effort to trivialize the coup attempt.[350] Even after the failure of the coup attempt, accusations such as *"danger of authoritarianism"* was made against President Recep Tayyip Erdoğan and the government. For example, an article written by Tim Arango and Ceylan Yeğinsu which was published in the US based New York Times, the allegation was made that *"President Recep Tayyip Erdoğan prevented the attempted coup with the Islamists coming out in the streets, however, in the future he will use this situation to clear out those who are opposed to him."* They willfully ignored the fact that people from all sides in Turkey resisted the coup. In the same newspapers twitter account abusive remarks were made on this topic, and a message was shared that insulted the Turkish people with the statement, *"Erdoğan's supporters are sheep, and they will follow whatever he says."*[351]

The British media, especially the BBC, chose to present the coup attempt as if it were part of a democratic debate and attempted to trivialize the connection between the coup and Fetullah Gülen. Even when it was understood that the coup attempt was stopped, the BBC continued to report as if the coup plotters had been successful. The BBC also used the headline *"How did they end up in a coup attempt?"* and started presenting a list of political discussions that happened in the last few years in Turkey. With this approach, the British television presented the military coup attempt as *"a natural and ordinary political result"*.

The Guardian, which is known as a *"liberal democrat"* British press newspaper evaluated the coup attempt against the elected government and the elected President as a "*detail*" and described the operations carried out by the state against the FETÖ/PDY members as a "*purge*". The Guardian which used the headline "*Aftermath of Turkey coup attempt will be bloody and repressive*" claimed that the rule of law will come to an end after the coup attempt was unsuccessful. In addition, they made the claim that the people who resisted the coup "*brutally*" attacked "*the people who opposed Erdoğan*" and "*the people who opposed the government*" and simply ignored the coup plotters' bloody attacks against the civilians.

The Times Newspaper chose to characterize the citizens who resisted the coup as "*Erdoğan supporters*", and leaving aside the coup attempt, accused President Erdoğan as "*opening the way to absolute power*" in news that was presented in a headline. In the newspaper's report, it was stated that, "*The Turkish military was the last strong opposition against Erdoğan*" and tried to simply legitimize the coup attempt by making an unbelievable claim that the army was in it for a democratic struggle against the democratically elected president and the government.

The Financial Times, on the other hand, completely ignored the epic struggle of the people for the protection of democracy and instead published news about a Turkish citizen, whose name was kept secret that feared the coup resisters, saying, that "*he/she was afraid to step outside of Etiler*". The British Independent Newspaper, forcing the limits of reason and logic in this regard published an article entitled, "*The Turkey coup: Conspiracy theorists claim power grab attempt was faked by Erdogan*". The British newspaper, The Daily Telegraph, made the allegation in their news article entitled "*Turkey Coup Attempt*" that world leaders warned President Erdoğan not to use this coup attempt as an excuse to oppress others. London based Economist magazine published a news article entitled *"Turkey's failed coup gives its president a chance to seize more power"* alleged that Erdoğan now had the opportunity to increase his authority after the coup attempt became unsuccessful.

The American Fox News published a news article entitled *"Turkey's last hope dies"* written by Ralph Peters on their website, which made the claim that the failed coup was Turkey's last hope to stop the Islamization of its society, and that the Western Leaders efforts condemning the coup attempt was useless and will only result in *"a poisonous Islamic regime that is at the door of Europe."*

DECLARATION OF STATE OF EMERGENCY AND THE EMERGENCY DECREE LAWS

Declaration of State of Emergency

The National Security Council, which met on the 20th of July 2016 after the coup attempt, in accordance with Article 120 of the Constitution[352], advised the Government to declare state of emergency.[353] The Council of Ministers, which convened on the same day under the chairmanship of President Recep Tayyip Erdoğan, declared a 90 day state of emergency starting from 01.00 on the 21st of July 2016 and the decision was published on the Official Gazette on the 21st of July and come into effect.[354] The decision of the Council of Minsters was approved by the Grand National Assembly of Turkey on the 21st of 2016, i.e. the same day.[355] The State of Emergency decision was extended 90 days on Wednesday the 19th of October 2016[356], on Thursday 9th of January 2017[357], on Wednesday 19th of April 2017[358], on Wednesday 19th of July 2017[359]and on Wednesday the 19th of October 2017[360] starting at 01.00.

Emergency Decree Laws Passed During the State of Emergency

By means of the emergency decree laws issued after the state of emergency, institutions belonging to the Fetullahist Terrorist Organization (FETÖ/PDY) and the institutions and organizations and non-governmental organizations whose affiliation or connections to FETÖ/PDY was ascertained were closed down. The members of the judiciary and other public officials who were evaluated by the National Security Council as having connections to Terrorist organizations or institutions or groups that act against the national security of the state, were removed from their offices. It was decided that these individuals could not be employed in the public service and that they would be removed within fifteen days from the public space or foundation statuses which they held, and, furthermore, firearm licenses, seamanship certificates and pilot's licenses held by them would be canceled. It was also stipulated that they in the future would not be allowed to found, be in partnership or be an employee of a private security company. In addition, students related to this context, who were studying abroad with state scholarship, were dismissed.[361]

The assets of the closed foundations were transferred to the Directorate General of Foundations, and the assets of higher education foundations, health application and research centers and other institutional corporations were transferred to the Treasury without any direct cost to them. A decision was made that under no circumstance shall any claim or demand related to any type of debts mentioned be made against the Treasury. It was also decided that the students enrolled in the higher education institutions that were closed should be placed by the Council of Higher Education in State-run universities or foundation-run universities.[362]

An issue of the stay order was passed in order to prevent the interruption of any struggle against terrorism by the cases opened in response to the decisions and actions taken in scope of the 667 numbered emergency decree law. In addition, such arrangements were made in many cases of detention, interrogation, investigation, trial, prosecution, defense, detention, conviction and judicial matters:[363]

1. The maximum period of detention was increased to thirty days.

2. Within the scope of the investigations carried out, allowing all suspects, victims and witness statements, including public officials, to be taken by judicial law enforcement officials, without any distinction between duties and titles within the scope of the investigations were carried out.

3. In the investigations and prosecutions carried out;

- During the statement taking and interrogation or at the hearing, at most 3 lawyers had to be present.

- To be able to read the entire or part of the indictment or documents that substitutes the indictment before the start of the trial

- Investigation of detention, appeal against detention and requests for release decisions were carried out through the case file

- In cases where the judge or court deems it appropriate, it was considered possible to question the suspect/defendant or to make them participate in the hearings using video and audio communication.

The revocation of the right of easement and the right of usufruct and the lease agreements by the related institutions and organizations were arranged, regarding the evaluation of the beneficiaries and tenants of all public real estate's being a member or being in connection with organizations, and networks that present a threat to the national security. It was stipulated that legal, administrative, financial and criminal responsibility will not arise due to the decisions and duties of the persons who make decisions and perform the duties within the scope of the emergency decree laws issued during the state of emergency.[364]

With the emergency decree law no. 668 declared on July 27 2016[365]; The public prosecutor may issue a direct arrest warrant, and the detention period for the persons apprehended upon the order issued shall be a maximum of 30 days (in order not to interfere with the investigations), and the detained persons shall be brought before the authorized judge or court upon completion of the proceedings. In order to ensure that the investigations remain inclusive, the persons who go into hiding domestically or abroad will be considered fugitives in the investigation phase without discrimination. In this way, the aim was to conduct the investigations effectively and to prevent disruptions. It was imposed that the objection to the detention decisions has to be evaluated in the maximum period of ten days and the release requests within a maximum period of 30 days.

In cases where there is peril in delay, searches can be conducted in domiciles, workplaces and non-public closed spaces upon an order by the public prosecutor. Seizures made by a public prosecutor shall be submitted to the qualified judge for approval within five days. In military zones, in cases where there is peril in delay searches and seizures can be carried out by law enforcement officers that are not military personnel without the participation of the public prosecutor upon the written order of a public prosecutor. The authority to examine the documents and papers which belong to the person concerning whom a search measure has been carried out was widened; and it enabled them to be examined by law enforcement officers. In order to prevent the terrorist activities and communication of the suspect or accused regarding a threat to national security, documents related to their communication with their relatives may be confiscated in this scope.

In cases where there is a strong suspicion that the terrorist organization used elements in its financing or obtained it through terroristic activities the public prosecutor may in cases where there is peril in delay, or in other cases, ask the judge or a court decision to carry out the seizure processes without waiting for the reports from institutions such as the Banking Regulation and Supervision Agency, the Capital Markets Board, the Financial Crimes Investigation Board etc. The requirement of the presence of a public prosecutor in the searches of the offices of lawyers was abolished. In these places, in addition to the decision of the judge, in cases where there is peril in delay, it was allowable to carry out searches by the decision of a public prosecutor.

Searches, copies and seizures regarding computers, computer programs and databases can be ordered by the public prosecutor as well, in cases where there is peril in delay. Such orders shall be submitted to the competent judge for approval within five days. When the order is not submitted or approved by a judge, the seizure shall be automatically lifted and these evidences cannot be used further in the case. In case the copying and backup process takes a long time, these tools and devices may also be seized. The devices seized shall be returned without delay once the process has been completed.

The defense counsel's right to examine the contents of the case-file or the right of the suspect in custody to see a defense counsel can be restricted by the decision of the public prosecutor, to ensure that the investigation is not compromised in accordance with national security. However, no statement shall be taken during this time. In cases where it has been deemed necessary for the verification of the information received, remand or sentenced inmates may be taken from penitentiary institutions for temporary periods by the order of the magistrate.

Amendments to some laws and emergency decrees laws were made such as: Military courts empowered to exercise judicial powers shall be established by the Ministry of National Defense by taking the opinion of the Force Commands; granting temporary authority to members of the military judiciary to meet the military judge's deficit; the temporary dismissal of the Turkish Armed Forces personnel up to one year with the approval of the minister; the relevant commanders can be taken to the Supreme Military Council regardless of the rank awaiting period and the appraisal requirement; abolishing the obligation to hold the Supreme Military Council meetings in August and holding the meetings at least once a year upon the call of the Supreme Military Council Chairman; changing the Supreme Military Council meeting date in 2016 to be held on July; removal of the "*maximum twice a year appointment limit*" regarding the employment of martyrs and veterans in the public sector benefiting from the rights under the Anti-Terror Law; and giving the possibility of appropriate appointment according to their profession, and issues relating to the appointment of contracted teacher and some other issues. In addition, the General Command of Gendarmerie and the Coast Guard Command were connected to the Ministry of Interior and these institutions were given the status of general law enforcement agencies.

With the emergency decree law no. 669 declared on July 31 2016[366]; the periods of time to initiate an investigation laid down in the governing legislation shall not be applied during the period of the state of emergency in respect of public officials who have been suspended after the 15th of July 2016 on the ground of national security considering the excessive number of detainees and the number of public officials in custody, the conduct of the investigation being multi-faceted and nationwide, and to ensure the administrative investigations being more sound and to prevent unjust treatment. With respect to the requests for postponement of bankruptcy filed prior to the announcement of the state of emergency, during the period of the state of emergency, postponement of bankruptcy cannot be ordered, no interim measure can be ordered and if such interim measure has been ordered, it shall be lifted immediately. With this decree, the University of Health Sciences was established, the Ministry of National Defense was restructured, and the restrictions on access to military schools were abolished and all vocational high school graduates were allowed to enter military schools. The military schools, and the military factories and shipyards were attached to the Ministry of National Defense; War Colleges, military high schools and training schools for noncommissioned officers were shut down, the structure of the Supreme Military Council was changed where the majority came from non-soldier background, the Force Commands were connected to the Ministry of National Defense, various regulations were made on military jurisdiction and the legislation on disciplinary proceedings of military judges were amended and the Ministry of National Defense was fully authorized in the process of appointment, personalization and dismissal. The criminal penalties regarding the civilian judges and prosecutors as of Law No. 2802[367], was also put it into practice to military judges. The personnel of the Turkish Armed Forces, who were victimized by FETÖ/PDY by changing their class and status with health reports, were given the right to be re-examined by the Ministry of National Defense and the Ministry of Health upon request. Arrangements were made for the President and the Prime Minister to receive information directly from their affiliates and to give orders if necessary. The Gülhane Military Medical Academy (GATA) and military hospitals were transferred to the Ministry of Health.

With the emergency decree law no. 670 declared on August 17 2016[368]; those who had been dismissed from the civil service of the Decree-Law no. 667 would not be able to use titles once received nor professional titles and capacities that they held and they cannot enjoy the rights provided in connection with those titles, professional titles and capacities. Among the public officials and civilians who were injured during the coup attempt and terrorist action carried out on the 15th of July 2016, and those injured while trying to be helpful and beneficial to ensure that further actions of this attempt be exposed, and prevented would be awarded compensation. In addition, with regard to the person who may be the one that has benefitted from the right of compensation, or their relatives stated in the article, shall be employed in public institutions or organizations.

The seven working days period referred to in Law no. 5549 on Prevention of Laundering Proceeds of Crime Revenues[369] which states that, *"In cases where the assets which are the subject of a transaction are suspected to be linked to offence of laundering or financing of terrorism, the Minister shall be authorized to suspend the transactions that is being attempted to be conducted or currently going on within or through obliged parties for seven work days or not to allow the performance of those transactions for the same period of time so that MASAK can verify the suspicion, analyze the transaction and convey the results of those analyses to competent authorities when necessary"* shall be applied in thirty working days during the course of the state of emergency in respect of persons, institutions and organizations that are considered to be a member of, or have relation, affiliation or connection with terrorist organizations, structures/entities, or groups established by the National Security Council as engaging in activities against the national security of the State.

It was arranged that offences falling within the scope of the Anti-Terror Law no. 3713, when a need for re-taking of statement of a suspect with regard to the same incident arises, due to determine the structure and formation of terrorist organizations in a sound manner and to accelerate the investigation and prosecution proceedings, this procedure may be carried out by Public Prosecutor or by law enforcement officers upon the written order of Public Prosecutor during the course of the state of emergency.

Appointments of persons that are determined to have unlawfully obtained the exam's questions and/or the answers before it is held or during the exam shall be annulled particularly for the Public Personnel Selection Examination in 2010 and other examinations.

With the emergency decree law no. 671 declared on the 17th of August 2016[370]; it was decided to upon preventing the transfer and assignment, establishing property rights, and to restrict power of disposal concerning the immovable or land, sea, or air transportation vehicles of the suspects or accused persons, with a view to compensating the damages suffered by the natural and legal persons as well as public institutions and organizations due to the crimes against the security of the state in the Turkish Penal Code, crimes against the constitutional order, crimes against national defense, crimes regarding state secrets and espionage and offences within the scope of the 3713 numbered Turkish Anti-Terror Law, and the offenses within the scope of this Code. This decision is put into action in the phase of the investigation by the Magistrate and in the phase of the proceedings, by the court. If the interlocutory injunction regarding the continuation of annotation given by the civil court is not presented within a year as of the date of annotation, the annotation shall be automatically lifted.

In order to meet the needs of pilots in the Turkish Armed Forces, the pilot officers were provided from external sources and the pilot officers who had previously left the Turkish Armed Forces or were dismissed were allowed re-appointment in the Armed Forces. Those who have the necessary conditions to be employed in special operations units are allowed to be admitted to the police vocational training centers with physical qualification and interview tests without seeking the conditions of Public Personnel Selection Examination.

Telecommunications and Communication Presidency was closed, its duties and powers were transferred to the Information and Communication Technologies Authority. The retirement age was increased from 72 to 75 and the duration of this practice was extended to 2020 in order to ensure that academicians did not have any difficulties in obtaining and strengthening the academic infrastructure in some universities. In the execution of the penalty by probation, the duration of the conditional release, which was initially 1 year was extended to two years. For those who had been condemned to imprisonment in order to benefit from conditional release, the rate that requires that two-thirds of his penalties expiate at the execution facility was halved.

With the emergency decree numbered 672[371] declared on the 1st of September 2016, many personnel working in some public institutions and organizations were expelled from public offices. With the decree Law no. 673[372] which entered into force on the same date a number of private education institutions and private student dormitories, which were closed with the list numbered (II) in the annex of the decree numbered 667, were allowed to be taken out of scope and reinstated. Re-appointed for those who have resigned on multiple occasions or retired from their posts as a judge or public prosecutor of their own will and who request to return to their previous positions was made possible. The membership of the presidents and members of the Monitoring Boards of Penitentiary Institutions and Detention Houses shall cease on the date of entry into force of this Article and a re-election shall be held. The period of one month prescribed for approvals for retirement shall not be executed during the state of emergency. Workers, having membership of, affiliation, link or connection with terrorist organizations or structure/entities, organizations or groups held by the National Security Council as engaging in activities against the national security of the State, will not ever be employed, direct or indirect participation, at enterprises, partnership and participations in the State or legal entities, and within the other legal entities where the State has shares.

With the decree numbered 674 declared on the 1st of September 2016[373]; for only once, those who have worked for at least six years in the preparatory course centers and study centers, it was ensured that they could be appointed to the contracted teaching positions in the first degree priority regions in the development with an oral examination without seeking KPSS. The Computer Forensics Specialization Department has been established within the Forensic Medicine Institute to provide a prompt, impartial and transparent system for experts on the matters requiring specialization in information technologies during judicial investigations. The interruptions of judicial services have been disallowed by assigning members from other chambers by the chairman, according to seniority and order in cases where it is not possible for the Regional Courts of Justice to convene on account of legal or factual reasons.

The Decree Law has removed the obligation of the public prosecutors at the Regional Courts of Justice to submit preliminary opinions in writing in order to prevent the backlog of cases before the public prosecutor's offices after they have been sent to the Regional Courts of Justice for judicial revive and enable them to promptly be brought before the bench of judges. However, the public prosecutors at the Regional Courts shall attend the hearings and continue to submit opinions during the hearings. The Code of Criminal Procedure has been amended and accordingly, the assize courts have been empowered to appoint a trustee in addition to its authority to seize immovable properties, rights and receivables.

The Law on Execution of Penalties and Security Measures[374] has been amended. Accordingly, the Chief Public Prosecutor's Offices shall be entitled to impose restrictions on the temporary leave from the penitentiary institutions of those who have been detained for or convicted of terror offences in case they provide opportunities for terrorist organization communication, and if it becomes assessed that it would be detrimental to the penal institutions, examination centers or school.

Following the entry into force of the Decree Law, the duties of trustees serving in the companies to which a trustee has been appointed on account of their membership, affiliation or connection to terrorist organizations shall be terminated and their powers shall be transferred to the Savings Deposit Insurance Fund (TMSF).

With the decree law numbered 675 declared on the 29th of October 2016[375]; concerning the cases against agencies, institutions, private radio and televisions, newspapers, magazines, publishing houses and distribution channels, which have been closed in accordance with the Emergency Decree Laws, and their real person or legal entity owners as well as the cases, the lawsuits and execution proceedings shall be rejected and reduced by the grounds of hostility. According to the interest of such requests, it will be forwarded to the Ministry of Finance or to the Directorate General of Foundations, if no response is made within 30 days or if the request is not fulfilled, a case may be filed in the administrative court. Again, from the 15th of July 2016 until the announcement of the state of emergency and during the time when the state of emergency was declared, among those that have been dismissed from their appointed positions, it is stipulated in the relevant legislation that the time limit prescribed for this measure will not be applied during the state of emergency.

The ranks of those, who retired while serving in the Turkish National Police, or those who were previously dismissed from the profession and who were found to be a threat to national security, were identified as belonging to the FETÖ/ PDY terrorist organization, whose affiliation, or contact with the terrorist organization were included in the list attached to this decree, have been revoked. Within the scope of the emergency decree the military ranks of the members of the military judiciary and of the military judges, who had previously been decided to be revoked, were also terminated under this decree. Among the students, who have been discovered to not have a connection with FETÖ/PDY, their dismissal of studentships in accordance with the emergency decree law no. 673 was settled and their status was returned. In accordance with the emergency decree law no. 668, the military officers in various ranks that were dismissed from their profession and those that have been dismissed in accordance with the decree law numbered 672 were returned to their professions. With the decree law no. 673, the procedures regarding the students who were studying abroad and whose objections were accepted and whose objections have been re-examined and which have been rejected provision and results have been finalized.

With the decree numbered 676 on 29th of October 2016[376]; in order to ensure that the proceedings would not impede in the prosecution phase and thus to ensure a fair trial, in the hearings of organized crime cases, the maximum representation was limited to three representatives.

Lawyers that were representing those what were referred to as a suspect defendant or convict for offenses referred to in Articles 220 and 314 of the TCK and terrorist crimes, would possible become prohibited from their duties in cases they were also in prosecuted or investigated against the same offences stated in the article. With this amendment made in Article 151 of the Code of Criminal Procedure, it was ensured that this measure was applied to persons who were evaluated as being a perpetrator or suspect rather that the condition of detention, and the requirement of initiating an investigation was brought instead of the requirement of prosecution for those lawyers involved in the duty defending the suspects.

Again with the amendment made in the Code of Criminal Procedure the right of the suspect in custody to consult with their lawyers may be restricted for twenty-four hours by the judge at the request of the public prosecutor in order to effectively combat the crime and prevent the delay of the investigations in cases where the suspects are in custody for; acting against the security of the state, the constitutional order, the functioning of this order, national defense, acting against state secrets, offenses covered by the Anti-Terror Law and crimes of manufacturing and trading drugs and stimulants. However, no statements can be taken during this time.

By amending the Code of Criminal Procedure, it was stipulated that requests to hear witnesses to prolong the cases may be rejected and the hearing may be resumed if the defense leaves the hearing without excuse. With the amendment to the Law on the Execution of Penalties and Security Measures it was stipulated that conversations between lawyers and convict cannot be heard, and that their notes and documents submitted cannot be taken.

On the other hand, in the case of offenses defined in Article 220 of the Turkish Penal Code and in the fourth, fifth, sixth and seventh sections of the second book and in the convicts conversations with the lawyers of those convicted of crimes under the scope of the Anti-Terror Law, some measures were allowed to be implemented in the event that information and instructions were given to the organization, and that the security of the community and the execution institution were compromised. In this context, the interviews can be recorded using voice and video, an attendant can be present in these meetings, documents given to the convict by the lawyer and the documents given to the lawyer by the convict can be confiscated, and the days and hours of their conversations can be limited. These measures may be taken by the decision of the judge of execution upon the request of the public prosecutor's office and may be applied for a period of three months, and according to evaluation can be extended if necessary.

In case of violation of the rules during negotiations, the prosecutor's request to the attorney general's office to meet with his lawyer may be barred for six months by the judge of the execution, and in this case the relevant bar association will appoint a new lawyer. These arrangements may also be applied during the period of detention under the same conditions. The authority on the application of these measures against the detainees belongs to the magistrate during the investigation phase and to the court at the prosecution stage.

Again by this decree, the definition of senior manager in the Ministry of National Defense has been reassessed in accordance with other ministries. The jurisdiction of the ministry supervisory unit was extended to all organs related to the ministry, and it was made possible to carry out temporary implementation to meet the need of necessary ministry's supervisory staff and experts. Security investigation and/or archive research has been made mandatory in entry into public offices.

With the decree law no. 677 declared on the 22nd of November 2016[377]; The members of the penal institutions who are detained or convicted due to the crimes committed within the framework of the membership of the terrorist organization or the activities of these organizations, by means of the central examinations applied throughout the country and all kinds of education/training institutions and public institutions and organizations, will not be able to take the examinations carried out inside or outside the penal execution institution. In addition, civil students who are going to graduate in the institutes of the war academies closed with the war schools will be placed in institutes and universities, which are suitable for their circumstances. A total of 16.409 students attending military high schools, military, maritime and air vocational schools and military schools were dismissed from the Turkish Armed Forces and placed in universities or secondary schools attached to the Ministry of National Education.[378]

The institutions and organizations closed for having membership to, affiliation, or connection with terrorist organizations or structures, formations or groups determined by the National Security Council to carry out activities against the national security, may under no circumstances claim compensation for being closed. The powers vested in the trustees taking office in the companies, in respect to article 133 of the Turkish Penal Code, that a trustee be appointed for having membership to, affiliation, or connection with terrorist organizations shall be transferred from the trustees to the Saving Deposits Insurance Fund.

In respect of the municipalities where a mayor or acting mayor has been appointed and their affiliated institutions and in respect of partnerships; in situations where the Directorate General of Security reports that the contractors, which are parties to all kinds of goods or service procurement contracts under the Public Procurement Contracts Law[379], have affiliation or connection with the terrorist organizations or in cases where it is determined that there has been an infringement of the municipal interest to a great extent due to these contracts, shall be unilaterally terminated by the mayor or the acting mayor.

With the decree Law No. 678 declared on the 22nd of November 2016[380]; in addition to the new provisions on the age limit and the legal consequences related to the security guards in accordance with the article added to the Village Law[381], the houses that were rented on a daily basis will be added under the scope of the necessity to keep records of identity and arrival-departure of the persons included in the Identity Reporting Law[382] and various provisions were introduced. In addition, new regulations regarding the Turkish Armed Forces, the General Command of Gendarmerie, the Coast Guard Command and the General Directorate of Security were introduced.

Those people who stood against the 15th of July 2016 dated terrorist coup attempt and the continuation of the coup attempt—even though they were not assigned to do so—among these martyrs, the ones whose male children are of the same father and mother, will not have to serve their military duty unless they are willing. And if they are unwilling, they will be released from their military duty.

With the amendments made to the Law on Trade Unions and Collective Bargaining Agreements[383], if the legal strike or lockout destabilizes the general health, national security, public transport services in metropolitan municipalities, banking services, economic or financial services, it is made possible for the Council of Ministers to postpone the strike and lockout for sixty day.

In the decree numbered 687 declared on 9th of February 2017[384], regarding the companies, that were decided on the appointment of a trustee and the authority delegated to the Savings Deposits Insurance Fund, in the cases where the company's shares or assets are decided to be confiscated due due to the offenses defined in the Turkish Penal Code and the offenses defined in the Anti-Terror Law and the Law on the Prevention of Terrorism Financing; The decision of confiscation should be conducted by Savings Deposit Insurance Fund by sale and liquidation of the shareholders shares and assets. In the process of sale and liquidation, it was decided to continue the management of the company by the appointed managers according to the relevant legislation and the revenues obtained from the sale of shares and assets and liquidation are stipulated to be recorded to the Treasury. The emergency decree also regulates other matters.

In the decree numbered 688 declared on the 19th of March 2017[385], 416 public officials, who were dismissed from profession in accordance with the previously enacted Emergency decree laws, have been reinstated to their duties. Accordingly, the actions taken against these persons shall be deemed to have ceased with all their effects and consequences as of the date of the publication of the relevant decree law.

In the decree numbered 689 declared on the 29th of April 2017[386], institutions and organizations, persons with membership or affiliations on grounds of being terrorist organizations or a threat to national security, have been removed from public offices without any further actions to be taken. Newspapers, journals, foundations, associations and private health institutions, which belong to the structure, formations or groups that are determined to be active through the terrorist organizations or acting against the national security of the state determined by the National Security Council, have been closed down. The movables and all kinds of property, receivables and rights, documents and documents were decreed to be transferred in relevance to the Directorate General of Foundations or to the Treasury without any compensation. The immovable properties were registered in the name of the Treasury or the Directorate General Foundations in relevance as being free from any restrictions and burdens in the land registry office. No rights and claims can be made from the Treasury or the Directorate General of Foundations in any way due to their debts. It was ascertained that the transactions related to the transfer shall be performed by the Ministry of Finance by obtaining the necessary assistance from all relevant institutions.

In addition, the relevant provisions of the decrees which came into force on the closure of the associations listed in the annex to this decree were abolished, valid from the effective date together with all provisions and results of these associations.

Students that are subjected to Law number 1416 dated the 8th of April 1929 regarding students that will be sent to foreign countries (*Ecnebi Memleketlere Gönderilecek Talebe Hakkında Kanun*)[387], which have been evaluated as being a member of, or have relation, connection or contact with terrorist organizations, or structures/entities, or groups established by the National Security Council as engaging in activities against the national security and those that have been registered in the list attached in the appendix (5) have been dismissed from studentship. Regarding these students, paragraph 2 and 3 of Article 4 of the Law no. 6749 dated 18th of October 2016 on Amendment and Acknowledgement of the Decree-Law on the Measures, was decided to be implemented. It was stipulated that equivalence procedures shall not be carried out regarding the trainings they have received and they shall not benefit from the rights related to their academic titles and degrees within the scope of these trainings. In addition, a total of 246 people were sent back to their duties in their public offices and the provisions of these decrees were repealed with all their conclusions.

With the decree Law No. 690 published on the 29th of

April 2017[388], new provisions concerning The Commission on Examination of the State of Emergency Procedures have been introduced, as well as, new regulations on national defense, domestic security, media services and other matters were completed.

With the decree law numbered 691 declared on the 22nd of June 2017[389], in order to increase flight safety against helicopter crashes, regulations for the height of vertical obstacles were made. Also those who are determined to be active members or have a relation to terrorist organizations or organizations that participate in actions against the state's national security by the National Security Council and those and those who are understood to be eligible for military service, who do not have a valid excuse written in the relevant law, including evading the draft and evading the examinations, have been decided to be taken under arms in accordance with the referral principles of the Ministry of National Defense. Additional amendments have been made to the provisions of the Military Penal Code[390], the Anti-Terror Law and the Turkish Commercial Code.

With the decree law numbered 692 declared on the 14th June 2017[391] and the decree law numbered 693 and 694 declared on the 25th of August 2017[392], institutions and organizations, persons with membership or affiliations on grounds of being terrorist organizations or a threat to national security determined by the National Security Council, have been removed from public offices without any further actions needed to be taken. The persons listed in the annex to the decree were returned to their duty in public offices. With the decree, amendments were made regarding the titles of Turkish Armed Forces personnel whose titles were revoked, students studying abroad, and security guards, military schools, National Defense University and many other laws and emergency decrees.

Institutions and organizations, persons with membership or affiliations on grounds of being terrorist organizations or a threat to national security determined by the emergency decree laws or the National Security Council can be removed from their public offices in cases which;

1. Personnel subject to the 926 numbered Law on the Turkish Armed Personnel[393], by the proposal of the relevant force commander, by the official letter of the Commander of the Turkish Armed Forces and the approval of the Minister of Defense.

2. Personnel subject to the 2803 numbered Law of on the Organization, Duties and Powers of Gendarmerie[394]; by the proposal of the Commander of the Turkish Gendarmerie Forces and with the approval of the Minister of Interior.

3. Personnel subject to the 2692 numbered the Coast Guard Command Law[395], by the proposal of the Commander of the Coastguard Command and with the approval of the Minister of Interior.

4. Personnel of the Ministry of National Defense, by the Minister of National Defense approval.

5. Personnel subject to 2914 numbered Law on Higher Education Personnel[396], by the Chairman of the Council of Higher Education's proposal and the approval of the Council of Higher Education; administrative personnel in higher education institutions, by the authorized supervisor and the approval of the Board of Directors.

6. Personnel of the local administrations, by the Council's proposal that is determined and chaired by the Governor and with the approval of the Minister of Interior.

7. All kinds of Personnel employed in all positions and status (including workers) that are subject to other legislations, that are subject to the 657 numbered Civil Servants Law[397] except those specified in Article 3 of the Decree Law, by the proposal of the Board formed by the affiliated, relevant or related Minister under the chairmanship of the top manager of the relevant institution or organization, and approval of the Minister.

8. Personnel that are employed in all positions and statuses (including workers) in any other relevant, related or unrelated ministry, by the proposal of the chief of the unit, and by the approval of the appointment supervisor.

As of July 17 2017, a total of 111,240 people have been dismissed from their public duties, 32,188 people have been suspended and 35,639 have been returned to public offices.[398]

After the 15th of July 15 attempt, 34 private health institutions, 1411 private educational institutions, 995 private student dormitories and boarding houses, 104 foundations, 1326 associations and their economic enterprises, 15 foundations of higher education institutions (universities), 31 unions, federations and confederations, 733 preparatory course centers, 70 private radio and television institutions, 109 newspapers, magazines, publishing firms, distribution channels and news agencies; a total of 4.724 institutions and organizations were closed on terms of being in connection, belonging to or being a member of the FETÖ/PDY.[399] The list of media, publishing and distribution companies under the control of the FETÖ/PDY is presented in Table 5.

Table 5: The FETÖ/PDY related media, printing, publishing, and distribution companies closed during the state of emergency.[400]

News Agencies	Cihan Haber Ajansı, Muhabir Haber Ajansı, Sem Haber Ajansı
Television Channels	Barış TV, Bugün TV, Can Erzincan TV, Dünya TV, Hira TV, Irmak TV, Kanal 124, Kanal Türk, MC TV, Mehtap TV, Merkür TV, Samanyolu Haber, Samanyolu TV, SRT Televizyonu, Tuna Shopping TV, Yumurcak TV
Radio Stations	Aksaray Mavi Radyo, Mavi Radyo, Berfin FM, Burç FM, Cihan Radyo, Dünya Radyo, Esra Radyo, Haber Radyo Ege, Herkül FM, Jest FM, Kanal Türk Radyo, Radyo 59, Radyo Aile Rehberi, Radyop Bamteli, Radyo Cihan, Radyo Fıkıh, Radyo Küre, Radyo Mehtap, Radyo Nur, Radyo Şimşek, Samanyolu Haber Radyosu, Umut FM, Yağmur FM
Newspapers	Adana Haber Gazetesi, Adana Medya Gazetesi, Akdeniz Türk, Şuhut'un Sesi Gazetesi, Kurtuluş Gazetesi, Lider Gazetesi, İşçehisar Durum Gazetesi, Türkeli Gazetesi, Antalya Gazetesi, Yerel Bakış, Nazar, Batman Gazetesi, Batman Postası, Batman Durum, Bingöl Olay, İrade, İskenderun Olay Gazetesi, Ekonomi, Ege'den Son Söz Gazetesi, Demokrat Gebze, Kocaeli Manşet, Bizim Kocaeli, Haber Kütahya Gazetesi, Gediz Gazetesi, Zafer Gazetesi, Hisar Gazetesi, Turgutlu Havadis Gazetesi, Milas Feza Gazetesi, Türkiye'den Yeni Yıldız Gazetesi, Yeni Yıldız Gazetesi, Hakikat Gazetesi, Urfa Haber Ajansı Gazetesi, Ajans 11 Gazetesi, Yeni Emek, Banaz Postası, Son Nokta, Mekür Haber, Millet, Bugün, Meydan, Özgür Düşünce, Taraf, Zaman, Today's Zaman

Magazines	Akademik Araştırmalar Dergisi, Aksiyon, Asya Pasifik, Bisiklet Çocuk, Diyalog Avrasya, Ekolife, Ekoloji, Fountain, Gonca, Gül Yaprağı, Nokta, Sızıntı, Yağmur, Yeni Ümit, Zirve Dergisi
Publishing and Distribution Companies	Altın Burç Yayınları, Burak Basın Yayın Dağıtım, Define Yayınları Dolunay Eğitim Yayın Dağıtım, Giresun Basın Yayın Dağıtım, Gonca, Gülyurdu, GYV, Işık Akademi, Işık Özel Eğitim Yayınları, İklim Basın Yayın Pazarlama, Kaydırak Yayınları, Kaynak Yayınları, Kervan Basın Yayıncılık, Kuşak Yayınları, Muştu Yayıncılık, Nil Yayınları, Rehber Yayınları, Sürat Basın Yayın Reklamcılık ve Eğitim Araçları, Sütün Yayınları Şahdamar Yayınları, Ufuk Basın Yayın Haber Ajans Pazarlama, Ufuk Yayınları, Waşanxaneya Nil, Yay Basın Dağıtım, Yeni Akademi, Yitik Hazine, Zambak Basın Yayım

Rights Provided to the Martyrs' Relatives, the Veterans and the Veterans' Relatives[401]

The rights granted to the relatives of the heroic martyrs who sacrificed their lives for their homeland and nation against the 15th of July coup attempt and are considered partially incapacitated are as follows: setting monthly payments, cash compensation payment, additional compensation or retirement bonus, right to employment, interest free mortgage, free travel right, discount on the cost of electricity and water, additional payments to educational aid, exemption from military service, exemption from special consumption tax, exemption from residence tax, providing free education in private education institutions for children, administrative leave on Martyrs and Veterans Day, the ability to use social facilities, entering museums, historical sites and state theaters (spouse and children) for free, priority in state dormitories and students loans, and exemption from higher education tuition fees and charges.

The rights granted to the veterans who fought heroically for their their homeland and nation against the 15th of July coup attempt are as follows: setting monthly payments, cash compensation payment, additional compensation or retirement bonus, right to employment, interest free mortgage, free travel right, discount on the cost of electricity and water, additional payments to educational aid, health assistance exemption from residence tax, providing free education in private education institutions for children, administrative leave on Martyrs and Veterans Day, the ability to use social facilities, entering museums, historical sites and state theaters (spouse and children) for free, priority in state dormitories and students loans, and exemption from higher education tuition fees and charges.

The rights granted to the veterans who fought heroically for their homeland and nation against the 15th of July 15 attempt and who were not wounded to be considered partially incapacitated are as follows: cash compensation payment, right to employment, interest free mortgage, free travel right, discount on the cost of electricity and water, additional payments to educational aid, health assistance, exemption from residence tax, providing free education in private education institutions for children, administrative leave on Martyrs and Veterans Day, using social facilities, entering museums, historical sites and state theaters (spouse and children) for free, priority in state dormitories and students loans, and exemption from higher education tuition fees and charges.

THE COUP ATTEMPTS IMPACTS
ON ECONOMIC AND SOCIAL LIFE[402]

The ban on the FETÖ/PDY's most common field of activity, which has been in the education sector for nearly 40 years, contrary to popular belief, did not have a great impact on social life. Education centers of the FETÖ/PDY, which has a very elitist and closed education structure, created in fact more substantial damage to the community. Students studying in these education centers were placed in other schools without any difficulties after the coup attempt by the Ministry of National Education and the Council of Higher Education.

Contrary to what some media organs claim regarding the society becoming more distant to religious institutions, personalities and practices after the 15th of July Coup Attempt, it is not the case. The results from the survey of social media networks and public opinion research show that the majority of the population has become more interested in religion and spirituality after the 15th of July. This also makes one think that the real intentions of the coup plotters were not related to religion at all.

The coup attempt brought together millions of patriots regardless of their religions, sects, political views and life-styles. These people fought against the coup plotters, side by side in the public squares, streets, road, airports and public in-stitutions. Even after the coup attempt was suppressed, mil-lions of people did not empty their squares for several weeks in all parts of the country. This was because the people want-ed to guard democracy and support the Grand National As-sembly of Turkey, which is the manifestation of the elected President, the Government and the National will. The people also wanted to say "*stop*" to the plots of FETÖ/PDY and the external forces even at the cost of their lives.

On the other hand, the majority of our people (86,5%) found the State of Emergency and the Emergency Decree Laws to be important to combat the *juntaists* and the FETÖ/PDY, and the majority of the people (96%) supported the ac-tions to get rid of FETÖ/PDY's existence within the state. Thus, restructuring the bureaucracy and all the institutions of the state, particularly the military, security and the judiciary in order for the government to keep control became among the most important expectations of our people (93.2%). The rate of those who believe that the failure of the coup attempt protected the national will is very high (97,4%). (Table 6)

Our people believed that if the coup attempt was success-ful, strong countries would have invaded Turkey (91,1%), sectarian and ethnic conflicts would have begun in Turkey and lasted years as in Syria (92%), and that belief in concepts such as democracy and human rights would have disappeared (97,3%). (Table 6).

The coup attempt increased public confidence in states-men and politicians who stood up and struggled against the coup, especially President Recep Tayyip Erdogan. For example, confidence in President Recep Tayyip Erdoğan increased from 78.7% to 85.5%, the confidence in Prime Minister Binali Yıldırım from 66% to 75.6% and the confidence in MHP Chairman Devlet Bahçeli increased from 47.5% to 70.3%. On the other hand, the ambivalent attitude of CHP leader Kemal Kılıçdaroğlu against the coup attempt was reflected in the confidence of the people and remained at 30.1%. The HDP Co-Chairperson Selahattin Demirtaş's confidence fell to 36%. (Table 6)

One of the most obvious effects of the coup attempt in the social life of society is the society's increased confidence in the state, the government officials and the Grand National Assembly of Turkey.

Table 6: Popular perception against the coup, and the confidence in statesmen and politicians.[403]

Criteria		Rate (%)
Could you please specify your reasoning's and expectations for joining the demonstrations against the coup attempt and the democracy watch	To stand against the coup, and protect democracy.	92,5
	To support the President and the elected government.	88,9
	To protect the national will and to take preventive actions against coup risks.	92,6
	To stop the plots of the FETÖ and the external forces.	91,9

I find it important to combat FETÖ with the State of Emergency and the Emergency Decree Laws.	86,5
I support the efforts to remove FETÖ from the state. (The average from the three different components have been taken.)	96,0
Government keeping everything under control by restructuring the bureaucracy and all the institutions, especially the army, the security and the judicial structures.	93,2
The superiority of the national will was preserved.	97,4
Confidence in President Recep Tayyip Erdoğan	85,5 (78,7 before the coup attempt)
Confidence in Prime Minister Binali Yılıdırm	75,6 (66,0 before the coup attempt)
Confidence in CHP Chairman Kemal Kılıçdaroğlu	30,1 (21,9 before the coup attempt)
Confidence in MHP Chairman Devlet Bahçeli	70,3 (47,5 before the coup attempt)
Confidence in HDP Co-Chairman Selahattin Demirtas	36,0 (57,0 before the coup attempt)

What would have happened if the coup attempt had been successful?	Certain powerful countries would partially or fully invade Turkey.	91,1
	Sectarian and ethnic conflicts would begin that would have lasted years, just as in Syria.	92,0
	Belief in concepts such as democracy and human rights would have disappeared.	97,3

The state of emergency, which was declared and implemented after the coup attempt, seems not to have affected the society a lot. Both the results obtained in the public opinion surveys and the comments in the open sources suggest that the state of emergency did not have strong effects in the socio-economic life of the society in general.

The coup attempt, on the other hand, reinforced the confidence of the society. Turkey, which had been surrounded by a ring of flames with the Arab Spring, despite the 15th of July coup attempt did not have its social cohesion disrupted nor its solidarity. In fact, not only did this event of solidarity and social cohesion renew Turkey's confidence but it also led to a spread of a message of unity and solidarity to its hinterland, as well as to the rest of the world.

Still, the coup attempt has had some effects on Turkey's international relations, and this situation has clearly affected its social life. In particular, the European Union (EU) countries ambivalent attitude at the beginning of the coup attempt was not met kindly by the masses and the majority believes that the EU was unfair to Turkey in this respect. However, this situation does not mean that Turkey's relationship with EU has come to an end. There is no doubt that reproach and disapproval has been rendered against the countries and officials who made public statements that belittled or trivialized the coup attempt, particularly the EU and the US. The majority believes that the EU and the US left Turkey all by itself and that they have not yet produced a social response in this regard. The comments reflected in the media platforms shows that the response of the Turkish society towards the West increased to a much higher level than before the 15th of July. There is a growing agreement in society that the coup attempt, which affected the country's internal relations, is an internal matter for Turkey, and that some EU officials are taking an advantage of this state of affairs by pressuring Turkey in the international field.

It must be said that the country assessed the situation accurately from the first moments of the 15th of July coup attempt, and reacted appropriately. In addition, it is evident that the society developed some social measures as well as formal measures to minimize the negative effects of the coup attempt. Some of these measures were; using a more careful and constructive language from the very first moment, giving no concessions to those that have positively been identified as being involved in the coup attempt, making meticulous inspections and then reacting to irregular conditions, trying to improve the image of the country, confirming the rule of law and the indispensability of the will of the people, prioritizing national values and accepting the fact that the coup attempt, if successful, would have had major devastating socio-economic consequences and therefore acting accordingly.

As a result of the impact of the coup attempt, the downtrend in financial markets occurred in the week of 18-22 July and significant losses were experienced. While Borsa Istanbul's Bist-100 Index depreciated by 13.4%, the average loss in Borsa Istanbul was 18.1% in the same period on the basis of the US Dollar. With the sale tendencies in the government domestic debt securities, on Friday the 15th of July, the benchmark bond rate which was at 8.55% at the close rose to 9.37% at the end of Friday the 22nd of July. Turkey's five-year US dollar denominated CDS[404] (credit default swap) rate, which indicates the risk rate in the international credit markets basis points increased from 224.7 to 275,2 between the 15th of July 15 and the 22nd of July. After the coup attempt, fluctuations in foreign exchange markets were recorded. While the US Dollar which was at 2.89 TL at the end of 15th of July, increased to 3.07 TL at the end of the 22nd of July; the Euro increased to 3.37 TL from 3.20 TL.

During the week of 18-22 July, there was an intense capital outflows in stocks, government domestic debt securities (DİBS) and repo. According to the data of Central Bank of Turkey; portfolio investments of non-residents, in other words, the market value of hot money decreased by 12.3 Billion USD during the week of 18-22 July. This reduction in market value of portfolio investments by foreigners was due to; 8.4 Billion USD in stock portfolios, 3.4 Billion USD in government domestic debt securities (DIBS) portfolios and the rest was due to the reduction in repo and deposit portfolios. According to the change in net cash, there was an outflow of 523 Million USD in the week of 18-22 July and 415.6 Million USD in the week of 25-29 July on the subject of the portfolio investments of foreigners. The market value of the portfolio investments of foreigners increased slightly due to the increase in stock prices despite the outflow of the week of 25-29 July. The market value of the previously mentioned hot money also increased in the second week of August.

The losses in the markets during the week of 18-22 July were compensated in the following weeks. Staying together against the coup attempts and by acting in unison, the Turkish People contributed to the improvement of the perception of Turkey's economy. Moreover, the total amount of foreign currency accounts in the banking sector decreased in July, August and September. In these three-month period 18.0 Billion USD of the total of 21.7 Billion USD reduction in the foreign currency accounts was attained in terms of deposit/participation fund accounts. Despite the increase in the exchange rates and the decrease in the amount of foreign currency accounts, that is, foreign currency deposit/participation fund accounts, the indications are that the Turkish people supported the Turkish Lira by selling foreign exchange after the coup attempt.

International credit rating agency Moody's started to monitor Turkey's credit rating in order to lower its credit rating, by assessing the medium-term impacts of the unsuccessful coup attempts effects on Turkey's economic growth, on the decision making bodies and on the external buffers. In a statement by Moody's dated the 21st of July 2016, the increasing tension in Turkey will possibly impact its already low investor confidence, effect its foreign direct investment negatively and the necessary foreign capital inflows that it will need in the next two-three year period will also be adversely impacted. In addition, it was also expressed that the coup attempts impact on Turkey's economy, in particular in consumer spending, will likely be felt in the third and fourth quarter of 2016.

Hence, Moody's on the 23rd of September 2016 downgraded the Government of Turkey's long-term issuer and senior unsecured bond rating level one rank from BAA3, which is the lowest rank of the "*investment grade*", to BA1. The reasoning was stated as, the increase in the risks related to the country's sizeable external funding requirements and the weakening in previously supportive credit fundamentals, particularly growth and institutional strength. In addition, the risk of a shock arising as a result of the country's weak external position became more pronounced, given the combination of persistently high political risks and volatile investor sentiment. However, two days prior to the announcement of the credit rating reduction by Moody's, it was stated that, "*The unsuccessful 15th of July coup attempt's shock on the economy is dispersed in large extent, however Turkey's problems will still continue in the long run*". Moreover, although Moody's Head of Sovereign Ratings Alastair Wilson's stated that, "*Turkey's credit note for the ongoing process of the review will be completed next month*", Turkey's credit rating was reduced suddenly within two days, which hints at this decision being politically oriented. International credit rating agency Standard and Poor's (S&P) reduced Turkey's credit rating one rank below and lowered its (BB+) rating level which was one rank below the "*investment grade*", to (BB) which was two ranks below the "*investment grade*" suddenly after the unsuccessful coup attempt on the basis of increasing risks.[405]

The FETÖ/PDY's propaganda and lobbying activities conducted for several years in order to destroy Turkey's reputation, which destroyed foreigners' confidence in the Turkish economy, made Turkey more susceptible to negative effects of the fluctuations in the world market than other countries. The fact that FETÖ/PDY is a crypto organization that has infiltrated critical positions in every institution of the country caused people to have trust issues after the coup attempt. The reflection of this trust issue to the economy has shown itself through a slowdown in commercial activities.

If we were to inquire to *"what would have happened to a country that faced even a small portion of the events that Turkey has faced recently"*, we can easily recognize the strong resilience of Turkey's economy. Turkey passed the stress test not by doing imaginary scenarios that even countries with very high levels could not pass, but instead passed this stress test by successfully overcoming it by personal experience and by being directly subject to it. Indeed, the FETÖ/PDY especially during the 17-25 December periods tried to harm the economy with all sorts of manipulations and plots. After the coup attempt failed to reach its objective, it continued its lobbying and defamation activities abroad in order to undermine the expectations, perceptions, trust and reputation of the Turkish economy.

UARDS TO INSURE THE DESTRUCTION OF THE ECONOMIC POWER OF THE FETÖ/PDY[406]

Several institutions, especially the Ministry of Finance, the Financial Crimes Investigation Board (MASAK), the Banking Regulation and Supervision Agency (BDDK), the Savings Deposit Insurance Fund (TMSF), and the General Directorate of Land Registry and Cadastre carried out several important operations before and after the 15th of July 2016. For example, Bank Asya (Asya Katılım Bankası A.Ş.), which played an important role in the financing of the organization, was put under close financial control and then transferred to the Savings Deposit Insurance Fund. The chronological course of the decisions taken in this process is as follows:

1. On the 28th of August 2014, the Banking Regulation and Supervision Agency in consequence of the *"occurrence of a situation requiring action"* stated in the Article 67 of the Banking Law No: 5411[407], put Bank Asya under the scope of the law in question covered in Article 70 regulating the adoption of restrictive measures.

2. On the 3rd of February 2015 the Banking Regulation and Supervision Agency decided to allow Bank Asya's sharehold-

ing rights of the privileged Group (A) shares except dividends of Meltem Tourism JSC's and other 122 shareholders to be used by the Savings Deposit Insurance Fund based on Article 18/5 of the Banking Law No: 5411. It also decided to dismiss the chairman and all of members of the board of directors and the CEO of Bank Asya and make new appointments for the chairman and member of board of directors' positions. The necessary appointments were made based on this decision and the management of the bank was taken over by the Savings Deposit Insurance Fund.

3. On the 27th of February 2015 the Banking Regulation and Supervision Agency decided to allow Bank Asia's shareholding rights of Group (A) shares except dividends of Sürat Publishing Trading JSC's and Forum Construction Tic. J. S. C's to be used by the Savings Deposit Insurance Fund based on Article 18/7 of the Banking Law No: 5411.

4. On the 29th of May, the Banking Regulation and Supervision Agency decided to transfer the Bank's shareholding rights except dividends, management and control to the Saving Deposit Insurance Fund in accordance with the provisions of clause (b) of the first paragraph of Article 71 of the Banking Law. Since then, the Savings Deposit Insurance Fund started to conduct the Bank's management and audit powers directly. Thus, Bank Asya was completely transferred to the Savings Deposit Insurance Fund.

5. Although the SDIF decided to dispose of the bank through the sale of shares, the Bank's activities were temporarily halted on the 18th of July 2016 as no participant made a bid on the tender held on the 15th of July 2016, and the bank's activity permit was requested to be removed from the BRSA. On the 22nd of July 2016, the BRSA abolished the Bank's operating license with the decision numbered 6947. With the

publication of the decision in the Official Gazette on the 23rd of July 2016, Bank Asya's liquidation process began.

The General Directorate of Land Registry and Cadastre established a special unit prior to the 15th of July 2016 after determining suspicious real estate sales related to the FETÖ/PDY foundations and universities. Regarding this subject; the Turkish National Police force units, the Directorate General of Foundations and the Council of Higher Education made the necessary initiatives as well as take severe measures in the General Directorate of Land Registry and Cadastre by contacting the trustees appointed to the institutions connected with the organization. In accordance with the measures taken, the directives of 18th of May 2016 and the 25th of May 2016 prevented the organizations or its members hiding their assets to a great extent.

In the first paragraph of Article 19 of the Decree Law no. 674; the trustee's authorities were transferred to judges or to the Saving Deposits Insurance Fund by the court for the companies whom it was decided to appoint a trustee pursuant to Article 133 of the Code of Criminal Procedure because of their belonging, affiliation or contact with the terrorist organizations before the entry into force of this article. In the second paragraph it was decided to appoint the Savings Deposit Insurance Fund as a trustee if it was necessary for an appointment of a trustee for the companies and entities for whom it was decided to appoint a trustee pursuant to Article 13 of this emergency decree law.

In article 7 entitled *"transfer of the power of trusteeship"* of the 677 numbered emergency decree law it was stated that, *"The powers vested in the trustees taking office in the companies in respect of which it was decided that a trustee be appointed pursuant to Article 133 of the Code of Criminal Procedure dated 4th of De-*

cember 2004 and no. 5271 for having membership to, affiliation, or connection with terrorist organizations before the entry into force of this decree law shall terminate on the date when this decree law is issued without seeking for a decision rendered by a judge or a court or a request, and the management of the companies shall be immediately transferred by the trustees to the Saving Deposits Insurance Fund".

Within the scope of decree laws 674 and 677, upon the request of court/judicial decisions or trusteeship, the trustee's authorities of 694 companies were transferred to the Savings Deposit Insurance Fund or the Savings Deposit Insurance Fund was assigned as a trustee to these companies, in Turkey's 33 different provinces.

A total of 4724 institutions and organizations were closed by the Ministry of Finance on the basis of the decree laws issued during the state of emergency in order to reveal and dissolve the structure and economic power of the FETÖ/PDY and their types and numerical distribution are as follows:

- 34 private health institutions and organizations

- 411 private education institutions and organizations

- 995 private student dormitories

- 1326 associations and their economic enterprises

- 15 higher education institutions that were run by foundations

- 31 unions, federations and confederation

- 733 preparatory course centers

- 70 private radio and television establishments

- 109 newspapers, magazines, publishing houses, distribution channels and news agencies

The commercial activities of the companies to which these institutions were connected to, were terminated, and these were transferred to the Savings Deposit Insurance Fund to be sold or liquidated. In addition, 4351 real-estates belonging to these were registered in the name of the Treasury and 2214 real-estates were registered in the name of the Directorate General of Foundations. Moreover, upon the request of the administrative authorities, 59,666 real-estates, and upon the request of judicial authorities, 154,030 real-estates, sale and transfer were blocked.

Until the transactions related to the evaluation of the real-estates acquired by the Treasury by allocation or other methods are established; it was decided that, private health institution would be temporarily used by the Ministry of Health, private education institutions and entities; and secondary education private dormitories and pensions would be temporarily used by Ministry of National Education; and higher education institutions that belongs to foundations except for health application and research centers would be temporarily used by Universities; and higher education private dormitories and pensions would be temporarily used by the Higher Education Credit and Hostels Institution.

According to the data from the Department for Fighting against Smuggling and Organized Crimes, the FETÖ/PDY conducted activities in Turkey with a total of 3257 associations and foundations in 81 provinces and achieved substantial revenue out of them. The most well-known associations and foundations of the FETÖ/PDY were the Kimse Yok Mu Foundation, the Journalists and Writers Foundation, the International Turkish Association, the Turkish Confederation of Businessmen and Industrialists (TUSKON) and the Aktif-sen. The organization also formed many federations by uniting associations. The Alevi Bektashi Federation and the Federation of Eastern Anatolia Industrialists and Businessmen Associations (DASİDEF) are some examples.

Following the failure of the 15th of July coup attempt, in accordance with the Regulation on Postponement of Transactions within the Scope of Prevention of Laundering Proceeds of Crime and Financing of Terrorism, on the 10th of August 2016, a list of 25,000 FETÖ/PDY members received from the General Directorate of Security and other lists of soldiers involved in the coup attempt, were forwarded to the banks by MASAK, and these persons on the lists were restricted from banking activities. Since the 29th of July, banks have been acting vigilantly in all transactions and after consulting the MASAK, it decides on the completions of such transactions.

The Republic of Turkey is working on achieving the objective to stop all FETÖ/PDY's activities in other countries and to advise these countries about the internal and secret objectives of the organization. In this context, informative studies have been conducted against the FETÖ/PDY in the presence of foreign governments. In addition, a comprehensive struggle against this organization's activities conducted abroad under associations, foundations, companies, lobby etc. have been carried out. In the first hours of the 16th of July, the Ministry of Foreign Affairs sent a transcript announcing that the coup attempt failed and it was sent to foreign representatives with translations in different languages and published on social media. After the coup attempt, as a result of external information and communication activities implemented by Turkey, messages of support from 111 countries and 6 international organizations were received, and delegations from over 30 countries and international organizations visited our country.

Examples of statesmen, politicians and international figures who visited our country are such as; the King of Bahrain, the President of Kazakhstan, the President of the Turkish Republic of Northern Cyprus, the President of Macedonia, the President of the Bosnia and Herzegovina Presidency Council, the Prime Ministers of Georgia, Qatar and Turkish Republic of Northern Cyprus, the Vice-President of the United States, the Crown Prince of Saudi Arabia, the Minister of Defense of Singapore, the Foreign Ministers of Lithuania, Saudi Arabia, Qatar, Iran, Moldova, Hungary, Palestine, Netherlands, Estonia, Slovakia, Singapore, Norway, England, Latvia, Denmark, Romania, Poland, Serbia, Italy, Spain, Germany and France, the Minister of State of Japan, the President of the Iraqi Kurdistan Regional Government, the Vice President of the People's Republic of China, the Pakistan Joint Parliamentary Committee, the President of the European Parliament, the NATO Secretary General, the Secretary General of the Council of Europe Parliamentary Assembly, the Council of Europe Human Rights Commissioner, the High Commissioner for Refugees of the United Nations, and the OSCEPA delegation and Heads of International Parliamentary Assemblies.

A detailed information note was prepared by the Ministry of Foreign Affairs on how the coup attempt was suppressed and then sent to foreign agencies. The Grand National Assembly of Turkey's anti-coup joint statement adopted at the extraordinary general meeting, was translated into English and announced to the whole world. In addition, an English transcript describing the evening of the coup attempt and its afterwards was sent to all representatives abroad to be published on their website, and the links of the brochure *"FETÖ's Coup Attempt: A Timeline"* prepared by Anadolu Agency were shared with all departments of the Ministry.

All Turkish agencies abroad were instructed to publish the following messages on their websites; entities related to FETÖ/PDY cannot be allowed to use logos and emblems of our public institutions, expressions such as "*Turkish*" or "*Turkey*" or use any such official symbols. Moreover, in order to combat the FETÖ/PDY's sinister propaganda that was conducted in the aftermath of the coup attempt, a circular was sent to representations in foreign countries that stated its support of the Ministry of Economy, the Foreign Economic Relations Board, the TUSIAD, the MUSIAD, the Turkey Exporters Assembly (TIM), the Turkey Contractors Association (TMB) and all activities of similar institutions/organizations in countries where they are located and accredited.

In order to inform the foreign counterparts of Turkey of the coup attempt carried out by FETÖ/PDY, official letters signed by the Minsters of Customs and Trade, Transport, Maritime Affairs and Communications, and Economy and Finance were sent to their counterparts through representations in foreign countries.

The main agenda of the meetings after the 15th of July with the counterparts at the level of the president, the prime minister and the foreign minister during all high-level visits in Turkey and abroad was the July 15 coup attempt and the FETÖ/PDY. Foreign counterparts were informed on the issue in multilateral platforms, particularly in G-20 summit in China, the Council of Europe meeting in Strasbourg, the United Nations General Assembly in New York, the Parliamentary Assembly of the Council of Europe and the NATO-Parliamentary Assembly.

The fight against FETÖ/PDY is carried out by representatives abroad and foreign counterparts in our country are regularly informed about this issue. In addition the website "*www.15.07.gov.tr*" has been put into service, and the Ministry of Foreign Affairs issued briefings on FETÖ/PDY for the members of the press from different locations who were invited by the Directorate General of Press and Information.

Turkey's operations conducted against FETÖ/PDY abroad focuses on the closure or transfer of schools related to this structure, to prevent activities of the foundations and associations, preventing people in connection with this organization to travel freely abroad and escaping from justice, freezing their assets and to wipe out their financial resources.

As a result of the initiatives of our country, the Organization of Islamic Cooperation made a historical decision on the 19th of October 2016 and declared FETÖ/PDY a terrorist organization. This organization was recorded as a threat to public order, security and stability to Turkey, the Muslim countries and other countries. In addition, member states were invited to take all necessary measures against the FETÖ/PDY and to cooperate with our country in this direction. Furthermore, a joint statement was published following the Ministerial Meeting of the Gulf Cooperation Organization held in Riyadh between 12-13 October. Upon Turkey's efforts, the determination of countering new terrorism forms such as FETÖ/PDY was confirmed, and the terrorist nature of this organization was put forward. In the declaration of the Asian Parliamentary Assembly (APA) meeting held in the city of Siem Reap in Cambodia during the 28th of November – 1st of December 2016, it was clearly stated that FETÖ/PDY is a terrorist organization, and a paragraph was added stressing full solidarity with our country in the fight against the terrorist organization in question and for the APA member states to take necessary measures against the terrorist organization in question.

As a result of Turkey's initiative, the business capacities

of companies connected with FETÖ/PDY decreased significantly. We have entered a period in which having connections with this organization has become a serious burden for the entities. Therefore, FETÖ/PDY elements who in the past did not hesitate to disclose these connections are now desperately trying to hide these links. In this context, schools, associations, foundations, companies etc. are changing their titles, changing their Board of Directors, shutting down their websites or trying to erase the information that shows that they are in connection at all with FETÖ/PDY - Fetullah Gülen.

Visits to various countries have been carried out by the Ministry of National Education and the Maarif Foundation authorities to address issues related to the FETÖ/PDY related schools. In this context, visits to Senegal, Mauritania, Sudan, Mongolia, Guinea, Pakistan, Afghanistan, Somalia, Bosnia and Herzegovina, Albania, Serbia, Thailand and Cambodia were organized. In some countries, it was agreed that the measures to be taken for FETÖ/PDY affiliated schools should be addressed in joint committees to be formed by the authorities of the countries concerned. As a result of Turkey's initiatives, schools in connection with FETÖ/PDY in Gambia, Azerbaijan, Libya, Jordan, Somalia and Sudan have been closed. Schools in connection with FETÖ/PDY in Guinea were transferred to the Turkish Maarif Foundation in October 2016 and schools in Chad were transferred to the Turkish Maarif Foundation in November 2016. Administration of schools operating in Pakistan was transferred to Pakistan, and Pakistani administrators were appointed to the Board of Directors. A representative was appointed in Pakistan by the Turkish Maarif Foundation and the application process for the foundation to operate in Pakistan was completed. The Sudan government decided to transfer the schools operated by the organization to the Turkish Maarif Foundation.

RESISTANCE BY FETÖ/PDY AGAINST MEASURES THAT THE STATE TOOK UPON THE COUP ATTEMPT[408]

The fight against terrorist organization which has crossed national boundaries and has global extent such as FETÖ/PDY requires a comprehensive and organized work. Unlike the typical difficulties encountered in combating terrorist organizations, combating against terrorist organization that the world has not seen before require some unconventional techniques. The external and domestic extensions of this organization, which seems fairly to be an espionage organization, are in an effort to disrupt the struggle of the state by conducting continuous perception operations, developing insidious techniques and setting traps. Some of the strategies, tactics and techniques implemented by FETÖ/PDY are:

1. To prohibit face-to-face meetings among members and to communicate through communication applications over the internet that has end-to-end encryption.

2. In order to keep morale high in the organizational base allegations have been put forward such as, "*there will be serious events and economic crisis in the country in the short term, and a second coup and/or assassination attempt will be made to the top-level state officials.*"

3. To instruct the detained members of the organization on how to testify and answer the questions.

4. To direct members of the organization in prisons on what kinds of *"attitudes and behaviors"* that they should follow, to keep members under control by establishing organizational hierarchy in prisons, to maintain ties with each other by using secret communication (notes, sending letters etc.) methods and to ensure that members act in unison.

5. To put pressure on politicians and state administrators by using the theme of the victimized public personnel that is subject to judicial/administrative procedures and their families, and to conduct perception management in the form of confusing the minds on public opinion.

6. By providing financial assistance to the families of those detained/convicted, displaying that the organization was still active and they are not alone.

7. To order members of the organization that work in public officials to exhibit anti FETÖ/PDY attitude and behavior in order to protect to their real denies being revealed in sight.

8. To ensure that members of the organization *"become members only in name"* of other religious communities to display themselves as being from different religious and social backgrounds.

9. To increase cooperation with other terrorist organizations and secret structures.

10. To try to maintain organizational commitment by maintaining communication with the students and their families, who have not yet graduated or those that have graduated in the closed schools of the organization.

11. Encourage members of the organization that have the possibility of being caught to flee abroad.

12. To transfer capital abroad.

13. To try to create social unrest by conducting psychological operations on social media.

14. To carry out new restructuring in public institutions, to work on the placement of people who are educated in educational institutions abroad and who are difficult to determine their organic ties with the organization in public institutions.

15. To exploit religious sensitivities and humanitarian aid issues in order to attract Syrians who are refugees in our country.

16. To reach out to political contacts in order to maintain its presence in the countries it operates and to assert that *"the organization does not have a connection with the coup attempt"*.

17. To display the investigations and impeachments conducted after the coup attempt in the foreign press in such a way that creates headlines against Turkey, and that creates the perception of themselves being victimized.

18. To carry out propaganda activities to promote the organization as a *"civil society movement"* that operates within the scope of *"moderate Islam"*.

19. To enable Fetullah Gülen giving interviews in different countries media that makes a call for the US, NATO and EU to put a pressure on the country, for the return to democracy in Turkey and setting up an international commission to investigate the coup attempt.

20. To force members of the organization to apply to in-

ternational organizations such as the United Nations and the European Court of Human Rights on basis of being *"unjustly treated"*.

21. To move the assets and members of the organization from countries where they live in distress to other countries or to transfer their assets to the people they find *"reliable"* in the related country.

22. To continue to manage and control in the background, while apparently transferring the educational institutions known to belong to the organization, in foreign countries.

23. To look out for members of the organization who have escaped from Turkey, in countries that they escaped to, by other members of the organization.

24. To continue the propaganda activities by establishing new media outlets or controlling other media outlets in the background.

25. To establish relations with other terrorist organizations abroad, and to make contact with powers, lobbies and diaspora's that are against the country.

26. To make propaganda that *"innocent Muslims"* are being intimidated by the emergency decree laws.

The organization tries to keep its activity lost in the country, alive and continue abroad. It has been observed that they make effective publicity, lobbying and influencing activities, reach political elites and media in every country they settle, especially in USA and European countries, and they can still use these tools even though their effects are gradually decreasing. FETÖ/PDY after July 15, have been trying to smear Turkey in the Western Public opinion by using all communication tools available to them. On the other hand they are trying to present themselves as "*A peaceful movement opposed to radical Islam and authoritarianism and ready to work with the West*".

FETÖ/PDY is able to maintain its presence in countries where its structuring abroad goes long way back and in countries where our citizens and kinsmen live intensively. This mainly due to the organization using the close relations it has established with local administrators for many years, seeing the positive results of their efforts to cling on to the country they are located and to have the support of our citizens in the places where there is a great number of Turkish citizens.

The organization maintains its own media activities in the countries where it has the opportunity, and it continues its efforts to make publications in the direction it wants with close relations developed with the local and national media in the countries where it does not have such opportunity. The organization is trying to shape public opinion in their own interest in various countries by publishing the articles/news in these counties by first publishing these in prestigious newspapers in countries such as USA, UK, Germany and France.

FETÖ/PDY carries out activities to develop dialogue with politicians, religious leaders, opinion leaders, bureaucrats and academicians by taking into account the conditions of the country in which it operates, as well as through propaganda activities carried out through media, through various NGOs and companies, and attaches special importance to shaping public opinion in favor of the organization. In this context, it provides interest to the organization through these people who can be used/directed by the lobbying activities, and more importantly, it aims to be able to continue its existence in the country in any condition, regardless of the political structure/governments.

The organization is working to reopen the schools through the companies belonging to the citizens of the country, in countries where there was an inadequate education system when the schools initially opened and have been closed as a result of Turkey's initiatives.

Prejudiced and unfair criticisms have been directed toward Turkey, by FETÖ/PDY's lobbying activities conducted in some countries abroad. In fact, in some countries, instead of reacting to the coup attempt, publications have been made that are being concerned about the coup plotters being put on trial, and accusing the Turkish people that have reacted against coups. The organization is using its lobbying power which is a strategic force effectively in both at home and abroad to disrupt expectations and perceptions regarding Turkey and the Turkish Economy.

FETÖ/PDY, which is organized in 45 of the 50 states in the USA, which is one of the countries where its lobbying activities are carried out most effectively in the world, operates in every field with its established network in USA. The e-mails and documents about Hillary Clinton, which the FETÖ/PDY openly supported in the US presidential elections, showed that this organization was in close contact with many politicians in the United States. The organization using *himmet* money collected in Turkey, it has established strong links with many politicians, bureaucrats and international lobbying organizations not only in the US but also in different countries of the world. FETÖ/PDY which is seeking to discredit Turkey in the international arena and to mobilize international criminal courts, they are carrying out their lobbying activities with their schools, associations, foundations, newspapers and even politicians bribed by them. For instance according to a news published in the England based Times newspaper dated August 1 2016[409], Garnier, a Conservative MP for Harborough received 115,994 pounds from FETÖ/PDY on February 2015 for a report titled *"Human Rights and the Rule of Law in Turkey"*.

Some of FETÖ/PDY members which have been placed in international economic/financial institutions in the past such as the Bank for International Settlements (BIS), the World Bank and the Islamic Development Bank have been dismissed from their positions due to Turkey's pressure, while others continue to work. These people are putting a great effort to ensure that these international organizations prepare negative reports about Turkey.

SAFEGUARDS TO PREVENT THE RISE OF ANY FETÖ/PDY TYPE OF ORGANIZATION[410]

The struggle against FETÖ/PDY should be accepted as a long-term effort and this struggle should be turned into a state policy. The measures to be taken for this purpose are explained below through main subheadings.

Measures to Be Taken by Intelligence Institutions

The Intelligence units in our country were unable to identify the 15th of July coup attempt during the preparatory phase - they became aware of it only by a tip-off received on the day of the coup. This state of affairs is the result of institutional problems as well as coordination problems between the intelligence agencies. Although, it seems as the MİT is the head of central intelligence in Turkey, there is no central figure responsible for intelligence; in fact, in practice there is a multi-headed structure. The problem of this multi-headed structure in security intelligence regarding the Gendarmerie, Turkish National Police and MİT should be eliminated; all information should be collected in one place. In this context, the National Intelligence Coordination Board (MIKK), which was established under the presidency of the President with the decree Law No. 694, is an important step towards this direction. In this respect, it is important to make new arrangements for the appointment of military personnel under MİT.

This new established central unit should especially have coordination capabilities along with analyzing abilities. In this center, there should be departments concerning different ideological elements. The intelligence units in our country lack analysis capabilities in general. In this center, strategic intelligence should also be produced, not only be reliant on tactical and operative intelligence. Also this intelligence should be able to be presented to the related political entities. Moreover, the intelligence units should have the authority to operate at home and abroad, in addition to collecting information within the scope of the country's security.

Safeguard to Be Taken Regarding Security

The FETÖ/PDY was able to hide itself within the Turkish Armed Forces and was able to quickly infiltrate it. This is mainly due to the fact that the Turkish Armed Forces has been operating in a closed system for decades, and is not open to external auditing, and does not allow state intelligence agencies to collect intelligence within the Turkish Armed Forces. In the event that any illegal formation takes root in such a structure, it is not easy for the institution to struggle with its internal dynamics and decision-making mechanisms, and external intervention is not possible because it is excluded from external auditing. In these cases where illegal organizations acquire positions, authorities and power it is almost impossible to regain it from them. Every office gained by external groups is considered a "*military position*", and an extraordinary effort will be made to prevent the loss of this position.

While the government did make significant number of dismissals of members of the organization within the Directorate General of Security after the dates between 17-25 December, the same dismissal processes could not be carried out in the Turkish Armed Forces due to the closed structure of the Turkish Armed Forces, which was strictly protected by the constitution and laws. In fact, even in the Gendarmerie and in the Coast Guard, which are inherently law enforcement agencies, dismissal procedures could not be carried out.

It is necessary to have the Turkish Armed Forces open to external, administrative, financial and intelligence external audits and to establish an internal audit system that effectively operates within this domain. In particular, it is of especial importance to establish a unit in which necessary intelligence information is compiled, evaluated and the information flow is provided. As a matter of fact, retired Commanders of the Turkish Armed Forces have also expressed the necessity of this matter. Within this context, the expansion of the powers of the National Intelligence Agency is an important step forward.

The issue of monitoring soldiers inside and outside the military post is another matter that should be examined. Currently, monitoring the soldiers in the military post is carried out under certain laws and this is merely conducted by observing attitudes, movements and statements of the personnel. The real problem is the identification and tracking of the soldiers in illegal formations. This determination and monitoring is only possible with the cooperation of the intelligence agencies of the military authorities and institutions. It is important to establish a military unit that can monitor all kinds of personnel inside and outside of the military posts and to organize it in the coordination of civilian and judicial authorities, and to enable the monitoring of personnel from a position to be established at the upper level of the institution and to get assistance from other intelligence units.

While the FETÖ/PDY is not considered to have the capacity to attempt a new coup, the possibility of the transformation of an organization into a marginal armed terrorist organization should not be overlooked considering the existence of the crypto elements that remain hidden in the Turkish Armed Forces and other law enforcement units. In case of the realization of this possibility, it is possible that some forces will take advantage of this situation and enter into cooperation with such terrorist organizations operating within Turkey.

Necessary Financial Safeguards

It is not possible to maintain the existence of any illegal organization without its financial resources. In the fight against FETÖ/PDY, the global financial structuring of the organization should be exposed. As a matter of fact, one of the weaknesses that the coup attempt revealed is that the financial dimension was not adequately addressed or ignored regarding the fight against organized crime organizations and terrorist organizations. This is due to the fact that terrorist organizations' existence depends on meeting its financial needs. The main reason for the failure in Turkey's fight against terrorism and organized crime is that the struggle is conducted one-dimensionally by only dealing with the perpetrators. As a result of ignoring the financial dimension in the background of the organizational structure with only focusing on the perpetrators in criminal investigations, a steady transformation of organized crime/terrorism, whose players are constantly changing, may threaten our country for decades.

Another reason for this situation is the institutional attitude observed in law enforcement units and public institutions. In other words, institutions do not trust each other and keep information to themselves. Obstacles arising from legislation prevent the sharing of information to institutions that want to share information. Thus, the unit dealing with the financial dimension of the offense, without knowing the position of the perpetrators in the organization, without knowing which perpetrators and which issue should be specifically focused on, puts forward a report only within the framework of the registered economic data of the people who were requested to be investigated, and therefore the efficiency of the financial investigation remains insufficiently low.

The duties of financial intelligence units in the fight against money laundering and terrorist financing are limited to accepting and analyzing suspicious transaction notifications and transferring the results to the relevant institutions. The transmission of suspicious transaction notifications to the prosecutors by the financial intelligence unit is considered a *'tactical intelligence'*. Reports generated at a tactical level may include the identity, communication and suspicious transaction information and database checklists. The *'operational intelligence'* is a process of making the report after analyzing the suspicious transaction notifications and other news and information obtained by using the tactical intelligence data and analyzing it after being linked to an existing event. At the level of "strategic intelligence", a wide range of issues and trends are addressed rather than individual cases.

Article 19 of the Law no. 5549 on Prevention of Laundering Proceeds of Crime Revenues that regulates the duties and authorities of the Financial Crimes Investigation Board (MASAK), does not permit any law enforcement or public bodies except for the prosecution authorities to share the results of analysis and evaluation produced as a result of suspicious transaction notifications and other data received. This situation is understood as an obstacle that may weaken the fight against organized crime and terrorist organizations. That MASAK is not mentioned as an intelligence unit in the legislation, that they have a lack of personnel, lack of autonomy, that their capacity of expert personnel in the institution regarding sharing information and authority is minimized, and that there are security issues in terms of related legislation are the main concerns in this area awaiting urgent resolution.

The aim of the restructuring of MASAK is to organize a unit that is able to accomplish significant deductions or inferences by collecting suspicious transactional notices and other data that are essential to financial intelligence in the battle against money laundering and financing of terrorism. Moreover, to be able to analyze the financial data and other situations of the individuals or companies, especially those related to crime, and be able to assess them with other data found. In this framework, the financial intelligence unit should have a multidisciplinary structure considering that criminal proceeds involves different areas of expertise and sectors, and therefore to combats all criminal proceeds effectively, experts from all different sectors and institutions are required within its unit.

Safeguards to Be Taken Considering the Public Personnel System

The FETÖ/PDY was able to infiltrate public offices mostly during the personnel recruitment of the related institutions. This kind of infiltration activities may be carried out by the candidate personnel concealing him/her, but also by the appointment of the members of the organization in the commissions that make the personnel recruitment of the institutions. Prior to the election of all civil servants, security investigation and archival research should be done more thoroughly for the candidate. The security investigation and archival research is conducted by the MİT, the Turkish National Police and the the Gendarmerie. Due to the high number of requests sent by the relevant institutions, the security investigation and archive research constitute an immense workload for the authorities. In addition to this, due to the fact that there is a time limit, it is unfortunately not possible to have in-depth research. Therefore, measures should be taken to increase the performance of the institutions that direct these research and investigation activities.

If the results of the security investigation and archive research are cleared as "*clear*", the personnel can be accepted as "*good*" and taken as government employees. However, this situation should not be considered sufficient, the appropriate personnel should be monitored in whatever institution the personnel is situated, and in case of doubtful situation, the relevant units should be requested to investigate the personnel again. According to the current legislation, the security investigation carried out at the initial recruitment of the personnel cannot be done again even if the demand is made within the personnel's time in office, and only archive research can be carried out by the MİT or the Turkish National Police if the institution deems it necessary.

The criterion for selecting and assigning civil servants to courses and employments in the country and abroad is only based on an assessment within the institution and this evaluation generally consists of the personnel file and opinions of the supervisor. However, the 15th of July coup attempt should be closely analyzed in terms of an *"environmental assessment"* of all activities considered *"suspicious"* of the government employees. According to the criteria of environmental assessment, the person interacting with his/her environment may have influence on his/her behaviors on duty or may have influence on his/her decisions. For example; it should be taken into consideration that even if there is no negative information in the investigations and research about a person, which has been raised in an neighborhood that looks positively to FETÖ/PDY and supports its activities, it should be taken into consideration the possibility of them being influenced by the environment in which the person was raised and that the person may sympathize with FETÖ/PDY.

The reassurance in the public personnel system, in particular the Civil Servants Law No. 657, prevents or delays the process of organizations members in the bureaucracy. Even for the institutions that have strategic importance, personnel recruitment procedures have not been checked for compliance with the requirements of the duties. Thus, the organization members' positioned itself within the bureaucracy. On the other hand, giving priority to political connections instead of *"qualification"* and *"merit"* for the promotion processes in the offices caused the members of the organization to cluster in the public institutions they desired. Therefore, the legislation regulating the public personnel system, especially the Civil Servants Law No. 657, should be rearranged in a way to encourage auditing and reward based on *"qualification"*, *"merit"* and *"performance"*.

Measures to Be Taken in the Education System

One of the measures to be taken in order to erase FETÖ/PDY's existence from all institutions and brackets of the state as well as to prevent the development of such illegal organizations is to carry out comprehensive training activities aimed at improving public awareness and understanding of democracy. Such educational activities should be implemented systematically starting from the elementary school years.

For the students in the formal education system, activities should be organized at the beginning of each academic year. These activities should consist of oral, written and visual presentations that give meaningful messages about democracy, the national will, elections, fundamental rights and different types of freedom, politics, parliament etc. Another study, which must be done in the context of the formation and development of democracy awareness, is to include these topics as subjects in textbooks or in the form of reading pieces in all the relevant textbooks. In addition, information should be given about different forms of tutelage; the implicit and explicit coups that have been carried out in the country and the 15th of July 15 attempt should be dealt with in detail, and the negative impacts of these on society, economy, human rights and freedoms should be explained.

Commemoration of the 15th of July coup attempt and the coups that have taken place in the past should be dealt with in each academic year through different activities (theater, cinema, travel programs, etc.) so that it can develop and strengthen the consciousness of democracy in the students.

Likewise, awareness-raising activities should be given regularly in a widespread education format for all segments of society, that are in different statuses (retirees, housewives, etc.) and that are separated from formal education institutions. A proper environment should be prepared in all kinds of education structures, where the relatives of the 15th of July martyrs and the veterans can reach the various sections of the people and speak of their experiences, and these activities should be repeated at regular intervals. Again, in both contexts, joint projects with the media should be carried out and support should be obtained from the arts and the sports community.

Strengthening the education infrastructure in state schools, reducing the number of students in classrooms, increasing the state incentives given to students going to private schools as well as the elimination of teacher shortages, strengthening state supervision in private schools, encouraging competition between private schools and controlling specific social groups or political - ideological sectors in private schools to prevent the cartelization, are also matters that should be focused on.

Measures to Be Taken in Religious Affairs

All the requirements of the social state must be ensured in order to prevent the rise of structures similar to FETÖ/PDY. This is because the FETÖ/PDY exploited religion and the belief sensitivity of the society since its establishment. Giving the impression of providing education, scholarship, shelter, accommodation and religious development opportunities to the poor and needy Anatolian children, the organization exploited the goodwill and charity of the Anatolian people and the destitution of the poor.

The emergence of the organization by appearing as a religious community and ensuring that the youth receive religious education which believes in "*saving the souls of the community by spreading the truth of faith*" enabled the organization to operate freely for many years. This fact has shown that the Religious Affairs Presidency, which coordinates the religious activities in our country, which has the legal responsibility to carry out the religious officials' professions, and is responsible for ensuring public awareness of the religious issues, should fulfill these duties more effectively.

Measures to Be Taken in the International Dimension

Turkey is fighting with an organization that has unprecedented global connections. It should always be kept in mind that the FETÖ/PDY elements abroad created effective communication mechanisms wherever they settled, especially in the US and in European countries. Therefore, they can still use these effectively and easily reach political decision makers and the media.

The FETÖ/PDY's schools abroad are the first line of work of the organization at the international level. It is important to be persistent in transferring these schools to the Turkish Maarif Foundation, to prevent the shortage of education services in case these schools abroad are closed, especially in countries where the quality of education is low. The development of the institutional capacity of the Turkish Maarif Foundation is also necessary.

The FETÖ/PDY, which tried to keep businessmen associations as a reference point, has seen this opportunity reduced with the efforts of our embassies and trade consultancy, as well as weakening the relations of the organization with Muslim communities and Islamic opinion leaders in countries where our religious services consultancy is effective with our embassies. Similarly, in the countries where the Yunus Emre Institute was established, it is observed that educational institutions, especially language courses, that used to belong to the organization has lost their effectiveness. In addition, it has also been observed that the publication of newspapers and magazines that supports our country has significantly reduced the influence of the media organizations in connection with FETÖ/PDY.

It is of utmost importance to continue to share evidences with other countries about the fact that FETÖ/PDY was behind the 15th of July Coup Attempt. Using the message that the organization poses a potential threat and danger to these countries due to its secretive structuring within a country may additionally help these countries see the real face of the organization.

It is of particular importance to prepare academic studies that support the findings of FETÖ/PDY with scientific data and to publish them in leading scientific publications in the world. Considering the close relations of the organization with the academic circles in the West, the scientific community in those countries seeing the true face and intentions of the organization and advocating it in their own scientific studies will work very well as persuasion and will make a serious contribution to the fight against FETÖ/PDY at the global level. In addition, it is important to inform think tanks, investigative journalists and leading representatives of the media in this respect. This is because the publication of articles, broadcasting series and news about the real intention of the organization in the media will provide great benefits in terms of raising public awareness of the public in those countries.

One of the key points of FETÖ/PDY's propaganda, especially in Muslim countries, are the claims that "*devout Muslims are under oppression in Turkey, they are being dismissed from their jobs, they are being imprisoned by made up courts, even their legitimate rights are taken away from them, their properties are being confiscated and they are subject to psychological torture*". In particular, the foreign offices of the Religious Affairs Presidency should carry out intensive work against such claims.

Information emphasizing the principles of human rights, democracy and the rule of law to shape the public opinion of developed countries, and lobbying efforts should be speeded up in the face of intensive propaganda and lobbying by the organization abroad. In other countries, approaches taking into account the specific conditions of those countries should be developed.

It can be argued that FETÖ/PDY started to evolve into a diasporic structure long ago. We are faced with an era where the base of the FETÖ/PDY internalizes the managers of the organization's hostile attitude towards Turkey and transforms it into an identity. This process will most likely result in a *"FETÖ diaspora"* that define themselves with hatred towards Turkey, similar to the Armenian Diaspora. The internalized hatred and alienation will most likely be provoked by political discourses that are formed by the pragmatic relationship established by the organization with the global networks (Allegations of human rights violations in Turkey, etc.) and through esoteric religious narratives for the disciples of the organization. In order to prevent this, the focus should be on the removal of the organization's members that do not have a direct relationship with the organization at the level of management from FETÖ/PDY's influence. Within this framework, efforts should be made to encourage those who wish to break out of the organization to benefit from the provisions of the effective amnesty law[411] in the Turkish Penal Code.

ENDNOTES

1   "Çatı İddianamesi," 06.06.2016, E. No: 2016/24769, Part 5; Komisyon Raporu (The report of the constituted Assembly Research Commission regarding the 15th of July 2016 coup attempt of the Fetullahist Terrorist Organization (FETÖ/PDY) and ascertaining the measures needed to be implemented by inspecting all aspects of the terrorist organization's activities.) (2017) Türkiye Büyük Millet Meclisi, Ankara, p. 41.

2   It has been asserted that the 'sick leave' report of Gülen was fabricated, and that Gülen was an informant placed in the military working on behalf of the intelligence service. He used the 'sick leave' report to complete his next task, which was to participate in the establishment of the Anti-Communism Association in Erzurum.

3   It has been asserted that the Anti-Communism Association was established by the CIA during the Cold War, and that it was financed by the US Embassy and some capital groups. It dissolved itself in 1977 on the grounds that it its function had become outdated.

4   Veysel Dinçer (2016), "27 Maddede Gülen Cemaati ve FETÖ'nün Dünü ve Bugünü", listelist.com, August 08, (http://listelist.com/gulen-cemaati-feto/, access: 09.08.2017).

5   "Cumhuriyetin 50 nci Yılı Nedeniyle Bazı Suç ve Cezaların Affı Hakkında Kanun" No. 1803, Date: 15.05.1974, Resmi Gazete, Date: 18.05.1974, Number: 14890 (mükerrer).

6   Ergün Diler (2016), "Caminin Sırrı", Takvim, October 11, (http://www.takvim.com.tr/yazarlar/ergundiler/2016/10/11/caminin-sirri, access: 15.03.2017).

7   Ergün Diler (2016), "Sızıntı", Takvim, (http://www.takvim.com.tr/yazarlar/ergundiler/2016/08/12/sizinti, access: 15.03.2017).

8   Kapani is a branch of Sabbataism.

9   Ergün Diler (2016), "Sızıntı", Takvim, 08/12/2016, (http://www.takvim.com.tr/yazarlar/ergundiler/2016/08/12/sizinti, access: 15.03.2017).

[10] M. Hakan Yavuz (2004), "Neo-Nurcular: Gülen Hareketi", Modern Türkiye'de Siyasî Düşünce: İslâmcılık, Volume 6, ed. Yasin Aktay, (İstanbul: İletişim Yayıncılık), ISBN: 9789750502545, p. 306.

[11] Mustafa Öztürk (2016), "FETÖ'nün Genel Karakteristiği ve Teolojisi", Türkiye Günlüğü, Issue: 127, Summer, pp. 28-52.

[12] The name of the coalition government in the public domain, founded by the Anavatan Partisi, the Demokratik Sol Parti and the Demokrat Türkiye Partisi.

[13] The name of the coalition government in the public domain, founded by the Demokratik Sol Parti, the Milliyetçi Hareket Partisi and the Anavatan Partisi.

[14] Latif Erdoğan, Sait Alpsoy, and Prof. Dr. Ahmet Keleş are examples of such people.

[15] Komisyon Raporu (2017), p.130

[16] Komisyon Raporu (2017), pp.96-97

[17] "The Gülen Case investigation/VII-Videotapes containing speeches of Gülen", https://tr.wikisource.org, (https://tr.wikisource.org/wiki/G%C3%BClen_davas%C4%B1_iddianamesi/VII-G%C3%BClen%27in_konu%C5%9Fmalar%C4%B1n%C4%B1_i%C3%A7eren_Video_Kasetler, access: 26.01.2017); Komisyon Raporu, 2017, pp. 40-42, 62, 94-97; Information provided by Chief of Adana Police Department, Osman Ak to the Commission, official report dated 08.12.2016, TBMM Tutanak Hizmetleri Başkanlığı, p.84; Zübeyir Kındıra (2016), İşkevlerinden Darbeye Fetullah'ın Coplan (Ankara: Altaylı Yayınları), ISBN: 9786059630030, p.10

[18] Komisyon Raporu (2017), pp. 130

[19] Komisyon Raporu (2017), p. 130

[20] In his meeting with Fetullah Gülen in private, Hüseyin Gülerce claimed that Fetullah Gülen informed him, "I am not a Nurcu". (See also http://www.risalehaber.com/huseyin-gulerce-f-gulen--me-ben-nurcu-degilim-dedi-295053h.htm, access: 08.03.2017). See also (Komisyon Raporu, 2017, p.49)

[21] Nurettin Veren (2016), "Gülen'in hiç bilinmeyen yemin metni", Yeni Akit, March 23. (http://www.yeniakit.com.tr/yazarlar/nurettin-veren/gulenin-hic-bilinmeyen-yemin-metni-14326.html, access: 28.05.2017)

[22] Latif Erdoğan, a TV program entitled Türkiye'nin Gündemi on the CNNTürk Television Channel, 05/28/2017); Information provided by Prof. Dr. Mustafa Öztürk to the Commission, official report dated 13.10.2016, TBMM Tutanak Hizmetleri Başkanlığı, p.51; Selim Çoraklı's statements in the "Çatı İddianamesi", (Komisyon Raporu, 2017, p. 48).

[23] "1960'tan beri tanışıyorlardı", www.yenisafak.com, (http://www.yenisafak.com/gundem/1960tan- beri-tanisiyorlardi-2115056, access: 25.05.2017).

[24] Information provided by the former MİT Undersecretary Emre Taner to the Commission, official report dated 09.11.2016, TBMM Tutanak Hizmetleri Başkanlığı, (Komisyon Raporu, 2017, p. 116.)

[25] Çatı İddianamesi, Witness Statements, (Komisyon Raporu, 2017, p. 49)

[26] "Fetullah Gülen'in 28 Şubat'taki utanç verici sözleri", www.sabah.com.tr, (http://

www.sabah.com.tr/gundem/2015/02/28/Fetullah-gulenin-28-subattaki-u-tanc-verici-sozleri, access: 28.05.2017).

27 Çatı İddianamesi, Chapter 8, (Komisyon Raporu, 2017, p. 49).

28 Komisyon Raporu (2017), p. 50

29 Members of the FETÖ/PDY believed that the light houses were mentioned in the 36th and 37th verses of the chapter al-Nur and they used these to reinforce their beliefs in the *ebced* calculations they held for many years. The English translation of the 36th and 37th verses of the chapter al-Nur: "In houses which Allah has permitted to be exalted and that His name may be remembered in them; there glorify Him therein in the mornings and the evenings, Men whom neither merchandise nor selling diverts from the remembrance of Allah and the keeping up of prayer and the giving of poor-rate; they fear a day in which the hearts and eyes shall turn about." English translation is by M. H. Shakir, http://www.theholyquran.org/?x=s_main&y=s_middle&kid=15&sid=49, access: 30.04.2019.

30 Çatı İddianamesi, Witness Statements, (Komisyon Raporu, 2017, p.50)

31 Çatı İddianamesi, (Komisyon Raporu, 2017, pp.42, 50, 96, 202, 618, 619)

32 Information provided by Prof. Dr. Mustafa Öztürk to the Commission, official report dated 13.10.2016 dated report, TBMM Tutanak Hizmetleri Başkanlığı, p.51; Fetullah Gülen (1979), *Asker*, Sızıntı, Issue 5, June 1979; Fetullah Gülen (1980), *Son Karakol*, Sızıntı, Issue 21, October 1980; Information provided by former MİT Undersecretary Emre Taner to the Commission, official report dated 09.11.2016, TBMM Tutanak Hizmetleri Başkanlığı, (Komisyon Raporu, 2017, p.145; "Fetullah Gülen'in 12 Eylülcüler'e destek yazısı", www.sabah.com.tr, (http://www.sabah.com.tr/gundem/2015/05/10/fetullah-gulenin-12-eylulculere-destek-yazisi, access: 28.05.2017).

33 Çatı İddianamesi, Organizational Structure of FETÖ, (Komisyon Raporu, 2017, p. 53).

34 Information provided by former MİT Undersecretary Emre Taner to the Commission, official report dated 09.11.2016, TBMM Tutanak Hizmetleri Başkanlığı, (Komisyon Raporu, 2017, p. 116).

35 Çatı İddianamesi, Witness Statments, Organizational Structure of FETÖ (Komisyon Raporu, 2017, p. 52).

36 Nurettin Veren (2007), *ABD'nin Truva Atı Fetullah Gülen Hareketi: Kuşatma* (İstanbul: Siyah Beyaz Yayınları), ISBN: 9789944490139.

37 Komisyon Raporu (2017), pp. 54, 153.

38 Komisyon Raporu (2017), p. 53.

39 World Council of Churches, (https://www.oikoumene.org/en, access: 11.04.2017).

40 Komisyon Raporu (2017), p. 56.

41 Komisyon Raporu (2017), p. 55.

42 Nurettin Veren (2007), *ABD'nin Truva Atı Fetullah Gülen Hareketi: Kuşatma* (İstanbul: Siyah Beyaz Yayınları), ISBN: 9789944490139.

43 Çatı İddianamesi, Organizational Structure of FETÖ, (Komisyon Raporu, 2017, p. 54).

[44] Çatı İddianamesi, Annex 3, (Komisyon Raporu, 2017, p. 56).

[45] Nurettin Veren (2016), "Gülen'in Papa 2. John Paul'a ortaklık mektubu", www.ye-niakit.com.tr, (http://www.yeniakit.com.tr/yazarlar/nurettin-veren/gulenin-pa-pa-2-john-paula-ortaklik- mektubu-13914.html, access: 28.05.2017).

[46] Nurettin Veren (2016), *FETO: İsimlerle ve Belgelerle 1966-2016* (İstanbul: Tekin Yayınevi), ISBN: 9786053111535, p. 69.

[47] The chapter Âl-Imrân, 3/28; the chapter al-Nisa, 4/139, 144; the chapter al-Ma'ida, 5/51; the chapter al-Mumtahana, 60/1.

[48] Diyanet İşleri Başkanlığı (2016), Dini İstismar Hareketi FETÖ/PDY (Olağanüstü Din Şurası Kararları), Din İşleri Yüksek Kurulu Başkanlığı, Ankara, p. 56, (https://webdosya.diyanet.gov.tr/anasayfa/UserFiles/Document/TextDocs/9a-7d78e1-1513-4ef7- b294-e24dd4151b33.pdf, access: 10.06.2017).

[49] Diyanet İşleri Başkanlığı (2016), ibid., p. 31.

[50] Diyanet İşleri Başkanlığı (2016), ibid., pp. 67-68; "Teröristbaşı Gülen 'Haçlı'nın ülkenizi işgal etmesi çok tehlikeli değildir.'", www.sabah.com.tr, (http://www.sabah.com.tr/webtv/turkiye/teroristbasi-gulen-haclinin-ulkenizi-isgal-etme-si-cok- tehlikeli-degildir, access: 10.06.2017).

[51] Komisyon Raporu (2017), p. 63.

[52] Stephen B. Bevans (2013), "Mission at the Second Vatican Council; 1962-1965", NTR, Volume 25, No.2, p.1, March, (http://newtheologyreview.org/index.php/ntr/article/view/54/260, access: 02/21/2017); Aytunç Altındal (2017), Vatikan ve Tapınak Şövalyeleri, 18. Edition, İstanbul: Alfa Yayınları, ISBN: 9786051067407, pp. 11-17, 68-75.

[53] Mahmut Aydın (2001), *Monologdan Diyaloğa-Çağdaş Hıristiyan Düşüncesinde Hıristiyan- Müslüman Diyaloğu* (Ankara: Ankara Okulu), ISBN: 9789058190379, pp. 90-92.

[54] Declaration on the Relation of the Church to Non-Christian Religions: Nostra Aetate; Proclaimed by His Holiness Pope Paul VI", www.vatican.va, (http://www.vatican.va/archive/hist_councils/ii_vatican_council/documents/vat- ii_decl_19651028_nostra-aetate_en.html. access: 19.04.2017).

[55] Redemptoris Missio, s. 55, www.goldringbooks.com, (http://www.goldring-books.com/?page=shop/flypage&product_id=8648, access: 22.04.2017).

[56] Çatı İddianamesi, pp. 108, 224, 368.

[57] Ahmet Keleş (2016), *FETO'nun Günah Piramidi* (Diyarbakır: Destek Yayınları), ISBN: 9786053111634, pp. 84-87.

[58] Çatı İddianamesi, pp. 368, 380.

[59] Komisyon Raporu (2017), pp. 124-125.

[60] Diyanet İşleri Başkanlığı (2016), ibid., pp. 31, 63, 67.

[61] Nurettin Veren (2016), ibid., p. 82.

[62] Komisyon Raporu (2017), p. 63.

[63] HSYK General Assembly Decision, Decision Date: 15.11.2016, Decision No: 2016/440.

⁶⁴ Komisyon Raporu (2017), p. 57.

⁶⁵ Diyanet İşleri Başkanlığı, ibid., p. 69.

⁶⁶ Fehmi Koru (2016), *Ben Böyle Gördüm: Cemaat'in Siyasetle Sınavı* (İstanbul: Alfa Basım Yayım), ISBN: 9786051712789, pp. 82-100.

⁶⁷ Ahmet Akgül (2014), "Fetullah Gülen Dosyası", ahmetakgul.net, (http://ahmetakgul.net/fetullah- gulen-dosyasi/, access: 29.05.2017); Komisyon Raporu (2017), p. 59.

⁶⁸ "Bir askerimiz atılacağına tüm imam hatipler kapansın", www.gazetevatan.com, (http://www.gazetevatan.com/-bir-askerimiz-atilacagina-tum-imam-hatipler-kapansin--997384- gundem/, access: 21.03.2017).

⁶⁹ Komisyon Raporu (2017), pp. 42, 58-59.

⁷⁰ Formerly known as Asya Finans Katılım Bankası.

⁷¹ Komisyon Raporu (2017), p. 57.

⁷² Mehmet Barlas (2000), "Gülen'den Çevik Bir'e Mektup", www.yenisafak.com, (http://www.yenisafak.com/arsiv/2000/ekim/16/dizi.html, access: 29.05.2017).

⁷³ Komisyon Raporu (2017), p. 58.

⁷⁴ Latif Erdoğan (2006), *Küçük Dünyam, Fetullah Gülen*, (İstanbul: Doğan Kitap), ISBN: 9789756065168, pp. 132- 133.

⁷⁵ "Telekulak operasyonu", www.turkiyegazetesi.com.tr, (http://www.turkiyegazetesi.com.tr/Genel/a7045.aspx, access: 30.05.2017).

⁷⁶ Komisyon Raporu (2017), p. 239.

⁷⁷ Çatı İddianamesi, (Komisyon Raporu, 2017, p. 60).

⁷⁸ Çatı İddianamesi, Section on Tip-Off's, (Komisyon Raporu, 2017, p. 60).

⁷⁹ "Gülen: Amerika'ya alâka duymamızın sebebi", www.yeniakit.com.tr, (http://www.yeniakit.com.tr/haber/gulen-amerikaya-alaka-duymamizin-sebebi-62309.html, access: 22.02.2017).

⁸⁰ "23 Nisan 1999 Tarihine Kadar İşlenen Suçlardan Dolayı Şartla Salıverilmeye, Dava ve Cezaların Ertelenmesine Dair Kanun", No. 4616, Date: 21.12.2000, Resmi Gazete, Date: 22.12.2000, Issue: 24268.

⁸¹ Komisyon Raporu (2017), p. 62.

⁸² Komisyon Raporu (2017), p. 62.

⁸³ Komisyon Raporu (2017), p. 63.

⁸⁴ Information provided by former MİT Undersecretary Emre Taner to the Commission, official report dated 09.11.2016, TBMM Tutanak Hizmetleri Başkanlığı, (Komisyon Raporu, 2017, p.299.

⁸⁵ Komisyon Raporu (2017), pp. 271-274.

⁸⁶ Komisyon Raporu (2017), pp. 236-239.

⁸⁷ Komisyon Raporu (2017), pp. 230-233.

88 "Türk Ceza Kanunu", No. 5237, Date: 26.09.2004, Resmi Gazete, Date: 12.10.2004, Issue: 25611.

89 Komisyon Raporu (2017), pp. 250-257.

90 Komisyon Raporu (2017), pp. 274-278.

91 The website http://www.velfecr.com.

92 HSYK Inspectors 07.12.2015 dated report; The transcript of the prosecution decision dated 10.12.2015 of the 2nd Department of HYSK.

93 The 07.04.2011 dated document sent to the Istanbul Chief Public Prosecutors Office Authorized by Article 250 of the Code of Criminal Procedure to the Istanbul Anti-Terror Branch Directorate.

94 The 02.09.2015 dated, 21575 numbered official response sent from İstanbul Anti-Terror Branch Directorate to Istanbul Chief Public Prosecutors Office.

95 "Terörle Mücadele Kanunu", No. 3713, Date: 12.04.1991, Resmi Gazete, Date: 12.04.1991, Issue: 20843 (mükerrer).

96 The 2015/110148 numbered investigation of the Ankara Chief Public Prosecutor's Office, 2015/48175 case file-2015/3110 numbered indictment.

97 Komisyon Raporu (2017), pp. 261-263.

98 "Gazeteci Haydar Meriç Cinâyetinin Firari Komiseri Yakalandı", www.hurriyet. com.tr, (http://www.hurriyet.com.tr/gazeteci-haydar-meric-cinâyetinin-firari-komiseri-yakalandi-40220325, access: 09.09.2016).

99 "Paralel Yapı Soruşturmalarında İlk Cinâyet Suçlaması", t24.com.tr, (http://t24. com.tr/haber/paralel-yapi-sorusturmalarinda-ilk-cinâyet-suclamasi,346868, access: 24.06.2016).

100 "Haydar Meriç Cinâyetinde Bylock İzine Rastlandı", www.yenicaggazetesi. com.tr, (http://www.yenicaggazetesi.com.tr/haydar-meric-cinâyetinde-bylock-izine-rastlandi- 149377h.htm, access: 31.10.2016).

101 "Gülen'in özel hayatını araştırırken öldürülen ismin bilgisayarından neler çıktı?", odatv.com, (http://odatv.com/gulenin-ozel-hayatini-arastirirken-oldurulen-ismin-bilgisayarindan-neler-cikti-0607161200.html, access: 11.05.2017).

102 Yavuz Selim Demirağ (2015), *İmamların Öcü, Türk Silahlı Kuvvetlerinde Cemaat Yapılanması* (İstanbul: Kırmızı Kedi Yayınları), ISBN: 9786059908931, p. 238.

103 "Devlet İstihbarat Hizmetleri ve Milli İstihbarat Teşkilatı Kanununda Değişiklik Yapılmasına Dair Kanun", No. 6278, Enactment Date: 17.02.2012, Official Gazette, Date: 18.02.2012, No: 28208.

104 Commission's 11.09.2016 dated official report, TBMM Tutanak Hizmetleri Başkanlığı, (Komisyon Raporu 2017, p. 299.

105 http://www.sabah.com.tr/gundem/2016/11/16/eski-hsyk-baskanvekili-hamsiciden-carpici- itiraflar#, access: 12.05.2017; http://www.ahaber.com.tr/gundem/2016/11/16/eski-hsyk- baskanvekili-hamsici-itirafci-oldu, access: 12.05.2017; http://www.hurriyet.com.tr/hsyk-eski- baskanvekilinden-feto-itiraflari-40279870, access: 12.05.2017; http://www.milliyet.com.tr/hsyk-eski-baskanvekili-hamsici-den-gundem-2346101/, access: 12.05.2017; http://www.sozcu.com.tr/2016/gundem/hsyk-eski-baskanvekili-hamsiciden-2011-yilin-

daki- yargitay-ve-danistay-uyelerinin-secimleriyle-itiraflar-1512499/, access: 12.05.2017.

[106] 2012/120653, 2012/125043 and 2013/24880 numbered investigation files.

[107] "Adli Kolluk Yönetmeliği", Resmi Gazete, Date: 01.06.2005, Issue: 25832, (http://mevzuat.basbakanlik.gov.tr/Metin.Aspx?MevzuatKod=7.5.8201&MevzuatIliski=0&sourc eXmlSearch, access: 12.05.2017).

[108] Investigation reports dated 21.10.2014 and 20.05.2016.

[109] 2012/120653 and 2013/24880 numbered investigation files.

[110] It was decided that it was not permitted for the testimonies to be taken in detail. For example: He told the Mayor of Fatih district Mustafa Demir that, "you only have 2 minutes, give your statement and leave", and upon Mustafa Demir's insistence on giving a detailed testimony, he was told that "you can explain yourself in court". Therefore, he did not accept the evidence presented to him, he did not read Süleyman Aslan's testimony taken in the police station, and his testimony was not even taken in any detail, Barış Güler was told that "you have the right to present 3 sentences, and do so in 5 minutes in total" when he was offering his testimony and again he was not allowed to give a detailed testimony. Moreover, he was not allowed to examine the evidence and the documents that were presented.

[111] Public Prosecutors Mustafa Erol and Ekrem Aydıner.

[112] Phone calls made between January 24 2013-December 17 2013.

[113] The Minister of Economy Zafer Çağlayan, The Minister of Interior Muammer Güler, and the Minister for EU Affairs Egemen Bağış.

[114] The 2012/125043 numbered investigation file carried out by Public Prosecutor Mehmet Yüzgeç.

[115] Cumhuriyet Newspaper.

[116] January 25,26,27,28,29,30 2015

[117] "1 numara 'Erdoğan'dı", www.gazetemanset.com, (http://www.gazetemanset.com/cumhuriyet- gazetesi/25-ocak-2015, access: 06/01/2017); "Yolsuzluğa yol oldular", www.gazetemanset.com, (http://www.gazetemanset.com/cumhuriyet-gazetesi/26-ocak-2015, access: 01.06.2017); "Odama giren çıkanı izlediler", www.gazetemanset.com, (http://www.gazetemanset.com/cumhuriyet- gazetesi/27-ocak-2015, access: 01.06.2017); "Bakan çocukları süt dökmüş kedi gibiydi", www.gazetemanset.com, (http://www.gazetemanset.com/cumhuriyet-gazetesi/29-ocak-2015, access: 01.06.2017).

[118] The slander that claimed that he was a leader and director of a criminal organization established for the purpose of corruption, bribery, money laundering and using its influence to increase advantage.

[119] Investigation files numbered 2012/120653 and 2013/24880.

[120] Minister of Environment and Urbanization Erdoğan Bayraktar.

[121] Phone calls made between October 22 2012-December 17 2013.

[122] Investigation files numbered 2012/120653 ve 2013/24880 carried out by the Public Prosecutor Celal Kara.

[123] Investigation files numbered 2012/120653 and 2013/24880.

[124] Investigation file numbered 2012/125043.

[125] December 24-25 2011, May 20 2012, August 26 2012, April 20-21 2013.

[126] Investigation file numbered 2012/656.

[127] "HSYK'dan açıklama geldi: Amirden izin anayasaya aykırıdır.", www.radikal.com. tr, (http://www.radikal.com.tr/turkiye/hsykdan-aciklama-geldi-amirden-iz-in-anayasaya-aykiridir-1168158/, access: 01.06.2017).

[128] Investigation reports dated September 22 2014 and April 28 2016.

[129] "Akkaş bildiri dağıttı, Öz gece emniyete geldi", www.hurriyet.com.tr, (http://www.hurriyet.com.tr/akkas-bildiri-dagitti-oz-gece-emniyete-geldi-27867350, access: 01.06.2017).

[130] Phone calls made between July 21 2012-November 29 2013.

[131] The Minister of Transport, Maritime Affairs and Communications Binali Yıldırım, the Minister of Energy and Natural Resources, Taner Yıldız, the Minister of Forestry and Water Affairs, Veysel Eroğlu, the Minister of Environment and Urban Planning, Erdoğan Bayraktar, and the Minister of Interior, Muammer Güler.

[132] Authorized by Article 10 of the Anti-Terror Law.

[133] The Indictment prepared by Adana Chief Public Prosecutors Office, Investigation No: 2014/19640, Indictment No: 2014/772; (Komisyon Raporu 2017, pp. 269-27.)

[134] "Devlet İstihabart Hizmetleri ve Milli İstihbarat Teşkilatı Kanunu", Kanun No. 2937, Enactment Date: 01.11.1983, Resmi Gazete, Date: 03.11.1983, Issue: 18210.

[135] Aksaray, Niğde and Mersin provinces.

[136] IHH stands for The Foundation for Human Rights and Freedoms and Humanitarian Relief.

[137] 2nd Department of the Council of Judges and Prosecutors General Assembly Decision dated 24.08.2016 and No. 2016/99.

[138] 2nd Department of the Council of Judges and Prosecutors investigation file No. 2016/99.

[139] Komisyon Raporu (2017), p.245

[140] "Ceza Muhakemesi Kanunu", No. 5271, 04.12.2004, Resmi Gazete, Date: 17.12.2004, Issue: 25673.

[141] Komisyon Raporu (2017), p. 245.

[142] Nedim Şener (2016), *Ergenekon Belgelerinde Fetullah Gülen ve Cemaat* (İstanbul: Destek Yayınları), ISBN: 9789944298957, p.193.

[143] Zübeyir Kındıra (2016), *Işıkevlerinden Darbeye Fetullah'ın Copları* (Ankara: Altaylı Yayınları), ISBN: 9786059630030.

[144] "Fetullah Gülen'in MHP notları ortaya çıktı", www.sabah.com.tr, (http://www.sabah.com.tr/gundem/2016/06/27/fetullah-gulenin-mhp-notlari-ortaya-cikti, Access: 27.06.2016); Çatı İddianamesi, p. 148, "(Komisyon Raporu," 2017, p. 282.

[145] Sabri Uzun (2015), İN; *Baykal Kaseti, Dink Cinâyeti ve Diğer Komplolar*, 3rd Edition, (İstanbul: Kırmızı Kedi Yayınları), ISBN: 9786059908320, pp. 105-106.

[146] Levent Kenez, Aziz Mahmut İstegün, İsmail Avcı and some of other persons.

[147] Reşat Petek (2016), Komisyon Başkanı Tutanakları, pp. 21-22.

[148] Information provided by Eskişehir MP Emine Nur Günay to the Commission, official report dated 25.10.2016, TBMM Tutanak Hizmetleri Başkanlığı, pp. 40-41.

[149] Komisyon Raporu (2017), pp. 309-310.

[150] Komisyon Raporu (2017), pp. 67,98,99

[151] Komisyon Raporu (2017), pp. 49, 52, 70-71, 80-81, 207; Sabri Uzun (2015), ibid., p. 31.

[152] These students' guides mostly stay in state-owned dormitories, and also study in state-owned schools. The main task of these guides is to invite and persuade other students to participate in *iftars*, religious conversations, activities and to invite students to study programs in the houses, in order to familiarize them with the organization's residences, to keep in touch with the organization's contact staff, to take care of successful students, and to transfer them to dormitories or houses belonging to the organization. The organization also has such students' guides in their dormitories, and they act as *belletmens'* assistants.

[153] The *belletmens* are those who specifically pay attention to the students residing in the organization's dormitories, who educate them on specific subjects, who instill the organization's ideology, who keeps them under surveillance, and presents reports on them to the Imam's of the dormitory or the *serrehber* of the dormitory.

[154] The *serrehbers* are those who organize religious conversations, preach sermons, recite whole Quran sessions, organize *iftars*, camp programs and other religious education activities, and who keep the morale and motivation high of the organization's members. In short, they brainwash the youth that join the organization, and are ordered to pay special attention to businessmen. They are at a higher rank than the *belletmens* of the organization.

[155] There were student Imams in every district, province and region. These Imams functioned under the authority of the Imams of the relevant district, province and region. There was also a student Imam, who was responsible for all the students in Turkey. Moreover, this Imam was responsible to the Imam of Turkey. Furthermore, there were Imam who assumed the responsibility for the high schools and university students according to their province or region. These were responsible to the Imam of the relevant district/province. There were also Imams responsible for the students who were intended to be placed staff int highly important institutions, such as in the security, the judiciary and the military institutions.

[156] This is the term coined by the author to express the units of the organization, which indicates the area of the responsibility covering more than one country in a continent.

[157] "FETÖ'nün Asya Pasifik ülkeleri sorumluları", aa.com.tr, (http://aa.com.tr/tr/info/infografik/2624, access: 10.03.2017)

[158] "Komisyon Raporu" (2017), pp. 193; Necip Hablemitoğlu (2008), *Köstebek* (İstanbul: Pozitif Yayıncılık), ISBN: 9789756461686, pp. 14-16; Hanefi Avcı (2010), *Haliç'te Yaşayan Simonlar: Dün Devlet Bugün Cemaat* (Ankara: Angora Yayıncılık),

ISBN: 9789752870758, pp. 433-435; information provided by the former Deputy General Director of Security Affairs, Emin Arslan to the Commission, official report dated 27.10.2016, TBMM Tutanak Hizmetleri Başkanlığı, ("Komisyon Raporu," 2017, pp. 205-206); Emin Arslan, *ibid.*, ("Komisyon Raporu," 2017, pp. 205-206); information provided by the former General Director of Security Affairs, Mehmet Kılıçlar to the Commission, official report dated 02.11.2016, TBMM Tutanak Hizmetleri Başkanlığı ("Komisyon Raporu," 2017, p. 206); information provided by the former General Director of Security Affairs, Celâlettin Lekesiz to the Commission, official report dated 08.11.2016, TBMM Tutanak Hizmetleri Başkanlığı, pp. 8-9; information provided by the former Minister of Internal Affairs Efkan Âlâ'nın to the Commission, official report dated 18.10.2016, TBMM Tutanak Hizmetleri Başkanlığı, ("Komisyon Raporu," 2017, p. 206); information provided by the Izmir member of the parliament, Hüseyin Kocabıyık, to the Commission, official report dated 09.11.2016, TBMM Tutanak Hizmetleri Başkanlığı pp. 97-98; the transcript sent by the General Directorate of Security Affairs, Department of intelligence services to the Ankara Provincial Security Directorate, Presidency of Inspectorate, dated 10.03.1992, with the number B.05.1.EGM.0.06.03.400/1 (79-92); the transcript sent by the Ankara Provincial Security Directorate to the State Security Court, Office of the Chief Public Prosecutor, dated 28.09.1992 with the number B.05.1.EGM.4.06.00.14 İll.ve Sor. (F).92/8303 and the summary of proceedings added to it, dated 28.08.1992, with the number B.05.EGM.0.06.01/15-92.

[159] This is prepared by using the decision of the Higher Council of Judges and Prosecutors, dated 15.11.2016 with the number 2016/440, the decision of the Constitutional Court dated 04.08.2016 with the number 2016/12 and Çatı İddianamesi. See also, "HSYK Başkanvekili Hamsici'den çarpıcı itiraflar", www.sabah.com.tr, (http://www.sabah.com.tr/gundem/2016/11/16/eski-hsykbaskanvekili-hamsiciden-carpici-itiraflar#, access: 27.02.2017); "HSYK eski Başkanvekili'nden FETÖ itirafları, flaş iddialar", www.hurriyet.com.tr, (http://www.hurriyet.com.tr/hsyk-eskibaskanvekilinden-feto-itiraflari-40279870, access: 02.27.2017); "HSYK eski üyesi Kerim Tosun itirafçı oldu", www.milliyet.com.tr, (http://www.milliyet.com.tr/hsyk-eski-uyesi-kerim-tosungundem-2345811/, access: 02.27.2017); "HSYK eski üyesi Özçelik'ten FETÖ itirafları", www.trthaber.com, (http://www.trthaber.com/haber/turkiye/hsyk-eski-uyesi-ozcelikten-feto-itiraflari-283236.html, access: 02.27.2017).

[160] Komisyon Raporu, (2017), p. 83.

[161] Ahmet Keleş (2016), *FETO'nun Günah Piramidi* (Diyarbakır: Destek Yayınları), ISBN: 9786053111634, pp. 128-230.

[162] Necip Hablemitoğlu (2008), *ibid.*, p. 14-16.

[163] IQ is the abbreviation for "intelligence quotient."

[164] Information provided by Hüseyin Gülerce to the Commission, official report dated 10.26. 2016, TBMM Tutanak Hizmetleri Başkanlığı, (Komisyon Raporu, 2017, p. 214).

[165] Information provided by Yavuz Selim Demirağ to the Commission, official report dated 19.10.2016, TBMM Tutanak Hizmetleri Başkanlığı, Komisyon Raporu (2017), p. 214.

[166] Information provided by the retired Gendarmerie executive colonel and author Mustafa Önsel to the Commission, official report dated 13.10.2016, TBMM Tutanak Hizmetleri Başkanlığı, Komisyon Raporu (2017), p. 214.

[167] Information provided by Deputy Chief of the Turkish General Staff, Ümit Dündar to the Commission, official report dated 18.10.2016, TBMM Tutanak Hizmetleri Başkanlığı, Komisyon Raporu, 2017, p. 213; information provided by retired Four-Star General İlker Başbuğ, official report dated 03.11.2016, TBMM Tutanak Hizmetleri Başkanlığı, Komisyon Raporu (2017), p. 214).

[168] SBS: Placement Test.

[169] TEOG: Placement Exam Test for High Schools.

[170] Deniz Zeyrek (2016), "Sayılarla Sızıntı", *Hürriyet Gazetesi*, 04 Agust, 2016.

[171] Komisyon Raporu (2017), p. 217.

[172] Komisyon Raporu (2017), pp. 210-211.

[173] Çatı İddianamesi, (Komisyon Raporu, 2017, p. 82).

[174] Information provided by Mustafa Önsel to the Commission, official report dated 13.10.2016, TBMM Tutanak Hizmetleri Başkanlığı, Komisyon Raporu (2017), p. 82).

[175] Çatı İddianamesi, "FETÖ'nün Teşkilat Yapısı," s. 78.

[176] Oktay Bingöl, Ali Birlik Varlık (2016), "FETÖ Darbe Girişiminin Askerî Analizi," Rapor-016 A, Merkez Strateji Enstitüsü, Ankara, pp. 15-16.

[177] When certain noncommissioned officers in Şemdinli were arrested in 2006, the conspiracy lawsuits started to be filed. Information provided by Yavuz Selim Demirağ to the Commission, official report dated 19.10.2016, TBMM Tutanak Hizmetleri Başkanlığı, Komisyon Raporu (2017), p.214.

[178] Information provided by the retired Four-Star General Işık Koşaner to the Commission, official report dated 26.10.2016, TBMM Tutanak Hizmetleri Başkanlığı, Komisyon Raporu (2017), p.215.

[179] Çatı İddianamesi, "Onikinci Bölüm: Örgütün İşlediği Suçlar", p. 5; information provided by Efkan Âlâ to the Commission, official report dated 18.10.2016, TBMM Tutanak Hizmetleri Başkanlığı, 2017, p.71.

[180] Çatı İddianamesi, "Haberleşme, Toplantılar, Basın Yayın, Arşivler," p. 8.

[181] Çatı İddianamesi, "Onuncu Bölüm: Fetullahçı Terör Örgütünün İdeolojisi," p. 59; Deliller, the 36th folder, evidence number 4.

[182] Çatı İddianamesi, "Genel Örgüt Bilgileri", s. 6; Deliller, the 10th folder, evidence number 9/d.

[183] Information provided by journalist-author Nedim Şener to the Commission, official report dated 25.10.2016, TBMM Tutanak Hizmetleri Başkanlığı, p.97).

[184] Çatı İddianamesi, "FETÖ'nün Teşkilat Yapısı", p. 78.

[185] Information provided by the retired Four-Star General Hilmi Özkök to the Commission, official report dated 19.10.2016, TBMM Tutanak Hizmetleri Başkanlığı, p.26); information provided by the retired Four-Star General İlker Başbuğ to the Commission, official report dated 03.11.2016, TBMM Tutanak Hizmetleri Başkanlığı, pp.98-99).

[186] Information provided by Prof. Dr. Nevzat Tarhan to the Commission, official report dated 19.10.2016, TBMM Tutanak Hizmetleri Başkanlığı, p.113).

[187] Oktay Bingöl, Ali Birlik Varlık (2016), *ibid.*, p. 14.

[188] Information provided by Mustafa Önsel to the Commission, official report dated 13.10.2016, TBMM Tutanak Hizmetleri Başkanlığı, Komisyon Raporu (2017), p.213).

[189] The news report posted on the internet site of the Sabah Gazetesi, on 04.09.2016.

[190] Oktay Bingöl, Ali Birlik Varlık (2016), *ibid.*, p. 15.

[191] Oktay Bingöl, Ali Birlik Varlık (2016), *ibid.*, p. 16.

[192] The television program, "Türkiye'nin Gündemi," which was attended by Latif Erdoğan and was broadcasted by the CNN Türk television channel, on 08.08.2016; information provided by Prof. Dr. Mustafa Öztürk to the Commission, official report dated 13.10.2016, TBMM Tutanak Hizmetleri Başkanlığı, p.51); Çatı İddianamesi, "Selim Çoraklı'nın ifadesi," Komisyon Raporu (2017), p. 48.

[193] "FETÖ militanlarını CIA ve FBI eğitti," www.yenisafak.com, (http://www.yenisafak.com/dunya/feto-militanlarini-cia-ve-fbi-egitti-2501159, access: 05.06.2017).

[194] Necip Hablemitoğlu (2008), *ibid.*, quoted in "Komisyon Raporu" (2017), p. 206.

[195] Çatı İddianamesi, quoted in "Komisyon Raporu" (2017), p. 229.

[196] Komisyon Raporu (2017), pp. 73-76; quoted from Çatı İddianamesi, in Komisyon Raporu (2017), pp. 117-118.

[197] Komisyon Raporu (2017), pp. 55, 78, 100, 143-152; Fehmi Koru (2016), *ibid.*, pp. 80-81, 103-104; Diyanet İşleri Başkanlığı (2016), *ibid.*, p. 60.

[198] Komisyon Raporu (2017), p. 132.

[199] "FETÖ'nün amacı, devletin kılcal damarlarına sızmak", www.dha.com.tr, (http://www.dha.com.tr/fetonun-amaci-devletin-kilcal-damarlarina-sizmak_1290498.html, access: 11.03.2017).

[200] Diyanet İşleri Başkanlığı (2006), *ibid.*, pp. 36-37.

[201] Komisyon Raporu (2017), pp. 83-84.

[202] *The Holy Qur'an*, chapter Âl- Imrân 3/28, the chapter al-Nahl 16/ 106, chapter Ghafir 40/28.

[203] Mustafa Öztürk (2015), *Tefsirde Ehl-i Sünnet ve Şia Polemikleri* (Ankara: Ankara Okulu Yayınları), ISBN: 9944162180, pp. 118-119.

[204] Fetullah Gülen (2010), *Diriliş Çağrısı, Kırık Testi 6* (Gazeteciler ve Yazarlar Vakfı), ISBN: 9789756714416, p. 245.

[205] This booklet, the author of which is known but the publication date is unknown, was prepared specifically for the student of the Police College in 1993. It was published with a limited number of copies. This booklet, which explains the ideology of the FETÖ/PDY, after being read by the students of the Police College, who were affiliated with the organization, was taken back. They took it back, because they feared that if the information given inside the book became public it could harm the organization. (Çatı İddianamesi, Tanıklar, the 5th Folder, evidence number 9, 10 and 12, pp. 234-235.).

206 Çatı İddianamesi, Gizli Tanıklar 19, pp. 30-31.

207 Çatı İddianamesi, Gizli Tanıklar 12, pp. 42-43, 155-156.

208 The term *yakaza* (*yaqaza*) is an Arabic term, which literally means "to be awake." It is used to indicate a state in between sleeping and wakefulness. And the term "yakaza âlemi" indicates all the states and events, which a person may percieve when he is in the *yakaza* moment.

209 Komisyon Raporu (2017), p. 131.

210 Said Alpsoy (2015), *Çelişkiler İnsam* (İstanbul: Umran Yayınları).

211 Komisyon Raporu (2017), p. 132.

212 Selahattin Adanalı (2014), "Cemaatin Psikolojik Kaosu", *Fetullah Gülen'in Dinî Söyleminin Eleştirisi*, ed. Mehmet Şahin (İstanbul: Evre Yayınları), ISBN: 6058503908, s. 170; Mustafa Öztürk (2016), *ibid.*, Türkiye Günlüğü, issue: 127, pp. 28-52.

213 "FETÖ'nün 30 yıllık evlilik kataloğu ortaya çıktı", www.hurriyet.com.tr, (http://www.hurriyet.com.tr/fetonun-30-yillik-evlilik-katalogu-ortaya-cikti-40488155, access: 15.04.2016).

214 Translation of the chapter al-Hujurat 49/ 12 of *the Holy Qur'an*: "O you who believe! Avoid most of suspicion, for surely suspicion in some cases is a sin, and do not spy nor let some of you backbite others. Does one of you like to eat the flesh of his dead brother? But you abhor it; and be careful of (your duty to) Allah, surely Allah is Oft-returning (to mercy), Merciful." English translation is by M. H. Shakir, http://www.theholyquran.org/?x=s_main&y=s_middle&kid=15&sid=49, access: 30.04.2019.

215 Hasan Sabbah (1034-1124) was one of the leading administrators of the Ismaili religious sect. He had his pupils carry out criminal actions to get rid of many state officers of the time. "İbrahim Karahan – Yazarın kitapları", www.kitapsihirbazi.com, (https://www.kitapsihirbazi.com/ibrahim-karahan-w63170.html, access: 10.06.2017); Okan Sezer (2014), "Alamut Kalesi: İnanılması Güç Bir Efsane Değil", arkeolojigazetesi.com, (http://arkeolojigazetesi.com/?author=5, access: 10.06.2017).

216 Çatı İddianamesi, Tanıklar, Folder 2, Witness 18, p. 74.

217 Yavuz Selim Demirağ (2015), *ibid.*, p. 57.

218 Komisyon Raporu (2017), p. 622.

219 Latif Erdoğan (2016), *Şeytamn Gülen Yüzü* (İstanbul: Turkuvaz Kitap), ISBN: 6056670800, p. 33.

220 *The Holy Qur'an*, Chapter Âl-Imrân 3/42-54; al-Mâide, 5/111; Tâ hâ, 20/37-39; al-Shura, 42/51.

221 Fetullah Gülen's sermons given on April 06, 1979, on July 09, 1979 and April 07, 1991.

222 https://www.youtube.com/watch?v=bW5Vj_N2dnk, access: 11.04.2017.

223 *The Holy Qur'an*, Chapter Saba 34/15.

224 Latif Erdoğan (2016), *ibid.*, pp. 127, 164-165.

[225] İmam Ahmed bin Hanbel (2014), *Müsned* (Istanbul: Ocak Yayıncılık), ISBN: 6054659081, pp. 122-123.

[226] İmam Muhyiddin en Nevevî, *Sahih-i Müslim Şerhi*, trans. Beşir Eryarsoy (İstanbul: Polen & Karınca Yayınevi), p. 45.

[227] Karar Gazetesi, 24.08.2016.

[228] Buhari, Tabir, 45; Müsned 2/96, 119.

[229] Translation of the chapter Âl-Imrân 3/64 of *the Holy Qur'an*: "Say: O followers of the Book! Come to an equitable proposition between us and you that we shall not serve any but Allah and (that) we shall not associate aught with Him, and (that) some of us shall not take others for lords besides Allah; but if they turn back, then say: Bear witness that we are Muslims." English translation is by M. H. Shakir, http://www.theholyquran.org/?x=s_main&y=s_middle&kid=15&sid=3, access: 30.04.2019

[230] Necip Hablemitoğlu (2008), *ibid.*, pp. 14-16.

[231] Komisyon Raporu (2017), p. 110-114.

[232] "İtirafçı general: Âdil Öksüz 6 gün darbe planı yaptı", www.hurriyet.com.tr, (http://www.hurriyet.com.tr/itirafci-general-âdil-oksuz-6-gun-darbe-plani-yapti-40193392, access: 12.04.2017).

[233] "The members of the FETÖ developed ByLock and turned it into an encrypted communication system. To enter into the ByLock system, which has three different systems of encryption, one needs a reference. Since the ByLock program keeps an archive of activities, information about the identity of the users and records of their communication could be obtained. When members of the FETÖ discovered that MİT decoded the encryption of the ByLock program, they started since January 2016 to use the 'Eagle' program to communicate among themselves,. The Eagle program was downloaded to laptop and regular computers. They did not install this program to cellular phones in order to safeguard from signal tracing. They did not use true information about their identity. One user of Eagle would give a code name and code number to another user. In this way they insured secrecy." (Abdülkadir Selvi (2016), "ByLock ve Eagle'de yeni gelişmeler var", www.hurriyet.com.tr, http://www.hurriyet.com.tr/yazarlar/abdulkadir-selvi/bylock-ve-eagleda-yeni-gelismeler-var40278849, access: 12.04.2017).

[234] The MİT worked on the ByLock until May 2016 and thus discovered it and decoded its inscription system. However, since the organization learned about MİT's efforts in this regard early on, they started using Eagle program since January 2016.

[235] Komisyon Raporu (2017), p. 114.

[236] "Darbenin şifresini FETÖ medyasına gömmüşler", www.yenisafak.com, (http://www.yenisafak.com/gundem/darbenin-sifresini-feto-medyasina-gommusler-2502774, access: 19.04.2017); "Zaman İddianamesi'nde flaş detay! Darbe mesajı reklam afişiyle verildi", www.medyaradar.com, (http://www.medyaradar.com/zaman-iddianamesinde-flas-detay-darbemesaji-reklam-afisiyle-verildi-haberi-662718, access: 19.04.2017); "Hürriyet Benim, Zaman Kardeşimin", www.pazarlamasyon.com, (http://www.pazarlamasyon.com/reklam/hurriyet-benim-zaman-kardesimin/, access: 19.04.2017).

[237] "Sızıntı Dergisi Kapağından Darbe Mesajı Verilmiş", www.kamutime.com,

(http://www.kamutime.com/gundem/sizinti-dergisi-kapagindan-darbe-mesaji-verilmish3402.html, access: 20.04.2017).

238 "Zaman Gazetesinin Darbe Habercisi Gülen Bebek Reklamı. Subliminal Mesaj", www.youtube.com, (https://www.youtube.com/watch?v=W5-t5R5qhZQ, erişim: 29.01.2017); "Zaman'ın 9 ay 10 gün önceki reklamı darbeyi haber mi veriyordu", www.abcgazetesi.com, (http://www.abcgazetesi.com/zamanin-9-ay-10-gun-onceki-reklami-darbeyi-haber-mi-veriyordu23577h.htm, access: 20.04.2017).

239 "Ekrem Dumanlı Darbe Tehdidi", www.youtube.com, (https://www.youtube.com/watch?v=bXeXSRajYyg, access: 29.01.2017).

240 "Kelebek 2009 yerli film izle", www.inndirmedenfilmizle.com, (http://www.inndirmedenfilmizle.com/kelebek-film-izle.html, access: 21.04.2017)

241 Komisyon Raporu (2017), p. 179.

242 "Eşrefpaşalı kan kardeşler", www.dunyabizim.com, (http://www.dunyabizim.com/sinema/15134/zihni-gri-sehir-insaninin-manzarasi-da-gri, access: 21.04.2017)

243 "Eşrefpaşalı kan kardeşler", www.dunyabizim.com, (http://www.dunyabizim.com/sinema/15134/zihni-gri-sehir-insaninin-manzarasi-da-gri, access: 21.04.2017)

244 Hakimler ve Savcılar Yüksek Kurulunun 24.08.2016 tarihli ve 2016/426 sayılı genel kurul kararının gerekçesi.

245 From Çatı İddianamesi, quoted in Komisyon Raporu (2017), p. 161.

246 Ahmet Şık (2017), *İmamın Ordusu* (Istanbul: Kırmızı Kedi Yayınları), ISBN: 9786052981030, pp. 32-34.

247 Komisyon Raporu (2017), pp. 162-163.

248 From Çatı İddianamesi, quoted in Komisyon Raporu (2017), p. 163.

249 From Çatı İddianamesi, quoted in Komisyon Raporu (2017), p. 163; "667 sayılı Olağanüstü Hal Kapsamında Alınan Tedbirlere İlişkin Kanun Hükmünde Kararname", Resmi Gazete, Date: 23.07.2016, Issue: 29779, (http://www.resmigazete.gov.tr/eskiler/2016/07/20160723.htm, access: 16.04.2017).

250 "667 sayılı Olağanüstü Hal Kapsamında Alınan Tedbirlere İlişkin Kanun Hükmünde Kararname", Resmi Gazete, Date: 23.07.2016, Issue: 29779, (http://www.resmigazete.gov.tr/eskiler/2016/07/20160723.htm, access: 16.04.2017); "677 sayılı Olağanüstü Hal Kapsamında Bazı Tedbirler Alınması Hakkında Kanun Hükmünde Kararname", Resmi Gazete, Date: 22.11.2016, Issue: 29896, (http://www.resmigazete.gov.tr/eskiler/2016/11/20161122-1.htm, access: 16.04.2017).

251 From Çatı İddianamesi, quoted in Komisyon Raporu (2017), p. 168.

252 From Çatı İddianamesi, quoted in Komisyon Raporu (2017), p. 169.

253 Çatı İddianamesi, Tanık İfadeleri.

254 Eren Ural (2015), *Fetö Sıfır Tüketiyor* (Istanbul: Elips Kitapları), ISBN: 9786051214276, p. 80.

255 "FETÖ, 'Peygamber salonda' deyip insanları kandırdı", www.haber10.com,

(http://www.haber10.com/guncel/feto_peygamber_salonda_deyip_insanlari_kandirdi-667982, access: 24.11.2016).

[256] Eren Ural (2015), p. 80.

[257] Fehmi Koru (2016), pp. 90-94.

[258] "Yardım Toplama Kanunu", No. 2860, Date: 23.06.1983, Resmi Gazete, Date: 25.06.1983, Issue: 18088); "Yardım Toplama Esas ve Usulleri Hakkında Yönetmelik", Resmi Gazete, Date: 27.12.1999, Issue: 23919.

[259] 667 sayılı kanun hükmünde kararname.

[260] "Cemaatin himmet tarifesini açıkladı", www.ahaber.com.tr, (http://www.ahaber.com.tr/gundem/2014/04/15/cemaatin-himmet-tarifesini-acikladi, access: 24.11.2016); quoted from Çatı İddianamesi, 9. Bölüm, in Komisyon Raporu (2017), p. 105.

[261] Çatı İddianamesi, "Örgütün Legal Görünümlü Yapısı", FETÖ Teşkilat Yapısı, p. 59-60.

[262] Komisyon Raporu (2017), p. 66, 142.

[263] Translation of the chapter al-Tawba 9/60 of *the Holy Qur'an*: "Alms are only for the poor and the needy, and the officials (appointed) over them, and those whose hearts are made to incline (to truth) and the (ransoming of) captives and those in debts and in the way of Allah and the wayfarer; an ordinance from Allah; and Allah is knowing, Wise." English translation is by M. H. Shakir, http://www.theholyquran.org/?x=s_main&y=s_middle&kid=15&sid=9, access: 30.04.2019.

[264] Komisyon Raporu (2017), pp. 287-288, 291-291, 310-312; "Mavi Marmara'yı yok sayan İsrail'i otorite sayan Fetullah Gülen", twitter.com (https://twitter.com/akitgazetem/status/442469635628072960, access: 11.06.2017); "Fetö'cü Zaman'ın Peres üzüntüsü", www.avamhaber.com, (http://www.avamhaber.com/2016/10/fetocuzamanin-peres-uzuntusu-h529.html, access: 11.06.2017)

[265] Mustafa Önsel (2016), *Aşil'in Topuğu FETÖ'nün "O Gece"si* (İstanbul: Alibi Yayıncılık), ISBN: 9786058337053, s. 95.

[266] Mustafa Önsel (2016), *ibid.*, p. 95.

[267] Information provided by Malatya Member of the Parliament, Nurettin Yaşar, to the Commission, official report dated 25.10.2016, TBMM Tutanak Hizmetleri Başkanlığı, p. 56.

[268] Information provided by Izmir Member of the Parliament, Hüseyin Kocabıyık, to the Commission, official report dated 25.10.2016, TBMM Tutanak Hizmetleri Başkanlığı, pp. 45-46.

[269] "Danıştay Kanunu İle Bazı Kanunlarda Değişiklik Yapılmasına Dair Kanun", No. 6723, Date: 01.07.2016, Resmi Gazete, Date: 23.07.2017 (mükerrer), Issue: 29779.

[270] T.C. Adâlet Bakanlığı, Basın ve Halkla İlişkiler Müşavirliği, "Yüksek Yargı Düzenlemesi TBMM'de Kabul Edildi", www.basin.adâlet.gov.tr, (http://www.basin.adâlet.gov.tr/Etkinlik/yuksek-yargi-duzenlemesi-tbmmde-kabul-edildi, access: 19.04.2017).

[271] Komisyon Raporu (2017), p. 321.

[272] T.C. Milli Güvenlik Kurulu Genel Sekreterliği, "26 Mayıs 2016 Tarihli Toplan-

tı", www.mgk.gov.tr, (http://www.mgk.gov.tr/index.php/26-mayis-2016-tarih-li-toplanti, access: 19.04.2017).

273 "FETÖ'nün işi YAŞ'ta bitecek", www.sabah.com.tr, (http://www.sabah.com.tr/gundem/2016/07/12/fetonun-isi-yasta-bitecek, access: 19.04.2017).

274 Oktay Bingöl, Ali Birlik Varlık (2016), *ibid.*, p. 2.

275 Komisyon Raporu (2017), pp. 317-321.

276 "Hürriyet ve Özkök Gülen'i övdü", www.kanalahaber.com, (http://www.kanalahaber.com/haber/medya/hurriyet-ve-ozkok-guleni-ovdu-51344/, access: 21.05.2017).

277 Veysel Dinçer (2016), "27 Maddede Gülen Cemaati ve FETÖ'nün Dünü ve Bugünü," listelist.com, (http://listelist.com/gulen-cemaati-feto/, erişim: 28.05.2017); "Dershane gerilimi tırmanıyor," www.hurriyet.com.tr, (http://www.hurriyet.com.tr/dershane-gerilimi-tirmaniyor25122934, access: 23.05.2017).

278 "Terörle Mücadele Kanunu Ve Ceza Muhakemesi Kanunu ile Bazı Kanunlarda Değişiklik Yapılmasına Dair Kanun," No. 6526, Date: 21.02.2014, Resmi Gazete, Date: 06.03.2014, Issue: 28933 (mükerrer).

279 Yüksek Seçim Kurulu, "10 Ağustos 2014 Pazar Günü Yapılan Onikinci Cumhurbaşkanı Seçimi İle İlgili Kesin Sonuçlar", www.ysk.gov.tr, (http://www.ysk.gov.tr/ysk/content/conn/YSKUCM/path/Contribution%20Folders/HaberDosya/2014CB-Kesin-416_d_Genel.pdf, access: 19.04.2017).

280 "Halklarımıza Acil Çağrı", twitter.com, (https://twitter.com/hdpgenelmerkezi/status/519175390443474944 access: 20.04.2017).

281 "6-7 Ekim olaylarının bilançosu", aa.com.tr, (http://aa.com.tr/tr/turkiye/6-7-ekim-olaylarininbilancosu/436002, access: 20.04.2017).

282 Yüksek Seçim Kurulu, "26. Dönem Milletvekili Genel Seçimi Sonucu; Siyasi Partilerin Çıkardıkları Milletvekili ile Bağımsızların Sayısı, www.ysk.gov.tr, (http://www.ysk.gov.tr/ysk/content/conn/YSKUCM/path/Contribution%20Folders/SecmenIslemleri/Secimler/2015MVES/96-E.pdf, access: 20.04.2017).

283 Komisyon Raporu (2017), pp. 329-331.

284 Anadolu Ajansı (2016), *Dakika Dakika FETÖ'nün Darbe Girişimi* (Ankara: Anadolu Ajansı Yayınları), 27, ISBN: 9786059075176, (http://aa.com.tr/uploads/TempUserFiles/pdf%2Ffeto_darbe_girisimi.pdf, access: 24.04.2017); T.C. Cumhurbaşkanlığı Genel Sekreterliği (2016), *15 Temmuz Darbe Girişimi ve Milletin Zaferi* (Ankara: Cumhurbaşkanlığı Yayınları), (https://www.tccb.gov.tr/assets/dosya/15Temmuz/15temmuz_tr.pdf, access: 24.04.2017); Komisyon Raporu (2017), pp. 331-355; the bulletin of the General Command of Gendarmerie, dated July 17, 2016; the presentation given by the Office of the Prime Minister to the Commission, dated 02.11.2016; information provided by the General Directorate of Security Affairs, Presidency of Special Operations Department, to the Commission, the official report dated 30.11.2016, BMM Tutanak Hizmetleri Başkanlığı, Kmisyon Raporu, p. 333; Hande Fırat (2016), *24 Saat: 15 Temmuz'un Kamera Arkası* (İstanbul: Doğan Kitap), ISBN: 9786050937732; http://www.15temmuzdarbegirisimi.com/ (access: 25.04.2017); "Dakika dakika darbe girişimi –15—16 Temmuz 2016", www.hurriyet.com.tr, (http://www.hurriyet.com.tr/dakika-dakika-darbegirisimi-15-16-temmuz-2016-40149409, access: 25.04.2017); "Savcılıktan darbe açıklaması: HSYK, Danıştay ve Yargıtay üyeleri hakkında gözaltı kararı", www.

karar.com, (http://www.karar.com/gundem-haberleri/hsyk-danistay-ve-yargi-tay-uyeleri-hakkinda-gozaltikarari-188522, access: 27.04.2017); Türkiye Büyük Millet Meclisi Basın Açıklamaları: Yabancı Basın TBMM'de", www.meclishaber.gov.tr, (http://www.meclishaber.gov.tr/develop/owa/haber_portal.aciklama?p1=137721, access: 26.04.2017).

[285] The name of the "Bosporus Bridge" was changed after the coup attempt to "15 Temmuz Şehitler Köprüsü" (July 15, Bridge of Martyrs) and on the hill next to the bridge, a monument was erected, and it is called "15 Temmuz Şehitler Makamı" (July 15, the Place of Martyrs).

[286] Anadolu Ajansı Arşivi, (https://www.anadoluimages.com/Search?keywords=10256474&typeid=1&categoryid=&startdate=&enddate=&languageid=1&partnerid=1#1, ID: 10256474, 16.07.2016).

[287] "Darbe girişimi gecesi MHP Genel Merkezi", www.turkiyegazetesi.com.tr, (http://www.turkiyegazetesi.com.tr/gundem/388650.aspx, access: 24.04.2017).

[288] HTS is the detailed report containing information about the phone calls of people.

[289] NTV television channel.

[290] "Başbakan Yıldırım: Bunu yapanlar en ağır bedeli ödeyeceklerdir", aa.com.tr, (http://aa.com.tr/tr/turkiye/basbakan-yildirim-bunu-yapanlar-en-agir-bedelio-deyeceklerdir/608244?amp=1, access: 25.04.2017).

[291] "Kılıçdaroğlu'ndan tepki: Demokrasimize sahip çıkıyoruz", www.internethaber.com, (http://www.internethaber.com/kilicdarogludan-tepki-demokrasimize-sa-hip-cikiyoruz1611019h.htm, access: 25.04.2017).

[292] Anadolu Ajansı Arşivi, (https://www.anadoluimages.com/Search?keywords=10256339&typeid=1&categoryid=&startdate=&enddate=&languageid=1&partnerid=1#1, ID: 10256339, 16.07.2016).

[293] Anadolu Ajansı Arşivi, (https://www.anadoluimages.com/Search?keywords=10289608&typeid=1&categoryid=&startdate=&enddate=&languageid=1&partnerid=1#1, ID: 10289608, 19.07.2016).

[294] CNN Turk television channel.

[295] Hande Fırat (2016), *ibid.*

[296] Anadolu Ajansı Arşivi, (https://www.anadoluimages.com/Search?keywords=10253357&typeid=1&categoryid=&startdate=&enddate=&languageid=1&partnerid=1#1, ID: 10253357, 16.07.2016).

[297] Turgut Özal University belonged to the FETÖ/PDY. Thus, it was closed after the 15th of July Coup Attempt by the Legislative Decree, number 667.

[298] Decoded data of A Haber Television program appended to the official transcript sent by the Radio and Television High Council to the Commission, dated 29.11.2016 with the number 44096195-622-E.30594.

[299] "Adâlet Bakanı: Fötrünü alıp kaçacak hükümet yoktur", www.posta.com.tr, (http://www.posta.com.tr/adâlet-bakani-fotrunu-alip-kacacak-hukumet-yok-tur-haberi-353432, access: 25.04.2017).

[300] Anadolu Ajansı Arşivi, (https://www.anadoluimages.com/Search?keywords=10268994&typeid=1&categoryid=&startdate=&enddate=&languageid=1&partnerid=1#1, ID: 10268994, 17.07.2016).

[301] Anadolu Ajansı Arşivi, (https://www.anadoluimages.com/Search?keywords=10303193&typeid=1&categoryid=&startdate=&enddate=&languageid=1&partnerid=1#1, ID: 10303193, 21.07.2016).

[302] See also, "Panik yapmadı, sakindi", www.milliyet.com.tr, (http://www.milliyet.com.tr/panikyapmadi-sakindi-ekonomi-2280638/, access: 29.04.2017).

[303] "Dakika dakika kâbus gibi gece", www.sozcu.com.tr, (http://www.sozcu.com.tr/2016/gundem/dakika-dakika-kabus-gibi-gece-1317042, access: 25.04.2017).

[304] "Başbakan Yıldırım: Havadaki Jetlerle Kurumlarımıza Mermi, Bomba Yağdıranlar Âdeta Bu Terör...", www.haberler.com, (https://www.haberler.com/basbakan-yildirim-havadaki-jetlerlekurumlarimiza-8613074-haberi/, 25.04.2017).

[305] "Çalışma ve Sosyal Güvenlik Bakanı Soylu: Hükümet işinin başındadır", aa.com.tr, (http://aa.com.tr/tr/15-temmuz-darbe-girisimi/calisma-ve-sosyal-guvenlik-bakani-soylu-hukumetisinin-basindadir/608369?amp=1, access: 25.04.2017).

[306] "Başbakan Yıldırım: Herkes demokraside, halkın birliğinde, ülkenin bekasında biraraya gelmiştir", www.akparti.org.tr, (https://www.akparti.org.tr/site/haberler/basbakan-yildirimherkes-demokraside-halkin-birliginde-ulkenin-bekasinda-bi/84962#1, access: 25.04.2017).

[307] Anadolu Ajansı Arşivi, (https://www.anadoluimages.com/Search?keywords=10260795&typeid=1&categoryid=&startdate=&enddate=&languageid=1&partnerid=1#1, ID: 10260795, 16.07.2016).

[308] "Başbakan Binali Yıldırım: Uçan her uçak füzeyle vurulacak", m.milatgazetesi.com, (http://m.milatgazetesi.com/basbakan-binali-yildirim-ucan-her-ucak-fuzeyle-vurulacak-haber89889, 25.04.2017).

[309] SAT: Turkish Underwater Offence Command

[310] SAS: Turkish Underwater Defense and Security

[311] "Türkiye'de askeri darbe girişimi! İşte dakika dakika tüm yaşananlar", www.gazetevatan.com, (http://www.gazetevatan.com/turkiye-de-sskeri-darbe-girisimi-iste-dakika-dakika-tum-yasananl967359-gundem/, access: 25.04.2017).

[312] Anadolu Ajansı Arşivi, (https://www.anadoluimages.com/Search?keywords=10257113&typeid=1&categoryid=&startdate=&enddate=&languageid=1&partnerid=1#1, ID: 10257113, 16.07.2016).

[313] "Cumhurbaşkanı Erdoğan: Oradan bu ülkeyi karıştırmaya gücün yetmeyecek", aa.com.tr, (http://aa.com.tr/tr/15-temmuz-darbe-girisimi/cumhurbaskani-erdogan-oradan-bu-ulkeyikaristirmaya-gucun-yetmeyecek/608624?amp=1, access: 28.04.2017).

[314] "Boğaziçi Köprüsü kısmen trafiğe açıldı", aa.com.tr, (http://aa.com.tr/tr/turkiye/bogazicikoprusu-kismen-trafige-acildi/608671, erişim: 28.04.2017).

[315] "Başbakan Yıldırım: Kalkışma bastırıldı, 161 şehidimiz var", www.trthaber.com, (http://www.trthaber.com/haber/gundem/basbakan-yildirim-kalkisma-bastirildi-161-sehidimizvar-261297.html, erişim: 28.04.2017).

[316] Anadolu Ajansı Arşivi, (https://www.anadoluimages.com/Search?keywords=10259478&typeid=1&categoryid=&startdate=&enddate=&languageid=1&partnerid=1#1, ID: 10259478, 16.07.2016).

[317] JFAC: Joint Force Air Component.

[318] Anadolu Ajansı Arşivi, (https://www.anadoluimages.com/Search?keywords=10261374&typeid=1&categoryid=&startdate=&enddate=&languageid=1&partnerid=1#1, ID: 10261374, 16.07.2016).

[319] The 2016/20190 numbered indictment of the T.C. İzmir Chief Public Prosecutors Office, the 2016/4413, 2016/2670 numbered investigation and the 2016/267 numbered indictment of Muğla Public Prosecutors Office; "FETÖ'nün suikast timine 'bombacı'dan çelik kapı tüyosu", www.aksam.com.tr, (http://www.aksam.com.tr/guncel/fetonun-suikast-timine-bombacidan-celik-kapi-tuyosu/haber-566894, access: 29.04.2017).

[320] "Erdoğan'ı darbe gecesi suikasttan kurtaran hava trafiğinin ayrıntıları ortaya çıktı", tr.sputniknews.com, (https://tr.sputniknews.com/turkiye/201612021026105042-erdogan-darbe-suikast/, access: 29.04.2017).

[321] Anadolu Ajansı (2016), ibid., p. 18.

[322] "Erdoğan'ın uçağı F-16'ları THY'nin kodu ile atlatmış", www.turkiyegazetesi.com.tr, (http://www.turkiyegazetesi.com.tr/gundem/387010.aspx, access: 30.04.2017); (Komisyon Raporu, 2017, p. 375.

[323] Information provided by the former General Director of Security Affairs Celâlettin Lekesiz to the Commission, official report dated 11.08.2016, TBMM Tutanak Hizmetleri Başkanlığı, pp. 8-9.

[324] CNN Türk Television Channel.

[325] Anadolu Ajansı Arşivi, (https://www.anadoluimages.com/Search?keywords=10334740&typeid=1&categoryid=&startdate=&enddate=&languageid=1&partnerid=1#1, ID: 10334740, 25.07.2016).

[326] Anadolu Ajansı Arşivi, (https://www.anadoluimages.com/Search?keywords=10584869&typeid=1&categoryid=&startdate=&enddate=&languageid=1&partnerid=1#1, ID: 10584869, 22.08.2016).

[327] Komisyon Raporu (2017), p. 378.

[328] "Milletimizin Emaneti Gazi Meclis Tek Yürek Görevinin Başında", Meclis Bülteni (Türkiye Büyük Millet Meclisi Aylık Bülteni), Issue: 215, July 2016, ISSN: 2146-7730, pp. 6-15, (https://www.tbmm.gov.tr/meclis_bulteni/s215.pdf, access: 03.05.2017).

[329] Oktay Bingöl, Ali Birlik Varlık (2016), ibid., p. 11.

[330] Darbe teşebbüsüne karşı tek ses için TBMM'de tarihi toplantı", www.ntv.com.tr, (http://www.ntv.com.tr/turkiye/darbe-tesebbusune-karsi-tek-ses-icin-tbmmde-tarihi- toplanti,MCxVvwua_E-10p_op2_nDQ, access: 05.05.2017).

[331] "Darbe gecesi Bekir Bozdağ: Yapacağımız şey Meclis'te ölmek", www.milliyet.com.tr, (http://www.milliyet.com.tr/darbe-gecesi-bekir-bozdag--gundem-2280927/, access: 09.05.2017).

[332] Komisyon Raporu (2017), p. 378.

[333] Komisyon Raporu (2017), pp. 367-374.

[334] "Darbe girişiminin ikinci dalgası Malatya'da nasıl engellendi?", www.hurriyet.com.tr, (http://www.hurriyet.com.tr/darbe-girisiminin-ikinci-dalgasi-malatyada-nasil-engellendi- 37310557, access: 15.05.2017).

[335] Oktay Bingöl, Ali Birlik Varlık (2016), ibid., p. 10; "Amaçları ve Neticeleriyle 15 Temmuz Darbe Girişimi", www.stratejidusunce.org, (http://www.stratejidusunce.org/Detay/Haber/1001/amaclari-ve-neticeleriyle-15-temmuz-darbegirisimi.aspx, access: 21.05.2016); (Komisyon Raporu, 2017, pp. 340-341, 354-355, 382, 385-386, 390-391; General Command of Gendarmerie's July 17 2016 dated report; İstanbul Provincial Security Directorate's dated 28.11.2016 41393 numbered transcript addressing the commission.

[336] Brigadier General Semih Terzi.

[337] NTV Television Channel, CNN Türk Television Channel.

[338] Anadolu Ajansı Arşivi, (https://www.anadoluimages.com/Search?keywords=12744778&typeid=1&categoryid=&startdat e=&enddate=&languageid=1&partnerid=1#1, ID: 12744778, 27.08.2016).

[339] "Devlet Bahçeli, Demokrasi ve Şehitler Mitingi / 7 Ağustos 2016.", www.youtube.com, (https://www.youtube.com/watch?v=qV9yYCbZ5dc, access: 15.05.2017).

[340] "Kemal Kılıçdaroğlu, Yenikapı Demokrasi ve Şehitler Mitingi Konuşması, 07 Ağustos 2016", www.youtube.com, (https://www.youtube.com/watch?v=0kcEhdjPpcM, access: 15.05.2017).

[341] "Binali Yıldırım, Yenikapı Demokrasi ve Şehitler Mitingi Konuşması", www.youtube.com, (https://www.youtube.com/watch?v=HCqOFw0Dvd8, access: 15.05.2017).

[342] "İsmail Kahraman, Yenikapı Demokrasi ve Şehitler Mitingi Konuşması", www.youtube.com, (https://www.youtube.com/watch?v=Hjj5Pd1xQgQ, access: 15.05.2017).

[343] "Cumhurbaşkanı Recep Tayyip Erdoğan, Yenikapı Demokrasi ve Şehitler Mitingi Konuşması, 07 Ağustos 2016", www.youtube.com, (https://www.youtube.com/watch?v=VZR3W5IIgr0, access: 15.05.2017).

[344] Anadolu Ajansı Arşivi, (https://www.anadoluimages.com/Search?keywords=12744778&typeid=1&categoryid=&startdat e=&enddate=&languageid=1&partnerid=1#1, ID: 12744776, 27.08.2016).

[345] "Darbe Girişiminin Ayak Sesleri! FETÖ'ye Yakın Gazetecilerin Paylaşımları Çok Konuşulacak", onedio.com, (https://onedio.com/haber/darbe-girisiminin-ayak-sesleri-feto-ye-yakin- gazetecilerin-paylasimlari-cok-konusulacak-721590, access: 29.05.2017).

[346] A Haber Television Channel, NTV Television Channel.

[347] CNN Türk Television Channel.

[348] Whatsapp.

[349] "Sosyal medya paylaşımlarının %8'i darbe yanlısı", www.iha.com.tr, (http://www.iha.com.tr/haber-sosyal-medya-paylasimlarinin-yuzde-8i-darbe-yanlisi-574718/, access: 02.06.2017).

[350] "Batı medyası telaşta", aa.com.tr, (http://aa.com.tr/tr/15-temmuz-darbe-girisimi/bati-medyasi-telasta/612114?amp=1, access: 29.03.2015).

[351] "New York Times'tan darbeye direnen Türk halkına hakaret", www.yenisafak.com, (http://www.yenisafak.com/dunya/new-york-timestan-darbeye-direnen-turk-halkina-hakaret!-2497230, access: 29.03.2017).

[352] The Constitution Of The Republic Of Turkey, article 120: "In the event of serious indications of widespread acts of violence aimed at the destruction of the free democratic order established by the Constitution or of fundamental rights and freedoms, or serious deterioration of public order because of acts of violence, the Council of Ministers, meeting under the chairmanship of the President of the Republic, after consultation with the National Security Council, may declare a state of emergency in one or more regions or throughout the country for a period not exceeding six months."

[353] Recommendation decision numbered 498 of the National Security Council dated July 20 2016. ("20 Temmuz 2016 Tarihli Toplantı, www.mgk.gov.tr, (https://www.mgk.gov.tr/index.php/20-temmuz-2016-tarihli-toplanti, access: 03.06.2017).

[354] Council of Ministers Decision, No. 2016/9064, Date: 07/20/2016, Resmi Gazete, Date: 21.07.2016, Issue: 29777, (http://www.resmigazete.gov.tr/eskiler/2016/07/20160721.htm, access: 03.06.2017).

[355] "Ülke Genelinde Olağanüstü Hal İlanına Dair Karar", Türkiye Büyük Millet Meclisi, No. 1116, Date: 21.07.2016, (https://www.tbmm.gov.tr/tbmm_kararlari/karar1116.html, access: 03.06.2017).

[356] "Olağanüstü Halin Uzatılmasına Dair Karar", Türkiye Büyük Millet Meclisi, No. 1130, Date: 11.10.2016, (http://www.resmigazete.gov.tr/eskiler/2016/10/20161013-1.pdf, access: 03.06.2017).

[357] "Olağanüstü Halin Uzatılmasına Dair Karar", Türkiye Büyük Millet Meclisi, No. 1134, Date: 03.01.2017, (http://www.resmigazete.gov.tr/eskiler/2017/01/20170105-2.pdf, access: 03.06.2017).

[358] "Olağanüstü Halin Uzatılmasına Dair Karar", Türkiye Büyük Millet Meclisi, No. 1139, Date: 18.04.2017, (http://www.resmigazete.gov.tr/eskiler/2017/04/20170418m1.htm, access: 03.06.2017).

[359] "Olağanüstü Halin Uzatılmasına Dair Karar", Türkiye Büyük Millet Meclisi, No. 1154, Date: 17.07.2017, (http://www.resmigazete.gov.tr/eskiler/2017/07/20170718M1-1.pdf).

[360] "Olağanüstü Halin Uzatılmasına Dair Karar", Türkiye Büyük Millet Meclisi, No. 1165, Date: 18.10.2017, (http://www.resmigazete.gov.tr/eskiler/2017/10/20171018M1-1.htm).

[361] "667 sayılı kanun hükmünde kararname"; "668 sayılı Olağanüstü Hal Kapsamında Alınması Gereken Tedbirler ile Bazı Kurum ve Kuruluşlara Dair Düzenleme Yapılması Hakkında Kanun Hükmünde Kararname", Resmi Gazete, Date: 27.07.2016, Issue: 29783, (http://www.resmigazete.gov.tr/eskiler/2016/07/20160727m2.pdf, access: 16.04.2017); "669 sayılı Olağanüstü Hal Kapsamında Bazı Tedbirler Alınması ve Milli Savunma Üniversitesi Kurulması ile Bazı Kanunlarda Değişiklik Yapılmasına Dair Kanun Hükmünde Kararname", Resmi Gazete, Date: 31.07.2016, Issue: 29787, (http://www.resmigazete.gov.tr/eskiler/2016/07/20160731.pdf, access: 16.04.2017); "670 sayılı Olağanüstü Hal Kapsamında Bazı Tedbirler Alınması Hakkında Kanun Hükmünde Kararname", Resmi Gazete, Date: 17.08.2016, Issue: 29804, (http://www.resmigazete.gov.tr/eskiler/2016/08/20160817.pdf, access: 16.04/2017); "671 sayılı Olağanüstü Hal Kapsamında Bazı Kurum ve Kuruluşlara İlişkin Düzenleme Yapılması Hakkında Kanun Hükmünde Kararname", Resmi Gazete, Date: 17.08.2016, Sayı: 29804, (http://www.resmigazete.gov.tr/eskiler/2016/08/20160817.pdf, access: 16.04.2017); "672 sayılı Olağanüstü Hal

Kapsamında Kamu Personeline İlişkin Alınan Tedbirlere Dair Kanun Hükmünde Kararname", Resmi Gazete, Date: 01.09.2016, Issue: 29818, (http://www.resmigazete.gov.tr/eskiler/2016/09/20160901m1.pdf, access: 16.04.2017); "673 sayılı Olağanüstü Hal Kapsamında Bazı Tedbirler Alınması Hakkında Kanun Hükmünde Kararname", Resmi Gazete, Date: 01.09.2016, Issue: 29818 (mükerrer), (http://www.resmigazete.gov.tr/eskiler/2016/09/20160901m2.pdf, access: 16.04.2017); "675 sayılı Olağanüstü Hal Kapsamında Bazı Tedbirler Alınması Hakkında Kanun Hükmünde Kararname", Resmi Gazete, Date: 29.10.2016, Issue: 29872, (http:// www.resmigazete.gov.tr/eskiler/2016/10/20161029.pdf, access: 16.04.2017); "677 sayılı Olağanüstü Hal Kapsamında Bazı Tedbirler Alınması Hakkında Kanun Hükmünde Kararname", Resmi Gazete, Date: 22.11.2016, Issue: 29896, (http:// www.resmigazete.gov.tr/eskiler/2016/11/20161122-1.htm, access: 16.04.2017); "679 sayılı Olağanüstü Hal Kapsamında Bazı Tedbirler Alınması Hakkında Kanun Hükmünde Kararname", Resmi Gazete, Date: 06.01.2017, Issue: 29940 (mükerrer), (http://www.resmigazete.gov.tr/eskiler/2017/01/20170106m1.htm, access: 16.04.2017); "683 sayılı Olağanüstü Hal Kapsamında Bazı Tedbirler Alınması Hakkında Kanun Hükmünde Kararname", Resmi Gazete, Date: 23.01.2017, Issue: 29957, (http://www.resmigazete.gov.tr/eskiler/2017/01/20170123. htm, access: 16.04.2017); "686 sayılı Olağanüstü Hal Kapsamında Bazı Tedbirler Alınması Hakkında Kanun Hükmünde Kararname", Resmi Gazete, Date: 07.02.2017, Issue: 29972 (mükerrer), (http://www.resmigazete.gov.tr/eskiler/2017/02/20170207m1.htm, access: 16.04.2017); "693 sayılı Olağanüstü Hal Kapsamında Bazı Tedbirler Alınması Hakkında Kanun Hükmünde Kararname", Resmi Gazete, Date: 25.08.2017, Issue: 30165, (http://www.resmigazete.gov.tr/ eskiler/2017/08/20170825.htm).

[362] 667 numbered emergency decree law.

[363] 667 numbered emergency decree law.

[364] 667 numbered emergency decree law; 668 numbered emergency decree law.

[365] 668 numbered emergency decree law.

[366] 669 numbered emergency decree law.

[367] "Hakimler ve Savcılar Kanunu", No. 2802, Date: 24.02.1983, Resmi Gazete, Date: 26.02.1983, Issue: 17971.

[368] 670 numbered emergency decree law.

[369] "Suç Gelirlerinin Aklanmasının Önlenmesi Hakkında Kanun", No. 5549, Date: 11.10.2006, Resmi Gazete, Date: 18.10.2006, Issue: 26323.

[370] 671 numbered emergency decree law.

[371] 672 numbered emergency decree law.

[372] 673 numbered emergency decree law.

[373] "674 sayılı Olağanüstü Hal Kapsamında Bazı Düzenlemeler Yapılması Hakkında Kanun Hükmünde Kararname", Resmi Gazete, Date: 01.09.2016, Issue: 29818 (mükerrer), (http://www.resmigazete.gov.tr/eskiler/2016/09/20160901M2-2. pdf, access: 16.04.2017).

[374] "676 sayılı Olağanüstü Hal Kapsamında Bazı Düzenlemeler Yapılması Hakkında Kanun Hükmünde Kararname", Resmi Gazete, Date: 29.10.2016, Issue: 29872, (http://www.resmigazete.gov.tr/eskiler/2016/10/20161029.htm, access: 16.04.2017).

375 675 numbered emergency decree law.

376 "676 sayılı Olağanüstü Hal Kapsamında Bazı Düzenlemeler Yapılması Hakkında Kanun Hükmünde Kararname", Resmi Gazete, Date: 29.10.2016, Issue: 29872, (http://www.resmigazete.gov.tr/eskiler/2016/10/20161029.htm, access: 16.04.2017).

377 677 numbered emergency decree law.

378 The Ministry of National Defense's TFŞ: 43624358-1040-416-16 numbered, dated December 08 2016 examination and investigation transcript addressed to the Commission.

379 "Kamu İhale Sözleşmeleri Kanunu", No. 4735, Issue: 05.01.2002, Resmi Gazete, Date: 22.01.2002, Issue: 24648.

380 "678 sayılı Olağanüstü Hal Kapsamında Bazı Düzenlemeler Yapılması Hakkında Kanun Hükmünde Kararname", Resmi Gazete, Date: 22.11.2016, Issue: 29896, (http://www.resmigazete.gov.tr/eskiler/2016/11/20161122.htm, access: 16.04.2017).

381 "Köy Kanunu", No. 442, Date: 18.03.1924, Resmi Gazete, Date: 07.04.1924, Issue: 68.

382 "Kimlik Bildirme Kanunu", No. 1774, Date: 26.06.1973, Resmi Gazete, Date: 11.07.1973, Issue: 14591.

383 "Sendikalar ve Toplu İş Sözleşmesi Kanunu", No. 6356, Date: 18.10.2012, Resmi Gazete, Date: 07.11.2012, Issue: 28460.

384 "687 sayılı Olağanüstü Hal Kapsamında Bazı Düzenlemeler Yapılması Hakkında Kanun Hükmünde Kararname", Resmi Gazete, Date: 09.02.2017, Issue: 29974, (http://www.resmigazete.gov.tr/eskiler/2017/02/20170209.htm, access: 16.04.2017).

385 "688 sayılı Olağanüstü Hal Kapsamında Bazı Tedbirler Alınması Hakkında Kanun Hükmünde Kararname", Resmi Gazete, Date: 29.03.2017, Issue: 30022 (mükerrer), (http://www.resmigazete.gov.tr/eskiler/2017/03/20170329m1.htm, access: 16.04.2017).

386 "689 sayılı Olağanüstü Hal Kapsamında Bazı Tedbirler Alınması Hakkında Kanun Hükmünde Kararname", Resmi Gazete, Date: 29.04.2017, Issue: 30052 (mükerrer), (http://www.resmigazete.gov.tr/eskiler/2017/04/20170429-M1-1.htm, access: 30.04.2017).

387 "Ecnebi Memleketlere Gönderilecek Talebe Hakkında Kanun", No. 1416, Date: 08.04.1929, Resmi Gazete, Date: 16.04.1929, Issue: 1169.

388 "690 sayılı Olağanüstü Hal Kapsamında Bazı Düzenlemeler Yapılması Hakkında Kanun Hükmünde Kararname", Resmi Gazete, Date: 29.04.2017, Issue: 30052, (http://www.resmigazete.gov.tr/eskiler/2017/04/20170429-M1-2.htm, access: 30.04.2017).

389 "691 sayılı Olağanüstü Hal Kapsamında Bazı Düzenlemeler Yapılması Hakkında Kanun Hükmünde Kararname", Resmi Gazete, Date: 22.06.2017, Issue: 30104 (ikinci mükerrer), (http://www.resmigazete.gov.tr/eskiler/2017/06/20170622M2-1.htm, access: 22.06.2017).

390 "Askeri Ceza Kanunu", No. 1632, Date: 22.05.1930, Resmi Gazete, Date: 15.06.1930, Issue: 1520.

[391] "692 sayılı Olağanüstü Hal Kapsamında Bazı Tedbirler Alınması Hakkında Kanun Hükmünde Kararname", Resmi Gazete, Date: 14.07.2017, Issue: 30124 (mükerrer), (http://www.resmigazete.gov.tr/eskiler/2017/07/20170714M1-1.htm, access: 14.07.2017).

[392] "693 sayılı Olağanüstü Hal Kapsamında Bazı Tedbirler Alınması Hakkında Kanun Hükmünde Kararname", Resmi Gazete, Date: 25.08.2017, Issue: 30165, (http://www.resmigazete.gov.tr/eskiler/2017/08/20170825-12.htm, access: 26.08.2017); "694 sayılı Olağanüstü Hal Kapsamında Bazı Düzenlemeler Yapılması Hakkında Kanun Hükmünde Kararname", Resmi Gazete, Date: 25.08.2017, Issue: 30165, (http://www.resmigazete.gov.tr/eskiler/2017/08/20170825-13.pdf, access: 26.08.2017).

[393] "Türk Silahlı Kuvvetleri Personel Kanunu", No. 926, Date: 07/27/1967, Resmi Gazete, Date: 10.08.1967, Issue: 12670.

[394] "Jandarma Teşkilat, Görev ve Yetkileri Kanunu", No. 2803, Date: 10.03.1983, Resmi Gazete, Date: 12.03.1983, Issue: 17985.

[395] "Sahil Güvenlik Komutanlığı Kanunu", No. 2692, Date: 09.07.1982, Resmi Gazete, Date: 13.07.1982, Issue: 17753.

[396] "Yükseköğretim Personel Kanunu", No. 2914, Date: 11.10.1983, Resmi Gazete, Date: 13.10.1983, Issue: 18190.

[397] "Devlet Memurları Kanunu", No. 657, Date: 14.07.1965, Resmi Gazete, Date: 23.07.1965, Issue: 12056.

[398] "İhraç edilen kamu görevlilerinin sayısı açıklandı.", www.cnnturk.com, (https://www.cnnturk.com/son-dakika-ihrac-edilen-kamu-gorevlilerinin-sayisi-aciklandi, access: 17.07.2017).

[399] Komisyon Raporu (2017), p. 435.

[400] Komisyon Raporu (2017), p. 454.

[401] 667 numbered emergency decree law; 668 numbered emergency decree law.

[402] Komisyon Raporu (2017), pp. 554-565.

[403] İstanbul Düşünce Vakfı (2016), 15 Temmuz'da Nasıl Değiştik?, (http://www.idv.org.tr/arastirmalar, access: 17.06.2017).

[404] Credit Default Swap.

[405] S&P (Standard & Poor's), Even though it does not have a contract with the Under Secretariat of Treasury, it performs a credit rating assessment on Turkey.

[406] Komisyon Raporu (2017), pp. 187-188, 418-457, 567-574.

[407] "Bankacılık Kanunu", No. 5411, Date: 10/19/2005, Resmi Gazete, Date: 01.11.2005, Issue: 25983 (mükerrer).

[408] Komisyon Raporu (2017), pp. 571-577.

[409] Hannah Lucinda Smith (2016), "The MP paid by group linked with Turkey coup", The Sunday Times, 01.08.2016, (http://www.thetimes.co.uk/article/mp-paid-by-group-linked-to-turkey-coup-88x0s07vc, access: 18.06.2017; "The MP paid by group linked with Turkey coup", www.thetimes.co.uk, (https://www.thetimes.co.uk/article/mp-paid-by-group-linked-to-turkey-coup-88x0s07vc, access: 18.06.2017).

[410] Information provided by the former MİT Undersecretary Emre Taner to the Commission, official report dated 09.11.2016, TBMM Tutanak Hizmetleri Başkanlığı, Komisyon Raporu (2017), p. 585; 694 sayılı Olağanüstü Hal Kapsamında Bazı Düzenlemeler Yapılması Hakkında Kanun Hükmünde Kararname, Articles 62, 67; ("Komisyon Raporu," (2017), pp. 582-616, 618-628; Information provided by retired Generals Hilmi Özkök, Işık Koşaner, İlker Başbuğ and Ümit Dündar to the Commission, official reports dated October 18,19,26 2016 and November 03 2016, TBMM Tutanak Hizmetleri Başkanlığı, Komisyon Raporu (2017), pp. 159, 213-216, 583-584; "Suç Gelirlerinin Aklanmasının Önlenmesi Hakkında Kanun", No. 5549, Date: 11.10.2006, Resmi Gazete, Date: 18.10.2006, Issue: 26323.

[411] "Türk Ceza Kanunu", No. 5237, Date: 26.09.2004, Resmi Gazete, Date: 12.10.2004, Issue: 25611, Article 221.

BIBLIOGRAPHY

"15 Temmuz'un Gizli Kahramanı", www.airkule.com, (http://www.airkule.com/haber/15- TEMMUZ-UN-GIZLI-KAHRAMANI/25563, erişim: 30.04.2017).

"1 Kasım 2015 seçimini AK Parti kazandı", kuaza.com, (https://kuaza.com/guncel-haberler/bizden- haberler/1-kasim-2015-secimini-ak-parti-kazandi, erişim: 01.06.2017).

"23 Nisan 1999 Tarihine Kadar İşlenen Suçlardan Dolayı Şartla Salıverilmeye, Dava ve Cezaların Ertelenmesine Dair Kanun", No. 4616, Tarih: 21.12.2000, Resmi Gazete, Tarih: 22.12.2000, Sayı: 24268.

"667 sayılı Olağanüstü Hal Kapsamında Alınan Tedbirlere İlişkin Kanun Hükmünde Ka-rarname", Resmi Gazete, Tarih: 23.07.2016, Sayı: 29779, (http://www.resmigazete.gov.tr/eskiler/2016/07/20160723.htm, erişim: 16.04.2017).

"668 sayılı Olağanüstü Hal Kapsamında Alınması Gereken Tedbirler ile Bazı Kurum ve Kuruluşlara Dair Düzenleme Yapılması Hakkında Kanun Hükmünde Kararname", Resmi Gazete, Tarih: 27.07.2016, Sayı: 29783, (http://www.resmigazete.gov.tr/eskiler/2016/07/20160727m2.pdf, erişim: 16.04.2017).

"669 sayılı Olağanüstü Hal Kapsamında Bazı Tedbirler Alınması ve Milli Savunma Üniversitesi Kurulması ile Bazı Kanunlarda Değişiklik Yapılmasına Dair Kanun Hükmünde Kararname", Resmi Gazete, Tarih: 31.07.2016, Sayı: 29787, (http://www. resmigazete.gov.tr/eskiler/2016/07/20160731.pdf, erişim: 16.04.2017).

"670 sayılı Olağanüstü Hal Kapsamında Bazı Tedbirler Alınması Hakkında Kanun Hük-münde Kararname", Resmi Gazete, Tarih: 17.08.2016, Sayı: 29804, (http://www.resmigazete. gov.tr/eskiler/2016/08/20160817.pdf, erişim: 16.04.2017).

"671 sayılı Olağanüstü Hal Kapsamında Bazı Kurum ve Kuruluşlara İlişkin Düzenleme Yapılması Hakkında Kanun Hükmünde Kararname", Resmi Gazete, Tarih: 17.08.2016, Sayı: 29804, (http://www.resmigazete.gov.tr/ eskiler/2016/08/20160817.pdf, erişim: 16.04.2017).

"672 sayılı Olağanüstü Hal Kapsamında Kamu Personeline İlişkin Alınan Tedbirlere Dair Kanun Hükmünde Kararname", Resmi Gazete, Tarih: 01.09.2016, Sayı: 29818, (http://www. resmigazete.gov.tr/eskiler/2016/09/20160901m1.pdf, erişim: 16.04.2017).

"673 sayılı Olağanüstü Hal Kapsamında Bazı Tedbirler Alınması Hakkında Kanun Hük-münde Kararname", Resmi Gazete, Tarih: 01.09.2016, Sayı: 29818 (mükerrer), (http://www. resmigazete.gov.tr/eskiler/2016/09/20160901m2.pdf, erişim: 16.04.2017).

"674 sayılı Olağanüstü Hal Kapsamında Bazı Düzenlemeler Yapılması Hakkında Kanun Hükmünde Kararname", Resmi Gazete, Tarih: 01.09.2016, Sayı: 29818 (mükerrer), (http:// www.resmigazete.gov.tr/eskiler/2016/09/20160901M2-2. pdf, erişim: 16.04.2017).

"675 sayılı Olağanüstü Hal Kapsamında Bazı Tedbirler Alınması Hakkında Kanun Hük-münde Kararname", Resmi Gazete,

Tarih: 29.10.2016, Sayı: 29872, (http://www.resmigazete. gov.tr/eskiler/2016/10/20161029.pdf, erişim: 16.04.2017).

"676 sayılı Olağanüstü Hal Kapsamında Bazı Düzenlemeler Yapılması Hakkında Kanun Hükmünde Kararname", Resmi Gazete, Tarih: 29.10.2016, Sayı: 29872, (http://www. resmigazete.gov.tr/eskiler/2016/10/20161029.htm, erişim: 16.04.2017).

"677 sayılı Olağanüstü Hal Kapsamında Bazı Tedbirler Alınması Hakkında Kanun Hük-münde Kararname", Resmi Gazete, Tarih: 22.11.2016, Sayı: 29896, (http://www.resmigazete. gov.tr/eskiler/2016/11/20161122-1.htm, erişim: 16.04.2017).

"678 sayılı Olağanüstü Hal Kapsamında Bazı Düzenlemeler Yapılması Hakkında Kanun Hükmünde Kararname", Resmi Gazete, Tarih: 22.11.2016, Sayı: 29896, (http://www. resmigazete.gov.tr/eskiler/2016/11/20161122.htm, erişim: 16.04.2017).

"679 sayılı Olağanüstü Hal Kapsamında Bazı Tedbirler Alınması Hakkında Kanun Hük-münde Kararname", Resmi Gazete, Tarih: 06.01.2017, Sayı: 29940 (mükerrer), (http://www. resmigazete.gov.tr/eskiler/2017/01/20170106m1.htm, erişim: 16.04.2017).

"6-7 Ekim olaylarının bilançosu", aa.com.tr, (http://aa.com.tr/tr/ turkiye/6-7-ekim-olaylarinin-bilancosu/436002, erişim: 20.04.2017).

"680 sayılı Olağanüstü Hal Kapsamında Bazı Düzenlemeler Yapılması Hakkında Kanun Hükmünde Kararname", Resmi Gazete, Tarih: 06.01.2017, Sayı: 29940 (mükerrer), (http:// www.resmigazete.gov.tr/eskiler/2017/01/20170106m1. htm, erişim: 16.04.2017).

"681 sayılı Olağanüstü Hal Kapsamında Milli Savuma ile İlgili Bazı Düzenlemeler Yapıl-ması Hakkında Kanun Hükmünde

Kararname", Resmi Gazete, Tarih: 06.01.2017, Sayı: 29940 (mükerrer), (http://www.resmigazete.gov.tr/eskiler/2017/01/20170106m1.htm, erişim: 16.04.2017).

"682 sayılı Genel Kolluk Disiplin Hükümleri Hakkında Kanun Hükmünde Kararname", Resmi Gazete, Tarih: 23.01.2017, Sayı: 29.957, (http://www.resmigazete.gov.tr/eskiler/2017/01/20170123-1.htm, erişim: 24.01.2017).

"683 sayılı Olağanüstü Hal Kapsamında Bazı Tedbirler Alınması Hakkında Kanun Hük-münde Kararname", Resmi Gazete, Tarih: 23.01.2017, Sayı: 29957, (http://www.resmigazete.gov.tr/eskiler/2017/01/20170123.htm, erişim: 16.04.2017).

"684 sayılı Olağanüstü Hal Kapsamında Bazı Düzenlemeler Yapılması Hakkında Kanun Hükmünde Kararname", Resmi Gazete, Tarih: 23.01.2017, Sayı: 29957, (http://www.resmigazete.gov.tr/eskiler/2017/01/20170123.htm, erişim: 16.04.2017).

"685 sayılı Olağanüstü Hal İşlemleri İnceleme Komisyonu Kurulması Hakkında Kanun Hükmünde Kararname", Resmi Gazete, Tarih: 23.01.2017, Sayı: 29957, (http://www.resmigazete.gov.tr/eskiler/2017/01/20170123.htm, erişim: 16.04.2017).

"686 sayılı Olağanüstü Hal Kapsamında Bazı Tedbirler Alınması Hakkında Kanun Hük-münde Kararname", Resmi Gazete, Tarih: 07.02.2017, Sayı: 29972 (mükerrer), (http://www.resmigazete.gov.tr/eskiler/2017/02/20170207m1.htm, erişim: 16.04.2017).

"687 sayılı Olağanüstü Hal Kapsamında Bazı Düzenlemeler Yapılması Hakkında Kanun Hükmünde Kararname", Resmi Gazete, Tarih: 09.02.2017, Sayı: 29974, (http://www.resmigazete.gov.tr/eskiler/2017/02/20170209.htm, erişim: 16.04.2017).

"688 sayılı Olağanüstü Hal Kapsamında Bazı Tedbirler Alınması Hakkında Kanun Hük-münde Kararname", Resmi Gazete, Tarih: 29.03.2017, Sayı: 30022 (mükerrer), (http://www.

resmigazete.gov.tr/eskiler/2017/03/20170329m1.htm, erişim: 16.04.2017).

"689 sayılı Olağanüstü Hal Kapsamında Bazı Tedbirler Alınması Hakkında Kanun Hük-münde Kararname", Resmi Gazete, Tarih: 29.04.2017, Sayı: 30052 (mükerrer), (http://www. resmigazete.gov.tr/eskiler/2017/04/20170429-M1-1.htm, erişim: 30.04.2017).

"690 sayılı Olağanüstü Hal Kapsamında Bazı Düzenlemeler Yapılması Hakkında Kanun Hükmünde Kararname", Resmi Gazete, Tarih: 29.04.2017, Sayı: 30052, (http://www. resmigazete.gov.tr/eskiler/2017/04/20170429-M1-2.htm, erişim: 30.04.2017).

"691 sayılı Olağanüstü Hal Kapsamında Bazı Düzenlemeler Yapılması Hakkında Kanun Hükmünde Kararname", Resmi Gazete, Tarih: 22.06.2017, Sayı: 30104 (ikinci mükerrer), (http:// www.resmigazete.gov.tr/eskiler/2017/06/20170622M2-1. htm, erişim: 22.06.2017).

"692 sayılı Olağanüstü Hal Kapsamında Bazı Tedbirler Alınması Hakkında Kanun Hük-münde Kararname", Resmi Gazete, Tarih: 14.07.2017, Sayı: 30124 (mükerrer), (http://www. resmigazete.gov.tr/eskiler/2017/07/20170714M1-1.htm, erişim: 14.07.2017).

"693 sayılı Olağanüstü Hal Kapsamında Bazı Tedbirler Alınması Hakkında Kanun Hük-münde Kararname", Resmi Gazete, Tarih: 25.08.2017, Sayı: 30165, (http://www.resmigazete. gov.tr/eskiler/2017/08/20170825-12.htm, erişim: 26.08.2017).

"694 sayılı Olağanüstü Hal Kapsamında Bazı Düzenlemeler Yapılması Hakkında Kanun Hükmünde Kararname", Resmi Gazete, Tarih: 25.08.2017, Sayı: 30165, (http://www. resmigazete.gov.tr/eskiler/2017/08/20170825-13.pdf, erişim: 26.08.2017).

"Adâlet Bakanı: Fötrünü alıp kaçacak hükümet yoktur", www.posta. com.tr, (http://www.posta.com.tr/adâlet-bakani-fotrunu-alip-kacacak-hukumet-yoktur-haberi-353432, erişim: 25.04.2017).

Adana Cumhuriyet Başsavcılığı'nca hazırlanan iddianame, Soruşturma No: 2014/19640, İddianame No: 2014/772.

Adana Emniyet Müdürü Osman Ak'ın Komisyon'a verdiği bilgi, 08.12.2016 tarihli tuta-nak, TBMM Tutanak Hizmetleri Başkanlığı.

ADANALI, Selahattin (2014), *Cemaatin Psikolojik Kaosu*, Fethullah Gülen'in Dinî Söyleminin Eleştirisi, ed. Mehmet Şahin, İstanbul: Evre Yayınları, ISBN: 6058503908.

"Adlî Kolluk Yönetmeliği", Resmi Gazete, Tarih: 01.06.2005, Sayı: 25832, (http://mevzuat.basbakanlik.gov.tr/Metin. Aspx?MevzuatKod=7.5.8201&MevzuatIliski=0&sourceXmlSea rch, 12.05.2017)

"Akkaş bildiri dağıttı, Öz gece emniyete geldi", www.hurriyet.com. tr, (http://www.hurriyet.com.tr/akkas-bildiri-dagitti-oz-gece-emniyete-geldi-27867350, erişim: 01.06.2017).

Alıcı, Mustafa, (2011), Müslüman-Hıristiyan Diyaloğu, 2. Baskı, İz Yayıncılık, İstanbul.

"Âli İmrân Suresi Kur'an Meali", www.kuranmeali.org, (http:// www.kuranmeali.org/kuran/ali- imran-suresi/, erişim: 11.06.2017).

ALTINDAL, Aytunç (2017), *Vatikan ve Tapınak Şövalyeleri*, 18. Baskı, İstanbul: Alfa Yayınları, ISBN: 9786051067407.

"Alvar imamı (Alvarlı Muhammed Lütfi Efe) kimdir?", www. haberler.com, (https://www.haberler.com/alvar-imami-alvarli-muhammed-lutfi-efe-kimdir-6859042-haberi/, erişim: 28.04.2017).

ALPSOY, Said (2015), *Çelişkiler İnsam*, İstanbul: Umran Yayınları.

"Amaçları Ve Neticeleriyle 15 Temmuz Darbe Girişimi", www. stratejidusunce.org, (http://www.stratejidusunce.org/ Detay/Haber/1001/amaclari-ve-neticeleriyle-15-temmuz-darbe- girisimi.aspx, erişim: 21.05.2016).

Anadolu Ajansı (2016), Dakika Dakika FETÖ'nün Darbe Girişimi, Ankara: Anadolu Ajansı Yayınları 27, ISBN: 9786059075176, (http://aa.com.tr/uploads/TempUserFiles/pdf%2Ffeto_ darbe_girisimi.pdf, erişim: 24.04.2017).

Anayasa Mahkemesinin 04.08.2016 tarih ve 2016/12 sayılı kararı.

Ankara Cumhuriyet Başsavcılığı, FETÖ / PDY Hakkında Çatı İddianamesi, 06.06.2016, E. No: 2016/24769.

Ankara Cumhuriyet Başsavcılığının 2015/110148 sayılı sor., 2015/48175 esas, 2015/3110 id. sayılı iddianamesi.

"Askeri Ceza Kanunu", No. 1632, Tarih: 22.05.1930, Resmi Gazete, Tarih: 15.06.1930, Sayı: 1520.

AVCI, Hanefi (2010), *Haliç'te Yaşayan Simonlar Dün Devlet Bugün Cemaat*, Ankara: Angora Yayıncılık, ISBN: 9789752870758.

AYDIN, Mahmut (2001), *Monologdan Diyaloğa-Çağdaş Hristiyan Düşüncesinde Hristiyan-Müslüman Diyaloğu*, Ankara: Ankara Okulu, ISBN: 9789058190379.

Bakanlar Kurulu kararı, No. 2016/9064, Tarih: 20.07.2016, Resmi Gazete, Tarih: 21.07.2016, Sayı: 29777, (http://www. resmigazete.gov.tr/eskiler/2016/07/20160721.htm, erişim: 03.06.2017).

"Bankacılık Kanunu", No. 5411, Tarih: 19.10.2005, Resmi Gazete, Tarih: 01.11.2005, Sayı: 25983 (mükerrer).

BARLAS, Mehmet (2000), "Gülen'den Çevik Bir'e Mektup", www. yenisafak.com, (http://www.yenisafak.com/arsiv/2000/ ekim/16/dizi.html, erişim: 29.05.2017).

"Başbakan Binali Yıldırım: Uçan her uçak füzeyle vurulacak", m.milatgazetesi.com, (http://m.milatgazetesi.com/basbakan-binali-yildirim-ucan-her-ucak-fuzeyle-vurulacak-haber-89889, 25.04.2017).

"Başbakan Yıldırım: Bunu yapanlar en ağır bedeli ödeyeceklerdir", aa.com.tr, (http://aa.com.tr/tr/turkiye/basbakan-yildirim-bunu-yapanlar-en-agir-bedeli- odeyecek-lerdir/608244?amp=1, erişim: 25.04.2017).

"Başbakan Yıldırım: Havadaki Jetlerle Kurumlarımıza Mermi, Bomba Yağdıranlar Âdeta Bu Terör...", www.haberler.com, (https://www.haberler.com/basbakan-yildirim-havadaki-jetlerle- kurumlarimiza-8613074-haberi/, 25.04.2017).

"Başbakan Yıldırım: Herkes demokraside, halkın birliğinde, ülkenin bekasında biraraya gelmiştir", www.akparti.org.tr, (https://www.akparti.org.tr/site/haberler/basbakan-yildirim-herkes- demokraside-halkin-birliginde-ulkenin-bekasinda-bi/84962#1, erişim: 25.04.2017).

"Başbakan Yıldırım: Kalkışma bastırıldı, 161 şehidimiz var", www.trthaber.com, (http://www.trthaber.com/haber/gundem/basbakan-yildirim-kalkisma-bastirildi-161-sehidimiz-var-261297.html, erişim: 28.04.2017).

"Batı medyası telaşta", aa.com.tr, (http://aa.com.tr/tr/15-temmuz-darbe-girisimi/bati-medyasi-telasta/612114?amp=1, erişim: 29.03.2015).

BEVANS, Stephen B. (2013), "Mission at the Second Vatican Council; 1962-1965", NTR, Cilt 25, No. 2, Mart, (http://newtheologyreview.org/index.php/ntr/article/view/54/260, erişim: 21.02.2017).

"Binali Yıldırım, Yenikapı Demokrasi ve Şehitler Mitingi Konuşması", www.youtube.com, (https://www.youtube.com/watch?v=HCqOFw0Dvd8, erişim: 15.05.2017).

BİNGÖL, Oktay, Ali Birlik Varlık (2016), FETÖ Darbe Girişiminin

Askerî Analizi, Rapor-016 A, Merkez Strateji Enstitüsü, Ankara.

"Bir askerimiz atılacağına tüm imam hatipler kapansın", www. gazetevatan.com, (http://www.gazetevatan.com/-bir-askerimiz-atilacagina-tum-imam-hatipler-kapansin--997384-gundem/, erişim: 21.03.2017).

"Boğaziçi Köprüsü kısmen trafiğe açıldı", aa.com.tr, (http:// aa.com.tr/tr/turkiye/bogazici-koprusu- kismen-trafiğe-acildi/608671, erişim: 28.04.2017).

Burdur Milletvekili Reşat Petek, Komisyon Başkanı Tutanakları.

"Cemaatin himmet tarifesini açıkladı", www.ahaber.com.tr, (http:// www.ahaber.com.tr/gundem/2014/04/15/cemaatin-himmet-tarifesini-acikladi, erişim: 24.11.2016).

"Ceza Muhakemesi Kanunu", No. 5271, 04.12.2004, Resmi Gazete, Tarih: 17.12.2004, Sayı: 25673.

"Ceza ve Güvenlik Tedbirlerinin İnfazı Hakkında Kanun", No. 5275, Tarih: 13.12.2004, Resmi Gazete, Tarih: 29.12.2004, Sayı: 25685.

"Cumhurbaşkanı Erdoğan: Oradan bu ülkeyi karıştırmaya gücün yetmeyecek", aa.com.tr, (http://aa.com.tr/tr/15-temmuz-darbe-girisimi/cumhurbaskani-erdogan-oradan-bu-ulkeyi-karistirmaya- gucun-yetmeyecek/608624?amp=1, erişim 28.04.2017).

"Cumhurbaşkanı Recep Tayyip Erdoğan, Yenikapı Demokrasi ve Şehitler Mitingi Konuşması, 07 Ağustos 2016", www.youtube.com, (https://www.youtube.com/watch?v=VZR3W5IIgr0, erişim: 15.05.2017).

"Cumhuriyetin 50 nci Yılı Nedeniyle Bazı Suç ve Cezaların Affı Hakkında Kanun", No. 1803, Tarih: 15.05.1974, Resmi Gazete, Tarih: 18.05.1974, Sayı: 14890 (mükerrer).

"Çalışma ve Sosyal Güvenlik Bakanı Soylu: Hükümet işinin başındadır", aa.com.tr, (http://aa.com.tr/tr/15-temmuz-darbe-girisimi/calisma-ve-sosyal-guvenlik-bakani-soylu-hukumet-isinin-basindadir/608369?amp=1, erişim: 25.04.2017).

"Dakika dakika darbe girişimi – 15 – 16 Temmuz 2016", www.hurriyet.com.tr, (http://www.hurriyet.com.tr/dakika-dakika-darbe-girisimi-15-16-temmuz-2016-40149409, erişim: 25.04.2017).

"Dakika dakika kâbus gibi gece", www.sozcu.com.tr, (http://www.sozcu.com.tr/2016/gundem/dakika-dakika-kabus-gibi-gece-1317042, erişim: 25.04.2017).

"Danıştay Kanunu İle Bazı Kanunlarda Değişiklik Yapılmasına Dair Kanun", No. 6723, Tarih: 01.07.2016, Resmi Gazete, Tarih: 23.07.2017 (mükerrer), Sayı: 29779.

"Darbe Destekçilerine Sosyal Medyada Sıkı Takip", Anadolu Ajansı, 20 Temmuz 2016.

"Darbe gecesi Bekir Bozdağ: Yapacağımız şey Meclis'te ölmek", www.milliyet.com.tr, (http://www.milliyet.com.tr/darbe-gecesi-bekir-bozdag--gundem-2280927/, erişim: 09.05.2017).

"Darbe girişimi gecesi MHP Genel Merkezi", www.turkiyegazetesi.com.tr, (http://www.turkiyegazetesi.com.tr/gundem/388650.aspx, erişim: 24.04.2017).

"Darbe girişiminin ikinci dalgası Malatya'da nasıl engellendi?", www.hurriyet.com.tr, (http://www.hurriyet.com.tr/darbe-girisiminin-ikinci-dalgasi-malatyada-nasil-engellendi-37310557, erişim: 15.05.2017).

"Darbe teşebbüsüne karşı tek ses için TBMM'de tarihi toplantı", www.ntv.com.tr, (http://www.ntv.com.tr/turkiye/darbe-tesebbusune-karsi-tek-ses-icin-tbmmde-tarihi-toplanti,MCxVvwua_E-10p_op2_nDQ, erişim: 05.05.2017).

"Declaration on the Relation of the Church to Non-Christian Religions: Nostra Aetate; Proclaimed by His Holiness

Pope Paul VI", www.vatican.va, (http://www.vatican.va/archive/hist_councils/ii_vatican_council/documents/vat-ii_decl_19651028_nostra- aetate_en.html. erişim: 19.04.2017).

DEMİRAĞ, Yavuz Selim (2015), *İmamların Öcü, Türk Silahlı Kuvvetlerinde Cemaat Yapılanması*, İstanbul: Kırmızı Kedi Yayınları, ISBN: 9786059908931.

"Devlet Bahçeli, Demokrasi ve Şehitler Mitingi / 7 Ağustos 2016". (https://www.youtube.com/watch?v=qV9yYCbZ5dc, erişim: 15.05.2017).

"Devlet İstihabart Hizmetleri ve Milli İstihbarat Teşkilatı Kanunu", Kanun No. 2937, Kabul Tarihi 01.11.1983, Resmi Gazete, Tarih: 03.11.1983, Sayı: 18.210.

"Devlet İstihbarat Hizmetleri ve Milli İstihbarat Teşkilatı Kanununda Değişiklik Yapıl-masına Dair Kanun", No. 6278, Kabul Tarihi: 17.02.2012, Resmi Gazete, Tarih: 18.02.2012, Sayı: 28.208.

"Devlet Memurları Kanunu", No. 657, Tarih: 14.07.1965, Resmi Gazete, Tarih: 23.07.1965, Sayı: 12.056.

DİLER, Ergün (2016), "Sızıntı", Takvim, 12 Ağustos, www.takvim.com.tr, (http://www.takvim.com.tr/yazarlar/ergundiler/2016/08/12/sizinti, erişim: 15.03.2017).

DİLER, Ergün (2016), "Caminin Sırrı", Takvim, 11 Ekim, www.takvim.com.tr, (http://www.takvim.com.tr/yazarlar/ergundiler/2016/10/11/caminin-sirri, erişim: 15.03.2017).

Diyanet İşleri Başkanlığı (2016), Dini İstismar Hareketi FETÖ/PDY (Olağanüstü Din Şurası Kararları), Din İşleri Yüksek Kurulu Başkanlığı, Ankara, (https://webdosya.diyanet.gov.tr/anasayfa/UserFiles/Document/TextDocs/9a7d78e1-1513-4ef7-b294- e24dd4151b33.pdf, erişim: 10.06.2017).

"Ecnebi Memleketlere Gönderilecek Talebe Hakkında Kanun", No. 1416, Tarih: 08.04.1929, Resmi Gazete, Tarih: 16.04.1929, Sayı: 1169.

"Ekrem Dumanlı Darbe Tehdidi", www.youtube.com, (https://www.youtube.com/watch?v=bXeXSRajYyg, erişim: 29.01.2017).

Emekli Jandarma Kurmay Albay ve Yazar Mustafa Önsel'in Komisyon'a verdiği bilgi, 13.10.2016, tarihli tutanak, TBMM Tutanak Hizmetleri Başkanlığı.

Emekli MİT Müsteşarı Emre Taner'in Komisyon'a verdiği bilgi, 09.11.2016 tarihli tutanak, TBMM Tutanak Hizmetleri Başkanlığı.

Emekli Orgeneral Hilmi Özkök'ün Komisyon'a verdiği bilgi, 19.10.2016 tarihli tutanak, TBMM Tutanak Hizmetleri Başkanlığı.

Emekli Orgeneral Işık Koşaner'in Komisyon'a verdiği bilgi, 26.10.2016 tarihli tutanak, TBMM Tutanak Hizmetleri Başkanlığı.

Emekli Orgeneral İlker Başbuğ'un Komisyon'a verdiği bilgi, 03.11.2016 tarihli tutanak, TBMM Tutanak Hizmetleri Başkanlığı.

Emniyet Genel Müdürlüğü İstihbarat Daire Başkanlığı'nca Ankara İl Emniyet Müdürlüğü ve Emniyet Genel Müdürlüğü Teftiş Kurulu Başkanlığı'na gönderilen 10.03.1992 tarih ve B.05.1.EGM.0.06.03.400/1 (79-92) sayılı yazı; Ankara İl Emniyet Müdürlüğü'nün Ankara Devlet Güvenlik Mahkemesi Cumhuriyet Başsavcılığı'na yazdığı 28.09.1992 tarih ve B.05.1.EGM.4.06.00.14 İll. ve Sor. (F).92/8303 sayılı yazı ve ekinde gönderilen 28.08.1992 tarih ve B.05.EGM.0.06.01/15-92 sayılı fezleke.

Emniyet Genel Müdürlüğü Özel Harekât Daire Başkanlığı'nın Komisyon'a verdiği bilgi, 30.11.2016, tarihli tutanak, TBMM Tutanak Hizmetleri Başkanlığı.

"Erdoğan'ı darbe gecesi suikasttan kurtaran hava trafiğinin

ayrıntıları ortaya çıktı", tr.sputniknews.com, (https://tr.sputniknews.com/turkiye/201612021026105042-erdogan-darbe-suikast/, erişim: 29.04.2017).

"Erdoğan'ın uçağı F-16'ları THY'nin kodu ile atlatmış", www.turkiyegazetesi.com.tr, (http://www.turkiyegazetesi.com.tr/gundem/387010.aspx, erişim: 30.04.2017).

ERDOĞAN, Latif (2006), *Küçük Dünyam, Fethullah Gülen*, İstanbul: Doğan Kitap, ISBN: 9789756065168.

ERDOĞAN, Latif (2016), *Şeytamn Gülen Yüzü*, İstanbul: Turkuvaz Kitap, ISBN: 6056670800.

Eski Emniyet Genel Müdürü Celâlettin Lekesiz'in Komisyon'a verdiği bilgi, 08.11.2016 tarihli tutanak, TBMM Tutanak Hizmetleri Başkanlığı.

Eski Emniyet Genel Müdürü Mehmet Kılıçlar'ın Komisyon'a verdiği bilgi, 02.11.2016 tarihli tutanak, TBMM Tutanak Hizmetleri Başkanlığı.

Eski Emniyet Genel Müdür Yardımcısı Emin Arslan'ın Komisyon'a verdiği bilgi, 27.10.2016 tarihli tutanak, TBMM Tutanak Hizmetleri Başkanlığı.

Eskişehir Milletvekili Emine Nur Günay'ın Komisyon'a verdiği bilgi, 25.10.2016 tarihli tutanak, TBMM Tutanak Hizmetleri Başkanlığı.

"FETÖ militanlarını CIA ve FBI eğitti", www.yenisafak.com, (http://www.yenisafak.com/dunya/feto-militanlarini-cia-ve-fbi-egitti-2501159, erişim: 05.06.2017).

"FETÖ'nün 30 yıllık evlilik kataloğu ortaya çıktı", www.hurriyet.com.tr, (http://www.hurriyet.com.tr/fetonun-30-yillik-evlilik-katalogu-ortaya-cikti-40488155, erişim: 15.04.2016).

"FETÖ'nün amacı, devletin kılcal damarlarına sızmak", www.dha.com.tr, (http://www.dha.com.tr/fetonun-amaci-devletin-kilcal-damarlarina-sizmak_1290498.html, erişim: 11.03.2017).

"FETÖ'nün Asya Pasifik ülkeleri sorumluları", aa.com.tr, (http://aa.com.tr/tr/info/infografik/2624, erişim: 10.03.2017).

"FETÖ'nün işi YAŞ'ta bitecek", www.sabah.com.tr, (http://www.sabah.com.tr/gundem/2016/07/12/fetonun-isi-yasta-bitecek, erişim: 19.04.2017).

"FETÖ'nün suikast timine 'bombacı'dan çelik kapı tüyosu", www.aksam.com.tr, (http://www.aksam.com.tr/guncel/fetonun-suikast-timine-bombacidan-celik-kapi-tuyosu/haber-566894, erişim: 29.04.2017).

"FETÖ, 'Peygamber salonda' deyip insanları kandırdı", www.haber10.com, (http://www.haber10.com/guncel/feto_peygamber_salonda_deyip_insanlari_kandirdi-667982, erişim: 24.11.2016).

"Fetullah Gülen'in 12 Eylülcüler'e destek yazısı", www.sabah.com.tr, (http://www.sabah.com.tr/gundem/2015/05/10/fetullah-gulenin-12-eylulculere-destek-yazisi, erişim: 28.05.2017).

"Fethullah Gülen'in 28 Şubat'taki utanç verici sözleri", www.sabah.com.tr, (http://www.sabah.com.tr/gundem/2015/02/28/fethullah-gulenin-28-subattaki-utanc-verici-sozleri, erişim: 28.05.2017).

"Fetullah Gülen'in MHP notları ortaya çıktı", www.sabah.com.tr, (http://www.sabah.com.tr/gundem/2016/06/27/fetullah-gulenin-mhp-notlari-ortaya-cikti, erişim: 27.6.2016).

Fırat, Hande (2016), 24 Saat; 15 Temmuz'un Kamera Arkası, İstanbul: Doğan Kitap, ISBN: 9786050937732.

"Gazeteci Haydar Meriç Cinâyetinin Firari Komiseri Yakalandı", www.hurriyet.com.tr, (http://www.hurriyet.com.tr/gazeteci-haydar-meric-cinâyetinin-firari-komiseri-yakalandi-40220325, erişim: 09.09.2016).

Gazeteci Hüseyin Gülerce'nin Komisyon'a verdiği bilgi, 26.10.2016 tarihli tutanak, TBMM Tutanak Hizmetleri Başkanlığı.

Gazeteci-yazar Nedim Şener'in Komisyon'a verdiği bilgi, 25.10.2016 tarihli tutanak, TBMM Tutanak Hizmetleri Başkanlığı.

Genelkurmay İkinci Başkanı Orgeneral Ümit Dündar'ın Komisyon'a verdiği bilgi, 18.10.2016 tarihli tutanak, TBMM Tutanak Hizmetleri Başkanlığı.

"Gülen: Amerika'ya alâka duymamızın sebebi", www.yeniakit.com. tr, (http://www.yeniakit.com.tr/haber/gulen-amerikaya-alaka-duymamizin-sebebi-62309.html, erişim: 22.02.2017).

"Gülen Davası İddianamesi/VII-Gülen'in konuşmalarını içeren video kasetler", https://tr.wikisource.org, (https://tr.wikisource.org/wiki/G%C3%BClen_davas%C4%B1_iddianamesi/VII- G%C3%BClen%27in_konu%C5%9Fmalar%C4%B1n%C4%B1_i%C3%A7eren_Video_Kasetler, erişim: 26.01.2017).

GÜLEN, Fetullah (1979), "Asker", Sızıntı, Sayı 5, Haziran.

GÜLEN, Fetullah (1980), "Son Karakol", Sızıntı, Sayı 21, Ekim.

GÜLEN, Fetullah (2010), Diriliş Çağrısı, Kırık Testi 6, Gazeteciler ve Yazarlar Vakfı, ISBN: 9789756714416.

"Gülen'in özel hayatını araştırırken öldürülen ismin bilgisayarından neler çıktı?", odatv.com, (http://odatv.com/gulenin-ozel-hayatini-arastirirken-oldurulen-ismin-bilgisayarindan-neler-cikti-0607161200.html, erişim: 11.05.2017).

HABLEMİTOĞLU, Necip (2008), Köstebek, İstanbul: Pozitif Yayıncılık, ISBN: 9789756461686.

"Hakimler ve Savcılar Kanunu", No. 2802, Tarih: 24.02.1983, Resmi Gazete, Tarih: 26.02.1983, Sayı: 17971.

Hakimler ve Savcılar Yüksek Kurulu Genel Kurulu'nun 15.11.2016 tarih ve 2016/440 sayılı kararı.

Hakimler ve Savcılar Yüksek Kurulu İkinci Dairesi'nin 2016/99 esas sayılı soruşturma dosyası.

Hakimler ve Savcılar Yüksek Kurulu'nun 24.08.2016 tarih ve 2016/426 karar sayılı Genel Kurul kararı ve gerekçesi.

"Halklarımıza Acil Çağrı", twitter.com, (https://twitter.com/ hdpgenelmerkezi/status/519175390443474944 erişim: 20.04.2017).

"Haydar Meriç Cinâyetinde Bylock İzine Rastlandı", www. yenicaggazetesi.com.tr, (http://www.yenicaggazetesi. com.tr/haydar-meric-cinâyetinde-bylock-izine-rastlandi-149377h.htm, erişim: 31.10.2016).

"HSYK'dan açıklama geldi: Amirden izin anayasaya aykırıdır.", www.radikal.com.tr, (http://www.radikal.com.tr/ turkiye/hsykdan-aciklama-geldi-amirden-izin-anayasaya-aykiridir-1168158/, erişim: 01.06.2017).

"HSYK Başkanvekili Hamsici'den çarpıcı itiraflar", www.sabah. com.tr, (http://www.sabah.com.tr/gundem/2016/11/16/ eski-hsyk-baskanvekili-hamsiciden-carpici-itiraflar#, erişim: 27.02.2017).

"HSYK eski Başkanvekili'nden FETÖ itirafları, flaş iddialar", www.hurriyet.com.tr, (http://www.hurriyet.com.tr/hsyk-eski-baskanvekilinden-feto-itiraflari-40279870, erişim: 27.02.2017).

"HSYK eski üyesi Kerim Tosun itirafçı oldu", www.milliyet.com.tr, (http://www.milliyet.com.tr/hsyk-eski-uyesi-kerim-tosun-gundem-2345811/, erişim: 27.02.2017).

"HSYK eski üyesi Özçelik'ten FETÖ itirafları", www.trthaber.com, (http://www.trthaber.com/haber/turkiye/hsyk-eski-uyesi-ozcelikten-feto-itiraflari-283236.html, erişim: 27.02.2017).

HSYK Genel Kurul Kararı, Karar Tarihi: 15/11/2016, Karar No: 2016/440.

HSYK Genel Kurul Kararı, Karar Tarihi: 15/11/2016, Karar No: 2016/440.

http://www.15temmuzdarbegirisimi.com/ (erişim: 25.04.2017)

http://www.risalehaber.com/huseyin-gulerce-f-gulen-bana-ben-nurcu-degilim-dedi-295053h.htm, erişim: 08.03.2017.

http://www.ahaber.com.tr/gundem/2016/11/16/eski-hsyk-baskanvekili-hamsici-itirafci-oldu, erişim: 12.05.2017.

http://www.hurriyet.com.tr/hsyk-eski-baskanvekilinden-feto-itiraflari-40279870, erişim: 12.05.2017.

http://www.milliyet.com.tr/hsyk-eski-baskanvekili-hamsici-den-gundem-2346101/, eri-şim: 12.05.2017.

http://www.sabah.com.tr/gundem/2016/11/16/eski-hsyk-baskanvekili-hamsiciden-carpici- itiraflar#, erişim: 12.05.2017.

http://www.sozcu.com.tr/2016/gundem/hsyk-eski-baskanvekili-hamsiciden-2011-yilindaki- yargitay-ve-danistay-uyelerinin-secimleriyle-itiraflar-1512499/, erişim: 12.05.2017.

"Hucurât Suresi Kur'an Meali", www.kuranmeali.org, (http://www.kuranmeali.org/kuran/hucurat-suresi/, erişim: 10.06.2017).

İçişleri eski Bakanı Efkan Âlâ'nın Komisyon'a verdiği bilgi, 18.10.2016 tarihli tutanak, TBMM Tutanak Hizmetleri Başkanlığı.

"İhraç edilen kamu görevlilerinin sayısı açıklandı.", www.cnnturk.com, (https://www.cnnturk.com/son-dakika-ihrac-edilen-kamu-gorevlilerinin-sayisi-aciklandi, erişim: 17.07.2017).

İMAM Ahmed bin Hanbel (2014), Müsned, İstanbul: Ocak Yayıncılık, ISBN: 6054659081.

İMAM Muhyiddin en Nevevî, Sahih-i Müslim Şerhi, çev. Beşir Eryarsoy, İstanbul: Polen & Karınca Yayınevi.

"İsmail Kahraman, Yenikapı Demokrasi ve Şehitler Mitingi Konuşması", www.youtube.com, (https://www.youtube. com/watch?v=Hjj5Pd1xQgQ, erişim: 15.05.2017).

İstanbul Düşünce Vakfı (2016), 15 Temmuz'da Nasıl Değiştik?, (http://www.idv.org.tr/arastirmalar, erişim: 17.06.2017).

İstanbul İl Emniyet Müdürlüğü'nün, Komisyon'a hitaben 28.11.2016 tarihli ve 41393 sayılı yazısı.

İstanbul İl Emniyet Müdürlüğü Terörle Mücadele Şube Müdürlüğü'nce İstanbul Cumhu-riyet Başsavcılığı'na gönderilen 02.09.2015 tarih ve 21575 sayılı cevabi yazı.

İstanbul Terörle Mücadele Şube Müdürlüğü tarafından İstanbul CMK'nun 250. Madde-siyle Yetkili Cumhuriyet Başsavcılığı'na gönderilen 07.04.2011 tarihli evrak.

"İşte istihbaratın yazdığı o rapor", i1.wp.com, (https://i1.wp.com/i. sozcu.com.tr/wp-content/uploads/2016/12/fetobelge1.jpg, erişim: 04.06.2017).

"İtirafçı general: Âdil Öksüz 6 gün darbe planı yaptı", www.hurriyet. com.tr, (http://www.hurriyet.com.tr/itirafci-general-âdil-oksuz-6-gun-darbe-plani-yapti-40193392, erişim: 12.04.2017).

İzmir Milletvekili Hüseyin Kocabıyık'ın Komisyon'a verdiği bilgi, 25.10.2016 tarihli tutanak, TBMM Tutanak Hizmetleri Başkanlığı.

İzmir Milletvekili Hüseyin Kocabıyık'ın Komisyon'a verdiği bilgi, 09.11.2016 tarihli tuta-nak, TBMM Tutanak Hizmetleri Başkanlığı.

Jandarma Genel Komutanlığı'nın 17 Temmuz 2016 tarihli ceridesi.

"Jandarma Teşkilat, Görev ve Yetkileri Kanunu", No. 2803, Tarih: 10.03.1983, Resmi Gazete, Tarih: 12.03.1983, Sayı: 17985.

"Kadir Topbaş: 17 belediye çalışanı şehit oldu", www.aksam.

com.tr, (http://www.aksam.com.tr/guncel/kadir-topbas-17-belediye-calisani-sehit-oldu/haber-533701, erişim: 26.05.2017).

"Kamu İhale Sözleşmeleri Kanunu", No. 4735, Tarih: 05.01.2002, Resmi Gazete, Tarih: 22.01.2002, Sayı: 24648.

Keleş, Ahmet (2016), FETO'nun Günah Piramidi, Diyarbakır: Destek Yayınları, ISBN: 9786053111634.

"Kemal Kılıçdaroğlu, Yenikapı Demokrasi ve Şehitler Mitingi Konuşması, 07 Ağustos 2017", (https://www.youtube.com/watch?v=0kcEhdjPpcM, erişim: 15.05.2017).

"Kılıçdaroğlu'ndan tepki: Demokrasimize sahip çıkıyoruz", www.internethaber.com, (http://www.internethaber.com/kilicdarogludan-tepki-demokrasimize-sahip-cikiyoruz-1611019h.htm, erişim: 25.04.2017).

KINDIRA, Zübeyir (2016), Işıkevlerinden Darbeye Fethullah'ın Coplan, Ankara: Altaylı Yayınları, ISBN: 9786059630030.

"Kimlik Bildirme Kanunu", No. 1774, Tarih: 26.06.1973, Resmi Gazete, Tarih: 11.07.1973, Sayı: 14591.

Komisyon Raporu (Fethullahçı Terör Örgütü'nün (FETÖ / PDY) 15 Temmuz 2016 Tarihli Darbe Girişimi İle Bu Terör Örgütünün Faaliyetlerinin Tüm Yönleriyle Araştırılarak Alınması Gereken Önlemlerin Belirlenmesi Amacıyla Kurulan Meclis Araştırması Komisyonu tarafından hazırlanan rapor) (2017), Türkiye Büyük Millet Meclisi, Ankara.

KORU, Fehmi (2016), Ben Böyle Gördüm: Cemaat'in Siyasetle Sınavı, İstanbul: Alfa Basım Yayım, ISBN: 9786051712789.

"Köy Kanunu", No. 442, Tarih: 18.03.1924, Resmi Gazete, Tarih: 07.04.1924, Sayı: 68.

Malatya Milletvekili Nurettin Yaşar'ın Komisyon'a verdiği bilgi,

25.10.2016 tarihli tutanak, TBMM Tutanak Hizmetleri Başkanlığı.

"Milletimizin Emaneti Gazi Meclis Tek Yürek Görevinin Başında", Meclis Bülteni (Türkiye Büyük Millet Meclisi Aylık Bülteni), Sayı: 215, Temmuz 2016, ISSN: 2146-7730, (https://www. tbmm.gov.tr/meclis_bulteni/s215.pdf, erişim: 03.05.2017).

Milli Güvenlik Kurulu'nun 20 Temmuz 2016 tarihli ve 498 sayılı tavsiye kararı. ("20 Temmuz 2016 Tarihli Toplantı, www. mgk.gov.tr, (https://www.mgk.gov.tr/index.php/20-temmuz-2016-tarihli-toplanti, erişim: 03.06.2017).

Milli Savunma Bakanlığı'nın Komisyon'a hitaben 08 Aralık 2016 tarih ve TFŞ: 43624358-1040-416-16 / İnc. ve Sor. D. sayılı yazısı.

Mustafa Önsel'in Komisyon'a verdiği bilgi, 13.10.2016 tarihli tutanak, TBMM Tutanak Hizmetleri Başkanlığı.

"Nur Suresi Kur'an Meali", www.kuranmeali.org, (http://www. kuranmeali.org/kuran/nur-suresi/âyet-36/2-diyanet-isleri-meali.aspx, erişim: 28.05.2017.)

"Olağanüstü Halin Uzatılmasına Dair Karar", Türkiye Büyük Millet Meclisi, No. 1130, Tarih: 11.10.2016, (http://www. resmigazete.gov.tr/eskiler/2016/10/20161013-1.pdf, erişim: 03.06.2017).

"Olağanüstü Halin Uzatılmasına Dair Karar", Türkiye Büyük Millet Meclisi, No. 1134, Ta-rih: 03.01.2017, (http:// www.resmigazete.gov.tr/eskiler/2017/01/20170105-2.pdf, erişim: 03.06.2017).

"Olağanüstü Halin Uzatılmasına Dair Karar", Türkiye Büyük Millet Meclisi, No. 1139, Tarih: 18.04.2017, (http://www. resmigazete.gov.tr/eskiler/2017/04/20170418m1.htm, erişim: 03.06.2017).

"Olağanüstü Halin Uzatılmasına Dair Karar", Türkiye Büyük

Millet Meclisi, No. 1154, Tarih: 17.07.2017, (http://www.resmigazete.gov.tr/eskiler/2017/07/20170718M1-1.pdf).

"Olağanüstü Halin Uzatılmasına Dair Karar", Türkiye Büyük Millet Meclisi, No. 1165, Tarih: 10.2017, (http://www.resmigazete.gov.tr/eskiler/2017/10/20171018M1-1.htm).

ÖNSEL, Mustafa (2016), *Aşil'in Topuğu FETÖ'nün "O Gece"si*, İstanbul: Alibi Yayıncılık, ISBN: 9786058337053.

ÖZTÜRK, Mustafa (2015), *Tefsirde Ehl-i Sünnet ve Şia Polemikleri*, Ankara: Ankara Okulu Yayınları, ISBN: 9944162180.

ÖZTÜRK, Mustafa (2016), *"FETÖ'nün Genel Karakteristiği ve Teolojisi"*, Türkiye Günlüğü, Sayı: 127, Yaz, ss. 28-52.

"Panik yapmadı, sakindi", www.milliyet.com.tr, (http://www.milliyet.com.tr/panik-yapmadi-sakindi-ekonomi-2280638/, erişim: 29.04.2017).

"Paralel Yapı Soruşturmalarında İlk Cinâyet Suçlaması", t24.com.tr, (http://t24.com.tr/haber/paralel-yapi-sorusturmalarinda-ilk-cinâyet-suclamasi,346868, erişim: 24.06.2016).

Prof. Dr. Mustafa Öztürk'ün Komisyon'a verdiği bilgi, 13.10.2016 tarihli tutanak, TBMM Tutanak Hizmetleri Başkanlığı.

Prof. Dr. Nevzat Tarhan'ın Komisyon'a verdiği bilgi, 19.10.2016 tarihli tutanak, TBMM Tutanak Hizmetleri Başkanlığı.

(http://www.demokrasivesehitlermitingi.com/2016/08/07/recep-tayyip-erdogan-konusmasi-yenikapi- demokrasi-ve-sehitler-mitingi/, erişim: 17.05.2017).

"Sahil Güvenlik Komutanlığı Kanunu", No. 2692, Tarih: 09.07.1982, Resmi Gazete, Tarih: 13.07.1982, Sayı: 17.753.

"Said Nursi'nin Dersim tepkisi", www.risalehaber.com, (http://www.risalehaber.com/said-nursinin- dersim-tepkisi-65908h.htm, erişim: 28.04.2017).

"Savcılıktan darbe açıklaması: HSYK, Danıştay ve Yargıtay üyeleri hakkında gözaltı kararı", www.karar.com, (http://www.karar.com/gundem-haberleri/hsyk-danistay-ve-yargitay-uyeleri-hakkinda- gozalti-karari-188522, erişim: 27.04.2017).

SELVİ, Abdülkadir (2016), "ByLock ve Eagle'de yeni gelişmeler var", www.hurriyet.com.tr, (http://www.hurriyet.com.tr/yazarlar/abdulkadir-selvi/bylock-ve-eagleda-yeni-gelismeler-var-40278849, erişim: 12.04.2017).

"Sendikalar ve Toplu İş Sözleşmesi Kanunu", No. 6356, Tarih: 18.10.2012, Resmi Gazete, Tarih: 07.11.2012, Sayı: 28460.

SEZER, Okan (2014), "Alamut Kalesi: İnanılması Güç Bir Efsane Değil", arkeolojigazete-si.com, (http://arkeolojigazetesi.com/?author=5, erişim: 10.06.2017).

SMİTH, Hannah Lucinda (2016), "MP paid by group linked with Turkey coup", The Sun-day Times, 01.08.2016, (http://www.thetimes.co.uk/article/mp-paid-by-group-linked-to-turkey-coup-88x0s07vc, erişim: 18.06.2017).

"Sosyal medya paylaşımlarının %8'i darbe yanlısı", www.iha.com.tr, (http://www.iha.com.tr/haber-sosyal-medya-paylasimlarinin-yuzde-8i-darbe-yanlisi-574718/, erişim: 02.06.2017).

"Suç Gelirlerinin Aklanmasının Önlenmesi Hakkında Kanun", No. 5549, Tarih: 11.10.2006, Resmi Gazete, Tarih: 18.10.2006, Sayı: 26323.

ŞENER, Nedim (2016), *Ergenekon Belgelerinde Fethullah Gülen ve Cemaat*, İstanbul: Destek Yayınları, ISBN: 9789944298957.

ŞIK, Ahmet (2017), *İmamın Ordusu*, İstanbul: Kırmızı Kedi Yayınları, ISBN: 9786052981030.

T.C. Adâlet Bakanlığı, Basın ve Halkla İlişkiler Müşavirliği, "Yüksek Yargı Düzenlemesi TBMM'de Kabul Edildi", www.basin.

adâlet.gov.tr, (http://www.basin.adâlet.gov.tr/Etkinlik/ yuksek- yargi-duzenlemesi-tbmmde-kabul-edildi, erişim: 19.04.2017).

T.C. Cumhurbaşkanlığı Genel Sekreterliği (2016), 15 Temmuz Darbe Girişimi ve Milletin Zaferi, Ankara: Cumhurbaşkanlığı Yayınları, (https://www.tccb.gov. tr/assets/dosya/15Temmuz/15temmuz_tr.pdf, erişim: 24.04.2017).

T.C. İzmir Cumhuriyet Başsavcılığı'nın 2016/2090 numaralı iddianamesi; Muğla Cumhuriyet Başsavcılığı Sor. No: 2016/4413, Esas No: 2016/2670 ve 2016/267 numaralı iddianamesi.

T.C. Milli Güvenlik Kurulu Genel Sekreterliği, "26 Mayıs 2016 Tarihli Toplantı", www.mgk.gov.tr, (http://www.mgk. gov.tr/index.php/26-mayis-2016-tarihli-toplanti, erişim: 19.04.2017).

"Telekulak operasyonu", www.turkiyegazetesi.com.tr, (http:// www.turkiyegazetesi.com.tr/Genel/a7045.aspx, erişim: 30.05.2017).

"Teröristbaşı Gülen 'Haçlı'nın ülkenizi işgal etmesi çok tehlikeli değildir.'", www.sabah.com.tr, (http://www.sabah.com.tr/ webtv/turkiye/teroristbasi-gulen-haclinin-ulkenizi-isgal-etmesi-cok-tehlikeli- degildir, erişim: 10.06.2017).

"Terörle Mücadele Kanunu", No. 3713, Tarih: 12.04.1991, Resmi Gazete, Tarih: 12.04.1991, Sayı: 20843 (mükerrer).

"Terörle Mücadele Kanunu Ve Ceza Muhakemesi Kanunu ile Bazı Kanunlarda Değişiklik Yapılmasına Dair Kanun", No. 6526, Tarih: 21.02.2014, Resmi Gazete Tarihi: 06.03.2014, Sayı: 28933 (mükerrer).

"Tevbe Suresi Kur'an Meali", www.kuranmeali.org, (http://www. kuranmeali.org/kuran/tevbe-suresi/, erişim: 11.06.2017).

"Tutuklu hakim Mustafa Başer'den Fetullah Gülen açıklaması", www.yeniakit.com.tr, (http://www.yeniakit.com.tr/haber/tutuklu-hakim-mustafa-baserden-fetullah-gulen-aciklamasi-66545.html, erişim: 04.05.2017).

"Tüm ayrıntılarıyla 7 Haziran 2015 Genel Seçim sonuçları", www.karar.com, (http://www.karar.com/gundem-haberleri/tum-ayrintilariyla-7-haziran-2015-genel-secim-sonuclari, erişim: 01.06.2017).

"Türk Ceza Kanunu", No. 5237, Tarih: 26.09.2004, Resmi Gazete, Tarih: 12.10.2004, Sayı: 25611.

Türkiye Büyük Millet Meclisi Basın Açıklamaları: Yabancı Basın TBMM'de", www.meclishaber.gov.tr, (http://www.meclishaber.gov.tr/develop/owa/haber_portal.aciklama?p1=137721, erişim: 26.04.2017).

"Türkiye Cumhurbaşkanlığı Seçimi Sonuçları 2014", trbuguntvhaber.blogspot.com, (http://trbuguntvhaber.blogspot.com/2014/08/cumhurbaskanlg-secim-sonuclar-canli.html, erişim: 01.06.2017).

"Türkiye'de askeri darbe girişimi! İşte dakika dakika tüm yaşananlar", www.gazetevatan.com, (http://www.gazetevatan.com/turkiye-de-sskeri-darbe-girisimi-iste-dakika-dakika-tum-yasananl-967359- gundem/, erişim: 25.04.2017).

"Türk Silahlı Kuvvetleri Personel Kanunu", No. 926, Tarih: 27.07.1967, Resmi Gazete, Tarih: 10.08.1967, Sayı: 12.670.

URAL, Eren (2015), *Fetö Sıfın Tüketiyor*, İstanbul: Elips Kitapları, ISBN: 9786051214276.

UZUN, Sabri (2015), *İN; Baykal Kaseti, Dink Cinâyeti ve Diğer Komplolar*, 3. Basım, İstanbul: Kırmızı Kedi Yayınları, ISBN: 9786059908320.

"Ülke Genelinde Olağanüstü Hal İlanına Dair Karar", Türkiye Büyük Millet Meclisi, No. 1116, Tarih: 21.07.2016, (https://

www.tbmm.gov.tr/tbmm_kararlari/karar1116.html, erişim: 03.06.2017).

VEREN, Nurettin (2007), A*BD'nin Truva Atı Fethullah Gülen Hareketi: Kuşatma,* İstanbul: Siyah Beyaz Yayınları, ISBN: 9789944490139.

VEREN, Nurettin (2016), *FETO: İsimlerle ve Belgelerle 1966-2016,* İstanbul: Tekin Yayınevi, ISBN: 9786053111535.

VEREN, Nurettin (2016), "Gülen'in hiç bilinmeyen yemin metni", Yeni Akit, 23 Mart. (http://www.yeniakit.com.tr/ yazarlar/nurettin-veren/gulenin-hic-bilinmeyen-yemin-metni-14326.html, erişim: 28.05.2017).

VEREN, Nurettin (2016), "Gülen'in Papa 2. John Paul'a ortaklık mektubu", www.yeniakit.com.tr, (http://www.yeniakit. com.tr/yazarlar/nurettin-veren/gulenin-papa-2-john-paula-ortaklik-mektubu-13914.html, erişim: 28.05.2017).

World Council of Churches, (https://www.oikoumene.org/en, erişim: 11.04.2017).

"Yardım Toplama Esas ve Usulleri Hakkında Yönetmelik", Resmi Gazete, Tarih: 27.12.1999, Sayı: 23919.

"Yardım Toplama Kanunu", No. 2860, Tarih: 23.06.1983, Resmi Gazete, Tarih: 25.06.1983, Sayı: 18088).

Yavuz, M. Hakan (2004), "Neo-Nurcular: Gülen Hareketi", Modern Türkiye'de Siyasî Düşünce: İslâmcılık, Cilt 6, ed. Yasin Aktay, İstanbul: İletişim Yayıncılık, ISBN: 9789750502545.

Yavuz Selim Demirağ'ın Komisyon'a verdiği bilgi, 19.10.2016 tarihli tutanak, TBMM Tutanak Hizmetleri Başkanlığı.

"Yükseköğretim Personel Kanunu", No. 2914, Tarih: 11.10.1983, Resmi Gazete, Tarih: 13.10.1983, Sayı: 18.190.

Yüksek Seçim Kurulu, "10 Ağustos 2014 Pazar Günü Yapılan Onikinci Cumhurbaşkanı Seçimi İle İlgili Kesin Sonuçlar",

www.ysk.gov.tr, (http://www.ysk.gov.tr/ysk/content/
conn/YSKUCM/path/Contribution%20Folders/
HaberDosya/2014CB- Kesin-416_d_Genel.pdf, erişim:
19.04.2017).

Yüksek Seçim Kurulu, "26. Dönem Milletvekili Genel Seçimi Sonucu;
Siyasi Partilerin Çıkardıkları Milletvekili ile Bağımsızların
Sayısı, www.ysk.gov.tr, (http://www.ysk.gov.tr/ysk/
content/conn/YSKUCM/path/Contribution%20Folders/
SecmenIslemleri/Secimler/2015MVES/96-E.pdf, erişim:
20.04.2017).

"Zaman Gazetesinin Darbe Habercisi Gülen Bebek Reklamı.
Subliminal Mesaj", www.youtube.com, (https://www.
youtube.com/watch?v=W5-t5R5qhZQ, erişim: 29.01.2017).

"Zekeriya Öz'den keşke PKK Gezi'de olsaydı tweeti", www.
ensonhaber.com, (http://www.ensonhaber.com/zekeriya-
ozden-keske-pkk-gezide-olsaydi-tweeti-2015-08-02.html,
erişim: 01.06.2017).

ZEYREK, Deniz (2016), "Sayılarla Sızıntı", *Hürriyet* Gazetesi, 04
Ağustos 2016.